Constructing Critical Literacies
Teaching and Learning
Textual Practice

D1428266

Judith Green, editor

Constructing Critical Literacies

Teaching and Learning Textual Practice

edited by

Sandy Muspratt
Griffith University

Allan Luke
University of Queensland

Peter Freebody
Griffith University

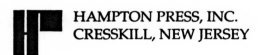

HAMPTON PRESS, INC.
CRESSKILL, NEW JERSEY

Printed in the United States of America

Library of Congress Cataloging-in-Publication Data

Constructing critical literacies : teaching and learning textual
   practice / edited by Sandy Muspratt, Allan Luke, Peter Freebody.
       p.   cm. -- (Language and social processes)
    Includes bibliographical references and indexes.
    ISBN 1-57273-102-8 (cl). -- ISBN 1-57273-103-6 (pbk.)
     1. Literacy--Social aspects. 2. Reading--Social aspects.
3. Sociolinguistics.   4. Critical pedagogy.   I. Muspratt, Sandy.
II. Luke, Allan. III. Freebody, Peter.   IV. Series: Language &
social   processes.
LC149.C67 1997
302.2 ' 244--dc21
                                           97-41752
                                             CIP

Hampton Press, Inc.
23 Broadway
Cresskill, NJ 07626

Contents

v

Series Preface

LANGUAGE AND SOCIAL PROCESSES

Judith Green, Editor
University of California at Santa Barbara

Associate Editors

Ginger Weade
University of Florida

Carol Dixon
**University of California
at Santa Barbara**

Language and Social Processes provides a forum for scholarly work that makes visible the ways in which everyday life is accomplished through discourse processes among individuals and groups. Volumes will examine how language-in-use influences the access of individuals and culturally, ethnically, and linguistically diverse groups to social institutions, and how knowledge construction and social participation across diverse social settings is accomplished through discourse.

Studies in education and other social institutions are invited from a variety of perspectives including those of anthropology, communication, education, linguistics, literary theory, psychology, and sociology. Manuscripts are encouraged that involve theoretical treatments of relevant issues, present in-depth analyses of particular social groups and institutional settings, or present comparative studies across social groups, settings or institution. Send inquiries to: Judith Green, Series Editor, Graduate School of Education, University of California, Santa Barbara, CA 93106, (805)893-4781.

Contributors

Carolyn Baker. Graduate School of Education, University of Queensland, Queensland 4072, Australia

Linda Christian-Smith. Department of Curriculum and Instruction, University of Wisconsin—Oshkosh, Oshkosh WI 52901-8664, USA

Nicholas Faraclas. Department of Language and Literature, University of Papua New Guinea, University NCD, Papua New Guinea

Peter Freebody. Faculty of Education, Griffith University, Queensland 4111, Australia

Jill Freiberg. Faculty of Education, Griffith University, Queensland 4111, Australia

James Paul Gee. School of Education, Clark University, Worcester MA 01610, USA

Pam Gilbert. School of Education, James Cook University of North Queensland, Townsville Queensland 4811, Australia

Bill Green. Faculty of Education, Deakin University, Geelong Victoria 3217, Australia

Mary Macken-Horarik. Department of English, Sydney University, New South Wales 2006, Australia

Ian Hunter. Faculty of Humanities, Griffith University, Queensland 4111, Australia

Barbara Kamler. Faculty of Education, Deakin University, Geelong Victoria 3217 Australia

Michele Knobel. School of Language and Literacy Education, Queensland University of Technology—Kelvin Grove, Red Hill Queensland 4059, Australia

Colin Lankshear. School of Language and Literacy Education, Queensland University of Technology—Kelvin Grove, Red Hill Queensland 4059, Australia

Alison Lee. Faculty of Education, University of Technology Sydney, Broadway New South Wales 2007, Australia

Allan Luke. Graduate School of Education, University of Queensland, Queensland 4072, Australia

Carmen Luke. Graduate School of Education, University of Queensland, Queensland 4072, Australia

Pat Moran. Faculty of Education, Central Queensland University, Rockhampton Queensland 4702, Australia

Sandy Muspratt. Faculty of Education, Griffith University, Queensland 4111, Australia

Annette Patterson. School of Education, Murdoch University, Murdoch Western Australia 6150, Australia

Fazel Rizvi. Faculty of Education, Monash University, Clayton Victoria 3168, Australia

M. Garbutcheon Singh. Faculty of Education, Central Queensland University, Rockhampton Queensland 4702, Australia

Parlo Singh. Faculty of Education, Griffith University, Queensland 4111, Australia

Terry Threadgold. Department of English, Monash University, Clayton Victoria 3168, Australia

Anna Yeatman. Department of Sociology, Macquarie University, New South Wales 2109, Australia

1
Critical Literacy and the Question of Normativity: An Introduction

Allan Luke
University of Queensland
Peter Freebody
Griffith University

HOW IS LITERACY SOCIAL?

The term *critical literacy* has come to refer to such a wide range of educational philosophies and curriculum interventions that their family resemblances and shared characteristics would be hard to pick. The chapters in this volume do not represent or advocate a canonical version of critical literacy. Nor do they subscribe to the appealing proposition that there is a single teaching method that can solve or resolve problems of students' reading and writing once and for all. *Constructing Critical Literacies* captures the locality and diversity of current approaches— approaches that have often been in theoretical, practical, and political contest with one another.

Although critical literacy does not stand for a unitary approach, it marks out a coalition of educational interests committed to engaging with the possibilities that the technologies of writing and other modes of inscription offer for social change, cultural diversity, economic equity, and political enfranchisement. There are shared assumptions across these chapters that literacy involves malleable social practices, relations, and events that can be harnessed in the service of particular pedagogical projects and agendas for cultural action and that, indeed, literacy education can make a difference in students' lives. There is also a shared understanding of the centrality of the institutions of schooling, government, the media, and work in the social construction of literacy.

1

Yet, at the same time there is heated debate over the exact directions and consequences of that cultural action and of these institutional formations. The key question that this volume asks is the question of normativity, of what should be: What prescriptive model of the literate person and the "social" should any approach to critical literacy aspire to? And, relatedly, on the basis of what theoretical and empirical, analytic and narrative grounds can such a model be constructed?

In the 1990s, the interest among educators in critical literacy has been hastened by the apparent failure of contemporary approaches to literacy education to address longstanding and tenacious classroom problems in the teaching of reading and writing. More specifically, there appears to be a disconnection of both traditional and progressive curricula from the educational needs and problems of significant groups of students, particularly those in historically "at-risk" groups of lower socioeconomic, cultural minority, and indigenous communities. Early reading failure and community-school transitions, the relationship of second language acquisition to literacy development, gender-differentiated literacy achievement, discipline-specific literacy demands of secondary curriculum, the connections between school and workplace textual practices, and the transparency of requirements of specialized writing for assessment and postsecondary entry are but some of the persistent issues facing school systems.

Our position here is that the "problem" cannot be taken up in terms of quantity, that is, in terms of "more or less" of a literacy conceived of in terms of universally comparable skills, competencies, or abilities. This quantitative approach has been adopted by projects as varied as the U.S. National Assessment of Educational Progress and most major international literacy programs of the postwar period. Rather, the problem has a powerful but frequently overlooked normative and qualitative dimension: What kinds of literate practices, for whom, fitted for what kinds of social and economic formations can and should be constructed and sanctioned through teaching? In this regard, the issues facing educators have their roots not in individual, educational, family, or cultural deficiencies and "lacks" but are visibly connected with changing demographics of communities, new and hybrid student bodies, connected with the overall impacts of social, cultural, and economic change on communities, identities, and actual institutional access and participation. This is precisely where many current approaches to literacy fall short, providing a microanalytic focus on fixing methods, texts, and learners rather than beginning by addressing the material consequences of selective traditions of curriculum—by taking up questions of what kinds of local textual practices can and should be forged in relation to larger social forces and dynamics, and how community, technological, and global change can form the very bases and objects of study of a critical literacy curriculum.

The contributors to this volume work from the notion that the "social" does not refer to a neutral site where linguistic and psychological activities occur, but rather is constitutive of and by material relations of discourse, power, and knowledge. By arguing that the contexts of literacy instruction are not "neutral," we argue that in contemporary conditions the contexts of literacy events are not necessarily "level playing fields" where all learners have comparable access to resources, whether construed as access to representational systems and mediational means, linguistic knowledge, and cultural artifacts, or in terms of access to actual financial capital, institutional entry, and status. The *social* thus is defined as a practical site characterized by contestations over resources, representation, and difference. These disputes over material and discourse resources are disputes over how and which forms of life are to be represented, and whose representations of whom are to "count" with what material consequences for literacy learners. They are also the basis for many of the political arguments in education, and, not surprisingly, they are at the heart of flare ups of "literacy crises" in the popular press, from debates over phonics and basic skills to debates over censorship and literary content, or, to take a current example, debates over the relationship between school literacy and the practices of new workplaces and technologies.

This is not to say that literate practices do not have cognitive accompaniments and behavioral characteristics, as Gee points out (chap. 16, this volume), or that they are not key elements in the formation of individual agency and subjectivity, as Kamler's (chap. 21, this volume), case study of a woman writer illustrates. It is to say that these are concomitants of what is a social activity, one that is tied to institutional projects of discipline and power. To say that literacy is socially constructed, then, is also to say that it is institutionally located. Our position is that institutional context is not benign or neutral, but rather must be seen as informed by social contracts and historical projects for molding, making, and disciplining human subjects, populaces, and communities—and for shaping and distributing cultural and material resources. Hunter's (chap. 18, this volume) work persistently reminds us that these historical projects of governmentality are not necessarily politically or culturally negative enterprises aimed at fettering an otherwise unfettered literacy and "natural" or unimpeded development of subjectivity and citizenship. Yet our view is that understanding of the historical linkages between forms of discipline, identity, and practice, on the one hand, and the differential distribution of representational and material resources, on the other, remains a crucial and necessary move in the analysis of current conditions.

By contrast, conventional approaches to literacy teaching tend to begin from presuppositions about the social and economic effects of textual practices, assuming the transfer, use, and value of educationally constructed practices in other institutional fields of power and capital (A. Luke, 1996). That is, even the most ostensibly apolitical approach to, say, early childhood language experience, process-oriented writing instruction, or early reading intervention and "recovery," is based on and prescribes particular versions of the literate person and accompanying visions of how she or he might use literacy to influence his or her life chances and trajectories in a particular material economy of textual and discursive relations. The functions and uses of literacy are never free standing and are always "restricted by factors other than the technology of writing itself" (Goody, 1977, p. 198). In this regard, instructional approaches that focus principally on the description of linguistic technologies of text and cognitive architectures for the construction and processing of text run the risk of mirroring or reproducing these sociocultural restrictions and constraints rather than elucidating and transforming them. The restriction described by Goody is tied to the historical dynamics of power and knowledge within communities and societies and there is compelling cross-cultural evidence that institutions gatekeep, distribute, and transmit differential kinds and levels of literacy for purposes both of governmentality *and* hegemony, authority and authorization (e.g., Barton & Ivanic, 1991; Besnier, 1995; Street, 1993).

Where psychological and depoliticized "social" and "cultural" approaches to instruction alike lack an explicit analysis of contemporary material conditions and social relations of power, issues of "transfer of training" tend to be treated as educational anomalies, to be solved by better and more precise instructional technologies and "methods," when they may be curricular artifacts and products of selective cultural traditions that are less than optimally connected in practice with these same contemporary conditions. Many literacy programs and instructional approaches attempt to provide "generic" textual tools and practices for what are emerging as definitely nongeneric, heterogeneous learners, places, conditions, and times. Furthermore, this dislocation and irrelevance is more than a simple waste or failure of instructional time and energy—it may actually succeed at constructing highly "restricted" literacies and literates, and at systematically excluding particular groups of learners.

Several of the chapters in this volume develop critiques of the sociological and historical assumptions of particular contemporary approaches to literacy education. Consider, for example, Hunter's (chap.

18) and Patterson's (chap. 19) critiques of personal growth and critical pedagogy models of English education that attempt to remake individual sensibilities in socially progressive directions (critiques that also apply to some of the normative claims and assumptions of this introduction). In her advocacy of genre-based writing instruction derived from systemic functional linguistics, Macken-Horarick (chap. 17, this volume) questions whether retheorizing the cognitive accomplishments of multidiscursivity, local textual practice, and critique will "make a difference" for secondary students whose very marginalization she links to lack of a vocabulary for talking about how texts and their affiliated institutions work.

It is the very adequacy of a pedagogical vocabulary principally based on linguistics that Lee (chap. 22, this volume) takes issue with, advocating a broader approach to classroom textual work that draws on poststructuralist and feminist framings of textuality and subjectivity. By contrast, P. Singh (chap. 5, this volume) critiques the capacity of some approaches to literacy based on feminist pedagogy to incorporate the distinctive interests and perspectives of postcolonial women. And Rizvi (chap. 10, this volume) raises serious questions about the degree to which neo-marxian economic analyses, on which many Freirian approaches to literacy education are based, in and of themselves can begin to describe the complexity and locality of change in postcolonial education.

Obviously, these are not just minor disagreements about practice or method. They raise unavoidable epistemological and political questions about the grounds and consequences of literacy education in new times. This is not a rehash of the "great debate" over approaches to reading and writing, a debate that, taken on its own terms as a binarist dispute over method (e.g., phonics vs. word recognition, skills vs. whole language, genre vs. process, liberal vs. conservative), just is not so "great" or relevant at explaining how literacy works in contemporary social conditions any longer. The issue of normativity is this: All models of literacy are predicated on and prescriptive of particular social logics, particular formulae for the economies of value and exchange for textuality in everyday life. These may include, for instance, Dick and Jane basal reader accounts of what might count as á "natural" or "normal" childhood; "common sense" about which genders "do" which textual practices and genres, as Gilbert's (chap. 4, this volume) work demonstrates; community-based folk wisdoms on, for instance, the value of literacy education for particular migrant groups; and, as the Lankshear and Knobel (chap. 6, this volume) and Singh and Moran (chap. 7, this volume) exchange indicates, particular values and beliefs regarding the state, citizenship, and "progress." In all of these cases, curriculum and instruction provides initiations for entry into linguistic and literate "markets" (Bourdieu, 1991), fields of power where particular statements and practices, texts, and discourses have local and contingent exchange value (cf. Carrington & Luke, in press). Approaches to critical literacy, then, are themselves expressions of normative "readings" of social, cultural, and economic worlds: analyses of how schools function as social institutions regulating access to resources and knowledge, and of how literacy can be made to count in the stratification of wealth and power in late capitalist societies. These are the key lessons of this volume, hardly new lessons, but certainly lessons worth continual reexamination in current educational conditions.

All of the contributors to *Constructing Critical Literacies* begin from a recognition of the social and political character of literacy education—we have indeed moved that far together. But they express skepticism toward all claims, including each others', about the product guarantees of approaches to critical literacy. Hence, this volume does not focus exclusively on a critique of traditional skills, cultural literacy, and personal voice approaches: the objects of various recent volumes on critical literacy (e.g., Baker & Luke, 1991; Cope & Kalantzis, 1994; Lankshear & McLaren, 1993). It turns an equally "critical" eye to ongoing debates over the claims of Freirian, community-based education, "genre" approaches based on functional linguistics and rhetorical theory, and discourse-analytic and semiotic approaches based on critical language studies, feminist theory, and cultural studies. In this regard, the debate over critical literacy has moved substantially since the beginning of the 1990s, towards self-criticism of many of the progressive and radical approaches undertaken in adult education, writing pedagogy, and early literacy instruction in the late 1980s. If indeed one of the principal characteristics of the particular moment we live in is openness to criticism, as Yeatman (chap. 23, this volume) argues, then the exchanges in this volume are indicative of, at once, a degree of normative uncertainty about what should be done, but agreement that, given the deteriorating economic and social conditions for many, there is an imperative that something more should be done.

If we begin, then, from this key proposition—that literacy education is not a technical/scientific problem but a normative social and cultural project—then the ways of constructing critical literacies likewise require a critical analysis of the material conditions facing teachers and students. The face-to-face normative decisions made by teachers and students in classrooms, examined by Baker (chap. 14, this volume), Freiberg and Freebody (chap. 15, this volume), are constrained by local pedagogic conditions. The contemporary conditions of teaching as work faced by teachers in schools and many universities across the United States, Canada, Australia, New Zealand, and the United Kingdom are shifting rapidly. Whatever their differences, teachers working in so-called Western educational contexts face the challenges of increasingly complex and hybrid student identities, youth cultures, and communities, the educational and economic imperatives of new communications media and technologies, and the need for curriculum that must address changing workplaces, and persistent patterns of unemployment and underemployment. As if these curricular challenges in and of themselves are not hard enough, they must be taken up in increasingly difficult working conditions dominated by the "new managerialism." In schools and other educational institutions, as in virtually all social service sectors, physical and administrative infrastructures are being cut back by public and private funding authorities, there are increasing demands for accountability via testing, assessment, and audits, and overall patterns of the deskilling and work intensification continue (Lingard, Knight, & Porter, 1993). These are the less glamorous material realities of teaching in fast capitalist conditions.

At the same time, longstanding ideological debates about what people should read and write persist, having been refocused in the 1990s on the speaking rights of marginalized cultural, gender, and minority groups (including various conservative and religious movements) and whose version of cultures, histories, and values should count in the curriculum. That is, the challenges presented by feminisms, multiculturalism, postcolonial, ecopolitical, and gay movements have had significant impacts not only on those conservatives interested in protecting a traditional Anglo/colonialist literary canon. As well, liberal theorists have offered a defense of academic freedom and more traditional rationalist philosophies to counter claims of the intrinsic validity and privilege of minority standpoint, and to critique notions of proprietary and essential rights of ownership or control over local or minority knowledges (B. Lee, 1995). This across-the-spectrum reaction against the knowledge claims of diasporic groups is one marker of the degree to which debates over the politics of representation, identity, and knowledge have disrupted longstanding left–right distinctions and historical educational coalitions built around class and regional alliances. The destabilization of canonical grounds for knowledge, the questioning of traditional disciplinary boundaries, and the so-called "political correctness" debate have powerful implications for all areas of school knowledge—including debates over the selection of children's and adolescent literature, phonics in early reading instruction, issues of textual representation in the history and practice of science, and the inclusion of women's and minority cultures' literatures and histories in mainstream curriculum.

If literacy debates and "crises" are routinely connected with larger social conflicts, we could ask: What is the catalyst for current debates about literacy? We would argue that the emergence of minority contention for a share of symbolic and material rights and resources in an era of ostensibly declining resources and increasing consumption has brought literacy education to a turning point, one as significant as the emergence of the human capital debate in the early 1960s, which forged the institutional link between literacy and the economy, or the successive recessions and structural unemployment in the 1980s, which set the conditions for a powerful ethos of "functional literacy," and later, "competency-based" approaches to adult literacy. What this postmodern and polycultural moment marks out is yet another critique of the very foundational assumptions of 20th-century secular literacy education: (a) that the practice of literacy is a universal human capacity above ideology and difference; (b) that literacy is amenable to and the rightful object of positivist scientific study; and (c) that politically charged contestation about the institutional construction and distribution of literacy can be resolved through the development of scientifically based technologies for curriculum, instruction, and evaluation.

The contributors to this volume offer various perspectives and descriptions of the educational imperatives of fast capitalism. What they would agree on is that there is a convergence of historical forces for change, unprecedented in pace and scale. Hybrid text forms, mixed modes of communication, and "multiliteracies" (New London Group, 1996) are developing in the contexts of new social relations, institutional structures, and practices. These contexts range from the new media mythologies built around software multinational entrepreneurs, Internet users, and online hackers/criminals—to the far less celebrated but ubiquitous end-user work of youth caught up in the MacJobs of the retail and service sectors. In this new civic and work environment, many of the possibilities for students, teachers, and their communities to use critical reading and analytic writing to gain strategic and tactical purchases over their life chances and trajectories are untested. But what is certain is that many of those same communities of students who were marginalized by the industrial division of print literacy—children of the urban and rural poor, recent migrants and cultural minority groups, girls and women, and indigenous peoples—remain at risk. New technologies, globalization of the economy, and the related breakup of many longstanding class, community formations, coalitions, and alliances have left many extremely vulnerable to new and residual forms of immiseration, marginality, and exclusion. Across the West, the very concrete social problems affiliated with youth unemployment, racial, and sexual discrimination, and actually declining standards of living for many families with school-age children remain on the table in school staffrooms and classrooms.

The questions raised here in part are about who gets access to which technologies and practices of writing and representation—and how schools and literacy education are active participants in the construction of the social division of textual and discursive work along these traditional fractures of gender, culture, and class, as C. Luke (chap. 2), Christian-Smith (chap. 3), Gilbert (chap. 4), Threadgold (chap. 20) and Lee (chap. 22) argue. Although the debate over the cognitive and social effects of a (theoretically) "unrestricted" literacy continues, what seems certain is that certified, visibly displayed levels of literate practice become requisite forms of cultural capital, necessary, if not sufficient, for entry into institutional and public life. Development of an array of flexible and context-sensitive reading and writing practices may provide no guarantees of such entry and participation—but in a text-saturated culture, not having access to such practices can systematically lock one out of linguistic and literate markets. The challenge then is not just one of equity of access (or lack of access) to such technologies and institutions, but also of the possibilities of using discourse and literacy to reinvent institutions, to critique and reform the rules for the conversion of cultural and textual capital in communities and workplaces, and to explore the possibilities of heteroglossic social contracts and hybrid cultural actions. The challenge is about what kinds of citizenship, public forums for discourse and difference are practicable and possible—as exchanges between Lankshear and Knobel (chap. 6), M. G. Singh and Moran (chap. 7), Gilbert (chap. 4), and P. Singh (chap. 5) here illustrate.

LITERACY AS A TECHNOLOGY FOR PUBLIC LIFE

Since the founding of mass secular education, literacy has become a cipher for constellations of valued cultural practices, for particular claims to moral, intellectual, and behavioral virtue. Literacy has been perceived as a central component of citizenship in the West since the first German campaigns of the Reformation, when Luther and colleagues forged the link between universal textual practices, spiritual enlightenment, and membership in the emergent nation-state (C. Luke, 1989). There is continuing evidence that the actual systematic deprivation of access to literacy continues to be a factor in colonialist and neocolonialist rule world-wide, as Faraclas (chap. 9), and A. Luke and Freebody (chap. 12) here suggest.

As the results of the international literacy campaigns of the 1970s and 1980s suggest, it is not as if these tenacious and longstanding patterns of exclusion are going to be absorbed in any linear path of national and multinational corporate development as promised by human capital models of domestic governments and international aid organizations, "trickle down" economic models forwarded by the World Bank, or by many of the promises of a post-Fordist restructuring of global and domestic economies. In fact, as Faraclas argues, the globalization of capital has extreme material consequences both in terms of the emergent practices and commodities of world media culture described by C. Luke (chap. 2) and Christian-Smith (chap. 3), and in terms of more rudimentary local access to civic participation and a basic degree of influence over one's life trajectory and economic destiny. Questions of who gets access to what kinds of discursive work, information, and knowledge and how these might or might not lead to jobs and voice in public forums are not simply local matters, negotiable or constructed in classrooms independently of larger forces and configurations of power.

The potentials and limits of literacy as a tool for cultural self-determination, raised in Luther's time, remain central to our exchanges here. But even while major segments of the world's population, predominantly female, and people in peasant economies, are continuing a slow move toward an industrial-style stratification of wealth and labor—there is a pressing need to begin describing and prognosticating the kinds of redivisions of wealth and power that are accompanying the shift toward service-sector and information-based corporate economies in Northern hemisphere countries. The issues of citizenship and normativity raised here, then, require a reexamination of classical and enlightenment models of democratic participation and social contracts, models that, feminists and postcolonialists have shown us, marked out some of the very historical conditions for a biased distribution of epistemic authority and material resources (e.g., Pateman, 1988; Young, 1990). They also require a reconsideration of those assumptions that have guided educators for the past century—about the centrality of print literacy for identity formation, "personal growth," and the establishment of "individual difference," about the universal value and transferability of rudimentary practices of reading and writing to new job places, about the significance of print media in community life, and most obviously, about the potential of (monolingual) reading and writing to build nation-state cohesion and economic productivity. If "universal literacy," "functional literacy," and so forth were very much legacies of historical convergences of, respectively, protestantism and the secular state and later, industrialism and capitalism—then it would appear that a reshaping of what will count as literacy in New Times is both necessary and inevitable.

Marx's 1844 analysis of alienated labor and species being is relevant, with its emphasis on the emergence of cultures and economies of tools for the transformation of the biosocial world. These tools would include language, writing, and those electronic media of communication that have increasingly been constitutive of the very relations of power and knowledge across and within societies for the past 50 years. The ownership and appropriation of the means of production are central to Marx's analysis of industrial conditions. What he could not have foreseen is that under the conditions of fast capitalism the means of production and modes of information have become the nexus of social relations and power. Literacy education plays a key role in influencing learners' access to and models for the mediational means and codes that situate them in relation to modes of information, and therefore, means of production. So what is socially constructed in classrooms is, *inter alia*, social relations to modes of information *and* means of production.

Many of Marx's insights are relevant, even, or especially as the conditions of work, the way people communicate, the lifeworlds of leisure, consumption and desire have changed. The issues now are as much ecological and semiotic ones as technical ones, as much concerned with matters of geography as history, physicality as mentality, body as consciousness. As a result, the basic vocabulary we have for describing literate practice and citizenship is up for grabs. The challenge of a political analysis of literacy in postmodern conditions is to move past Cartesian models of citizens as free wills and "class-conscious" mentalities, beyond Fordist models of students and workers as carriers of "skills," "competencies," and "abilities"—with writing the technology par excellence for the separation and classification of minds and bodies—and to move toward a reconsideration of human subjects as ecotechnical embodied subjects (Conley, 1993) in an emergent information order that brings to bear a new set of contingent factors not just about ownership of the media and political participation, but about how to live relationally in an era of cultural juxtaposition, shift and mixture, scarcer resources, limits to development, ill effects of industrial development, and with the competing and, at times, bewildering desires and novel, unprecedented affiliations and loyalties that accompany these new environments. As Wilden's (1982) ecosystemic model of communication explains, mediation and constraint go hand in hand and they are necessarily both political and environmental (in terms of how they influence relations of production and relations of exchange, including the matter/energy transformations of human labor and the ecosystem). Learning to work with codes, then, is not a simple matter of mastery of reason and skill, competence and genre. In Wilden's account, it involves developing strategies and tactics to remediate and "repunctuate" relations of exchange in ecosystems, which in turn may influence the distribution and construction of both symbolic and material resources in the interests of sustainable ecological and social systems. Following Wilden's lead, any theory of a general economy of literacy would have to reconsider the flows and exchange of capital as we conventionally construe it (wealth, resources), how linguistic/literate capital is valued in institutions, the relationship of discourse change and material change, and the ramifications of these for systems of biological/physical exchange necessary for sustainable futures. [1]

If our argument about the need for any approach to literacy to take up the challenge of normativity holds—in an age where such calls are increasingly viewed as politically risky and intellectually unchic—then indeed it is impossible to take up fully that challenge without engaging in some speculative analytic and narrative work, utopian and dystopian, and some science fiction. Our normative position is that the challenge of constructing critical literacies is in part a challenge to our capacity to re-envision new kinds of public spaces, institutional structures that might facilitate discourse exchange, and new forms of hybrid and nomadic cultural identity as part of a reshaping and redistribution of material and symbolic resources (Mouffe, 1993). At the least, such a project will require a stronger sociological imagination than that that has guided literacy education in the past, as Lankshear and Knobel (chap. 7) comment. Yet educational responses to the institutional fields and economies of schools, universities, teacher education programs, and so forth have been limited in the extent to which they have been able to reenvision what might count as literacy in a full blown political economy and lived reality of information, with all of its heteroglossic quirks and crashes, inequities and enabling conditions. As Green (chap. 13) concludes, this limitation is reflected in this volume with its continued insistence on print literacy and its conventional grammars of explanation as a matrix and starting point for discussion.

CRITICAL LITERACY AS A LOCAL CURRICULUM AND POLICY ISSUE

Given the degrees of economic and cultural uncertainty plaguing many communities, one would expect that literacy would be the focus of public controversy and moral panic. Nor should it be surprising that teachers of literacy at all levels—from early childhood to university, from literature studies to English as a Second Language—have cast about for new approaches. The resultant strategies and their affiliated "literacies" are various, from an emphasis on "media literacy" to "visual literacy," from the recent enthusiasm for "generic skills" and "key competencies" to developments in multicultural curriculum.

---

[1]The idea of a "general economy" that includes material, biological, libidinal, and representational resources is the focus of theoretical and practical development by Tony Fry and colleagues at the Ecodesign Foundation, Sydney, Australia.

Throughout the 1970s and early 1980s, the term *critical literacy* was probably most strongly affiliated with the work of Freire and colleagues, first in neocolonial contexts and later in the United States and other nations. Freire outlined an orientation to education that began from the proposition that language and literacy, and control over how issues, problems and aspects of the world are "named," are directly tied to issues of political power, and that, reconstructed, literacy education could therefore be used as a force for political liberation and emancipation for disenfranchised social groups. Many of the curriculum projects described here attempt to bring an explicitly political dimension to the teaching of reading and writing, fields that have been presented to successive generations of educators as fundamentally neutral and discipline-bound, whether to psychology, literary studies, or linguistics.

Although *critical literacy* might retain some of these political connotations, in Australia it has gradually moved from the margins to become part of the official knowledge of state curriculum, a concern of teacher educators, professional developers and inservice educators, policymakers, regional consultants, and school administrators. What is of interest here is the extent to which critical literacy has moved from the status of a "heretical discourse"—a family of unruly and dangerous practices pushing the boundaries of school and university orthodoxy—to the status of an authorized discourse: "heretical discourses . . . derive their power from their capacity to *objectify* unformulated experiences, to make them public—a step on the road to officialization and legitimation" (Bourdieu, 1977, pp. 170-171).

Bourdieu explained that "heretical power," although it may have "liberating potency" in the provision of an economy for the expression of the "usually repressed," is necessarily constructed in relationship to the "authorized, authorizing language." By this account, it would be impossible for discourses of critical literacy to engage with state school systems, to move from an oppositional position to one within mainstream institutions without generating new, incorporated meanings and practices, meanings and practices mutated and appropriated by that complex political economy of schooling and education, by what Kenway (1990) termed "temporary settlements between diverse, competing and unequal forces within civic society . . . and between associated discursive regimes" (p. 59).

There are two lessons to this. First, that similar curriculum discourses, whether at the level of policy or practice, may be "heretical" in one context (e.g., Republican-era U.S. or Conservative-ruled U.K. politics) and "official" and authorized in another (e.g., Australian Labor governments), revolutionary in one and conservative in another. Second, the transformation of these discourses into actual "official knowledge" (Apple, 1993) will be done in context of the "temporary settlements" of local, regional, and national educational politics.

In this way, the debate over literacy education reflects current methodological and epistemological problems in sociological and cultural studies: the need to theoretically and empirically describe the relationship between broader, global political economies of information and their local, face-to-face instances and mediations. Both real and perceived imperatives of economic globalization, new technologies and workplaces, declining and shifting roles of state intervention and the financing of public infrastructure, and the emergence of corporatist economies, are connected with how literacy will be constructed in "local sociologies" by school boards, curriculum writers, state government ministers, publishers, and parents (A. Luke, 1995), a point taken up in Threadgold's (chap. 20) commentary on the possibilities for curriculum reform and transformation within bureaucratic constraints. To return to Bourdieu's metaphor, there is a political economy by which "the counter-gift" is transformed into the "project of the gift," by which the heretical discourse is "institutionally organised and guaranteed" into an authorized discourse. At the same time, this transformation is profoundly local and ambiguous, a moment in the politics of the local described by Yeatman (1990) where there are possibilities for shifting, renaming, and redefining the discourses of literacy and literacy education in interests other than those that they have historically served.

We find this ambiguity and polysemy of the key words *critical literacy* in Australian curriculum guidelines and teacher development packages for the teaching of primary reading and writing, secondary English, and adult education programs. The term has been applied to different programs and ideas in the last decade, and has been used to develop a range of curricular interventions and positions, including instructional approaches designed to promote textual expressions of identity and self-esteem; to teach explicitly the rhetorical structures and linguistic features of conventional text forms; to teach reading comprehension in ways that generate reflective textual metacognition; to teach students to identify emotive terms, bias, stereotypes, and other aspects of textual representation; and to develop critical research and the writing of what M.G. Singh (1989) called *counter-constructions* as part of social studies education programs. The range of approaches covered here should show how the term *critical literacy* has been combined, in the rhetoric relatively effortlessly, with other recent approaches to literacy education, including whole language approaches to elementary school reading and language arts, genre-based approaches to the teaching of writing, and even, so-called "critical" components in standardized reading and curriculum packages. It has also found direct and productive affiliations with equity-based programs designed to promote gender equity both in the contexts of mainstream and "disadvantaged" schooling, as Gilbert's (chap. 4) work here illustrates

Recalling our second point about curriculum reform and local sociologies, what might count as critical literacy in schools and classrooms is, of course, contingent on the national, local, and regional politics of the curriculum—the enabling historical conditions that generate change in educational ideologies and practices. Different interests have appropriated and assimilated the concept of critical literacy, putting it to work to service particular pedagogical agendas, ranging from liberal projects for the promotion of individual access and development within capitalism, postmodern calls for the analysis and critique of power relations, neo-marxian interventions for a broader, more egalitarian redistribution of wealth and power, to conservative projects for the increased production of capital. All but the latter are represented in this volume. The discourses and contexts for curriculum policy in the United States, United Kingdom, and Canada differ considerably, each presenting to literacy educators particular sets of practical possibilities, community cultural resources, and local political thresholds that constrain what will count as "official knowledge," literate practice and competence. But because of the policy settings set out by a now past decade of Labor federal and state governments, Australian education has been a unique laboratory for the development, study, and implementation of varied "critical" approaches to literacy education, literature study, civics, and social studies, and various areas of second language instruction and adult basic education. In the Australian context, at least, we are looking at a diverse collection of activities that have already seen broad, although hardly comprehensive, curriculum application, appropriation, and so forth, and that already have been the subject of widespread theoretical and practical debate, substantive aspects of which are represented in this volume.

Finally, the local possibilities for teachers and students to use and learn about literacy differently that this polysemy might enable are issues in the face-to-face literacy teaching and learning described by Baker (chap. 14), Kamler (chap. 21), and others. Baker (chap. 14), and Freiberg and Freebody (chap. 15) debate whether critical literacy can and should be characterized procedurally in terms of visible patterns of classroom talk and interaction. Matching the "temporary" agreements and compromises that constitute school knowledge, classroom literacy events may entail the development of what A. Lee (1996) termed *interim literacies*, transient ensembles of practice that students develop in order to meet the procedural and disciplinary demands of schooling. In this light, the classroom talk described by Baker, and Freiberg and Freebody may capture the very locality and stabilized-for-now character of normative decisions about the shaping of school literacy. Our point here is that even the analysis of the face-to-face social construction of literacy returns us back to larger normative questions about the kinds of social formations, institutions, and identities classroom practice should develop.

A HISTORY AND READING POSITION FOR THIS BOOK

It would be ironic to produce a book on critical literacy that was not fraught with criticism, argument, debate, and in this case, fire. *Constructing Critical Literacies* does not purport to develop a new consensus about what should count as critical literacy, nor does it presuppose that critical literacy can be fixed with any final certainty and determination, nor that there is a right way of doing this in classrooms and communities. This book embodies debate, dissonance, and difference—crucial aspects of what might count as critical reading and writing.

We owe our readers some explanatory notes about the history of the construction of this text. All of the authors and respondents were participants in a series of conferences on critical literacy at Griffith University in 1992 and 1993, organized by Peter Freebody and Sandy Muspratt. Sandy Muspratt subsequently managed the editing of this book and the direct textual work with authors. Many of the chapters were composed and edited in 1993 and 1994, and the responses were compiled and edited in 1994 and 1995. As you read through some of the exchanges, you will see that these responses are not in the "rubber-stamp" or panegyric genre that often arises when people have written, taught, and worked together over a period of time, as many of our contributors have. Quite the contrary. The conferences and this book became forums where we discovered, articulated, and worked through—if not always to some sort of theoretical and practical closure—substantive political and pedagogical agreements and differences between us. Because of the complexity of the issues and perspectives involved in many of the responses, at series editor Judith Green's suggestion, we invited all of the authors further right of response in mid-1995, which several took up.

This, then, is a book with a history. And we would add that many of the authors have further developed or shifted their positions on critical literacy, in some cases directly as the result of our encounters and exchanges in the conferences, papers, and editorial work. We thank the authors, our series editor and publisher for their patience and encouragement in developing what has been for us a difficult and extremely worthwhile project. As a result of its history—this book is a live document, embodying and articulating critical literacies and differences, rather than simply talking about them.

ACKNOWLEDGMENTS

The authors thank David King of Thuringowa State High School for discussion of the ideas in this introduction, Judith Green for her editorial suggestions, patience, and advice.

REFERENCES

Apple, M.W. (1993). *Official knowledge*. New York: Routledge.

Baker, C. D., & Luke, A. (Eds.). (1991). *Towards a critical sociology of reading pedagogy*. Amsterdam: John Benjamins.

Barton, D., & Ivanic, R. (Eds.). (1991). *Writing in the community*. London: Sage.

Besnier, N. (1995). *Literacy, emotion, and authority*. Cambridge, UK: Cambridge University Press.

Bourdieu, P. (1977). *Outline of a theory of practice* (R. Nice, Trans.). Cambridge, UK: Cambridge University Press.

Bourdieu, P. (1991). *Language and symbolic power* (J. B. Thompson, Ed.; G. Raymond & M. Admanson, Trans.). Cambridge, UK: Polity Press.

Carrington, V., & Luke, A. (in press). Literacy and Bourdieu's sociological theory: A reframing. *Language and Education*.

Conley, V.A. (1993). Eco-subjects. In V. A. Conley (Ed.), *Rethinking technologies*. Minneapolis: University of Minnesota Press.

Cope, B., & Kalantzis, M. (Eds.). (1994). *The powers of literacy*. London: Falmer Press.

Goody, J. (1977). *The domestication of the savage mind*. Cambridge, UK: Cambridge University Press.

Kenway, J. (1990). *Gender and education policy*. Geelong, Australia: Deakin University Press.

Lankshear, C., & McLaren, P. L. (Eds.). (1993). *Critical literacy*. Albany: State University of New York Press.

Lee, A. (1996). *Gender, literacy, curriculum*. London: Taylor & Francis.

Lee, B. (1995). Critical internationalism. *Public Culture, 7*(3), 549-593.

Lingard, B., Knight, J., & Porter, P. (Eds.). (1993). *Schooling reform in hard times*. London: Falmer Press.

Luke, A. (1995). Getting our hands dirty: Provisional politics in postmodern conditions. In R. Smith & P. Wexler (Eds.), *After postmodernism*. London: Falmer Press.

Luke, A. (1996). Genres of power? Literacy education and the production of capital. In R. Hasan & G. Williams (Eds.), *Literacy in society*. London: Longmans.

Luke, C. (1989). *Pedagogy, printing and protestantism: The discourse on childhood*. Albany: State University of New York Press.

Mouffe, C. (1993). *The return of the political*. London: Verso.

New London Group. (1996). A pedagogy of multiliteracies: Designing social futures. *Harvard Educational Review, 66*(1), 60-92

Pateman, C. (1988). *The sexual contract*. Cambridge, UK: Polity Press.

Singh, M. G. (1989). A counter-hegemonic orientation to literacy in Australia. *Journal of Education, 171,* 34-56.

Street, B. V. (Ed.). (1993). *Cross-cultural approaches to literacy*. Cambridge, UK: Cambridge University Press.

Wilden, A. (1982). *System and structure: Essays on communication and exchange* (2nd ed.). London: Tavistock.

Yeatman, A. (1990). *Bureaucrats, technocrats, femocrats*. Sydney, Australia: Allen & Unwin.

Young, I. M. (1990). *Justice and the politics of difference*. Princeton, NJ: Princeton University Press.

2
Media Literacy and Cultural Studies

Carmen Luke
University of Queensland

One important dimension of children's culture and learning that is commonly overlooked in current literacy debates is popular culture. Youth culture in particular is usually, and historically, seen by parents and educators as dangerous, as morally corrupting. Television, for example, has long been used as a scapegoat on which to pin blame for a litany of individual and social problems such as teenage promiscuity, increased violence, reduced creativity and imagination, and falling literacy standards. Educators, as defenders of print, have a particular and longstanding historical problem with TV and popular culture more generally. For the most part, teachers claim that they do not watch "low-brow" commercial TV, they refuse to teach with it or about it. Most will only acknowledge it as a significant part of children's lives and an important part of their social and cultural learning in terms of TV's negative content and social consequences.

Television is today's mass social educator and it does have a powerful influence on social life, politics, consumer behavior, and the shaping of public sentiment. Consider, for instance, the kind of global response elicited by months of TV images of starvation in Ethiopia in the mid-1980s, which culminated in the global "Live-Aid" broadcast. In the early 1990s, TV coverage of Somalia brought on a similar flood of global sympathy and charity (and military intervention). Contemporary politics in the West is all about image crafting and carefully orchestrated 15-second soundbites. Today, political debate and building voter constituencies occurs on TV, not in town halls, school gyms, or public parks. Television structures the practice of family life in ways that remain largely common sense and imperceptible to people: Children have to finish homework before watching their favorite programs; family meals coincide with the evening news; weekend programming is organized for men, daytime weekday programs and commercials for women. Family members may not watch the same programs together, but their favorite programs do become topics of family and peer group conversations at home, work, and in the playground (C. Luke, 1993b; Lull, 1990; Press, 1991). Viewers act upon TV information in powerful ways: Viewer call-ins respond to the scripted death of a soap star, documentary specials on domestic violence elicit an avalanche of calls to local crisis hotlines, consumers rush out en masse in response to advertised products and/or sales. The flurry of marketing and product development in relation to the O. J. Simpson trial exemplify the power of television to commodify news, identity, and information. Advertising works and people do respond to TV product promotion. Although children are not direct income earners, they are in charge of more (pocket) money than in the past, and they also exert significant power over parental purchase choices. On any day, one can witness parents and children fighting over toy or snack food purchases in supermarket and toy store aisles. The toy, snack food, and entertainment industries capitalize on the bourgeois family's obsession with giving children what they want and have carved up the child market into increasingly smaller (and younger) consumer niches (Kline, 1993; Seiter, 1991).

Children today have more money to spend than ever before. In the United States in 1984, children aged 4 to 12 spent more than $4 billion on snacks, toys and games, fun machines, movies and sports, and gifts (McNeal, 1987). Total national average "income" for U.S. children in 1984 was $4.7 billion: 4-year-olds apparently earned an average of $1.08 per week and 12-year-olds earned an average of $5.49 per week (McNeal, 1987). No comparable data is available for Australian children, but it is not unreasonable to assume that, after adjustment for population size, Australian children spend a comparable amount on the same items. And if we consider the cross-media marketing of cartoons and movies, snack foods, actions figures, and video games, it becomes clear that children's consumer behavior and their socialization into commodity desires are lessons learned early from TV advertising and programs. I will discuss this in detail later in the chapter.

Given the pervasiveness of Western mass media and mass culture that children grow up with—the electronic, symbolic, commodity, and ideological signification system of popular culture—it is my position that TV cannot be ignored by schooling but must be treated seriously as a social text, as cultural icon, and as social practice. Part of what a critical social literacy should entail is an understanding of how the public texts of everyday life construct our understandings of the world, and position persons to take up various social, political, and cultural identities. How this can be accomplished is what I explore in this chapter.

THEORETICAL FRAMEWORKS

Media literacy curricula and debates have been around since the 1970s. In fact, educational psychologists first began arguing in the late 1920s for media literacy in terms of what was then called *aesthetic appreciation* of the silent pictures (C. Luke, 1990a). Academic and educational arguments for the curricular inclusion of media studies are not new. Yet, recent theoretical shifts in social and cultural theory (i.e., some versions of cultural postmodernism), in feminist theory, and certainly at the level of cultural production, provide a renewed framework for arguing not only for media studies pedagogy, but for a cultural studies pedagogy. By this I mean a critical literacy of the cultural present—not of the canonized past—of which media literacy is just one component. This kind of literacy is not the kind advocated by cultural preservationists such as Hirsch (1987), but rather one that focuses on the critical study of the mass media imagery and iconography of children's popular culture.

Theoretically, then, there are some aspects of feminism and postmodernism that are useful for arguing for a critical literacy of the cultural present. Feminist theory has contributed much to current understanding of the masculinist (mis)representation of the feminine as "other" in media texts and imagery, in social and natural science, literary and philosophical discourses (de Lauretis, 1987). Central to feminist theoretical arguments against male textual rule is the near seamless historical repression of a female authorial voice. That is, women's historical representations, whether in print or visual texts, have been primarily male-authored versions of girls, women, and "things feminine." The historical silencing of female authorship authority, in turn, has led to a fetishization and objectification of "the feminine" that, in various textual forms, reflects a collective male gaze and desire. Cultural industries in particular have a long history of male cultural productions of feminine stereotypes and misrepresentations that conceptualize women primarily either as object of male adornment, pursuit, and domination, or as mindless domestic drudges, mentally vacant bimbos, or saintly supermoms. Feminist scholarship has repeatedly shown over the past two decades that, whether through the eye of the camera or the eye of theory, the socially situated epistemological standpoint of masculinity dominates the "making" of history and the present: materially, textually, visually, and symbolically. Feminist theories of representation, then, provide the conceptual support for analyzing standpoint and authorship, exclusion, inclusion, and marginalization, and the cultural production of gendered desires.

Aspects of postmodernist theory relevant to my discussion here fall roughly into three areas: philosophical, cultural, and economic postmodernism. I outline briefly each in turn, mindful that such a brief survey cannot adequately address the complexities of various strands within postmodernist thought. Philosophical postmodernism rejects Enlightenment totalizing theories and cultural "stories" that, under "modernist" narratives, explained the world from a centered and privileged position of male power and knowing. This strand within postmodernism claims that modernist explanations could only account for all those not marked as white, male, and of European descent, as "less" and "other" than the centered object of study of its own theories that spoke to and for those who authored these discourses in the first place. Postmodernism rejects the master narratives of modernity and, instead, argues for multiplicity, difference, heteroglossia, and specificity. This focuses theory and political action on local sites, on microcapillaries of power and oppression, and on the multiple differences that characterize specific contexts and persons. The postmodernist human subject is seen as situated in a collective social body that is constituted through and in difference (of identity and location), not sameness. All that which historically has been associated with the supremacy of the White and male bourgeois subject (e.g., high culture and "art," objectivity, universalisms, detachment, industrial, and military rationality, etc.) has come under the critical scrutiny of both feminist and postmodernist scholars, who have shown the exclusionary nature of modernist discourses.

Cultural postmodernism is concerned primarily with culture, cultural productions, and the cultural subject. Of particular concern in terms of this discussion is the postmodernist insistence on the media(ted) construction of the social subject. In metaphoric terms, mass mediated technoculture of the present is seen as an infinite house of electronic mirror screens, each deflecting and yet projecting images and symbols of desire and identity on human subjects. In other words, the human subject is the "screen" on which electronic imageries project symbolic identities, needs, and wants (Grossberg, 1984). The subject is seen as a product of cultural symbols and signification systems that are said to have no referent to any concrete "real" material objects or relations in the world. Images and signs are seen by postmodern cultural theorists to refer only to other images and signs, and it is within this cross-referential system of culturally constructed meanings that the social subject is situated and acts in the world (Baudrillard, 1983). For Baudrillard and others, there is no "real" dimension to social experience, only "simulated" experiences and identities. So, for instance, the "real" time and social relations constructed around watching TV, shopping in malls, constructing an identity through designer labels, or kids playing

"Barbie" or "Alien," are simulated experiences that have no concrete referent in the "real" world. In this regard, the cultural postmodernist position argues that the subject of postmodernity is nothing more than a "simulacra"—a simulation (Baudrillard, 1983). The social subject is a cultural artifact and bodily/material ground for the inscription (indeed, embodiment) of mass-produced symbolic meanings and the "tie-in" commodities that make those meanings concrete through purchase and ownership.

The third theoretical dimension of postmodernism relevant to my discussion here is best exemplified by Harvey (1989) and Lash (1990), who explain the postindustrial moment as postcapitalism or economic postmodernism. The logic of modern capitalism was based on centralization of human and industrial resources; the logic of postmodern capitalism is based on off-shore and decentralized human and resource investments. The worker under industrial capitalism invested in lifetime specialization of skills, whereas the postmodernist worker is encouraged to develop "multiskilling" abilities. Under modernist capitalism, women and men labored under an industrial regime producing the "hardware" of an industrial economy. Postmodernist capitalism, by contrast, is now widely characterized as an information economy in which the primary object of labor (and, around which social relations are structured) is information. In the postmodern age, the "software" of information is the privileged currency of exchange. And, unlike print, its simulated (soft- and hardware dependent), nonmaterial electronic character makes it highly permeable across time and space. The intensity, globalization, and intertextuality of information regimes (e.g., finance, media coverage, advertising) makes having information of the right and potentially lucrative kind the core principle of contemporary capitalist logic.

How, then, does a postmodernist theoretical position help support arguments for media and cultural literacy? One key aspect of postmodernist theory relevant to a media and cultural literacy is the elimination of the high culture-low culture distinction that characterized the study of popular culture and culture industries since the 1930s (e.g., Horkheimer & Adorno, 1972). With the postmodernist turn away from Eurocentric notions of "high culture" and "high theory," academic inquiry—itself imbued with high culture "distinction" (Bourdieu, 1984)—has finally begun to take serious those mass cultural artifacts and practices that are of daily relevance to most people.

A second important insight of postmodern theory is the shift from centrist and relatively static notions of culture to global, corporate, and electronic culture that is in a constant state of renewal and reinvention. That is, the acceleration of change in style, "the look," and the commodities that enable continuous personal reinvention, is primarily achieved through increasingly globalized and standardized media messages, all of which refer to other sign systems (of status, success, "in"-groupness). Despite important theoretical differences among modernist and postmodernist theorists, they all agree on the increasingly central role of audiovisual and commodity imagery that appear in ever increasing social sites of everyday life. The pastiche of contemporary cultural life is no longer confined to the urban landscape but has extended its reach into the most far flung rural villages across the globe. For instance, in 1993 MTV Networks announced the creation of 24-hour Spanish language MTV, to be distributed to Mexico, the Carribean, Central and South America. Five other global MTV networks are already in place: MTV Europe, MTV Brazil, MTV Australia, MTV Japan, and MTV Asia. Educational cable programming with commercials is already well underway in U.S. schools. In airports, hospitals, sports stadiums, restrooms, shopping malls, urban public transport, and soon, in our own cars, screens pumping out information are commonplace. Coke or Mattell toy ads beam into the most remote hamlets around the globe. Homer Simpson, Ninja Turtles, Barbie, or *Beverly Hills 90210* are available to kids around the world on TV screens and in their merchandise transformations. Paradoxically, the intensity and global proliferation of primarily Western cultural signs and symbols seem on one level to de-emphasize national cultural differences and interests. Yet, the pan global commodification of cultural symbols and meanings (associated primarily with soft drink, toy, fast food, or entertainment empires) appears also to generate increasing resistance to the globalization of culture and increasing insistence on national and ethnic difference and identity. How diverse Australian childhood experiences fit in with American TV visions of childhood and adolescence, is one obvious question a critical study of media and culture would address.

As noted earlier, part of the postmodernist moment (in cultural, literary, and feminist studies) is the turn away from the canonization of "great books," "great authors," and "great art" precisely because those texts excluded and marginalized, indeed denigrated, all groups except the Euro-American male subject. The collapse of distinctions between high and low culture, and the demystification of high culture as a self-referential masculinist myth of self-glorification, has also begun to cast some light on the kind of modernist preoccupation with print text—with "good" books—in the school. Modern pedagogy, after all, is organized around print text and print literacy skills that are seen as applicable to and indispensable in a predominantly print culture. However, as we move from an industrial to a postindustrial information economy (Harvey, 1989), one in which print literacy is not obsolete but certainly substantially transformed, then surely we need a broader notion of a cultural and technological literacy that includes a study of the intertextuality of imageries, texts, and artifacts of media and popular culture.

Advertisements are one good illustration of media imagery playing on other media imagery, of the intertextual, cross-referential character of contemporary cultural texts and icons. Media advertising is one of the most sophisticated areas of image production given the huge amount of money, application of state-of-the-art computer graphic technology, and human resources it consumes both at the level of production and reception. And, as most would agree, advertising is itself one of the most powerful "public" pedagogies that teach us about needs and wants, desire and identity, the production of consumption, product, and self-renewal. The network of commodity and visual symbolic sign systems within which we live is already so dense and pervasive that we fail to take much note of it (e.g., how TV structures daily life). Yet the new cultural forms do have a massive and significant impact on our and our children's identity development, on our world views, politics, social relations, and actions. Not to attend to these new cultural forms and texts, not to teach children the value and the constructedness of our media and mediated understandings of how these texts structure experience, knowledge, and social relations, is pedagogically and politically irresponsible. It is irresponsible in an age when current generations are inheriting a technologically mediated world of work and leisure that is significantly different from how most of us grew up.

CHILDREN AND TELEVISION

That TV is today's mass social educator is without dispute. We might read about the Los Angeles riots, famine in Africa, or middle east and east bloc wars, but how we emotionally contextualize the "facts," how we "vision" what we read, comes directly from powerful screen images. Few of us have lived through war or in famine-stricken regions, but we all know "the look" of starvation and war. Such contextual visual knowledge that frames facts are not derived from books, newspapers, or magazines, but from TV. With 99% of Australian households owning a TV set, 60% of households owning two or more sets, and 72% of all TV households owning a VCR, clearly everyone is exposed to TV's version of social reality. And, unlike books, TV knowledge cuts across the boundaries of class, gender, race, nationality, and geography (Lull, 1990). McLuhan's moment is here: We participate in immediate and global communication, in instant and live war, sports events, famine, inaugurations, entertainment awards, and beauty pageants.

A brief overview at some common TV viewing patterns among Australian families and children will show the extent to which we consume the public pedagogies of media lessons. In Australian households, TV sets are turned on some 30 to 35 hours per week (C. Luke, 1990b). Depending on what statistics are consulted, school-aged children watch on average between 18 and 30 hours a week. Many children watch much more, and many watch far less. By age 18, the average viewer has watched some 14,000 hours of TV, and yet during that same time has spent only 12,000 hours in the classroom in front of teachers and texts. The average viewer sees some 20,000 ads per year, and by age 6, the average viewer has seen some 14,000 violent on-screen images. Television takes up more of children's time than any other activity except sleeping. As Wartella and Mazarella (1990) found in a comparative historical study of U.S. children's use of leisure time, children in the 1980s were spending 51% of their leisure time on media-related activities (TV: 46%; reading: 5%). These figures do not include the time children spend playing video games, or playing with media spin-off toys.

In terms of televisual representation, men outnumber women across all program genres by 3 to 1 (C. Luke, 1990b). Domestic pets appear on screen more frequently than people of color. Men dominate voice-overs regardless of product. Men "age" on screen, whereas women virtually disappear at about age 30 only to be revived in grandmotherly roles. Men solve most political and social problems, whereas women generally wait to be rescued, to be told how to do something right, or to be pursued. In advertising texts, women for the most part have their heads stuck in ovens looking for hidden dirt, they sniff the family's laundry, agonize over product choice, and gain their identity and the loving admiration of the family through domestic accomplishments that always hinge on their embodiment in the correct product choice. Indigenous Australians are absent from the screen: Apparently they do not eat, drive cars, or live in any of our neighborhoods. As one senior advertising executive said, "if we showed Aborigines eating . . . biscuits, nobody would buy them." For the most part, their occasional presence is constructed either as a "social problem" (e.g., deaths in custody, land rights demonstrations) or as anthropological curiosities (e.g., ceremonial dance, craft). Televisual lessons on gender, race, sexuality, power, and politics are inscribed across all TV genres and may well be far more powerful social lessons than those taught at school.

Clearly, 6-year-olds begin their schooling with an already well-established set of values and understandings that have been learned from family, from thousands of hours with TV, and from the artifacts of popular culture with which they grew up. The media-saturated commercialization of children's programming and play, and youth culture more generally, which is so centrally pivoted around televiewing, may be linked to cognitive and behavioral changes and outcomes. As Watkins suggested, in Vygotskian terms, TV may be the dominant activity and experience society provides for the young: it "define[s] important issues, events and values and insure[s] practice in developing socially valued behaviors and thoughts" (Watkins, cited in Wartella & Mazarella, 1990, p. 189). These media(ted) experiences that provide behavioral, social, and cognitive repertoires, begin in infancy as babies attend to the flicker on the screen and, later, when as toddlers they enter the world of the "kidvid" ghetto of TV, video, and the magic world of toy (in)corporations.

TV is not the only source that helps shape identity and world views. Of equal significance are the artifacts of popular culture to which media texts cross-reference and that, together, create an intertextual universe of what Engelhardt (1986) called a *network of desire*. It is in this intertextual network between TV and commodities in which childhood is played out and that, in fact, constructs childhood and youth more generally. In the early 1960s, Engelhardt noted, TV began marketing to increasingly younger audiences, and introduced toy-related programming. Children's programming was transformed into program-length commercials (e.g., *Ghostbusters, Strawberry Shortcake, HeMan, Transformers, Masters of the Universe*, etc.), and children's play (i.e., play narratives and the "toy" action figures central to those narratives) was transformed into simulations of TV programs. As Engelhardt pointed out, "if you take single lines of toys backed by TV programs, enormous advertising budgets, and a universe of product tie-ins, the results are . . . impressive" (p. 79). He noted, for instance, that licensed character products generated $8.5 billion in the United States in 1985, and that $100 million was generated in the first year of Transformer toy marketing (following the launch of the TV series), which is widely considered the most successful toy launch in history. Engelhardt is worth citing at length as he outlined the scope of commercial networking in the United States. But if we consider export markets, global links to off-shore subsidiaries, product dumping in third-world markets, and the endless life and royalty returns of TV reruns and video markets, the scope of the financial empires of children's popular culture takes on enormous proportions. Engelhardt (1986) wrote:

> The linking of such giant toy companies into TV production companies into advertising companies, now often overseeing the actual production of TV series for their toy company clients, tied into distribution companies (some owned by the above) linked

either to a nation-embracing set of independent television stations or directly to the networks, linked to a series of product licensees (sometimes up to one hundred or more per successful character)— this whole chain has had the effect not just of creating a few simple, recognisable images, attachable to almost any object in a child's world, but also of vastly upping the ante for successfully launching new toy lines, which now [in 1986] need an estimated $20 million to $30 million in start-up backing. (pp. 79-80)

WALL-TO-WALL NINJAS

At age 4, children begin the turn to adult programming because children's programming (e.g., *Sesame Street, Playschool*) no longer fulfill their maturing cognitive demands, and because adult programs have a much higher financial investment and therefore deliver state-of-the-art production that children find appealing. But even before that age, children already have grown up in an intertextual universe that ties TV programs to toys, tee shirts, slippers and shoes, games, crayons, coloring books, bed linens, pencil cases, lunchboxes, and even wallpaper. What Ang (1985) called wall-to-wall Dallas is as applicable to the child's world in terms of wall-to-wall *Simpsons, Teenage Mutant Ninja Turtles*, or *Garfield*. Consider, for instance, the hugely successful Garfield icon that has crossed the child–adult divide. Garfield is on every conceivable greeting card (except condolence cards), it is a cartoon, he (and he is male) comes in the shape of birthday cakes, on children's slippers, pajamas, and tee shirts, on pencils, pencil cases, and stationary, in coloring books, as wallpaper, and he is stuck on car bumpers and windows. Bart Simpson or Ninja Turtles similarly fill children's visual landscape.

Television shapes the child's entry into narrative and consumption by being located in the center of family life (however families may be constituted), and by assimilating and cross-referencing to other narrative forms such as movies, stories, comic books, video games, music videos (often movie soundtracks), of which toys are an integral extension. In that regard TV serves as a kind of clearinghouse for both the texts and artifacts of consumption. For children, the jump from narrative to commodities (e.g., from the *Transformer* cartoon to Transformer toys; from *Muppet* cartoons to McDonald's give-aways of Muppet Babies; or from Spielberg movies to spin-off cartoons or fast food outlet contests) seems relatively natural. It is natural and naturalized because it is the background cultural tapestry in which childhood occurs, and one in which (social or biological) parents collude and experience childhood with their children.

Buying into the system, whether the Nintendo, Teenage Mutant Ninja Turtles, Garfield, Strawberry Shortcake, Cabbage Patch, Barbie dolls, Roger Rabbit, or Muppet Babies "system," means both buying into particular ideological narratives (of family structure, gender roles, power relations), and into a social construction of reality that is real, material, and constitutes the lived experiences of childhood and adults (Kinder, 1991). Parents do take their children to McDonald's and purchase the latest figurines; parents do shop at Coles and save their receipts so that their children's school can purchase Mac computers; girls do respond to the cultural images of femininity and starve themselves to get "the look"; parents do buy the cereal or peanut butter children insist on to avoid embarrassing conflicts in the supermarket. These everyday consumer and social practices constitute the lived reality and material relations between parents and children.

If we look at the scope of children's popular culture—not at the adult romanticized version of what children's culture is or should be—then we can begin to see that children spend a lot of their waking hours with TV and the video games, comic books, and toy spin-offs from TV or movies. From infancy, children are indeed immersed in the texts of popular culture, and their understanding of narrative, of good versus evil, of heroes and heroines, gender, race, and social power, is learned from those texts. As pointed out previously, many parents, educators, and social critics find TV, and youth culture more generally, objectionable and politically suspect. However, not all texts and viewing contexts are as morally bankrupt, politically "incorrect," or socially corrupting as "child specialists" often claim. I believe that it is important for teachers and teacher educators to balance their generally negative views of media, popular and youth culture by developing an informed perspective that draws on a range of research findings and theoretical positions. In this next section, I provide an overview of research and some of my own work that has focused on more positive aspects TV and other forms of popular culture.

THE FLIPSIDE OF "NEGATIVE EFFECTS"

Negative public reactions to new communications technologies have a long history. Plato, for instance, was concerned about the cognitive and intellectual consequences of the alphabet because it would eliminate the need for rote memorization of information. If one could "look it up" in print, there would be no need to engage in intellectual dialogue to arrive at knowledge and truth. Similar fears were expressed in the 16th century by many educational reformers following the advent of the printing press and the mass availability of books (C. Luke, 1989). The printing press was seen by many as the work of the devil in undermining the sanctity of holy scripture and the clergy empowered to interpret scripture. Others feared that reading, rather than oral recitation and memorization, would make children cognitively lazy. The advent of the silent pictures in the 1920s, radio in the 1930s and TV in the 1940s, generated the same kinds of negative responses in terms of children's cognitive and social development (C. Luke, 1990b). Social critics, particularly educators, also feared that movies would herald the end of reading, that movie content would undermine the moral and social fabric, and that the movie palace itself posed a health threat to youngsters because they would sit side by side in stuffy and dark theaters unable to talk to each other. Comic books were accused of simplifying and "bastardizing" language. It was claimed that comic book illustrations would reduce children's imagination. So, in many ways, media of communication (which were not always seen as "popular culture" in the way we use the term today) have always generated heated public and academic debate, particularly in relation to the effects on children.

When home video games were first available, many parents and educators warned of the social and health effects of playing the games: the risk of joystick arthritis, the elimination of social interaction, and the potential of video game addiction. However, contrary to public perceptions, video game playing does not isolate children and make them antisocial but they do in fact foster social interaction (Mitchell, 1985). Home video games such as Nintendo apparently bring families together for shared play and interactions, children play against each other, take turns, teach each other new moves and strategies to beat the odds and obstacles, and in schoolyard talk children discuss those texts and textual strategies. Research suggests that when used in moderation, video games can improve children's visual memory, eye–hand coordination, spatial skills, and problem-solving skills (Greenfield, 1984; Mitchell, 1985). The cognitive demands of some video games can augment development of cognitive processes such as processing of visual information from multiple perspectives; decoding iconic spatial representations; reading and manipulating representations in three-dimensional space; and conceptualizing a problem and thinking ahead visually to solve problems (e.g., maze; Greenfield, 1984). Such skills potentially provide the kind of accelerated cognitive challenges that can move the child through a Vygotskian zone of proximal development; that is, cognitive demands that do not limit but are in advance of development and ability (Vasquez, 1994).

Commercial TV, as most would agree, leaves much to be desired. However, alongside much "quality" programming on noncommercial stations, there is much on commercial TV that is eminently educational and prosocial. Although some of this material may, at first glance, look ideologically suspect, spending some time with children and adolescents' favorite programs reveals that not all is as bad as it looks. Not all rock music, for instance, is exclusively about boy-meets-girl, urban alienation, or countercultural resistance. Much current African-American rap music is concerned with social transformation through politically positive lyrics such as pro-education messages that encourage kids to stay in school. Many rock videos promote antiracism, antiviolence, antidrug, and pro-environment messages. MTV news and current affairs deals with political issues in ways that engage young viewers more effectively than the more traditional and often staid talking heads news programs. On MTV a few years ago, Madonna encouraged viewers to vote, Magic Johnson talked about AIDS, and MC Hammer talked about the importance of getting an education and saying no to drugs and gangs. Kids pay attention to their favorite bands and their music: they buy music and fan magazines to follow the social life of their favorite musicians, movie and TV stars. What music or performance artists have to say on issues of importance to teens is, in many ways, more influential than what parents or teachers have to say. Moreover, as research into viewers of American MTV has shown, teens do not watch rock video programs passively and individually; they watch primarily in groups, interact with each other over content, and commonly lip-sync, dance, and interact with the music (Aufderheide, 1986; Sun & Lull, 1986). Along similar lines, cyberpunk music, movies, and novels tend to focus on utopian, often high-tech futures where urban decay, drug cultures, violence, and youth unemployment are the nightmare history of the 20th century. In the face of current and increasing gloom and doom, adolescents find these kinds of texts a positive escape (cf. Rosenthal, 1991).

Many teen TV shows (e.g., *DeGrassi Junior High, Beverly Hills 90210, The Heights, E Street*) and family shows also deal with topics that are important to kids; topics that they wonder about and which parents might be reluctant to raise. These programs deal constructively with alcoholism, drunk driving, abuse in families, birth control, breast cancer, racism, divorce, working parents, single-parent families, and so forth. These programs are important pedagogical texts for kids because they deal with issues that effect young people's lives in important political ways. The Australian screening in 1990 of the documentary on sexual abuse, *Without Consent*, generated a barrage of phone calls nationwide to crisis and counseling hotlines. Viewer response to that program led to follow-up items on current affairs shows that focused on the massive number of call-ins seeking help. Under the production and casting veneer of what may appear like bourgeois complacency and affluence, many of these programs do tackle social justice issues—from racism and poverty, to sexism and disability—which TV may well teach more effectively than the school.

For preschool and primary school-aged children, moderate and mediated TV viewing has been found to enhance young children's play strategies. Moderate preschool viewers apparently devise more complex characterizations, more options and subplots in group play and games. Children who watch moderate amounts of prosocial programs tend to display more awareness of positive family and peer values such as trust, reliance, cooperation, and verbal negotiation as problem solving. In households that are not "print-rich" environments, and where verbal exchanges between adults and children might be minimal, TV can provide access to language, to stories and, for many children, TV provides companionship. In terms of conceptual learning, TV can teach concepts such as transformation and spatial configurations in three-dimensional space much better than print ever will. There are significant differences between seeing the growth of alfalfa sprouts in time-lapse photography and reading about it. From documentaries and popular science programs, children can learn about the inside of the body (via a trip down the oesophagus), the depths of the ocean, about children in other cultures, or the social life of ant colonies, long before they have the literacy skills with which to read about such phenomena. Finally, TV is an irreplaceable source of language, social, and cultural learning for children and adults whose first language is not English. My own experience has taught me that learning another language, culture and cultural idioms is much easier from TV than from books.

All of this is to suggest that TV and popular cultural texts are neither all "bad" nor all intellectually edifying. What is important, however, is that if TV is treated seriously, as a text worthy of serious study, then children will read it differently. As Salomon (1979) pointed out, if we give children some analytic skills and reasons for viewing, they do put more mental effort into viewing, and the visual literacy skills they develop do become part of their viewing/reading repertoire. If we show students how media construct our understandings, how media texts can mean different things to different people, then we can begin to give them the kind of critical social literacy that can emancipate them from some of the forms of domination that structure identity and identity politics. Moreover, it gives teachers the opportunity to use the texts that children are so eminently familiar in order to move toward some of the print-based literacy skills that still remain fundamental to the educational enterprise. TV is such a central part of children's lives that it does not make sense not to capitalize on and extend that knowledge. I discuss this in more detail in the following section.

MEDIA LITERACY: DEBATE AND DEFINITIONS

In English and language arts classrooms around the country, children are taught from short stories, novels, and dramas in order to show what makes them work and how meanings are constructed. Plot, setting, characterization, written, and spoken language are just as present in televisual texts as in other textual forms. But there is a grammar to audiovisual texts that is not present in print texts, and these visual grammars or conventions, kids know quite well. Yet, teachers never ask them to use that knowledge. In fact, "TV talk" is commonly censored in classroom discourse, and if it is "allowed" as part of classroom discourse, it is often used to denigrate TV content and children's viewing.

What is *media literacy*? Many definitional variations abound yet all media literacy curricula generally include four broad aspects: the study of texts; political economy; audience; and production.

At its most rudimentary, media literacy includes the study of all forms of media but is primarily concerned with making students critical of TV's messages, its conventions, genres, and technical features, audience demographics, and their own viewing habits. Because of the pervasiveness of TV and because of the inordinate amount of time children spend watching TV, most media literacy curricula focus heavily on TV literacy. The central aim of TV literacy is to make students critical and selective viewers who are able to reflect critically on TV's messages, their own reasons for viewing, and to use those critical skills in the production of their own print and electronic texts. Core analytic questions are meant to interrupt students' unreflective acceptance of text and to develop new strategies for thinking about the meanings TV transmits, and how viewers construct meanings for themselves from those texts. Within this framework, students are commonly asked to consider the following: How are society, culture, and persons portrayed? What attitudes, values, and conceptions of pleasure and desire do certain texts/programs promote? What technical (semiotic) features are used to generate meanings (e.g., mood, emotion, consumer desire)? How might others, watching from different sociocultural positions, view a certain text/program and what might it mean to them (e.g., stereotyped, racist, homophobic portrayal)? Developing a critical understanding of how texts position individual students must always extend to helping them understand how others might read texts, construct and/or resist textual meanings (see Luke & Freebody, chap. 10, this volume).

Teaching children to take the point of view of others is a skill taught from early primary school and is therefore not a particularly new or difficult concept to introduce. It is a central epistemological strategy in all antiracist, antisexist, and antihomophobic pedagogies. As media educators have repeatedly acknowledged, "students are hungry for dialogue about what they see on television. As soon as it becomes a legitimate research topic, discussion in class intensifies; an opportunity to discuss television immediately provokes student participation; television is a subject about which students believe they can talk and write with experience and authority" (Morris, 1989, p. 40). Students labeled *reluctant readers* or more generally *reluctant* students, might well be reached and transformed into active participants through the incorporation of media studies into classroom work. Giving them access to a medium in which they are experts, one they have watched for years and that comprises a significant part of the prior knowledge they bring to school with them, can open intellectual gateways to concepts and skills that students often resist when presented in the more abstract and middle-class codes of print-based school knowledge.

MEDIA LITERACY: PEDAGOGICAL STRATEGIES

What, then, are some of the more specific features of media literacy? The study of media texts is the most common form of media studies programs. This usually entails a study of the symbols, codes, language, narratives, and genres of particular of films, TV programs, and genres. These analyses can be quantitative (frequency counts of words, speech acts, news items, product brand names, etc.), sociological (content analysis of occupational representation, age groups, gender, race, class, etc.), and/or semiotic analysis (study of sign/symbols signification systems). Quantitative analyses are often used in primary media literacy studies as a lead-in to more qualitative and interpretive analyses. So, for instance, children might be asked to count the number of times a product name appears in a print ad, on the screen or mentioned by the voice-over. The point of this kind of exercise would be to open the way for discussions about the need for repetition and foregrounding in order to persuade the viewer/reader, and to associate the product promises with the product name. Alternately, children might be asked to count and list the number of superlatives in a given ad in order to show how an "old" product (e.g., Colgate) reinvents itself by claiming to be new, improved, and better. This strategy can then also lead into discussions about persuasive intent and writing for an audience. This kind of learning would inform children's subsequent efforts at production of a print or video ad. Primary school students might be asked to prepare an ad for good foods such carrots, raisins, or cheese. In small group work such a project would entail story boarding a short narrative that would include the repetition of key words associated with the product the ad tries to sell (e.g., raisins), and it would include persuasive strategies such as a list of health or social benefits. A simple analysis of frequency counts, then, can lead to more sophisticated textual production and print-related literacy skills.

Sociological analysis provides a broad framework for looking at the representation of groups in society that commonly lead into studies of cultural stereotypes. Identification and description of stereotypes in various media are a common feature of media studies across the grade levels. An analytic focus on how difference (gender, cultural, racial, national, etc.) is culturally constructed—in which kinds of narratives, power relations, and in which genres—enables students and teachers to approach issues related to identity politics, and social justice issues more generally. For instance, analyses of how disability, gender, nationality, or racial/ethnic identity is "stereotyped," marginalized, or excluded in mainstream media texts, can enable student understanding of how "common sense," public attitudes toward difference are inscribed in the media texts of everyday life. Complementing such broad, thematic, and ideological interpretations of stereotyping, semiotic and linguistic analyses can show the microtextual features that underpin the making of stereotyped meanings. We are all semioticians, living in a material and social world coded with endless symbolic meaning systems from traffic signs and clothes to the symbolic meaning systems of classrooms and lounge rooms. The way we combine meanings in how we dress and represent ourselves, and the cultural-specific symbolics and nonverbal communications of facial and bodily gestures, constitute complex sign systems that people produce and "read off" one another. Kids of all ages develop their own "in-group" language and symbolism from the colour of shoelaces and gestural repertoires to clothing regimes that signify fashion statements, group membership and, commonly, a countercultural position from which youth derives its identity of difference from "adult" status quo culture. Semiotics is a way of making the self and reading the world that is part of everyone's everyday social practices. The central conceptual aspect of semiotics is the notion of opposition as intrinsic to all meaning and representation. Again, children of all ages are well familiar with the most fundamental textual strategies based on oppositions (e.g., good vs. bad guys; black associated with evil, white associated with good). All narratives begin with a problem and end with problem resolution: Ads feature a social or individual problem, the product resolves the dilemma, and the narrative closes with a happy and smiling consumer. "Doing semiotics," then, is not something abstract and outside the lived world of most kids.

For instance, technical features such as camera angles, lighting, music, pacing, or uses of colour can reveal a kind of semiotic shorthand used to construct gendered texts. The use of pinks and pastels, fade-ins, slow pacing, and soft music predominate in commercials aimed at girls and women (e.g., in toy, cereal, and feminine hygiene product ads). By contrast, ads targeted at men and boys are characterized by primary colors, quick jump shots, close-ups, fast pacing and hard (often metal) music (e.g., Transformer toys, Iron Man cereal, car ads). Shots of women commonly use downward camera angles, often over the visible shoulder of a male. Such positioning frames women as shorter than males, as diminutive, powerless, and in symbolic and actual need of protection and rescue. Men are usually framed in upward angle camera shots that signify the male as tall, powerful, authoritative, and someone literally and symbolically to "look up to." Simple linguistic or discourse analysis of women's and men's on-screen speech, or female and male "voice" in print ads, can reveal the gender differences between male uses of active verbs, a directive and instructional speech style compared to women who make greater use of passive verbs, question more frequently and provide endless supportive comments to male statements.

At more advanced levels of study, TV texts can be analyzed for their syntagmatic and paradigmatic features: how relationships and signs are selected to hold the narrative together across a particular scene or set of scenes (paradigmatic), and how the semiotic structure of particular bits of text are associated to each other in order to bind the narrative historically (syntagmatic). In terms of more everyday experience, one would view the selection of food, for instance cereal or fruit, at the exclusion of all other choices, as a paradigm that includes the selection of the appropriate dishes and utensils. The bowl of fruit or cereal subsequently enters into syntagmatic association with other signs and sequences associated with a meal, and all the attendant material, social, and cultural rituals and relations. The study of metaphor is common to most English and language arts content areas and is also a key element in media studies syllabi. The study of metaphor and metonymy helps to decode texts at the microtextual level for analysis of meaning and difference. Students, even very young ones, have little trouble identifying what simple symbolisms stand for, or how certain images and genre-specific codes are used to substitute for literal meaning. Thus, the use of laugh tracks in comedy genres signals that a particular scene or line is to be read as humorous. Rolling thunder and lightning, depending on the narrative genre, might signal immanent danger, suspense, or fear. The sign "heart" might denote romance or love in one genre (e.g., dating game shows), or health, exercise, and good nutrition in a heart foundation or fitness promotion. The symbolic shorthand often used with news programs are easy for young students to analyze and can also be used to lead into discussions about stereotyped media constructions of social reality. For instance, the common use of the cricket bat as a logo to signify upcoming sports news might be used to discuss how that particular icon comes to stand for "sports" more generally, and how it subsumes and yet excludes a wide range of other sports (particularly women's sports). Another example might be the common use in news broadcasts of a black-and-white logo of barbed wire signaling an upcoming news item on South Africa. This particular image signifies in very simple terms black and white, division and apartheid, conflict and difference. This kind of semiotic simplification of South Africa's complex historical, racial, and cultural legacy necessarily glosses over those complexities. Analyses of this kind can help students understand how a lifetime of repeated reading and viewing of countless such images from a variety of media sources fill out our frames of reference and help shape our world views.

Central to most senior media studies programs is the political economy of media institutions. Easily dovetailed into social education syllabi, political economic analyses include the study of media ownership legislation, electronic and print media as industries, industry regulations, censorship, viewer classifications, and so forth. Teaching about media institutions leads on to broader issues such as national and global circulation of information, information control and dissemination, corporate ownership and sponsorship, the cultural, social, and economic implications of transnational broadcasting and film distribution. Teachers might consider inviting a local TV station representative to speak to the class about the economics of ratings and the links between ratings and commercial sponsorship. Where available, teachers can make use of local TV stations or production studios and provide students with firsthand experience of how media texts are produced professionally, and how network stations operate. Importantly, the study of media institutions should not solely be focused on students' accumulation of financial figures, corporate names, legislative bodies, or "important" dates and names. Rather, it should extend to helping students develop an understanding of how the globalized world of images and popular cultural artifacts produced by Disney, Mattell Toys, or McDonald's frame particular experiences of childhood and adolescence, or of growing up female or male.

Tied to the study of political economy, the study of media technology is a common component in such units. In order to consider and analyze the mass circulation of media texts, "technological possibilities, constraints, and choices are always capable of opening up questions such as: What kinds of technology are available to whom? How are they used? What difference do these technologies make to the final product?" (Bazalgette, 1992, p. 210). Importantly, technological choices affect meaning and audience-consumer accessibility.

Technological literacy is not confined to computer skills, or editing and camera skills in the media classroom, but includes a critical understanding of technological hardware, costs and ownership, questions of control, selection, exclusion, and distribution.

The study of audience is the study of how audiences are made and sold, the social and personal uses of media, and reader positioning. Most primary media studies programs begin with personal uses. That is, children are asked what they watch and why, what their favorite TV characters are and why. The aim at this level of study is to enable children to talk about their likes and dislikes, to enable discussion about family viewing rules, what they consider "good" and "bad" about TV. Conceptually, most media studies at primary level aim to help children understand the difference between fantasy and reality, to understand that media texts are made by people with specific intents (e.g., to sell, to entertain), and to become aware of how much and what kinds of TV children in this age group watch. From this early "making conscious" of the role of TV in their lives, children are encouraged to produce alternate media texts much like they are asked to produce written text with a topic or audience in mind. Making simple viewing logs of what each child or the entire family watches aims to encourage a self-reflective understanding of how much time is actually spent in front of the TV. A cumulative class graph on students' total viewing could lead to a maths activity, to considerations of what other activities children could pursue instead of TV, and how to begin viewing selectively rather than compulsively.

Even with very young children, semiotic analyses can help reveal how texts position viewers, how certain generic conventions frame specific messages. So, for instance, young children are quite adept at explaining how certain ads make appeals to viewers by the use of imagery and sound. Appeals to thirst and hunger are common among commercials targeted at children: Soft drink ads use sounds and visuals to simulate heat and dryness to which the product responds in representational frames signifying thirst quenching sounds of liquid and fizziness to accompany huge icy condensation drops slipping slowly down the side of a soft drink can or bottle. Toy and snack food ads appeal to children through the use of happy children, themes of fun, friendship, upbeat music, laughter, and good times. The message in these ads, children readily point out, is that "if you have this toy or snack, all your friends will come around and you will laugh and have fun." Appeal strategies, then, target particular audiences through the identification of a lack or negative state (no good snack, pimples, or thirst), the product as problem solver, and the social benefits associated with that product. Children know this textual grammar well, although they lack the technical vocabulary with which to interpret the text. But they do understand narrative, generic conventions, and the semiotic structuring of meaning (cf. Hodge & Tripp, 1986).

At primary school levels, the central aim is not primarily to provide children with the "correct" technical language and interpretation but, rather, to move them towards an understanding that televisual texts are cultural texts worthy of serious study: in the ways by which meaning is made through language, image, and sound. Early visual literacy teaching aims to give children the opportunity to observe and talk about what they see and hear. Much as print literacy is centered on the production of print text, media literacy curricula include the production of media texts (from photomontages and newspaper ads or editorials to video productions). Production is an essential feature of media literacy studies although too often teachers get locked into text analyses and interpretation because such teacher-directed activities enable pedagogies of control.

English and language arts teaching focuses on genre study, on point of view, on the study of drama, novels, poetry, and short stories, on aspects of plot, setting, and characterization features that make a "good story." Because both English and media studies are primarily concerned with the study of language, interpretation, and meaning—the decoding and encoding of texts—there is nothing incompatible about making children literate in print and media-specific conventions. Teachers generally index classroom study to out-of-school examples and to contemporary culture more generally. Children are readers of both print (literature) and electronic media texts (contemporary culture) and, therefore, teachers should provide children with opportunities to become literate in and producers of both print and audiovisual texts. The making of video texts is not confined only to the English or media classroom, but cuts across the curriculum and grade levels. In senior social education, for instance, students can produce a video segment (augmented with written work) on local or endangered architecture and urban (mis)planning; as a "social science" project, students can prepare, organize and videotape interviews with any number of experts: from town planning, waste recycling and disposal, women's shelters, tertiary education institutions, or community and welfare agencies. In the science classroom, units on climate, environmental protection and sustainable development, electricity, or the circulatory system similarly lend themselves to student media productions (e.g., videotape, slides, photomontages).

All such activities require group work and collaborative research: Students allocate tasks, story board, undertake preliminary library research on specific topics, organize equipment, write letters requesting an interview with relevant experts, prepare charts, graphs, or essays to accompany a videotape or slide production and, finally, present the finished product to the class. Primary school-aged children are keen actors in front of the camera and they are generally less self-conscious and self-critical in seeing themselves on screen. Moreover, as many teacher educators working in media studies report, "many teachers are already familiar with the experience of discovering that five-year-olds know more about video recording and playback than they do" (Bazalgette, 1992, p. 41). And because role-playing and, often, short stage (usually Christmas) plays, are common fare in the primary classroom, these are ready-made opportunities for teachers to videotape short productions.

The next step is to incorporate some of the elements of decoding advertisements as outlined earlier, and to have children prepare a short video text such as an ad for a healthy food or drink, an antilitter campaign for the school, an announcement for an upcoming fete or school play, or a "tourist guide" of the classroom or primary school wing. Older children can work on conceptually and technically more advanced ads or public service announcements: a tinned food or recycled clothing drive for the local shelter; an information clip on the school (e.g., its history, grounds, facilities, interviews with teaching and ancillary staff, etc.); a segment on national literacy or disability week; a bulletin on upcoming school events (fete, play, musical, sports, parent meetings, invited speakers, etc.). All such activities break the traditional boundaries between book knowledge and the social world to which that knowledge allegedly refers. Moreover, such activities enable students to combine critical and practical skills by encouraging collaboration about how a "story" is to be framed; how a message is best transmitted through language, sound, and image; how medium-specific conventions, codes, and genres can be combined in the production of alternative texts that do not conform to the traditional TV stereotype of sensationalized violence as the only means by which to gain and maintain viewer attention. Importantly, media production as a way of producing knowledge opens classroom learning to explorations of contemporary out-of-school culture alongside the study of more traditional text-bound learnings.

CULTURAL STUDIES IN THE CLASSROOM

Teaching with and about media should not be seen as focused only on the study of media and popular culture. Teachers not uncommonly associate media literacy with, for example, the study of soap operas, the Madonna signifier, or ads to "expose" ideology at work from which the teacher will liberate children with the correct analytic tools. These common misperceptions of what media studies is all about ignore the productive potential of teaching with and about media. That is, as long as teachers operate from the marxian false consciousness notions of ideology as fundamental premises of media studies, then all classroom activities based on the study and use of media will remain locked into a model in which TV is the ideological culprit, and students the "duped" viewers who must be emancipated from "bad habits" and "incorrect readings" (Williamson, 1981-1982). This approach positions the teacher as an objective knower and interpreter in contrast to students who cannot "see through" the text when, in fact, it is often teachers who cannot see through the text beyond its object-level representations. Pedagogy then becomes a tool leveled against students' pleasures derived from TV programs, from rock music, and popular culture more generally. As Buckingham (1993) pointed out, students then quickly learn to conceal their liking for and interpretations of the texts and practices they are asked to respond to, and merely give the teacher what he or she wants in the way of a politically correct position and terminology. The point is that a critical cultural and social literacy, one that includes a critical understanding of media texts, industries, and the production of meaning, must balance discourse critique with giving students opportunities for alternative readings and text productions.

Such alternatives should not rely solely on the teacher's definition of what is appropriate but, rather, should fit into a negotiated framework of acceptable limits within which students' definitions of "alternatives" can find an expressive space. In other words, a class might agree that racist and sexist content is not something students should reproduce in any expressive mode. Here, teachers need to strike a morally responsible balance between their own values and socialized tendencies toward censorship, and the pedagogical imperative of attending to student difference: all those socially marked differences that mark out various reading, writing, and meaning-making positions. Specific guidelines for alternative texts, then, for what is ruled in and out in classroom discourse, cannot be prescribed here because such injunctions would defeat the contextual demands of any classroom situation. However, this does not mean the absence of some common standards applicable to all classrooms that would ensure observation of some fundamental principles of human rights and dignity (e.g., exploitative characterization of women, AIDS victims, lesbians and gays, persons of color, religious groups, etc.).

To envision what students' alternative media texts and readings might be requires that teachers give up their generally negative attitudes towards TV, popular and youth culture, and that they spend time with and develop an interest in the cultural texts, artifacts, and practices that are so important to the age group that they teach. Teachers can provide students with the analytical tools to become critical TV viewers and consumers of mass culture without ruining the pleasures they derive from popular culture. However, it requires teachers and teacher educators to take a less denigrating attitude toward TV, youth and popular culture, and accept that there is much of questionable value but also much that is socially positive and educational. Academic cultural studies since the 1970s has helped explain a lot of what goes on in schools, and there is no reason why teachers and teacher educators cannot translate some of those insights into a cultural studies pedagogy (Green & Bigum, 1993). A study of the political economy of media and popular culture, of audience and text, lends itself a cultural studies approach to pedagogy and curricular content. The study of popular culture enables teachers to reveal the culturally situated structures of world views, to get students to start questioning who counts as socially and politically relevant, and how persons learn to objectify and reinvent themselves in products and the lifestyles they promise.

A cultural studies approach to knowledge can help show students how identities—people's senses of selves and others—are cultural products coproduced by various media, community and peer culture, the school (texts and practices), in the shopping mall or playground, and by bodily self-inscriptions. Cultural studies is a perspective and set of analytical tools that aim to deconstruct everyday cultural practices and texts in which everyday life is lived in uniquely "individual" and collective ways. In my estimation, the kind of social and cultural literacy presupposed as pedagogical ends of cultural studies is not something that should be left to university level studies, but is eminently applicable to and politically important for primary and secondary school studies. As I have tried to show so far, the sociocultural construction and marketing of childhood in mass consumer culture begins long before they start school, transforms them during their schooling into what counts as adolescence and young adulthood, and certainly constructs material and discursive possibilities for them as adult women, men and, later, perhaps as parents.

CRITICAL MEDIA LITERACY: SO WHAT?

Much research, mostly British, has shown that kids are not the cultural dupes adults often judge them to be (Alvarado & Boyd-Barrett, 1992; Buckingham, 1993; Lusted, 1991). In fact, kids are astute (and often critical) viewers who, however, may not have the technical "deconstructive" vocabulary teachers consider appropriate for textual analysis (see Green, chap. 11, this volume). One recent development in scholarly debates over media education has been a concern with the politics of pleasure. Media studies scholars have noted that the relocation of children's and adolescents' "leisure/pleasure" texts into the classroom for formal intellectual scrutiny, potentially subverts and belittles whatever pleasure kids derive from such texts and the social relations within which such texts are consumed. Buckingham, for instance, quite rightly pointed out that kids know very well that adults (particularly teachers) disapprove of TV content and, by association, of TV viewing. By asking children in the public forum of the classroom to undertake ideology critique of the texts that are important to them and that usually form a subversive counterpoint to the discourse of schooling, teachers unwittingly position students to reveal and possibly disavow their "secret pleasures." In other words, by giving students the technical skills with which to dismantle and dismiss ideologically incorrect texts—to identify stereotyping, class bias, sexist or racist content—we ask them to expose and confess to desires, and publicly to confess their dislike of programs that they probably like a lot. Getting students to admit to liking anything, then, can easily slip into giving the teacher what he or she wants (see Baker, chap. 12, this volume): that is, claiming to like educationally edifying content such as documentary or "quality" adult programs, and claiming disdain for soaps, rock videos, or talk shows. Moreover, by making the familiar unfamiliar by intellectualizing mundane TV content through abstract conceptual terminology can imply that kids are immature or stupid. Because teachers ask students to "see through" media texts with politically correct analytical lenses, teachers imply that students cannot do so on their own, and that what they watch is believed to be real.

Any adult asking children questions about TV—particularly in classroom contexts—is likely to cue a critical response that is often an outright lie. As with any "critical" discourse (including that of critical pedagogy more generally), school and university students are quick to talk a good antisexist, antiracist, pro-equity game. As teachers are well aware, what students write in the essay or what they tell us in classroom discussion is no measure of what goes on in their heads. Boys can easily show outrage at the sexist portrayal of women in the media, much as White kids can feign to be appalled at racist portrayal. Not surprisingly, there appear to be class distinctions in children's "critical responses" to media. As with print literacy instruction, middle-class children are more likely to produce the abstract, critical interpretations of text that teachers expect. Buckingham (1993), for instance, found that middle-class children are much more adept at reproducing critical readings of TV, and of publicly distancing themselves from the texts that they may well like. Working-class kids, on the other hand, make less of an effort to put themselves "above" the text. Instead, they take great pleasure out of celebrating their pleasure in the face of teachers' common distaste for and critical readings of students' favorite texts and genres: from horror and slasher films to "low value" game shows, talk shows, or soaps. Working-class students' refusal to conform to and confirm the teachers' critical interpretations of media texts he or she judges as "low brow" or politically incorrect, easily positions them and their work outside of what are considered appropriate critical responses. This scenario is reminiscent of Willis' (1977) working-class resistance scenario that guaranteed educational failure, not success.

Media studies is often seen as a curricular area inclusive of the experiences and knowledges of working-class and minority cultures. However, without a politicization of the economy of value and information exchange that goes on in the classroom, critical studies and pedagogies can easily exclude and repress the very content and sociocultural practices it claims to center. The most damning critics of TV - those students who can display the most contempt for popular TV and, by association, its audiences—are those who win out with the teacher. Those students are overwhelmingly from middle-class and upper class origins (Buckingham, 1993).

In the process of teaching students to become critical of "low-brow" mass culture, middle-class kids cultivate bourgeois taste and accumulate cultural capital that distinguishes them from others. And whether middle-class students actually read popular texts critically or not, the point is that they are rewarded for those critical judgments and readings. I would suggest, however, that the cultural and class divisions of knowledge reproduction in the classroom are not confined to media and popular cultural studies. What is different about media studies is that it advocates critical practice that can border on condemning youth's cultural terrain that adults commonly associate with "dangerous" meanings and pleasures. Unlike typical English, science, mathematics, or social education syllabi, which most students treat as "school knowledge," as mostly "unreal" and unconnected to their lived experience, popular culture is a sphere of meaning and practice distinctly separate from school, adults, parents. And although social critics and theorists might talk about contemporary culture and the subject within it as *simulacra*, a mirror world of simulations and inauthentic cyborg identities, it is nonetheless a very real dimension of experience for today's children and teens. To take that experience into the classroom and show its cultural constructedness, its ideological fabrication, myths and countermyths, is potentially to encourage a critical practice suspicious of students' meanings and pleasures, and the making of a critical viewer who can only recognize pleasure as a form of deception and for whom there isn't much left to enjoy.

WHAT IS TO BE DONE?

What, then, can be done to prevent or at least minimize such outcomes? I do not believe that, within the present sociopolitical organization of mass schooling, there are practical ways to escape the imperatives of assessment, hierarchical relations of power and control, normative definitions of what is to count as "school knowledge," or normatively defined "critical readings." But an acknowledgment of the school's political functions of normalization and selection should not, in principle, prevent teachers from making a committed effort to address difference among students on several important cultural levels.

First, teachers and teacher educators need to confront and accept the fact that today's students have grown up in a technological and cultural world radically different from generations who have grown up in the 1950s and 60s. As Green and Bigum (1993) aptly put it, what appear to today's teachers as "aliens in the classroom" are a consequence of educators' refusals to engage with the cultural and subcultural experiences, identities, skills, and knowledges with which kids come to school. An understanding of the sociocultural and discursive construction of youth and childhood culture is an essential first step in making educators aware of the profound difference between the lived technocultural experiences of students, and the experiences schooling offers through a fundamentally monologic, linear, static, and text-based curriculum. The move then is toward an understanding of student differences of (gender, sexual, racial and ethnic) identities, and of class and cultural locations from which children differentially enter into the broader mass cultural discourses. For example, Nintendo's *Super Mario Brothers 4*, *Indiana Jones and the Temple of Doom*, *Total Recall*, or *Karate Kid* games address a male audience and thereby provide very different experiences for girls. Or, as Turnbull (1993) pointed out, classroom deconstruction of feminine stereotypes may mean very different things to Anglo-Australian and migrant girls. Migrant girls, Turnbull noted, are often caught in contradictory positions by having to denounce politically incorrect media images of women in classroom work. Yet, secretly they value and aspire to such images and visions of autonomous, "carefree" women because they stand in direct opposition to the traditional gender roles they are expected to conform to at home. Difference in popular cultural experience, then, is not only a profound knowledge gulf between many teachers and students, but students' gender identity, class, and ethnic cultural locations make for very different experiences and readings of popular culture among students. What this suggests is the urgent need for educators to engage constructively with media, popular and youth culture to better understand how these discourses structure childhood, adolescence, and students' knowledge.

Second, as critical sociological accounts of schooling have long argued, teachers need to come to terms with and actively intervene in the exclusionary and divisive consequences of their own pedagogical practices that continue to distribute knowledge, privilege, and educational rewards unequally. And although these kind of prescriptions for change since the 1970s, targeted at teachers, classroom practice and curriculum, have guided arguments in much academic work that claims to take a critical social theoretical position, the target for change should not reside only with teachers but ideally should to begin in teacher education programs. The incorporation of a cultural studies approach in teacher education enables not only the teaching of media and popular culture, cultures of childhood and adolescence; it theoretically enables the teaching of all other "sacred" educational theories and concepts as historical and cultural constructs, as provisional interpretive schemata, and as both derivative and constitutive of the era, cultural and epistemological moment from which and for whom such theories speak.

Third, and in specific relation to teaching with and about media and popular culture, unless analyses and production are related to students' own experiences, then media studies will remain a purely academic exercise. Whether popular cultural texts are used as a vehicle into a content area or are studied in their own right, the realities of students' and teachers' situatedness in the cultural politics of everyday life should remain the pedagogical core of constructing classroom knowledge and final learning "objectives." A critical cultural and media literacy, divorced from the cultural and contradictory experiences of everyday life, can readily deteriorate into another set of unimaginative print-based exercises in which students "do" images of Aborigines, women, or sporting heroes, much like they are asked to "do" Napoleon, Captain Cook, or bushrangers. The need for curricular and pedagogical "relevance" reaches beyond the primary and secondary classroom and includes undergraduate preservice and postgraduate inservice teaching . Returning teachers, perhaps more so than preservice undergraduates, require a theoretical updating and initiation into the texts and pedagogical strategies for teaching with and about the postmodern cultural spheres their students inhabit that are far more complex than and incomparable to the world they entered as beginning teachers.

Fourth, teachers need to take seriously and to acknowledge students' different readings of and pleasures derived from popular culture while guarding against potential slippage into a vacuous celebration of individual taste, pleasure, or personal responses. As mentioned previously, this is not an easy task because so much of progressive pedagogies, and English teaching in particular, valorize personal voice and growth. Not unrelated, feminist pedagogy too argues for a politics of voice and difference articulated by and for women and girls. However, the postmodern turn to difference and heterogeneity does not mean that "anything goes" (C. Luke, 1993a). What it does mean is that a commitment to social justice principles should guide teacher work in enabling students to come to their own realizations that homophobic, racist, or sexist "opinion" or "readings," quite simply, oppress and subordinate others. Providing students with theoretically and historically grounded frameworks from which to approach cultural and textual constructs of identity gives students the discourse analytic tools with which to interrogate the sociocultural and historical contingencies of difference, exclusion, and marginalization (see Kamler, chap. 19, this volume). Such critical interrogation should focus not only on media and popular cultural texts, but should be used to interrogate all school texts from basal readers to science, geography or history texts in order that students question the politics of constructs such as "science," "progress," "History," "discovery," "populations," "society and the individual," and so forth.

Ultimately, I believe that if schooling refuses to deal with the texts of everyday life—which include media and school texts—then educators will indeed widen, not bridge, the experiential and knowledge gap between both teacher and student "aliens." If we resist the changes currently underway as part of the postmodernist moment of technological change, economic and cultural upheaval, and if we continue to conceive of literacy as narrowly print defined and applicable only to a print culture of an earlier time, then teachers and teacher educators will be teaching a generation of kids conceptualized according to an outdated concept of the child—kids who no longer exist in our classrooms, homes, and on the streets.

REFERENCES

Alvarado, M., & Boyd-Barrett, O. (Eds.). (1992). *Media education*. London: British Film Institute/Open University Press.

Ang, I. (1985). *Watching Dallas: Soap opera and the melodramatic imagination*. London: Methuen.

Aufderheide, P. (1986). Music videos: The look of the sound. *Journal of Communication, 36*(1), 57-78.

Baudrillard, J. (1983). Simulations. *Semiotext(e)*, 1-13, 23-49.

Bazalgette, C. (1992). Key aspects of media education. In M. Alvarado & O. Boyd-Barrett (Eds.), *Media education*. London: British Film Institute/Open University Press.

Bourdieu, P. (1984). *Distinction: A social critique of the judgement of taste*. New York: Routledge & Kegan Paul.

Buckingham, D. (1993). *Children talking television: The making of television literacy.* London: Falmer Press.

de Lauretis, T. (1987). *Technologies of gender.* Bloomington: Indiana University Press.

Engelhardt, T. (1986). Children's television: The shortcake strategy. In T. Gitlin (Ed.), *Watching television.* New York: Pantheon Books.

Green, B., & Bigum, C. (1993). Aliens in the classroom. *Australian Journal of Education, 37*(2), 119-141.

Greenfield, P. (1984). *Mind and media: The effects of television, video games, and computers.* Cambridge, MA: Harvard University Press.

Grossberg, L. (1984). "I'd rather feel bad than not feel anything at all": Rock and roll, pleasure and power. *Enclitic, 8*, 95-111.

Harvey, D. (1989). *The condition of postmodernity.* Oxford,UK: Blackwell.

Hirsch, E. D. (1987). *Cultural literacy.* New York: Random House.

Hodge, B., & Tripp, D. (1986). *Children and television.* Cambridge, UK: Polity.

Horkheimer, M., & Adorno, T. (1972). *Dialectic of enlightenment* (J. Cumming, Trans.). New York: Herder & Herder.

Kinder, M. (1991). *Playing with power in movies, television and video games: From Muppet Babies to Teenage Mutant Ninja Turtles.* Berkeley: University of California Press.

Kline, S. (1993). *Out of the garden: Toys and children's culture in the age of TV marketing.* Toronto: Garamond Press.

Lash, S. (1990). *Sociology of postmodernism.* New York: Routledge.

Luke, C. (1989). *Pedagogy, printing and protestantism: The discourse on childhood.* Albany: State University of New York Press.

Luke, C. (1990a). *Constructing the child viewer: An historical study of the discourse on television and children.* New York: Praeger Press.

Luke, C. (1990b). *TV and your child.* Sydney, Australia: Angus & Robertson.

Luke, C. (1993a). The politicised I and depoliticised "we": The politics of theory in postmodern feminisms. *Social Semiotics, 2*(2), 1-20.

Luke, C. (1993b). Television curriculum and popular literacy: Feminine identity politics and family discourse. In B. Green (Ed.), *The insistence of the letter: Literacy studies and curriculum theorizing.* London: Falmer Press.

Lull, J. (1990). *Inside family viewing: Ethnographic research on televisions' audiences.* New York: Routledge.

Lusted, D. (1991). *The media studies book.* New York: Routledge.

McNeal, J. (1987). *Children as consumers.* Lexington, MA: Lexington Books.

Mitchell, E. (1985). The dynamics of family interaction around home video games. *Marriage and Family Review, 8*(1-2), 121-135.

Morris, B. (1989). The television generation: Couch potatoes or informed critics? *English Journal, 78*(8), 35-41.

Press, A. (1991). *Women watching television: Gender, class, and generation in the American television experience.* Philadelphia: University of Pennsylvania Press.

Rosenthal, P. (1991). Jacked in: Fordism, cyberpunk, marxism. *Socialist Review, 21*(1), 79-104.

Seiter, E. (1991). Toys are us: Marketing to children and parents. *Cultural Studies, 6,* 232-247.

Sun, S., & Lull, J. (1986). The adolescent audience for music videos and why they watch. *Journal of Communication, 36*(1), 115-125.

Turnbull, S. (1993). The media: Moral lessons and moral careers. *Australian Journal of Education, 37*(2), 153-168.

Vasquez, O. (1994). The magic of La Clase Magica: Enhancing the learning potential of bilingual children. *Australian Journal of Language and Literacy, 17*(2), 120-128.

Wartella, E., & Mazarella, S. (1990). A historical comparison of children's use of leisure time. In R. Butsch (Ed.), *For fun and profit: The transformation of leisure into consumption.* Philadelphia: Temple University Press.

Williamson, J. (1981-1982). How does girl number twenty understand ideology? *Screen Education, 40,* 83-84.

Willis, P. (1977). *Learning to labour: How working class kids get working class jobs.* Farnborough, UK: Saxon House

3
Pleasure and Danger:
Children, Media and Cultural Systems
Response to Carmen Luke

Linda Christian-Smith
University of Wisconsin

Recently, 5-year-old Austin Messner from Ohio set a fire in his mobile home that killed his 2-year-old sister. This tragedy received unprecedented coverage in the national television news, major newspapers, and the tabloids. Television itself and its influence on child viewers was on trial. It was alleged that an episode of MTV's popular *Beavis and Butt-head*, featuring two unconventional teens of the same names, may have been a factor in the events in Ohio. Beavis and Butt-head's recurring fascination with fire culminated in a torch scene in an episode that the Ohio boy had viewed. According to the boy's mother, Austin was "obsessed" with Beavis and Butt-head and tried to imitate their actions ("Cartoon on MTV," 1993).

Although MTV denied any responsibility, it promised to delete references to fire in the show and to re-examine the show's contents in general. At risk were millions of dollars of licensing deals held by MTV. A school in Sioux Falls, South Dakota had already banned clothing and the memorabilia bearing likenesses of Beavis and Butt-head (Schwed, 1993). Mike Judge, creator of *Beavis and Butt-head*, conveyed that the show was not meant for small children and should have aired in a later time slot. MTV has since moved the show to late evening. In all the press coverage of the Ohio tragedy, more details of Austin's life and his perspectives are yet to become public. What do young viewers think of Beavis and Butt-head? Children interviewed for the TV program *Inside Edition* conveyed that they watch *Beavis and Butt-head* because the characters are "very funny," "gross," "hostile," and "express how we feel." Beavis and Butt-head may represent some youth's resentment of adult authority, and their alienation in postindustrial societies with diminished opportunities for youth. In another sense, Beavis and Butt-head enact the extremes of alienation: prejudice and violence. The *Beavis and Butt-head* controversy encapsulates many of the varying perspectives and positions the media and popular culture occupy in the lives of youth discussed by C. Luke in chapter 2.

The current moral panics over *Beavis and Butt-head* are equally about the social construction of childhood in postmodern societies as they are about the influences of the media, especially television. There is little new in the current perceptions in many English-speaking countries that segments of youth culture are dangerous, morally corrupt, out of control, and that the media is at fault. Forerunners of today's media-oriented youth cultures such as soap opera fans, romance-fiction readers, devotees of MTV, *Beavis and Butt-head*, and rap can be found in early rock and roll's young enthusiasts. They, too, formed youth cultures from the discourses of records, fan magazines, movies, TV and other commodities, in relation to broader discourses of gender, class, race, ethnicity, sexuality, family, and age.

Luke is correct in her assessment that the continuing social uneasiness with television relates to larger issues of children, power, control, and the plurality of children's interpretations of the media. Popular media represents the areas that many youth have claimed as their own, where they may feel in most control, and out of reach of parents' and teachers' surveillance and power. Christian-Smith (1993a) and Nilan (1993) found that for some White young women and young women of color from the working class, reading teen romance fiction and viewing teen programs and soap operas are important vehicles for expressing competence and working out their relations with families, peers, and romantic partners. These findings complement Luke's position that children are neither passive nor unsophisticated consumers of media; their perceptions are often critical and astute. However, Buckingham (1993) suggested that many children are very protective of the television they view. They recognize adult disapproval of their viewing choices and what this viewing says about themselves and their backgrounds.

MTV's fears of consumer backlash over *Beavis and Butt-head* are rooted in the media's understanding that much of youth culture is commodified culture. In many peer groups, consumer goods such as brand-named clothing, athletic shoes, and sports team jackets demarcate and sharpen social class boundaries. Children and youth often embody in their clothing and talk, images and discourses from commercially successful enterprises such as *Barney* and *Beverly Hills 90210*. Luke neither celebrates nor condemns the commodification of youth culture. Her interest is in exploring how TV constructs consumer positions and establishes tastes and desires in children from early on. Luke's emphasis on the intertextual formation of subjectivities in the context of families as consumer units represents a promising direction for future research and media education—a direction taken up by several other contributors to this volume. She links TV with other popular culture forms and commodities to theorize childhood as a network of material and discursive relations in late capitalism. Children enter into these relations within family life where TV frequently occupies a central position. According to Luke, parents are an important link in this consumption process. They purchase for children and themselves the very products TV promotes thus bringing market relations into the center of family life. However, these same commodities associated with television, such as video games, video movies, and cable TV, now provide the means for many parents to keep their children at home and away from the increasing violence, racism, and sex crimes on the streets of larger cities and in suburbia. Ironically, children may still confront these in TV programming and through familial relations that merge with the uncertainties they feel growing up today.

Kaplan's (1987, p. 5) statement regarding the ways "MTV addresses the desire, fantasies and anxieties of young people growing up in a world in which all traditional categories are being blurred and all institutions questioned—a characteristic of postmodernism" summarizes a number of issues raised here. According to Walkerdine (1984, p. 167), fantasy is a process featuring "active engagement and construction" of a wish and its fulfillment, which are linked to unconscious desires and scenes. Fantasy as the imaginary world and its contents provides a means of dealing with emotions, working out conflicts and life solutions to difficult problems where secret hopes and dreams come true (La Planche & Pontalis, 1986). Early commentators on alienation in industrial societies predicted the extremes of nihilism represented by the *Beavis and Butt-head* show in communities where few opportunities exist for youth and where futures are limited. The case is more acute for young working-class women and men of color who frequently do not have access even to diminished resources and who face bleaker futures.

With lived social experiences becoming more painful, TV and other popular media become the means for reshaping identities and experiences according to one's desires and fighting back against social systems through fantasizing other worlds. This "mild form" of protest (Radway, 1984) may leave conditions unchanged. Nevertheless, given their circumstances, this may be all that some children can do. Nilan (1993) noted that the genres young women prefer, such as soap operas and romance fiction, recognize and focus on the concerns of great importance to them within forms that bring to the fore aesthetic pleasure and emotional engagement. Popular media work on the levels of consciousness and desire, areas that male youth in particular protect from the scrutiny and possible ridicule of adults and peers, especially when that exposure could occur in school. Students are acutely aware that pleasure and desire in the classroom are mediated by restraint, policed and often punished. Yet, pleasure and desire are central to developing the kind of critical media literacy Luke advocates.

Now that TV's position as mass educator and leisure pursuit is becoming more pronounced, there is a crucial need for critical media education. Luke's proposal draws its framework from cultural studies, postmodernisms, feminist poststructuralisms, and critical literacy research. They are tools for analyzing the different meanings and social positions consumers of written and visual texts construct for themselves in everyday life. However, these perspectives also pose challenges for serving as a basis for cultural politics and classroom practice. Luke skillfully combines these often contradictory perspectives into a framework that does not sacrifice the strengths of any one perspective or gloss over the tensions among them.

Cultural studies provides an interdisciplinary approach for the study of subjectivities that views popular culture as a site of social differences and struggle (but see Hunter, chap. 16, this volume). Popular culture forms are connected to economic and social relations, power and oppression, particularly in terms of gender, class, race, ethnicity, sexuality, and age. Although these features of cultural studies strengthen Luke's approach to critical media studies, there are some limitations in television research within cultural studies. Television research has only lately combined audience studies with textual studies and moved away from analyzing audience responses as false consciousness or acts of resistance to dominant ideologies (Buckingham, 1993; Fiske, 1989; Luke, 1988). With its focus on the ideological and economic, cultural studies has neglected until recently the politics of pleasure and desire (Christian-Smith, 1993b; Grossberg, 1986), which are integral to children's TV viewing.

Feminist poststructuralisms and postmodernisms occupy the ground between these positions, suggesting that for any social event ,a multiplicity of readings and meanings are possible. Luke identifies three relevant strands of postmodernism: philosophical, cultural and economic. These strands provide ways for theorizing and analyzing the emergence of dynamic, new forms of social, political and economic arrangements from global perspectives. However, Hall (1986) claimed that postmodernism in general has focused on Western sign systems, particularly those associated with U.S. capitalism, thereby abetting and reproducing its dominance. Luke's inclusion of postcolonial discourses connects global imageries with the local histories and the struggles of oppressed groups (see P. Singh, chap. 5, this volume).

Hall (1986) and McRobbie (1986) have also extensively criticized the postmodernism associated with Baudrillard, particularly his notion of *simulacra* and its relation to subjectivity formation. Summarizing Baudrillard (1993) in this regard, Luke (chap. 2, this volume) explains that "the subject is seen as the product of cultural symbols and signification systems that are said to have no referent to any concrete "real" material objects or relations in the world" (p. 22). The notion of *simulacrum* may draw too tight a boundary around the meanings of cultural processes associated with the media, reducing them to cause–effect relationships enveloping individuals and inspiring pessimism (Grossberg, 1986). This could lead to resignation, making concrete struggles around cultural symbols and signification systems even more difficult. Yet, it is equally difficult to deny that simulated experiences are not the basis for many everyday actions where fantasies are planned out as in the *Beavis and Butt-head* controversy.

Many feminists have embraced postmodernism's and poststructuralism's rejection of a unified self in favor of multiple, fluid subjectivities (see Gilbert, chap. 4, this volume). However, Code (1991) suggested that behind this freedom is a new form of determinism in which "human agents are swept along by a tide of discourse that they are powerless to resist"(p. 180). These features of poststructuralism and postmodernism trouble many feminists because of their relativism and the difficulty of forging a political practice and effecting change in an atmosphere of constantly shifting subjectivities (Code, 1991; Fraser, 1989). A way around these dilemmas is the notion of *positionality* that Luke endorses. This allows for subjectivities to change in response to different contexts, to become sufficiently stable to permit active political involvement, and remain open to negotiation and redefinition (Code, 1991). Positionality is an important analytical concept for media education because it furthers individuals' and groups' understandings of the interrelationships of contexts, media, and subjectivities formation.

The theories and practices discussed here form the basis of critical literacy studies as conceptualized by Luke and the other contributors to this volume. By connecting media education to critical literacy, Luke greatly strengthens her proposal through the considerable explanatory powers of critical literacy studies. Critical literacy emphasizes the socioeconomic and political relations constructed through literate practices within the politics of everyday life (Baker & Luke, 1991). TV is one component of literacy, introducing children to narrative structure and preparing them for their interaction with print media. This focus on everyday media consumption infuses new vitality into the customary study areas of media education—texts, political economy, audiences, and production. Engaging with the TV that children watch and enjoy can enhance Luke's (chap. 2, this volume) goals for critical media education:

> If we show students how media construct our understandings, how media texts mean different things to different people, then we can begin to give them the kind of critical social literacies that can emancipate them from some of the forms of dominations that structure identity and identity politics. (p. 32)

When these goals are articulated through the proposed theoretical framework, children can obtain access to powerful discourses for understanding how the texts of everyday life construct their knowledge of the world and the various social positions they occupy. Yet, teachers face some challenges stemming from the social and political dynamics of classrooms, peer groups, and students' diverse backgrounds. In teaching ways to deconstruct popular media, care must be taken to accommodate, without privileging the setting, pleasures children derive from TV. This can become a thorny issue when pleasures stem from socially problematic practices, as in some fans' endorsement of Beavis and Butt-head's fascination with things ablaze, cruelty to animals and insensitivity to difference. Incorporating media texts popular with children (e.g., *Beavis and Butt-Head, The Simpsons*) that are subversive of the discourses of schooling, can be contradictory. These programs can be one means for critical examination of the differential distribution of rewards in schools and for incorporating students' knowledge and experiences into the curriculum. As versions of postmodern youth, Bart Simpson, and Beavis and Butt-head may speak compellingly to students already highly alienated from academics, thus further distancing them from schooling in a time plagued by overall diminished options for youth.

Buckingham (1993) and Nilan (1993) maintained that media studies can sharpen class and racial differences based on the differential distribution of knowledge in the larger society and classrooms where some children invoke class-based hierarchies to disparage others' knowledge and insights, especially those of working-class students. In the presence of social hierarchies in teenage peer groups, some students may disguise or distort the character of their media knowledge to maintain their positions with peers. At the same time, students' resistances to "emancipatory" pedagogies is well documented elsewhere by Luke and Gore (1994). Children may tell teachers what they want to hear out of a sense of fulfilling teachers' expectations for a more critical discourse and what Luke calls the "imperatives of assessment." As Luke notes, hierarchical relations of power in schools and normative definitions of school knowledge may pose very large challenges for developing and implementing critical media curriculum and pedagogies.

Acknowledging these circumstances should not prevent teachers from embarking on critical media education across the curriculum. Luke's chapter provides a comprehensive and compelling proposal for teachers in a variety of settings that articulates well with students' diverse backgrounds, knowledge, aesthetic pleasures and interests. As children's popular culture increasingly constructs subject positions across national boundaries that may run counter to local histories, values, and knowledge, it is imperative to examine the media's role in all of this. Teachers and students alike, even Beavis and Butthead, will find much to recommend here.

REFERENCES

Baker, C. D., & Luke, A. (Eds.). (1990). *Towards a critical sociology of reading pedagogy*. Amsterdam: John Benjamins.

Baudrilland, P. (1983). Sulutalions. *Semiotext(e)*, 1-13, 22-49.

Buckingham, D. (1993). *Children talking television: The making of television literacy*. London, UK: Falmer Press.

Cartoon on MTV blamed for fire. (1993, October 10). *The New York Times*, p. 30.

Christian-Smith, L. K. (1993a). Sweet dreams: Gender and desire in teen romance novels. In L. K. Christian-Smith (Ed.), *Texts of desire: Essays on fiction, femininity and schooling*. London: Falmer Press.

Christian-Smith, L. K. (1993b). *Texts of desire: Essays on fiction, femininity and schooling*. London: Falmer Press.

Code, L. (1991). *What can she know?* Ithaca, NY: Cornell University Press.

Fiske, J. (1989). *Reading the popular*. London: Unwin Hyman

Fraser, N. (1989). *Unruly practices: Power, discourse and gender in contemporary social theory*. Minneapolis: University of Minnesota Press.

Grossberg, L. (1986). History, politics and postmodernism: Stuart Hall and cultural studies. *Journal of Communication Inquiry, 10*, 61-77.

Hall, S. (1986). On postmodernism and articulation: An interview with Stuart Hall. *Journal of Communication Inquiry, 10*, 45-60.

Kaplan, E. A. (1987). *Rocking around the clock*. London: Methuen.

La Planche, J., & Pontalis, J. B. (1986). Fantasy and the origins of sexuality. In V. Burgin, J. Donald, & C. Kaplan (Eds.), *Formations of fantasy*. London: Verso.

Luke, C. (1988). *Television and your child*. Toronto, Canada: Kagan & Woo.

Luke, C., & Gore, J. (Eds.). (1994). *Feminisms and critical pedagogy*. New York: Routledge.

McRobbie, A. (1986). Postmodernism and popular culture. *Journal of Communication Inquiry, 10,* 106-116.

Nilan, P. M. (1993). *At the interface of talk and text: The social construction of gender in classroom interaction.* Unpublished doctoral dissertation, University of Newcastle, Newcastle.

Radway, J. (1984). *Reading the romance.* Chapel Hill: University of North Carolina Press.

Schwed, M. (1993, October 23). "Beavis and Butt-head" on the griddle. *TV Guide,* p. 53.

Walkerdine, V. (1984). Someday my prince will come: Young girls and the preparation for adolescent sexuality. In A. McRobbie & M. Nava (Eds.), *Gender and generation.* London: Macmillan.

4
Discourses on Gender and Literacy: Changing the Stories

Pam Gilbert
James Cook University of North Queensland

Texts addressing the specific relationship between gender and literacy have featured in a number of professional discourses over the past decade. Publications from the United Kingdom, such as *Alice in Genderland* (National Association for the Teaching of English [NATE], 1985), and the more recent *Language, Literacy and Gender* (Minns, 1991)—published as support for the National Curriculum—have been paralleled both in the United States with Sheridan's (1983) *Sex Stereotypes and Reading* (1983) and in Australia with *Gender, Literacy and the Classroom* (Gilbert, 1989). These texts, noticeably different in the ways in which they have approached questions of gender, literacy, and education, and in the discourses they have drawn on for explanation, reflect the impact on education over the past decade from sex difference data, equity and social justice debates, socialization theories, discourse theory, poststructuralism, and various forms of feminism.

More recently, another professional Australian publication (Gilbert, 1993) reviewed, synthesized, and tracked shifts that have occurred in discussions about gender, literacy, and classrooms—the "stories" that have been told—using the lens afforded through a poststructuralist position, about the ways in which subjects (researchers, students, and teachers alike) are constituted and reconstituted through discourse. The argument in this study has been that the "telling of stories" about gender and literacy—the production of a variety of texts exploring the connections between language, education and the construction of femininities and masculinities—has made possible a new signifying space (see Kristeva, 1986) from which to speak about language. Discourses on gender and literacy have, so to speak, made it possible to tell many stories about language and literacy—stories that offer not only a challenge and critique to existing language practices, but also a positive alternative to the gendered language order.

CRITICAL LITERACY AND GENDER

It could well be argued that understandings of the ways in which gender impacts upon language practices, and is itself constructed largely through language practices, are crucial in an exploration of critical literacy. A grasp of critical literacy—of what could be called the social contextualization of language practices—necessitates a grasp of how language operates in a social sense. To work with a commitment to critical literacy inevitably necessitates an engagement with the politics of language practices, and examples from Lankshear (1989), Freebody (1993), and Walkerdine (1990) have demonstrated what this might reveal in terms of group oppression through ethnicity, socioeconomic status, or, of course, gender. To explore the social context of language practices is inevitably to explore the networks of power that are sustained and brought into existence by such practices. It is to explore how language practices are used in powerful social institutions like the state, the school, the law, the family, the church, and how those practices contribute to the maintenance of inequalities and injustices. For teachers, it means engaging with issues that are often controversial, certainly contemporary, and perhaps volatile.

However, an interest in the gendered nature of literacy practices does make it possible to come quite easily to concepts of *critical literacy*: to issues that are political and problematic. The social construction of gender through language practices provides an obvious window through which to interrogate the authority of a text, and an obvious window through which to explore how social practices and language practices are entwined. It is therefore easier to see that language practices are far from neutral, value-free, or innocent. It becomes much simpler, for instance, to recognize the ideological form of language—to denaturalize the natural, and to problematize the common and everyday. It also becomes easier to recognize that there is differential access to certain powerful literacy practices and that many of the public, formal, and high status genres in our culture—particularly in the church, in law, and in government—prominently position men as speaking subjects. It is also more obvious to readers, positioned within feminist discourses, that common social and popular language forms or genres are derived from patriarchal discourses that objectify women, and construct narrow versions of femininity, and that the words and social language practices needed to relate women's experiences are often unknown or unfamiliar.

In a recent study (Gilbert, 1993), I explored the implications of these various forms of recognition in terms of my own history with language, gender, and education. In this study I reflected on the ways in which I have read, re-read/written, re-written a particular boys' story text produced in a primary classroom. I argued that each time that I returned to the story, I could read it differently, and that different readings of the story event were made possible by the different access I had as a social subject to various discourses about language, schooling, sex-difference, gender construction, feminisms, subjectivity, and so on.

I argue in this study that it had been my initial positioning in front of the story as a woman—and a woman inscribed by feminism—that first interrupted my reading and made it impossible for me to read the story as part of an ungendered corpus of children's writing. Feminism, as a discourse, had disrupted and challenged my "common sense" reading of the text. The misogyny and male aggression in the story—both of which I suspect would have not been so easily foregrounded through the discourses that usually operate in a primary school site—were able to be read and able to be recognized because of the reading position that I could then take up in relation to the boys' text.

This framework through which cultural practices can be read, can also be used to read our own discursive construction as gendered subjects who are continually being constituted and reconstituted through language and the stories of our culture. As Davies (1993) noted:

> we not only read and write stories but we also live stories. Who we take ourselves to be at any one point in time depends on the available storylines we have to make sense out of the ebb and flow of being-in-the-world along with the legitimacy and status accorded to those storylines by the others with whom we make up our lives at any one point in time. (p. 41)

If we accept that constructs like femininity and masculinity are constructed in and through textual practices, that both are indeed "fictions"—but fictions lived, as Walkerdine (1990) reminded us, as if they were "real," felt deeply as though they were universal truths of the psyche—then it becomes important to denaturalize and problematize these fictions or stories; to be able to recognize that they are tales not truths, and that there are other ways of telling about experience. It also becomes important to look toward the ways in which cultural stories become legitimated and authorized through social practices and social institutions. And it is here that schooling has clearly played a powerful role.

READING "GENDER" THROUGH LANGUAGE PRACTICES

In early literacy classrooms, one of the most obvious demonstrations of the gendered dimension to literacy is marked out in the texts children write. Here, the differences between girls' and boys' writing, in terms of subject matter selection, preferred generic patterns, and agency and action, can be very noticeable. These extracts from children's texts collected by Dwyer (1992) in a third-grade Australian classroom are clear demonstrations of this.

> One day there was a little girl called Kathleen. She found a gold pot. It was a useful pot. She rubbed it. A genie came out of it. The genie said "You have three wishes."
> "I wish I had the prettiest dress in the whole world."
> "But now it's your second wish."
> "I wish I had long blonde hair."
> "I wish I was a princess in a castle."
> Then she got her three wishes. Then she was happy. In the castle the next day she got married with a handsome prince and they lived happily ever after.
> THE END
> (8-year-old girl)

> Ace is going for a walk in the forest. Suddenly the Cobra planes start firing. Ace runs for shelter. He tells the Boss. He said, "Go to bed." Deep goes diving. He blew up the Cobras' underwater base. Ace calls Complex. He says, "I'm on my way." They go into the Cobra's house. Ace and Complex go to the Cobra's base and get into a plane. They find a Cobra plane. They shot it down. They shoot the Cobra base. Metalhead touched metal. He blew it up.
> (8-year-old boy)

It is difficult not to notice initially the differences here: not to notice the difference in story structure with the girl's clear alignment with printed children's stories ("One Day there was . . . "), and her use of storybook characters and mechanisms ("The genie said, 'You have three wishes' "), compared with the boy's present tense recount ("Ace is going for a walk . . . "), and his alignment with commercial boys' (U.S.) military style toys. Whatever form of analysis we might try with these two texts, we could read "difference": difference in narrative style, in character selection, in syntactic choices, in subject matter, in literary competence, in sentence length, in vocabulary choice. And the difference—which in these two texts is quite marked—comes down predominantly to a gender difference: to a gendered difference in the way in which these two children have drawn on their cultural worlds to construct classroom stories.

The differences in language use are not just noticeable in children's story writing. There is a considerable body of research that attempts to demonstrate differences in women's and men's speech (see, e.g. Poynton, 1985; Spender, 1980), in women's and men's writing (Showalter, 1977), in women's and men's reading practices (Flynn & Schweickart, 1986), in women's and men's viewing styles (Modleski, 1984). And there is a similar body of research that documents gender differences in texts produced for particular gendered groups: pulp and generic fiction (Christian-Smith, 1990; Cranny-Francis, 1992), reading materials for classrooms (Gilbert with Rowe, 1989), and television serials and films (Modleski, 1991). There is also the lived difference of a culture that operates along clear lines of distinction between girls and boys in the production of toys, hobby kits, electronic games, clothes, books, jewelry, stationery, greeting cards, and so on.

But what does this difference mean? Over the past decade, questions have been asked about how might we read difference. Does it matter? What does it signify? Whose interests are best served by such a dualistic polarization in textual practices? Are we able to write differently, to read differently, to construct other stories than these intensely polarized forms? And what conditions make that possible?

I would suggest that the questions that need to be addressed now about gender and literacy are questions like these. They are questions that examine the implications of living and operating in a culture where a dualistic construction of gender is so entrenched; of living and operating in a culture where the taking up of a position as a woman or a man becomes one of the first divides in the construction of the self as a social subject; of living and operating in a culture where to take up a position as a woman or as a man, means automatically to accept restrictions and limitations on the potential plurality and diversity of the social subject.

To examine issues of gender and literacy, however, I borrow and appropriate a framework developed by Kristeva (1986) in an article called *Women's Time*, a framework that has also been adopted by Davies (1989a) in relation to gender and education. Kristeva argued that the feminist struggle can be seen historically and politically as a three-tiered one, and she located three phases of the women's movement: a first phase, in which suffragists and "existential feminists" sought to gain an insertion into history and the symbolic language order; a second phase in which the male symbolic order was rejected as women sought to "give a language to the intrasubjective and corporeal experiences left mute by culture in the past"; and a third phase, that rejects the "metaphysical dichotomy between masculine and feminine and hopes instead for the disintegration of the concept of a single, or sexual identity."

Kristeva did not suggest that these three phases are necessarily chronological, or necessarily hierarchical, although her clear preference is for the attitude toward women made possible within the third phase. Rather, she argued that each phase or stage should have a "parallel existence" in the same historical time, or even be "interwoven one with the other." Kristeva's separation of these three stages, yet her suggestion that they be "parallel" and "interwoven," seems to be particularly relevant for work in gender and literacy. Her suggestion offers not only a way of sorting out and framing the work that has been achieved in the broad field of gender and literacy—but also a way of seeing what else might need to be done; of establishing an agenda for further action.

If we appropriate Kristeva's argument for discourses on gender and literacy, we could argue that the first phase has been predominantly occupied with recognizing and redressing obvious inequalities and issues of marginalization. Here we might place attempts to provide equal linguistic space to girls, or equal access to various forms of literacy, or equal textual representation of gender in classroom materials. And I would suggest that work like this needs to continue: There is a need for information about how access to the symbolic order may be restricted for women and girls. The omission of women's experiences from textbooks—or the silence of girls in classrooms—are still important issues to document. But more than this is needed.

Different stories about gender and literacy have been told at different historical moments, in response to different political agendas. Much of the work of the early 1980s, for instance, was concerned with inequality and injustice: with sexist books and classroom materials (as in NATE, 1985; Sheridan, 1983), unfair classroom language practices (Spender & Sarah, 1980), discriminatory teacher expectation and perception of student competence and achievement on the basis of sex differences (Stanworth, 1984). Later work built on this data of inequality to explore relationships between gender and language in a variety of different ways: to explore the role of language practices in the formation of gendered subjectivities (Davies, 1989b, 1993); the conscious and unconscious "fictions" that girls and women struggle over as they live out their lives (Walkerdine, 1990); the complex interactions girls make with the texts of their culture as they attempt to play out their lives in positive and resourceful ways (Christian-Smith, 1990; Gilbert & Taylor, 1991; Moss, 1989).

Such work documents what it has been possible at various times to speak and to name; what it has been possible to see as an agenda for action. The past decade or more of research and theorizing has produced various discourses about gender and literacy that have constructed a signifying space from which to continue to speak about inequity; to continue to challenge social structures; to continue to add to the project that seeks nondualistic social subjectivity. The work must of necessity overlap and fold into itself. We can consider the significance of practices that have fought for equity and access—and how important such work still is; we can critically consider elements and features of the language order that access has been fought for—and look for ways in which we might have other needs of the language order; and we can look toward a future where the potential of all of us as social subjects is not limited by oppositional constructions of gender.

EQUITY, ACCESS AND THE MAPPING OF SOCIAL DIFFERENCE

Some of the most widely publicized and recognized work in gender and literacy has come from this first phase of "time," and the argument can strongly be made that the time for this work has not run out: The mapping and documenting of inequalities and imbalances still needs to be done. However understandings made possible for gender and literacy from other periods of "time" have lent new lenses through which such inequality and imbalance might be reframed.

Initially, we could define three broad areas that became obviously areas of concern in terms of the struggle for entry to the symbolic order: the struggle to gain access to a full range of linguistic practices. Initially, the construction of printed classroom materials in terms of sexist stereotypes and of the omission of women and women's experiences became an obvious target for analysis and critique. Parallel to this concern for access to print resources, came also a concern for access to classroom talk. Whose voices were heard and whose were not? Which students were encouraged to take risks and to learn through language, and which were not? And, as well, educators became aware of the different ways in which girls and boys appropriated linguistic structures in their writing: What was the extent of this difference? What was its result?

Printed Classroom Material

Much of the research work on printed classroom materials has been popularized and become familiar. There have been analyses of basal reading schemes that have indicated the gendered narrowness within such texts of character construction (Anderson & Yip, 1987; Graebner, 1972), of occupational example (Children's Rights Workshop, 1976; Gilbert with Rowe, 1989), and of syntactic choices in the construction of the "male" and the "female" child (Baker & Freebody, 1989). Similarly, there have been examples of studies that have demonstrated the unequal portrayal of female and male characters and of female and male story action within children's picture books and adolescent literature (Gilbert with Rowe, 1989; NATE, 1985; Sheridan, 1983).

Although serious and deliberate attempts have been made over the past decade by many publishing houses (and by many writers) to shift these stereotypical patterns, and to produce guidelines for books with less stereotypical constructions (see Bissland & Pittway, 1986; Dellitt, 1984), the construction of female and male characters within children's literature, and within basal reading materials, still bears careful scrutiny (see Pearce, 1991). In addition, many of the older materials of the 1970s and early 1980s are still commonly used in classrooms, and found on library shelves. The construction of gender within reading materials for children still provides clear evidence of the often unequal access that has been provided for alternative constructions of femininity and masculinity within classroom print materials.

Classroom Talk Space

Early work in the 1970s and 1980s published by researchers like Spender and Sarah (1980) and Stanworth (1984) made it clear that female students often had unequal access to teacher time, to question type, and to classroom linguistic space. More recent work by Graddol and Swann (1989), Sadker, Sadker and Donald (1989), and Baker and Davies (1989), confirms that such inequality still exists. This more contemporary work documents, however, the increasingly complex ways in which children are positioned in gendered ways in classroom interactions.

Studies of classroom practices, such as that by Clark (1989) or Gilbert and Taylor (1991), indicate some of the ways in which "naturalized" classroom practices contribute toward unequal linguistic access in classrooms, but work by Baker and Freebody (1989), Baker and Davies (1989), and A. Luke (1993) also indicate the power of the teacher's role in moving children toward certain acceptable ("authorized") stories. As Davies (1993) remarked in her most recent study of the construction of gendered identities:

> For teachers to introduce critical literacy into their classrooms and for students to begin to deconstruct the text and to talk through the ways in which they are constituted, a great deal has to change. Assumptions about the teacher's interpretive authority and the authority of texts, assumptions about the nature of authorship, the nature of student–teacher interaction, the texts made available to students, methods of assessment and the understanding of the relations between knowledges and the person must all come under critical scrutiny. (pp. 39-40)

Quite clearly children do not have equal access to teachers' time, and interest, and to classroom opportunity, but methods of reading the discursive site of the classroom—and of altering classroom relationships—are still being explored.

Classroom Writing

Studies of children's school writing predominantly produce sex-differences within such writing, indicating that children's readings of gender and gendered language practices (particularly story practices) plays a significant role in the ways in which they construct written texts. Children do not seem to have equal access to a full range of character construction or to narrative genre choice. American work by Romatowski and Trepanier-Street (1987), Tuck, Bayliss, and Bell (1985), and Mulac, Studley, and Blau (1990), and British work by White (1986) indicates how constructions of character traits, setting, motivation for action, and genre form, are often significantly different in texts constructed by female and male students. Australian work by Poynton (1985), Gilbert (1989), Dalley (1991), Dwyer (1992) and Kamler (1993) portrays a similar picture in Australian children's work.

Some of these differences might be best synthesized by summary statements such as the following by Poynton (1985):

> Girls and boys write about different things almost from the start, with the difference increasing with age and the common ground becoming smaller. Girls write about home activities, . . . dress and appearance, romance, and fantasy worlds inhabited by fairies, witches, characters from children's stories, . . . commercial toys, . . . and talking animals and objects. Boys write about playing or watching sport and other physical activities such as bike-racing. . . . Boys' fantasy worlds are inhabited by creatures from outer space, assorted monsters (preferably of the kind that kill people unexpectedly and messily, with lots of blood), everyday burglars, kidnappers, and murderers—and when the writer himself is a character in an adventure story then he is usually accompanied by a group of his male class-mates. . . . Boys also write about topics that do not lend themselves to "story"-writing e.g., the solar system, dinosaurs, radios. (pp. 34-35)

Although the differences are obvious, the impact and significance of these differences is beginning increasingly to be questioned and interrogated (see Gilbert, 1994; Poynton, 1985). Poynton, for example, suggested that fictional text construction—as one of the very areas in which girls excel as students and as writers—may not be a very valuable area of excellence.

> Telling fairy stories, even telling good fairy stories very well . . .
> simply doesn't count. The positions of real power and influence in
> our society necessitate command of genres for which boys'
> educational experience provides an appropriate preparation and
> girls' doesn't . . . girls' genre competence at primary school is not
> merely irrelevant but positively disabling. (p. 36)

As Poynton suggested, equity and access are not the only issues
that need to be addressed in questions of gender and literacy. Access to
"what"—or equality to participate in "what"—have become areas that
clearly need also to be addressed.

CHALLENGING AND CRITIQUING THE LANGUAGE ORDER

As Kristeva (1986) noted, the first phase of women's work fought to
achieve access to a patriarchal system, finding, as it did so, that the
system itself was not a system that supported and represented women's
needs or experiences. Access to the symbolic order will not provide
automatic equality. Access can bring a different set of problems that
Kristeva considered in her second phase of women's time. Being able to
read, write, and talk like men or boys is not perhaps a great
achievement. Although it might open doors to some avenues of power,
it will not necessarily to others.

And it involves, as has been noted of and by women writers (see
Rich, 1980), almost a sense of betrayal of intrinsic ways of being and
knowing, for existing language forms or genres assume certain sets of
gender relationships for their intelligibility and coherence. To write
within the forms of our culture can often mean to write against
women—to betray a potentially "essential" feminine self—and
Kristeva's second phase looks toward ways in which women might
develop their own "language" or ordering of the world. The second
phase of women's work—although continuing to fight for equity of
access—became involved in foregrounding marginalizing practices and
constructing alternatives.

An increasing understanding of, and focus on, the relations
between language and power through discourse theory and
poststructuralism, has been particularly valuable for this stage of work
in gender and literacy. The specific language practices of powerful social
institutions—like the family, school and popular media—have been able
to come under closer scrutiny and to be subjected to more careful and
illuminating forms of analysis. For instance, critical discourse theories
such as those proposed by Kress (1985) and Fairclough (1989, 1992)
made it possible to make different "readings" of the social: to

denaturalize the apparently "natural" language forms we seem to swim in so effortlessly. They have made it possible for us to disrupt the readings we were making, and to read "differently."

Through approaches like these, it becomes possible to foreground the constructed nature of language practices, and how they work against women's interests. For example, earlier work I completed with student teachers (when they had surprising difficulty writing nonstereotypical children's stories; Gilbert, 1985), and with student writers (when girl writers had trouble writing adventure stories with independent female characters; Gilbert, 1989) demonstrates how "naturalized" have become narrative conventions that are stereotypical and demeaning for women. Similar examples can be found in popular cultural texts, where gendered relationships have become the "naturalized" and expected conventions (see Cranny-Francis, 1992).

It could well be argued that the social constructedness of stories needs to be foregrounded, and the power of cultural storylines to "naturalize" and therefore mask the gendered dynamics of language made visible (see Davies, 1993; Gilbert, 1994). Interesting and compelling research directions for gender and literacy have come from work that attempts to expose the workings of stories: to unravel the workings of social language practices, by recognizing connections between powerful language forms, and the appeal many of them have to some of our most deeply held desires and needs.

For instance, Walkerdine (1990) suggested that our understanding of ourselves as gendered social subjects, is predominantly achieved through the fictions or stories that we take on, through living and operating in our culture.

> It is not that we are filled with roles and stereotypes of passive femininity so that we become what society has set out for us. Rather, I am suggesting that femininity and masculinity are fictions linked to fantasies deeply embedded in the social world which can take on the status of fact when inscribed in the powerful practices like schooling, through which we are regulated. (p. xiii)

However, increasingly, women have realized that a change of stories—even a change of the practices through which the stories are regulated and authorized—is a larger project than it first appeared. As social subjects, we are still read through the stories of our culture. Even if women attempt a reordering of the social, perhaps partly through parody or through play with conventional forms, the way such play is read will usually still be from within frameworks of conventional gender dualisms. As the Australian novelist Thea Astley (cited in Gilbert, 1988) remarked:

Partly it is because I am a woman—and no reviewer, especially a male one, can believe for one split infinitive of a second that irony or a sense of comedy or the grotesque in a woman is motivated by anything but the nutrients derived from "backyard malice." Assuming these particular qualities—sense of irony, the eye for the comic or the grotesque—are an indication of intelligence and believing a priori that no woman is intelligent, critics assign the evidence of humour, irony or comedy to darker forces at work; the Salem judgment comes into play and the lady writer most certainly is for burning. (p. 111)

In other words, as social subjects we are still positioned by our gender, and read through our gender, even when we try to write outside of, or beyond, gendered dualisms and patriarchal meaning systems. Within our culture, gender becomes an inevitable first divide when taking up subject positions within social practices. We cannot, as Weedon (1987) warned, "escape the implications of femininity. Everything we do signifies compliance or resistance to dominant norms of what it is to be a woman" (p. 87). However, as she also said:

The range of ways of being a woman open to each of us at a particular time is extremely wide but we know or feel we ought to know what is expected of us in particular situations. . . . We may embrace these ways of being, these subject positions whole-heartedly, we may reject them outright or we may offer resistance while complying to the letter with what is expected of us. (p. 86)

READING BEYOND GENDER

Kristeva's (1986) argument is that it is within a third phase of woman's time that we might be able to get beyond such a dualistic approach to gender that pigeonholes human subjects in terms of their biological sex and provides them with a single sexed identity. Such a time would instead regard human subjects as capable of multiple subjectivities and would look toward ways in which such plurality might be made possible. With this as perhaps a goal, language classrooms could be regarded as arenas of space within which dualistic gender positions are not sanctioned, supported, legitimated; within which "gender" becomes a construct to critically examine and undermine.

By unravelling some of the "fictions" of our lives, and the "powerful practices" through which they are regulated, it is possible to straddle Kristeva's three tiers: to document the differences in the fictions that are available to women and to men; to challenge and critique the construction of gendered subjects that they bring into being; and to look to a future that might be different—a future in which an oppositional hierarchical gendered order is broken down. We can then look towards the location of classroom space within which constructions of gender can be read and recognized, and within which students have options of operating beyond dualistic regimes of gender.

But this space must be fought for and will need to be constantly protected, given the sheer weight and dominance of so many "stories" or fictions from our culture that would not acknowledge that "difference"—that would construct and read femininity and masculinity narrowly within a dualistic ordering of gender; and would position women, for instance, within what Davies (1993) described as a romantic storyline of possibility. As I have argued (Gilbert, 1994), some readings of the stories from our culture—or, as Walkerdine (1990) suggested, the "fictions" constructing the facts of femininity—become dominant and authorized because they are constantly repeated. These dominant readings are often naturalized as the common sense lore of our culture. The other "quieter" stories are more difficult to hear: more difficult to find. Classrooms will need deliberate strategies that will open out the constructedness of language practices: the sets of social conventions on which they have drawn, and the cultural set of meanings through which they are read. And they will need deliberate strategies to help students find other stories by which they might construct their lives: ways of taking up positions as human subjects other than in stereotypically gendered ways.

Comparison and juxtaposition can make it possible to read the historical specificity of many common and familiar language practices, and contemporary re-tellings of traditional tales, fables, or fairy tales are valuable source texts here (see Mellor, Hemming, & Leggett, 1984). Similarly, the paradigms of possibility that exist in different story constructions—as in the construction of a "quality" children's literary text, or a teen romance novel, or an early graded reader, or a *Sixty Minutes* story, or a *Woman's Day* feature—can be explored. What is likely to be included in each of these stories, and what is not? And why? How culturally and historically specific are decisions like these? How are certain assumptions about gender implicit in these decisions? Stories from magazines, newspapers, TV quiz shows, soap operas, popular films, jokes, gossip, pulp fiction, and radio talk-back programs can then be read as the "fictions" of daily life that construct the "facts" of femininity and masculinity. To operate beyond dualistic frameworks of gender, there is a need to make language practices more explicit in classrooms, and to offer students ways of critically reading—and of re-writing—the popular stories of their culture.

If we appropriate Kristeva's argument for discourses on gender and literacy, we could argue that the first phase has been predominantly occupied with recognizing and redressing obvious inequalities and issues of marginalization. Here, we might place attempts to provide equal linguistic space to girls, or equal access to various forms of literacy, or equal textual representation of gender in classroom materials. And, as I have suggested earlier, work like this needs to continue: there is a need for information about how access to the symbolic order continues to be restricted. The omission of women's experiences from textbooks—or the silence of girls in classrooms—are still important issues to document. But more than this is needed.

We need to place on the agenda a critical assessment of the language order that we seek access to for our students. We need to consider how the socially based language practices of our culture 'naturalize' and obscure the construction of dualistic gendered patterns; how the "stories" of our culture become the "facts" we learn of femininity or of masculinity. What we have—through a consideration of work on literacy in this way—is an argument in support of a number of different approaches to critical literacy. Approaches that still redress inequalities of language opportunity in terms of access, space, power; approaches that acknowledge that such access brings with it a new set of difficulties and will need to be accompanied by a recognition of the limitations of existing language practices in terms of naming experiences in positive and affirming ways; and approaches which look toward breaking down dualistic positioning of human subjects in terms of biological sex.

Discourses on gender and literacy have given us different stories through which we can read language practice. They have made it possible to change not only the stories we use as classroom resources, but also the stories we might build and construct to position ourselves differently—as researchers, as teachers, as students. By "changing the stories" and offering us other ways of reading the social, discourses on gender and literacy make an important contribution to work on critical literacy.

REFERENCES

Anderson, J., & Yip, L. (1987). Are sex roles represented fairly in children's books? A content analysis of old and new readers. *Unicorn*, 13(3), 155-61.

Baker, C. D., & Davies, B. (1989). A lesson in sex roles. *Gender and Education*, 1(1), 59-76.

Baker, C. D., & Freebody, P. (1989). *Children's first schoolbooks: Introductions to the culture of literacy*. Oxford, UK: Basil Blackwell.

Bissland, J., & Pittaway, C. (1986). *Picture books to grow on: An annotated bibliography of non-sexist picturebooks.* Melbourne, Australia: Prahran College of TAFE.

Children's Rights Workshop. (1976). *Sexism in children's books: Facts, figures and guidelines.* London: Writers and Readers Publishing Cooperative.

Christian-Smith, L. (1990). *Becoming a woman through romance.* New York: Routledge.

Clark, M. (1989). *The great divide: The construction of gender in the primary school.* Canberra, Australia: Curriculum Development Centre.

Cranny-Francis, A. (1992). *Engendered fictions: Analysing gender in the production and reception of texts.* Kensington, NSW: NSW University Press.

Dalley, L. (1991). *Regulating gender through genre: A study of the construction of gender in school narrative writing tasks at the year ten level.* Unpublished bachelor of education honours thesis, School of Education, James Cook University of North Queensland, Townsville, Australia.

Davies, B. (1989a). Education for sexism: A theoretical analysis of the sex/gender bias in education. *Educational Philosophy and Theory, 21*(1), 1-19.

Davies, B. (1989b). *Frogs and snails and feminist tales.* Sydney, Australia: Allen & Unwin.

Davies, B. (1993). *Shards of glass: Children reading and writing beyond gendered identities.* Sydney, Australia: Allen & Unwin.

Dellitt, J. (1984). *Strong females in adolescent fiction: An annotated bibliography.* Adelaide: South Australian Department of Education.

Dwyer, B. (1992). *The construction of narrative within one year three classroom.* Unpublished master of education thesis, School of Education, James Cook University of North Queensland, Townsville, Australia.

Fairclough, N. (1989). *Language and power.* Harlow, UK: Longman.

Fairclough, N. (Ed.). (1992). *Critical language awareness.* London: Longman.

Flynn, E., & Schweickart, P. (Eds.). (1986). *Gender and reading: Essays on readers, texts and contexts.* Baltimore, MD: The Johns Hopkins University Press.

Freebody, P. (1993). Social class and reading. In A. Luke & P. Gilbert (Eds.), *Literacy in contexts.* Sydney, Australia: Allen & Unwin.

Gilbert, P. (1985). Stereotypes for the classroom: student teachers write sexist children's stories. *Australian Journal of Reading, 8*(1), 14-20

Gilbert, P. (1988). *Coming out from under: Contemporary Australian women's writing.* Sydney, Australia: Allen & Unwin.

Gilbert, P. (1989). Stoning the romance: Girls as resistant readers and writers. In F. Christie, R. Maclean, D. Morris, & P. Williams (Eds.), *Writing in schools: Reader*. Geelong, Australia: Deakin University Press.

Gilbert, P. (1993). The stories we tell. In P. Gilbert (Ed.), *Gender stories and the language classroom*. Geelong, Australia: Deakin University Press.

Gilbert, P. (1994). "And they lived happily ever after": Cultural storylines and the construction of gender. In A. Dyson & C. Genishi (Eds.), *The need for story*. Urbana, IL: NCTE.

Gilbert, P., with Rowe, K. (1989). *Gender, literacy and the classroom*. Carlton: Australian Reading Association.

Gilbert, P., & Taylor, S. (1991). *Fashioning the feminine: Girls, popular culture and schooling*. Sydney, Australia: Allen & Unwin.

Graddol, D., & Swann, J. (1989). *Gender voices*. Oxford, UK: Basil Blackwell.

Graebner, D. (1972). A decade of sexism in readers. *The Reading Teacher, 26*, 52-58.

Kamler, B. (1993). Constructing gender in the process writing classroom. In P. Gilbert (Ed.), *Gender stories and the language classroom*. Geelong, Australia: Deakin University Press.

Kress, G. (1985). *Linguistic processes in sociocultural practice*. Geelong, Australia: Deakin University Press.

Kristeva, J. (1986). Women's time. In T. Moi (Ed.), *The Kristeva reader*. Oxford, UK: Basil Blackwell.

Lankshear, C. (1989). *Literacy, schooling and revolution*. London: Falmer Press.

Luke, A. (1993). Stories of social regulation: The micropolitics of classroom narrative. In B. Green (Ed.), *The insistence of the*. London: Falmer Press.

Mellor, B., Hemming, J., & Leggett, J. (1984). *Changing stories*. English Centre/Scarborough, WA: Chalkface Press.

Minns, H. (1991). *Language, literacy and gender*. London: Hodder & Stoughton.

Modleski, T. (1984). *Loving with a vengeance: Mass-produced fantasies for women*. New York & London: Methuen.

Modleski, T. (1991). *Feminism without women: Culture and criticism in a "postfeminist age"*. New York & London: Routledge.

Moss, G. (1989). *Un/popular fictions*. London: Virago Press.

Mulac, A., Studley, L., & Blau, S. (1990). The gender-linked language effect in primary and secondary students' impromptu essays. *Sex Roles, 23*(9/10), 439-469.

National Association for the Teaching of English (NATE). (1985). *Alice in genderland*. Sheffield: Author.

Pearce, S. (1991). Growing up gender-wise: What we give to girls. *Magpies, 6*(5), 10-14.

Poynton, C. (1985). *Language and gender: Making the difference.* Geelong, Australia: Deakin University Press.

Rich, A. (1980). *On lies, secrets, silences.* London: Virago Press.

Romatowski, J., & Trepanier-Street, M. (1987). Gender perceptions: An analysis of children's creative writing. *Contemporary Education, 59*(1), 17-19.

Sadker, M., Sadker, D., & Donald, M. (1989). Subtle sexism at school. *Contemporary Education, 60*(4), 204-212.

Sheridan, E. M. (Ed.). (1983). *Sex stereotypes and reading.* Newark, DE: IRA.

Showalter, E. (1977). *A literature of their own: British women novelists from Bronte to Lessing.* Princeton, NJ: Princeton University Press.

Spender, D. (1980). *Man-made language.* London: Routledge.

Spender, D., & Sarah, E. (Eds.). (1980). *Learning to lose: Sexism and education.* London: Writers and Readers Publishing Co-operative.

Stanworth, M. (1984). Girls on the margins: a study of gender divisions in the classroom. In A. Hargreaves & P. Woods (Eds.), *Classrooms and staffrooms.* Milton Keynes, UK: Open University Press.

Tuck, D., Bayliss, V., & Bell, M. (1985). Analysis of sex stereotyping in characters created by young authors. *Journal of Educational Research, 78*(4), 248-52.

Walkerdine, V. (1990). *Schoolgirl fictions.* London: Verso.

Weedon, C. (1987) *Feminist practice and poststructuralist theory.* Oxford, UK: Basil Blackwell.

White, J. (1986). The writing on the wall: Beginning or end of a girl's career? *Women's Studies International Forum, 9*(5), 561-74.

5

Reading the Silences within Critical Feminist Theory[1]
Response to Pam Gilbert

Parlo Singh
Griffith University, Queensland

This chapter initially written in July 1994 is a critical response to Gilbert's "Discourses on Gender and Literacy: Changing the Stories" written in August 1993. The criticism is historically contextualized and therefore situates this text in the wider corpus of discourses on gender and literacy produced under the authorship of Gilbert (1989a, 1989b, 1992) and Gilbert and Taylor (1991). The theorization in this chapter is aimed at opening up, rather than closing off, the issues within feminisms and education in Australia. Consequently, this chapter examines the theoretical limitations in the corpus of work, focussing specifically on the chapter "Discourses of Gender and Literacy: Changing the Stories".

FEMINISM AS COUNTER DISCOURSE

For me, as for many, research on gender and literacy (specifically Gilbert 1989a, 1989b) has opened up a set of reading practices that enable me, as a woman, to read from a position that is Other to the "Other" of patriarchy (Irigaray, 1992, 1993). This writing has given me a means of speaking and understanding myself that contests and challenges the deficit constructions of woman in relation to man. By giving me this discursive resource, that is, a critical feminist reading practice, the

---

[1]Since writing this response, I have been alerted to work undertaken within critical feminist literacy that "gives voice to" girls from a range of different race, class, and ethnic positions. I also acknowledge that critical feminist theorists are genuinely struggling with issues of difference among women.

research on gender and literacy has enabled me to view social reality, my social identity, and my social relationships differently. These feminist writings have shown me that gender differences are socially and culturally produced. Gender differences are not natural nor are they the way the world was meant to be.

Furthermore, this corpus of work has persistently challenged the everyday or common sense practices of schooling and encouraged teachers and policymakers to view this social reality from a feminist or *girl-friendly* perspective. This can never be an easy process. Gender identities, constructed in and through the everyday practices of schooling, often remain unquestioned. To challenge established practices, that is, to contest the power relations of patriarchy is likely to be met with resistance and opposition. Under these circumstances, and relentlessly for many years, theorists working in the area of gender and literacy (specifically Gilbert 1989a, 1989b, 1992) have persistently brought to the attention of educators the gendered construction of reality.

For example, Gilbert (1989a, 1989b), and Gilbert and Taylor (1991) analyzed the invisible or naturalized power-knowledge relations invested in discourses of liberal and child-centered literacy classrooms. They proposed that the social construction of educational discourses as "natural," "individualist," "personalized," and "child-centered" mitigates against the possibility of equitable practice. Positioned within liberal educational discourse, the teacher cannot gain access to ways of identifying and dealing with inequitable relations of power and gender production. Institutionalized inequality is naturalized and personalized so that it becomes hegemonic (Gilbert, 1989a).

Despite the need to contest or deconstruct gendered practices, these critical feminist positions do not overly dwell on the regulatory practices of patriarchy. By drawing on their own personal and professional experiences, feminists in the area of gender and literacy argue that discourses of patriarchy can be disrupted. For example, Gilbert proposes that feminist literature gives her the language and a set of meanings to view practices of patriarchy differently. And this different way of reading the word and the world has been and continues to be empowering.

Gilbert translates her personal empowering experience with feminist literature to the practical reality of classroom practice. Gilbert and her colleagues (Freebody, Luke, & Gilbert, 1991; Gilbert, chap. 4, this volume; Gilbert & Taylor, 1991) propose that the empowerment of girls, is achieved through the acquisition of strategies of "reading against the grain" or deconstructing the phallogocentrism within discourses. *Phallogocentrism* refers to the logic of binary oppositions that center the phallus or self of man as the norm and woman as the negative or deficit "Other." Drawing on the work of Derrida, poststructural feminists have proposed that the structure of Western language is based on the binary oppositional logic of gendered difference. Within this logic "woman" signifies or means something "Other" than, or different from "man." And because the logic of the Western symbolic system places man at the center, "woman" is read or interpreted as negatively different from "man." The logic of this language system, however, can be deconstructed and reconstructed so that the sign of "woman" is produced through *differance*. In this context, Derrida's use of *differance* implies that the meaning associated with a sign, for example in this instance "woman," is constantly deferred or suspended and therefore capable of being reconstructed to mean something Other than the "Other" of "man" (cf. Grosz, 1989; Irigaray, 1992; Whitford, 1991).

In their study of teenage girls, popular culture, and literacy practices, Gilbert and Taylor (1991) found that not all girls read romance novels in the same way. Reading practices are learned because children learn to take up various subject positions that allow the text to be framed in specific ways. Gilbert and Taylor (1991) argued that if reading positions are socially constructed, then girls should be taught how to read against the grain of patriarchal texts. That is, students need to question the natural construction of gendered difference.

This process of challenging common sense views of gendered identity and practices must begin with students' experiences. Only by working on students' personal constructions of gender can teachers attempt to challenge feminine subordination. However, challenging students' constructions of gendered identity is not simply a matter of rational, logical debate. The power of gender ideologies lies in the fact that they work at an emotional level, through the structuring of desires, as well as at a rational level. Deconstructing emotional attachments through analysis of personal lives, however, is problematic. It is personally threatening for many students to place their lives under scrutiny as their very sense of themselves is at stake (Gilbert & Taylor, 1991).

Within this theoretical perspective, challenging students' personal constructions of gender is only the first stage in the process of contesting gender difference. The second stage is to enable students to "try out" or experiment with different gendered positions. In other words, students are encouraged to read and write from different discursive positions. That is, girls are encouraged to take on the role of the lead character in a story, be adventurous and take risks. Boys can try to write about topics other than war and action heroes, and place female characters in the center of their texts rather than in subservient roles.

These stages in challenging patriarchy and reconstructing discourses that provide powerful speaking and writing positions for boys and girls are based on Kristeva's (1986) theoretical work. Gilbert proposes that Kristeva's three-phase model of women's work provides a guide by which women can challenge and incorporate their voices within the current literacy curriculum. Briefly, the first level of challenge to the patriarchal literacy curriculum is to gain access to the dominant symbolic order. The second phase is to set up oppositional knowledge(s) and construct alternative symbolic order(s) that represent the interests and lived experiences of marginalized groups. The third phase operates on the principle of incorporating alternative meaning systems into the dominant symbolic order. That is, women must create and incorporate alternative ways of reading, writing, and speaking in order to express their lived experiences. Moreover, using this theoretical framework, Gilbert proposes that women must challenge the patriarchal symbolic order that operates on the Cartesian logic of male-female dualisms to create multiple stories and ways of being and living. In this way, both men and women will have available to them, alternative stories by which they can construct their subjectivities and practices.

FEMINISM AS A DISCOURSE OF EXCLUSION

> Don't you just hate it when reviewers or critics write about what you did not say rather than what you did? (Ball, 1994, p. 108)

This theoretical analysis of "fashioning" gendered identities as an instrument of patriarchy has helped me to come to terms with the constructedness of what I had been socialized and educated to believe were natural instincts and behaviors without which I could not be a "proper" or "good" woman. But for all that this research has given me, it also has taken something away. What this research has taken from me is my racialized, socioeconomic, gendered identity. By constructing difference as a gendered difference and silencing "Other" differences of race and class that interweave with gender; my identity, my voice, my practices have been silenced. And power-knowledge relations work through these silences. What remains unspoken in this theoretical analysis are the differences within the category "woman." And from this position, no matter how I now look at this theoretical work, the pain of being excluded from the Western feminist "Other" leads me to suggest that critical feminist discourse (of the variety practiced within this theoretical model) does not have an agenda of inclusivity.

On this subject, du Cille (1994) writing about the meaning of Adrienne Rich's (1986) poetry *Of Woman Born: Motherhood as Experience and Institution* for herself as a Black woman writes:

I "discovered" this essential book at a critical moment in my life and in the development of my feminism: on the eve of my fortieth birthday, as I wrestled with the likelihood of never having a child. . . . But for all that Rich's book gave me, it also took something away; and what it snatched from me, ironically and perhaps a little unfairly, has come to mean almost as much to me as what it gave. . . . To the double silences of sexism and racism Rich adds a third: the silence and blindness of feminism. Like Jane Gallop, who I am sure meant to praise Deborah McDowell, Adrienne Rich no doubt means to honor the woman who cared for her as a child. But the poetry of her prose should not disguise the paternal arrogance of her words or mask the annihilating effect of her claim on the being she resurrects and recreates as "my Black mother." (p. 613)

du Cille (1994) also argued, "Even ten years later (in the revised edition of the book) Rich has failed to recognize that she is talking about another woman—another woman who is not her black mother but a laborer whose role as mammy is also socially, politically and economically constructed" (p. 613).

Similarly, I propose that despite all that I have gained from the theoretical research on the social construction of gender and literacy I feel that, as a subject positioned by race, social class, and gender, I have been silenced. And I propose that if educational feminisms are to be inclusive of all women, not just the minority of White bourgeois women, then these silences within feminisms, the differences within the category "woman," must be debated and researched.

Currently, counterdiscourses within the academy, the "Other" of the speaking subject, Western feminisms make distinctions between White women and "women of color." In the discourses of the Western academy, White lady is the symbol of purity, innocence, sexual chastity, virginity—the princess with blonde hair in the castle. This focus on the desires and lived reality of the White middle-class woman is explicit in the selection, organization, and interpretation of data within the Gilbert text:

One day there was a little girl called Kathleen. She found a gold pot. It was a useful pot. She rubbed it. A genie came out of it. The genie said "You have three wishes."
"I wish I had the prettiest dress in the whole world."
"But now it's your second wish."
"I wish I had long blonde hair."
"I wish I was a princess in a castle."
Then she got her three wishes. Then she was happy. In the castle the next day she got married with a handsome prince and they lived happily ever after.
THE END
(8-year-old girl).

Within the Gilbert text there is no detailed theorization of this data. Rather, the reader is called on to "read difference." The power-knowledge relations by which "difference" is constructed within this text are naturalized, so that the reader is positioned to notice only gendered difference: "it is difficult not to notice initially the differences here: not to notice the difference in story structure . . . storybook characters and mechanisms" (chap. 4, this volume, p. 62).

Power speaks through silences. The selection, organization and interpretation of this data silence differences within the category "boy" and "girl." Also silenced is the complexity of economic and racial discourses that construct the Australian rural cultural world from which the children construct their stories. The theorization within this text therefore is complicit in silencing the multiple differences that are erased in the cultural world of a white blonde girl princess living in a castle waiting for a prince.

The "Other" of the white princess, the woman who is silenced—the Black, brown, olive, dark, yellow woman—the "woman of color" is base. In this fantasy, the "woman of color" as sexual object is not valuable, is either unworthy of being rescued by the prince, or must be rescued from her own "uncivilized kind" to serve the interests of the White male. The "woman of color" is the symbol of sexual promiscuity, the oversexed Black Jezebel, repressed sexuality waiting for liberation from the White phallus—"or more precisely, the yellow girl—represents the mirror image of the white woman on the pedestal. Together, white and black women stand for woman as madonna and whore" (Painter, 1992, p. 207).

Hall (1992) also wrote about the politics of representation in terms of the Black subject. The play of identity and difference positions the Black subject not only in relation to class, gender, nation but also in relation to sexuality and desire. Hall proposed that:

> Just as masculinity always constructs femininity as double—simultaneously Madonna and Whore—so racism constructs the black subject: noble savage and violent avenger . . .
>
> This double fracturing entails a different kind of politics because . . . black radical politics has frequently been stabilized around particular conceptions of black masculinity, which are only now being put into question by black women and black gay men. (p. 256)

Represented by the signifier "woman of color," "racialized subject," "subaltern sexed subject" I have become an object either suppressed through silence within the category of "universal woman" that signifies only bourgeois White woman, or objectified as the "etc." or the arithmetic add-on of patriarchal oppressions. For example, Gilbert and

Taylor (1991) theorized about the triple oppression of race, class, and gender for Aboriginal working-class girls. This theorization does not even begin to examine the relationality produced in and through discourse that constructs the categories of White middle-class Anglo-Australian and Aboriginal working-class girls. This theorization does not raise questions about the ideological representation of dominant and subordinate groups.

> By representation I refer not only to mimesis or the presence or absence of images of minorities and third-world people in textbooks. More broadly, I refer to the question of power that resides in the specific arrangement and deployment of subjectivity in the artefacts of formal and informal culture. This is what Louis Althusser (1971) calls the "mise-en-scene of interpellation"—the way in which the orchestration of cultural forms in textbooks and in the popular culture generates the capacity to speak for whole groups; to arraign these groups, as it were, before a deeply invested court of appeal, draining social life of its history and naturalizing dominant/subordinate relations in the process. (McCarthy, 1994, p. 8)

Within the text "Discourses of Gender and Literacy: Changing the Stories," the signifier of White girl writing about a White princess with blonde hair is used as representative of all girls. This text identifies a significant difference in the construction of stories written by boys and girls in primary schools. Within this specific theorization of gender and literacy it is argued, "And the difference—which in these two texts is quite marked—comes down predominantly to a gender difference: to a gendered difference in the way in which these two children have drawn upon their cultural worlds to construct classroom stories" (chap 4, this volume, p. 62).

However, gender difference is not the only difference produced in these particular children's stories, neither is it the most significant difference. The children's stories to which the theorization refers draw not only on gendered discourses, but also racialized and socioeconomic discourses. The children's texts (re)produce the power relations of a post-industrial capitalist society with its inherent oppressions. Although gender power relations in the texts are constructed and now read as visible, other interweaving oppressions, such as race, class, and sexual preference speak through the power-knowledge relations of silence, of invisibility.

By colluding in the process of silencing "Other" differences, this theorization on gender and literacy does not acknowledge the complexity and hybridity of discourses that construct gendered subjectivities. I propose that a gendered analysis that only examines sexual difference between White men and White women, fails to acknowledge the sexual difference on which racial and classed difference is constructed. That is, sexual difference constructed through the binary male–female is also constituted in the difference of White woman-colored woman, White woman-colored man, White man-colored man, White man-colored woman.

The signifier "color" is used here to refer to "non-White." European colonization is based on the scientific, economic project of modernity that incorporates the centrality of the White phallus. That is, the logic of modernity is based on the discursive construction of binary opposites in which the second of the binary pair denotes the negative. In addition, the logic of modernity, logocentrism, is centered on the self of the European male constructed during the Enlightenment. The logic of this discourse is captured in Spivak's (1988) statement: "White men are saving brown women from brown men" (p. 296). What this means is that Spivak's "brown woman" or "sexed subaltern subject" is constituted through imperialist discourses. Imperialism's image as the establisher of the good society is marked by the espousal of the woman as object of protection from her own kind (Spivak, 1988).

I am not implying that the signifier "color" encapsulates and represents the racialized experiences of all "non-White" subjects. Clearly, there exist differences and hierarchies of oppressions within the category "the subject of color." As Luke (1995) suggested, race and racial identity are historically generated and socioculturally produced regimes of difference and power. From the vantage of those persons invested with the power to define the terms of difference, the discourse of the "White Australia Policy" aimed to exclude all non-White, namely non-British and non-European people from entry into Australia. At the same time, discourses about Australia's Indigenous or First Nations people negated the differences of language, location, sociocultural practices under the category "Aboriginal and Torres Strait Islander" and used pseudoscientific techniques of blood sampling to ascertain degree of "Aboriginal authenticity."

What I am proposing is that the project of European expansion was based not only on an ideology of patriarchy but also of imperialism in which White bourgeois women colluded in the oppression of "non-White," of "colored" subjects. On this point, and referring to the forms of feminism in educational theory, Tsolidis (1990) argued that "the analysis which has dominated the girls' education debate has, by and large, been ethnocentric. It operates within a schema which defines Australian in dominant cultural terms only. To be Australian is to be Anglo-Celtic and to be female and non-Anglo-Celtic is to be pitied" (p. 57).

WOMEN'S TIME: READING RACIALIZED GENDERED *DIFFERANCE*

In this section, I use Barthes' (1977) notion of the death of the author and the birth of the reader to provide an alternative reading of Kristeva's (1986) concept of *women's time*. I propose, following Barthes (1977), that the truth of a text cannot be ascertained from the authorial voice. The birth of the reader must be at the cost of the death of the author. Spivak (1993) proposed:

> Barthes is writing here not of the death of the writer (although he *is* writing, quite copiously, of writing) or of the subject, or yet of the agent, but of the *author*. The author, who is not only taken to be the authority for the meaning of a text, but also, when possessed of authority, possessed *by the fact* of "moral or legal supremacy, the power to influence the conduct or action of others;" and, when authorizing, "giving legal force to, making legally valid." (pp. 217-218)

Barthes (1977) announced the birth of the reader who "is simply that *someone* who holds together in a single field all the traces by which the written text is constituted" (pp. 145-146). The writer is, in this sense, a reader at the performance of writing.

In other words, there can never be only one truth, one authorial voice, or one reading of Kristeva's (1986) work. If I want to know the truth about Kristeva's text my task is not to scrutinize the text for insight about Kristeva's true intent. Rather, I am interested in the discursive conditions that allowed Kristeva to produce this text, as well as the discursive conditions in which I am positioned to interpret this text in specific ways (cf. Spivak, 1993).

In contrast to the theoretical interpretation of Kristeva (1986) in the text "Discourses on Gender and Literacy: Changing the Stories," which I have already outlined here, I suggest an alternative reading using the discourse of post- and anticolonial writers (cf. Bhabha, 1990). I am not suggesting that post- or anticolonial discourse is homogeneous. Indeed, writers who position themselves as postcolonial have vastly contradictory responses to Kristeva's work. Spivak (1993), an Indian/Bengali–U.S. writer, has this to say:

> I'm repelled by Kristeva's politics: what seems to me to be her reliance on the sort of banal historical narrative to produce "women's time"; what seems to me Christianizing psychoanalysis; what seems to me to be her sort of ferocious Western Europeanism; what seems to me to be her long-standing implicit positivism; naturalizing of the chora, naturalizing of the presemiotic. I'm so put off by this that I can't read her seriously anymore, so it is more my problem. I mean, I'm not generous and catholic enough to learn from her anymore. (p. 17)

Similarly, Chow (1991) a Chinese–U.S. postcolonial writer, criticized Kristeva for her interpretation of the Chinese practice of maiming women's bodies through foot binding. Chow argued that Kristeva's Eurocentric interpretation of this practice suggests that Chinese women become men's equal in the symbolic order through the practice of foot binding. Instead of seeing women in an active discursive role expressing discontent with this practice, Kristeva's reading says that in your suffering you are the bearers of Chinese culture (cf. Ram, 1993).

Although I agree with both of these interpretations of Kristeva's writing, I offer an alternative reading of "Women's Time" by using the research of Bhabha (1990), an Indian-British postcolonial writer. Rather than deconstructing Kristeva's text for its Eurocentric assumptions and arguing that it has nothing to offer educators in Australian schools, I want to build on the theoretical research in the area of gender and literacy.

What I am proposing then is a reading of Kristeva (1986) that attempts to erase the Eurocentric bias and enable an understanding of the differences within the category "woman." In "Discourses on Gender and Literacy: Changing the Stories" a critical feminist reading of Kristeva's (1986) theory has been articulated. I suggest that an alternative reading, that is a postcolonial reading (Bhabha, 1990) of the same text, will enable an analysis of the differences within the category "woman," which have not been recognized in Gilbert's reading of children's writing practices. Consequently, the differences within the category "woman" have been silenced and suppressed, and only the differences between the category "woman" and "man" have been made visible.

I have both a personal and professional desire to speak about the differences that have been erased in the theoretical analysis articulated in "Discourses on Gender and Literacy: Changing the Stories." I am one of those women whose gendered ethnic difference has been violently suppressed. And under these circumstances I believe that we should no longer ask the question: "Why are ethnic people, Indigenous people, people of color silent from literary practices, textual representations?" The question that needs to be asked is: "What symbolic violence has been committed to erase the presence of 'people of color' in a society seething with their presence?" (Carby, 1989; Morrison, 1989).

Postcolonial, anticolonial, and Black feminist theory has evolved out of a desire to raise these questions, that is, shift the problem from one that focuses solely on patriarchy as the source and site of oppression. Postcolonial theory attempts to understand and give meaning to the lives, experiences, and identities of people once the objects of colonization. Since World War II, during which, for the most part, the decolonization of the European empires has taken place, there has been an accompanying attempt to decolonize European thought and the forms of its history. This project, Young (1992) argued, could be said to have been initiated in 1963 by Fanon's *The Wretched of the Earth*. I am not implying that new forms of colonial practices (i.e., neocolonialism and postcolonialism) do not exist. What I am saying is that the political, economic, and cultural relationship of Empire and colony, center and periphery has changed. There is no going back.

Decolonization and the accompanying resurgence of Asian-Pacific economies, languages and cultures has ushered in a New World Order (West, 1993). Japan has emerged as an economic leader. And South East Asian countries, recently represented as undeveloped, too traditional or third world are now the fastest growing economies in the world (cf. Alexander & Rizvi, 1993; Hall, 1992). In addition, mass worldwide immigration has dislocated and relocated people from the former colonies of Europe. That is, mass immigration has produced nations such as Australia with a multicultural identity. The immigrant people in the Australian nation constitute part of the diaspora. As diasporic people they have been objects of colonization and immigration. They have been scattered across the globe but still retain some relationship with traditional or home cultures, even though these relationships are fraught with ambiguity. At the same time, the people of the diaspora are constantly producing, negotiating, and reconstructing their ethnic identities. That is, their ethnic identity is not traditional or primitive in relation to Anglo-Australian identity that has been constructed as the norm, but lives with and through difference, by hybridity.[2]

Let me be clear. Academic theorizing does not exist in isolation. The context of my struggle as an Asian-Australian woman is not only patriarchal discourses, but also the racist trajectory that has constructed the imagined community (Andersen, 1991) of the Australian nation as

---

[2]The experiences of gendered ethnic subjectivity in postcolonial spaces and times have been captured well in the following literary works:

Ang, L. (1983). *The butcher's wife*. London: Penguin.

Castro, B. (1983). *Birds of passage*. Sydney: George Allen & Unwin.

Hong Kingston, M. (1981). *The woman warrior. Memories of a girlhood among ghosts.*

Seth, V. (1993). *A suitable boy*. London: Phoenix.

Tan, A. (1989). *The Joy Luck Club*. London: Manderin.

Tan, A. (1991). *The Kitchen God's wife*. London: Flamingo.

Xiaoqui, D. (1993). *Maidenhome*. Melbourne: Hyland House Fiction.

Yahp, B. (1994) In 1964. In W. Jenkins (Ed.). *Reading from the left*. Fremantle: Fremantle Arts Centre Press.

White British. Within this racialized historical context, women's bodies are marked by social class, race, sexual preference, mental and physical difference, and age. Of principal concern to me here is the way women's bodies are racially marked as "White middle-class" and "woman of color". These communities are imaginary in that they exist inside people's heads, naming groups that are far too large to know each other personally; yet they presuppose connectedness and belonging among in-group members (Pettman, 1992). I do not propose that these communities, within which the bodies of "White women" and "women of color" are located, are fixed or static. Rather the signifiers of "whiteness" and "color" are ambiguous and shifting (Perera, 1992). "Color" has never been just there waiting to be discovered as the site of oppression or authentic identity. As Hall (1992) said, "It has always been an unstable identity, psychically, culturally, and politically. It, too, is a narrative, a story, a history. Something constructed, told, spoken, not simply found" (p. 45).

Moreover, signifying particular bodies as "colored" has real material consequences for those who are so named and represented (Hall, 1992).

Now let me return to Kristeva. A postcolonial interpretation of Kristeva's (1986) theory of how the sign or representation of "woman" is constructed enables me to analyze the "difference" within the category "woman," not only the relational "difference" symbolically constructed between "man" and "woman." Kristeva proposed that in the space of the postmodern nation, such as Australia, symbolic representation in the form of the sign of "woman" is constituted in and through three temporal relations. Kristeva's three temporal relations can be described as:

1. Monumental time (eternity) produces a sign or symbol with an inherited history (mythology, religious beliefs, scientific discourses). So for example, the sign of "woman" in monumental time refers to the biblical representations of woman, "woman" as inferior to "man" in Darwin's theory of survival of the fittest, and "Black woman's" sexual deviancy as incorporated in the theories of 19th-century medicine and science.[3]

---

[3]Gilman (1992) argued that Virey and Cuvier in the early 19th century summarized their (and their contemporaries') views on the sexual nature of Black females in terms of acceptable medical discourse.

According to (Virey), their "voluptuousness" is "developed to a degree of lascivity unknown in our climate, for their sexual organs are much more developed than those of whites." Elsewhere, Virey cites the Hottentot woman as the epitome of this sexual

2. Cyclic time represents the biological difference of woman to man that is understood, interpreted, or read in specific ways. The cycle, the biological rhythm of woman that conforms to that of nature has often been interpreted as a "natural difference" to the norm of man.
3. Linear or cursive time is the time of language, enunciation, a sequence of words from the space of articulation to the site of performance or reception. It is within linear or cursive time and space that the gendered sign is disrupted and reconstructed.

Consequently, the present of women's time (monumental, cyclical, and linear) is a zone of representational instability. That is, the representation of women in and through the sign "woman" becomes the site of continual challenge and reconstruction. It is from this instability of cultural signification that the literary canon comes to be articulated as a dialectic of various temporalities—modern, colonial, postcolonial, feminist, postfeminist, poststructural feminism(s), "native," traditional—that cannot be a knowledge that is stabilized in enunciation. In this time, "woman" does not signify the female body as an a priori historical presence, a discursive object; but a discursive subject constructed in the performance of the narrative.

The gendered sign constructed in the grand narratives, the literary canon of patriarchal discourses is constantly disrupted in performance. The repetition of the gendered sign in discourses of patriarchy is disrupted in linear or cursive time (Kristeva, 1986) by discourses of difference—gendered difference, racialized difference, homosexual difference, socioeconomic difference. The space of representation threatens the binary division of grand narratives with its difference, its "Othering," through the continual production and re-articulation of difference. The signs of difference—women, minorities—

---

lasciviousness and stresses the relationship between her physiology and her physiognomy (her "hideous form" and her "horribly flattened nose"). His central proof is a discussion of the unique structure of the Hottentot female's sexual parts, the description of which he takes from the anatomical studies published by his contemporary, Georges Cuvier. According to Cuvier, the black female looks different. Her physiognomy, her skin colour, the form of her genitalia label her as inherently different. In the nineteenth century, the black female was widely perceived as possessing not only a "primitive" sexual appetite but also the external signs of this temperament— "primitive" genitalia.

These discourses, which attribute a primitive sexuality to Black women, have been reconstructed into different versions of racist discourses today.

move from the space of the "Other," the margin, and disrupt the center. The "Other" has to be faced, difference has to be incorporated. Difference can no longer be "Othered" (cf. Bhabha, 1994; Kristeva, 1986).

This is the representational space of women's double time. By the concept *double time* I mean that the sign of "woman" is not simply or automatically reproduced as "object of patriarchy". Rather, the sign of "woman" is contested and challenged by different women in and through their practices, for example, their speaking and writing practices.

The gendered sign produced in the pedagogic discourses of the literary canon, the grand cultural narratives, is not simply reproduced in linear time, in representational space. The gendered sign is rewritten in the representational space of performance. And this rewriting, re-articulation of the gendered sign doubles back to the space of pedagogic discursive construction, the grand narratives, as an add-on that cannot be reincorporated within the totalizing boundaries of patriarchy. That is, feminist, postcolonial, Indigenous women's writing cannot be simply added onto the master discourses. By their very nature, these counterdiscourses disrupt the workings of patriarchy and colonialism. In addition, the different voices of women disrupt any attempt to stabilize meaning around "universal womanhood." The sign of "woman" is continually the site of contestation and struggle because it constitutes the site of identity construction.

In the postmodern nation, difference is incorporated within the category "woman" and is signified by a succession of plurals such as White, Anglo, Black, colored, Indigenous, Asian, mentally and physically challenged, lesbian, and so forth. Such a pluralism where difference returns as the same, is contested by the signifier's "loss of identity" that inscribes the narrative of woman in the ambivalent, "double" writing of the performative and the pedagogical (cf. Irigaray, 1993). That is, the sign of woman can no longer signify the universal experiences of all women. At the same time, incorporating difference by words such as Black, physically and mentally challenged, lesbian, and so forth, challenges the very meaning of the sign "woman." The differences of woman cannot be simply dismissed and incorporated back into the liberal notion that we are all individual women with our individual differences. The differences produced by social, historical, cultural, and economic circumstances that constitute different categories of "woman" can never be incorporated back into the universal sign of "woman"— women who experience "similar oppressions" under patriarchy. Different groups of women do not experience the same kinds of oppressions. Patriarchy takes on different forms and is realized in different ways for different groups of women. That is, the experiences of racialized, ethnicized women are profoundly different from those of White bourgeois women and are manifested in profoundly different social, cultural, and economic practices.

This does not mean, however, that under some political circumstances the symbolic category "women as a collective" should not be evoked to make a strategic, political difference. But the question must always be posed—in whose interests is difference and commonality being celebrated?

Now if I return to "Discourses on Gender and Literacy: Changing the Stories," I can demonstrate how this particular text, through the use of a specific reading of Kristeva's theoretical model, disrupts and alters the workings of patriarchy. Woman is not simply added on as an afterthought in the discourses of patriarchy but significantly disrupts the workings of these discourses. Similarly, my challenge of opening up the category of "woman" to examine the racial and socioeconomic differences within "woman" means that the sign of woman can no longer return as the same. In Kristeva's terms the racialized or Black woman is not simply the negative or silent other of White woman.

It is from this position that I urge feminists who are rewriting patriarchal discourses to examine the contradictions within the gendered subject—the *differance* within the symbolic category "woman," the voices of minority women, the supplementary discourses that refuse to be added on, discourses that disrupt and fragment the pedagogic discourse of feminisms (cf. hooks, 1991). As Kristeva (1986) said, "the time has perhaps come to emphasize the multiplicity of female expressions and preoccupations so that from the intersection of these differences there might arise . . . the real fundamental differences between the two sexes" (p. 193).

SUMMARY

In this chapter I proposed that critical feminist theory has contributed significantly to an analysis of the social construction of gender within schooling and literacy practices. However, I argue that the construction of gender deployed within this corpus of work is not inclusive because it does not theorize (apart from simple arithmetic calculations of triple oppression) the differences within the category "woman." I propose an alternative reading of Kristeva that enables the multiplicity and differences within the category "woman" to be articulated. If critical feminist theory is to achieve its objective of democratizing literacy and schooling practices, then it is imperative that we hear and not suppress the voices of all women.

REFERENCES

Alexander, D., & Rizvi, F. (1993). Education, markets and the contradictions of Asia-Australia relations. *The Australian Universities' Review, 36*(2), 16-20.

Anderson, B. (1991). *Imagined communities*. London: Verso.

Ball, S. (1994) What is criticism? A continuing conversation? A rejoinder to Miriam Henry. *Discourse: The Australian Journal of Educational Studies, 14*(2), 108-110.

Barthes, R. (1977). *The death of the author* (S. Heath, Trans.). New York: Hill & Wang.

Bhabha, H. K. (1990). DissemiNation: Time, narrative, and the margins of the modern nation. In H. K. Bhabha (Ed.), *Nation and narration*. London: Routledge.

Bhabha, H. K. (1994). *The location of culture*. London: Routledge.

Carby, H. (1989). The Canon: Civil war and reconstruction. *Michigan Quarterly Review, 28*, 1.

Chow, R. (1991). *Woman and Chinese modernity. The politics of reading between West and East*. Minnesota: University of Minnesota Press.

du Cille, A. (1994). The occult of true black womanhood: Critical demeanour and black feminist studies. *Signs: Journal of Women in Culture and Society, 19*(3), 591-629.

Fanon, F. (1963). *The wretched of the earth*. London: Pelican.

Freebody, P., Luke, A., & Gilbert, P. (1991). Reading positions and practices in the classroom. *Curriculum Inquiry, 21*(4), 435-457.

Gilbert, P. (1989a). Personally (and passively) yours: Girls, literacy and education. *Oxford Review of Education, 15*(3), 257-265.

Gilbert, P. (1989b). *Writing, schooling and deconstruction. From voice to text in the classroom*. London: Routledge.

Gilbert, P. (1992, October). *Gender and literacy: Key issues for the nineties*. Paper prepared for the Victoria Australia Ministry of Education.

Gilbert, P. & Taylor, S. (1991). *Fashioning the feminine. Girls, popular culture and schooling*. Sydney, Australia: Allen & Unwin.

Gilman, S. (1992). Black bodies, white bodies: Toward an iconography of female sexuality in late nineteenth-century art, medicine and literature. In J. Donald & A. Rattansi (Eds.), *"Race," culture and difference*. London: The Open University Press.

Grosz, E. (1989). *Sexual subversions*. Sydney, Australia: Allen & Unwin.

Hall, S. (1992). New ethnicities. In J. Donald & A. Rattansi (Eds.), *"Race," culture and difference*. London: Sage.

hooks, bell (1991). Sisterhood. Political solidarity between women. In S. Gunew (Ed.), *A reader in feminist knowledge*. London: Routledge.

Irigaray, L. (1992). *Elemental passions*. London: The Athlone Press.

Irigaray, L. (1993). *je, tu, nous. Towards a culture of difference.* New York: Routledge.

Kristeva, J. (1986). Women's time. In T. Moi (Ed.), *The Kristeva reader.* Oxford, UK: Blackwell.

Luke, C. (1995). White women in interracial families: Reflections on hybridization, feminine identities, and racialized othering. *Feminist Issues, 14*(2), 49-72.

McCarthy, C. (1994). The politics of culture: Multicultural education after the content debate. *Discourse. The Australian Journal of Educational Studies, 14*(2), 1-16.

Morrison, T. (1989). Unspeakable things unspoken: The Afro-American presence in American literature. *Michigan Quarterly Review, 28*(1), 34.

Painter, N. I. (1992). Hill, Thomas and the use of racial stereotype. In T. Morrison (Ed.), *Race-ing justice, En-gendering power. Essays on Anita Hill, Clarence Thomas and the construction of social reality.* New York: Pantheon.

Perera, S. (1992, November). *Making difference: Language corporeality and the protocols of conferencing.* Paper presented at the Dealing with Difference Conference, University of Melbourne, Australia.

Pettman, J. (1992). *Living in the margins. Racism, sexism and feminism in Australia.* Sydney, Australia: Allen & Unwin.

Ram, K. (1993). Too `"traditional" once again: Some poststructuralists on the aspirations of the immigrant/third world female subject. *Australian Feminist Studies, 17,* 5-28.

Spivak, G. C. (1988). Can the subaltern speak? In C. Nelson & L. Grossberg (Eds.), *Marxism and the interpretation of culture.* Chicago: University of Illinois Press.

Spivak, G. C. (1993). *Outside in the teaching machine.* London: Routledge.

Tsolidis, G. (1990). Ethnic minority girls and self-esteem. In J. Kenway & S. Willis (Eds.), *Hearts and minds. Self-esteem and the schooling of girls.* London: Falmer Press.

West, C. (1993). The new cultural politics of difference. In S. During (Ed.), *The cultural studies reader.* London: Sage.

Whitford, M. (1991). *Luce Irigaray. Philosophy in the feminine.* London: Routledge.

Young, R. (1992). Colonialism and humanism. In J. Donald & A. Rattansi (Eds.), *"Race," culture and difference.* London: The Open University Press.

6

Critical Literacy and Active Citizenship

Colin Lankshear
Michele Knobel
Queensland University of Technology

In this chapter we suggest some possible components of classroom reading and writing practice that are integral to the educational goal of promoting active citizenship, and that can reasonably be identified as components of a critical literacy. We begin with some introductory remarks about literacies as discursive constructions, and explain why we address the development of classroom approaches to critical literacy in the context of a larger concern of education for active citizenship in the 1990s.

   We then discuss active citizenship as contested discursive terrain by outlining an account of active citizenship advanced by an Australian Senate Standing Committee and drawing on competing views to mount a critique of that account. Proceeding from this critique, we identify some important demands imposed on citizens in what have been termed *New Times* and develop an alternative account of active citizenship as an educational goal. The chapter concludes with our attempt to identify some components of a critical classroom literacy consonant with our view of the active citizen.

   Understanding of literacy has expanded dramatically since the early 1980s with the emergence of the "new literacy studies" (Gee, 1996). Developments from a range of social theory perspectives have progressively chipped away at the virtual monopoly over educational research of text-based practices previously exercised by psychologists of one type or another. Freed from the stranglehold of positivist technicism, those working from a new literacy studies perspective have come to appreciate the radically plural and discursive character of literacy (cf. A. Luke, 1995).

Literacies are many, not singular. Moreover, what all cases of literacy seem to have in common—such as a basis in a technology (e.g., print, alphabetic script), or a set of techniques or competencies, or some combination of these—is now widely seen as in many ways less significant than the *differences* among literacies. We now understand literacies as socially created constitutive elements of larger human practices—discourses—that humans construct around their myriad purposes and values. It is precisely these human purposes and values that give point to developing and working with certain kinds of texts in certain kinds of ways. Equally, these socially constructed ways of working with texts contribute, dialectically, to shaping the larger practices, processes, beliefs, attitudes, and so on, by and through which human purposes and values are "lived."

This is readily apparent from an historical standpoint. Rich historical data reveals how, for example, in late 18th-century England the opposing political values and purposes of the Corresponding Societies and the Church and King Clubs, respectively, gave rise to polarized political Discourses whose associated literacies were as different from one another as chalk and cheese (Lankshear & Lawler, 1989; Willinsky, 1993). Historians of literacy, sociolinguists, and ethnographers from several disciplines have documented, individually and comparatively, many cases of social practices and their related constructions of reading and writing (see, e.g., Gee, 1990; Graff, 1979, 1981; Heath, 1983; Kress, 1985; A. Luke, 1988; Scribner & Cole, 1981; Street, 1984; Willinsky, 1989). They have, in other words, traced in close detail important aspects of the relationship between what Gee (1991, 1992–93, 1996, see chap. 14, this volume) called *Discourses* (with a capital D) and *discourses*.

By Discourses we mean socially constructed and recognized ways of being in the world, which integrate and regulate ways of acting, thinking, feeling, using language, believing, and valuing. By participating in Discourses we take up social roles and positions that other human beings can identify as meaningful (cf. Gee, 1996), and on the basis of which personal identities are constituted. It is in and through Discourse that *biological* human beings are constituted as ("identitied") *social* human beings.

This is not to imply that the "rules" governing a Discourse and membership "within" it are necessarily precise, still less to imply that they are settled or immutable. What constitutes being in or out of a particular Discourse is often highly contested. This, as we show later, is true of active citizenship as Discourse. Discourses are dynamic, alive. Living in and through them is very much a process of constantly renegotiating them. Discourses are profoundly dialectical. At the same time, discrete Discourses are identifiable as such, together with the sorts of identities they make possible. Discourses, then, are of widely varying types and scope. In his list of typical Discourses, Gee (1991) included:

> (enacting) being an American or a Russian, being a man or a woman, being a member of a certain socio-economic class, being a factory worker or a boardroom executive, being a doctor or a hospital patient, being a teacher, an administrator, or a student, being a member of a sewing circle, a club, a street gang, a lunchtime social gathering, or a regular at a local watering hole. (p. 4)

To these we add "being an (active) citizen."

discourses (with a small d) are the language—or the "saying/ writing/listening/reading/viewing"—components of Discourses. Discourse is "always more than just language" or "discourse"; but "discourse" is always and necessarily present in Discourse (Gee, 1990, p. 142). Although Gee himself advanced a different, and much more elaborate view, we define *literacy* for our purposes here as those "language bits" (in Discourses) that involve text. Literacies, then, are the "textual components" of discourses: that is, texts and textual practices.

In their relationship, Discourse and discourse are mutually constitutive. As a locus of meaning-making a Discourse both shapes and is shaped by its discourse. This is to recognize that making meaning requires purposes and means as well as a medium. The important points for us here are that we can conceive of literacies only in conjunction with cogenerative integrated Discourses. This helps explain why we are grounding our attempt to construct elements of a critical literacy in the larger discursive context of educating for active citizenship. Practicing active citizenship, we argue, presupposes an orientation toward texts and certain capacities for meaning-making that are increasingly being identified with conceptions and practices of critical literacy.

There is more, however. Once we understand Discourses and literacies for what they are, and in their relationship to each other, we can self-consciously engage in framing and constructing (new) Discoursal visions—which, as we have seen, incorporate literacies, in the same way as it has long been argued people can enter consciously into making and transforming history and culture once they understand history and culture for what they are.

The dialectic noted earlier applies here. Teaching a critical social literacy is part of what is involved in educating students for active citizenship for an anticipated multicultural republican Australia (Kalantzis, 1992/1993). Our conception of this critical social literacy is partly shaped by our vision of the active citizen. At the same time, however, our evolving vision of active citizenship is itself partly constituted out of attitudes, values, competencies, and so on, that we already recognize as aspects of "reading and writing the social" from a critical perspective. What follows is an attempt to "play out" this dialectic imaginatively on the surface texture of this text.

ACTIVE CITIZENSHIP: CONTESTED DISCURSIVE TERRAIN

Right now citizenship is a high profile educational concern in the United States and Britain, as well as in Australia. Following the release of the *Report of the Senate Standing Committee on Employment, Education and Training* (Department of Employment, Education and Training, 1989. See also *Active Citizenship Revisited*, Department of Employment, Education and Training, 1991), the Australian Education Council ratified a citizenship education goal among its 10 *Common and Agreed National Goals for Schooling in Australia*: namely, to "develop knowledge, skills, attitudes and values which will enable students to participate as active and informed citizens in our democratic Australian society within an international context." All state and territory education systems in Australia have responded at some level to this goal.

Broadly speaking, citizenship marks a domain of Discourse at the intersection of state (or "political society") and civil society. More specifically, however, we can identify multiple extant competing discursive constructions of citizenship, within and between societies, as well as attempts to "reframe" new Discourses of citizenship that go beyond those currently in evidence.

Something of the contested nature of active citizenship as Discourse is revealed in the debate surrounding the release of the Senate Committee's 1989 report, *Active Citizenship*, and subsequent developments in Australia associated largely with the prospect of that country becoming a republic. As Trinca (1993) noted, at the level of discourse at least, monarchies (and their colonies) are about constituting subjects: the discourse of republics espouses constituting citizens. According to the Senate Committee, education for active citizenship must ensure students (a) understand how government works (at the commonwealth, state and local levels), (b) appreciate the role of community groups and non government organizations, and (c) be motivated to be active citizens. Such an education was seen by the Committee as necessary to counteract a number of growing concerns, including the following:

1. Media ownership and presentation trends are restricting the range of information and viewpoints represented on matters pertaining to government, and emphasising "personalities and image" over "issues" (Department of Employment, Education and Training, 1989, p. 8).

2. Many migrants have only experienced political structures and traditions quite different from Australia's. Not all "necessarily share our democratic traditions." Some may actually "fear the political process" (p. 8).
3. Many young people feel alienated from community affairs, lacking skills and interest to participate in formal community processes and decision making. Many young people, failing to see "any direct link between . . . government . . . and their own lives," do not register to vote (pp. 9, 14).
4. Unacceptably high levels of "political ignorance," especially among young Australians, have been proclaimed, indicating "indifference and apathy towards political dimensions of experience," and an attitude of leaving it to "other people" to take care of governance. Where "accountability is weak" and power concentrates "in the hands of a few," the "quality of democracy [comes] under threat" (p. 14).

In the view of the Senate Committee, for citizenship education to be effective in helping counteract such concerns certain things would have to be observed. According to the report, "active citizenship" means more than mere knowledge of political–governmental and community affairs. Education for active citizenship must not revert to "old-style 'civics' courses," merely force-feeding facts about the political system. Rather, active citizenship is about believing in the concept of a democratic society and being "willing and able to translate that belief into action." In this context, the report stresses upholding and participating in formal democratic processes, noting that for migrants this begins with taking up Australian citizenship. Beyond knowledge of (formal) political structures and processes at government and community levels, "being active" as a citizen calls for relevant skills and attitudes including, notably, respect for rights and duties that have evolved constitutionally and institutionally throughout Australia's colonial history.

The report maintains that sufficient curriculum policy already exists to underwrite the syllabus and pedagogical requirements of active citizenship education. Rather, the need is to reduce the gap between policy rhetoric and action, and to extend citizenship education beyond books alone and out into civil society. Teacher education must prepare teachers to educate for citizenship (Department of Employment, Education and Training, 1989, chap. 3). Appropriate curricular resources must be developed (chap. 4, esp. p. 51). Curriculum and resource developers, teacher educators, and teachers themselves, must identify and build on available exemplars of pedagogy and resources for active citizenship (chap. 4).

Unfortunately, the report glosses complex and contested ideals and, consequently, masks the extent to which concepts like *democracy, politics, participation, public versus private sphere,* and *being active* denote what adds up to hotly contested discursive terrain. Three focal points of competition and dispute are sufficient to make the point.

- The notion of active commitment to democracy is vague and open to quite different discursive renderings. Respondents to the 1989 report distinguished, significantly, between "protectionist" and "participatory" approaches to democracy, as well as between a "party politics and representative democracy" ethos on the one hand, and a "personal and community politics" ethos on the other. John Fien and Wayne Kippin made it clear in their individual submissions to the original report that without careful attention to concepts and definition "it is impossible to sustain a consistent analysis" of the issues involved in education for active citizenship, or to develop "a coherent solution to the perceived problems of school curricula and teacher education" that arise in this area (Department of Employment, Education and Training, 1991, pp. 4-5). Moreover, the Committee's explicit and practically exclusive focus on formal public practices of democracy undermines its avowed concern that students learn to "appreciate the role of community groups and non-government organisations" (see Faraclas, chap. 8, this volume). Despite scattered references in the subsequent 1991 report to wider "activities and values which constitute the culture of a community", and through which "a community seeks both to preserve and transform itself" (p. 6), the Committee's overwhelming emphasis is on developing familiarity with "institutionalised aspects of parliamentary democracy." Certainly, this is the ground on which the Committee speaks most clearly and convincingly. The level of conceptual development of "community" and related concepts is very low in both reports, and illustrative examples of the possible role of community and nongovernmental organizations in citizenship education are impoverished.
- Both *Active Citizenship* and *Active Citizenship Revisited* have been charged with advancing an essentially conservative, unduly narrow, and conceptually underdeveloped position on the relationship between the "political" and the "personal" and the relative significance of the "public" and "private" spheres with regard to active citizenship (Department of Employment, Education and Training, 1991).

Some opponents of the Senate Committee's framing of active citizenship advocate "a holistic view" that is not confined to "the arena of civic or public concerns" but stresses individual and private as well as collaborative and public dimensions of being an active citizen. The wider view acknowledges elements of "the personal" as having political significance, and posits dialectical links between power, social arrangements, and personal life.

> Politics . . . is not simply a matter of who occupies the Lodge or what issues are attracting public lobbying activity, but [also of] who (for example) decides and who accepts responsibility for the household chores and why one particular type of household "agreement" on these matters is common. Personal life is undoubtedly political and any attempt to deny this must be seen as a political act in itself. (Department of Employment, Education and Training, 1991, p. 6)

From this standpoint, struggles within the private sphere to win a more equitable distribution of domestic work and decision-making power inside the family, and struggle by migrants to negotiate a viable and satisfying identity within their new life situation, become facets of actively constructing and practicing citizenship.

Against this, the Committee digs in and asserts the grounding of citizenship in the public sphere. "To be a citizen is to participate in the public practices which sustain, *and to a large extent define,* a community" (p. 6, italics added). The reports explicitly recognize the formal processes of parliamentary democracy: those "concrete social and historical forms through which . . . participation and transformation are currently effected" (p. 7). Yet matters that are emerging ever more obviously as major issues of citizenship in New Times—like the morally and politically significant dimensions of constructing and negotiating identity and loyalties across borders (Kalantzis, 1992/1993)—go unrecognized.

- In "Citizenship Education after the Monarchy," Kalantzis (1992/1993) identified pressing citizenship issues emerging at this juncture in Australia's national history that are quite absent in the Senate Committee's ruminations. These relate to constructing citizenship around a (shifting) dialectic between national identity and the identities of persons and groups. The current preoccupation among social theorists worldwide with discourses of "the Post"— the postmodern, postcolonial, postindustrial, poststructural, and so on—reflects a growing awareness that we have reached an historical conjuncture: a crossroads between "past" ways of doing things and opportunities to negotiate new discursive orders across a wide spectrum of human experience (Slattery, 1993). For all the fuzziness that remains around the edges, it is widely accepted that we have, in a significant sense, entered New Times.

Berman (1982) and Hall (1991) captured key features of the age that speak directly to citizenship. Hall recognized global trends toward "greater fragmentation and pluralism, the weakening of older collective solidarities and block identities and the emergence of new identities associated with greater work flexibility, the maximisation of individual choices through personal consumption" (p. 58). Berman documented ways in which and the extent to which "modern environments and experiences cut across all boundaries of geography and ethnicity, of class and nationality, of religion and ideology." These boundaries are not so much destroyed as weakened and undermined. The overall effect is an erosion of, in Hall's (1991) words, "lines of continuity which hitherto stabilised our social identities" (p. 58).

Kalantzis' work on citizenship in Australia resonates with these themes. She identifies two factors bearing on citizenship in Australia that demand a new Discourse. These are the extent of *local diversity* in Australia, brought about largely, although not entirely, by mass immigration and the fact that Australians are having to live with an "increasingly proximate global diversity as our economic, cultural and civic associations increasingly and more comfortably cross national borders" (1992/1993, p. 29). Her call for an approach to citizenship based on rights and responsibilities located in geographic space rather than on a sense of national loyalty predicated on assumptions of singularity, highlights the importance of constructing and negotiating identities and loyalties across borders.

Clearly, active citizenship is assuming a new urgency, but at the same time is well and truly due for a major discursive overhaul. In its attempt to frame the Discourse of active citizenship, however, the Senate Committee has simply failed to comprehend the scope and depth, and to grasp the mood of New Times. The challenge issued by the Committee must be taken up, but in much wider discursive terms than it envisages, and beginning from a more adequate purview of the life of our age. This calls for building a Discourse of active citizenship in which developing and teaching a critical literacy has a central place.

CITIZENSHIP DISCOURSE IN NEW TIMES

Obviously there is much more to be said about New Times than is possible here. We intend only to identify three important contemporary trends that impact directly on citizenship, and to trace some of their discursive implications. These are:

- social changes calling for enhanced understanding of institutions in their relationship to the lives of individuals and groups, and for revitalized civic participation in institutional life;
- trends in communications media that create impediments to making meanings (from text) that promote the common good;
- increased proximity to and intensified experience of diversity, calling for new approaches to negotiating identities and loyalties and to learning to live productively and harmoniously with difference (Kalantzis, 1992/1993).

Social Change and Institutional Life

Social changes during recent decades have heralded a decline in numerous institutions, wrought change in others, and thrown the validity of still others into doubt. Many older established means of "hooking people up" socially have been eroded, often without new means emerging to take their place.

For example, the near complete entry of women into the paid workforce in many "developed" societies has had an important impact on community life and prior institutional arrangements. To date, little institutional adjustment has occurred to ensure such things as (a) provision for the unpaid work of child care, (b) care of the elderly, (c) the maintenance of neighborhood ties, and (d) the elaborate system of voluntary community activity previously undertaken by women. Much of what continues to be done in these areas is still carried out by women. Men's work hours have not decreased. There has been little growth in compensatory community services. Not surprisingly, then, the women who continue such work (and their families) endure considerable stress. Alternatively, "the [important] community-related tasks are often abandoned" (cf. Levett & Lankshear, 1992, p. 45).

Social theorists working from quite different perspectives advance sobering analyses of civic life in crisis. Drawing on work by Lyotard (1984), Baudrillard (1981), and on related theoretical developments that stress the centrality of the communications revolution to the "postmodern condition," Hinkson (1991) observed the extent to which in postmodern times institutions and social groupings associated with modernity are experienced as "anachronisms," and even as "forms of dogmatic imposition." Two related aspects stand out from this so far as the institutional life of citizens is concerned.

First, the "logic of information" and image demands the absence of structural or systemic constraints ("noise") to the free flow of messages and image signifiers. Second, computer and hi-tech media communications generate and constitute "social relations which are essentially *networks of temporary or fleeting interchange*" (p. 9). One way of demarcating the social settings of modernity from their postmodern counterparts is in terms of the relative significance and foregrounding of network (social) relations. Hinkson (1991) made the point well:

> [T]he network in modernity as a structured form of relation was significantly offset by relations which were structured in other ways—relying on forms of social bonding which held together self and other through inter-generational norms, for example.
>
> What happens in postmodern settings is the emergence of a social space which holds out the possibility—by virtue of the structuring possibilities of information and the flow of images—of reconstituting social life around the network to such a degree that the social group is experienced as an anachronism (and a form of dogmatic imposition). It is as though the network relation which was always an aspect of the more comprehensive group is filleted off . . . and under the influence of the power of the new technologies moves into the foreground as a means of structuring a society which works on principles quite different from those of other known social forms. (pp. 9-10)

The implication of this logic for some important familiar institutions of modernity is obvious. They become discredited as "out of time"; as so much "noise"; as impediments to postmodern individuality, autonomy, and mobility. Add to this the construction of postmodern selves through engagement with disembodied, image-mediated Others, in accordance with intense pressure to define one's *self* over and *against* Others through individualized consumption, and the threat posed to institutional life as we have known it becomes even more apparent (Kellner, 1991).

From a rather different angle, Bellah, Madsen, Sullivan, Swidler, and Tipton (1991) reported from the United States a widespread loss of faith in institutions, and emphasized the implications of this for citizenship. They argued that modern societies have been overly dependent on technical means for solving problems. We need to balance technique with a deeper understanding of "moral ecology." This means understanding how much we live our lives within institutions, recognizing that enhancing our lives presupposes better institutions, and "surveying our present institutions . . . to discern what is healthy in them and what needs to be altered" (p. 5). The challenge of New Times, then, is to reform existing institutions, and build new ones where necessary, in response to changed and changing demands. A good society is "an open quest" calling for the active participation of all citizens, because "the common good is pursuit of the good in common." The age calls for nothing less than "a new experiment in democracy, a newly extended and enhanced set of democratic institutions, within which we citizens can better discern what we really want and what we ought to want to sustain a good life on this planet for ourselves and the generations to come" (p. 9).

This calls for resisting current trends toward ideologies and Discourses of robust individualism, and opening ourselves up instead to an invigorating and fulfilling sense of social responsibility. Beyond merely calling for people to get involved—reminiscent, perhaps, of the Senate Committee's pleas to match our rhetoric of citizenship education with practice—it will be necessary to *create and maintain institutions* that enable such participation, encourage it, and make it fulfilling as well as demanding. For Bellah and colleagues, the question facing citizenship education is "how to educate ourselves as citizens so that we really can 'make a difference' in the institutions that have such an impact on our lives" (p. 19).

Media, Meanings, and the Common Good

The Senate Committee's concerns about media trends in Australia resonate with growing interest among educationists in promoting critical media literacy as an integral aspect of education for active citizenship. As has often been noted, theorists spanning the range from Fredric Jameson to Jean-Francois Lyotard identify "the dominance of image, appearance [and] surface effect over depth; . . . the blurring of image and reality . . . [and] the erasure of a strong sense of history" as key features of the postmodern condition (Hall, 1991, p. 60; cf. Harvey, 1989). Communications media are strongly implicated—as simultaneously cause and effect—in these patterns of dominance. Not surprisingly, critical media literacy is being heralded as a counterforce to this postmodern logic that, like the growing emphases on network relations, presents serious challenges to maintaining and reconstructing Discourses of active and informed political and civic involvement (see C. Luke, chap. 2, this volume).

Kellner (1991) commented on the rise of the image to dominance by reference to Postman's (1985) argument that early this century Western society began to abandon print culture and enter an "Age of Entertainment" grounded in a culture of the image. This shift heralded a "dramatic decline in literacy [and] a loss of the skills associated with rational argumentation, linear and analytical thought, and critical and public discourse—resulting in 'degeneration of public discourse and a loss of rationality in public life' " (p. 64; cf.; Enzensberger, 1992). Kellner advocated classroom activity aimed at expanding "literacy and cognitive competencies" in ways that enable us to counteract the subject constitutive effects of the deluge of media messages, images, and spectacles we encounter daily. He identified elements in hermeneutics and postmodern theory that provide relevant insights into how we are constituted socially, and techniques by which to deconstruct texts and images. From these, he argued, we can and should move to construct and teach a critical media literacy "which will empower individuals to become autonomous agents, able to emancipate themselves from contemporary forms of domination and able to become more active citizens, eager and competent to engage in forms of social transformation" (Kellner, 1991, p. 64; see Lankshear, 1993; A. Luke, 1995, for further discussion of problems in recipes for "empowerment").

Identities and Loyalties in Contexts of Diversity

The need in New Times to rethink citizenship radically—that is, from the roots—is nowhere more apparent than with regard to the themes of diversity, the new complexity of personal and group identities, and the need to constitute a citizenry accepting of and comfortable with difference. Economic, telecommunications, travel, migration, and political trends during recent decades have coalesced to produce situations in many societies worldwide, including Australia, where citizens are having to live with "increasingly proximate global diversity" and heightened local diversity (Kalantzis, 1992/1993, p. 29). This, as Kalantzis made clear, poses three specific challenges having profound educational implications. First, societies like Australia must "leave [their] boundaries open to the negotiation of global diversity" as their associations, economic and otherwise, move inevitably across national borders. This requires on the part of citizens acceptance of and ease with ethnocultural diversity.

Second, given the complex multicultural character of modern populations, many citizens are likely to develop and experience "'multiple senses of loyalty and affinity." In New Times the state must be able to recognize and accommodate multiple layers of loyalty and affinity in ways that extend to "new" citizens the full enjoyment of rights and execution of their duties as citizens. Against the backdrop of war between rival ethnic factions in places like Bosnia, Kalantzis suggested that reconstituting civic life around such an accommodation may be the best route to stability and the surest safeguard against "internecine ethnic craziness." Indeed, having many links "to diverse geographic spaces and ethnic roots" can enhance stability, "diffusing and defusing past animosities," as citizens "negotiate and live with difference" (p. 29).

Third, for these conditions to be met, citizens in New Times require particular understandings and capabilities. They must understand processes by which they have been formed morally and politically so that they can "disentangle the multiple layers of their identities and political loyalties" (p. 31). They must also be able to negotiate across boundaries of ethnicity, gender, and countries. In short, they need a more elaborate, New Times equivalent of what Mills (1959)—in earlier times—called a *sociological imagination*.

ELEMENTS OF EDUCATION FOR ACTIVE CITIZENSHIP IN NEW TIMES

On the basis of the ideas just sketched, we see a need to reframe citizenship around active commitment to understanding and evaluating social institutions and practices (i.e., Discourses), in both the public and private spheres, in relation to the requirements for promoting the common good in New Times. Beyond this, active citizenship involves working to modify, build, and maintain institutions that are conducive to pursuing the common good. Moreover, as we have seen, the common good has become the good of an increasingly diverse citizenry. So far as pursuit of the common good is "the pursuit of the good in common," the discursive processes, structures, relations, and values—the *institutions*—in and through which this good is pursued must accommodate such diverse cultural, ethical, and political traditions as meet the legitimate demands of an ethical human order.

In what remains, we focus on two key implications of all this for citizenship education.

1. Education for active citizenship calls for fostering a sophisticated "sociological imagination" that incorporates (what we call) institutional imagination, political imagination, cultural imagination, and moral imagination.
2. Practicing active citizenship presupposes being competent in handling media texts of varying types (e.g., news reports, public notices, advertisements, and commentaries) in a range of ways (e.g., analysis, evaluation, synthesis, criticism). Of course, active citizens need to be competent with other sorts of texts as well: such as policy documents, political party manifestos, voting papers, bureaucratic forms, funding applications, by laws, and many others. We are simply highlighting media texts here.

We agree with Kalantzis that teaching a critical social literacy is integral to any such education for active citizenship. And with Kellner we recognize the necessity of a critical media literacy, as an essential dimension of critical social literacy. To put things in terms of the conceptual frame we have been working with here, we are calling for a reconstituted Discourse of active citizenship, and for classroom education to support other sites within which future adults are apprenticed to this Discourse. Critical social (and media) literacy is a key element of the discourse integral to enacting the Discourse of being an active citizen. Becoming critically literate is integral to being apprenticed to a New Times Discourse of active citizenship.

Yet, both the new Discourse of active citizenship and the critical social literacy element of the discourse of active citizens are currently underformed. They are very much still-to-be-constructed. We have clues to follow in constructing them, however. And we know that they are necessarily constructed together and dialectically. Consequently, in order to conceive potential components of a critical social literacy that simultaneously informs and is informed by the practice of active citizenship, we need to grasp the nature and requirements of a sociological imagination for New Times. Because our notion of sociological imagination is derived directly from Mills' work in earlier times, it is useful to begin from Mills' original conception. Mills (1959) addressed the recurring phenomenon of people encountering troubles in their daily lives and feeling immersed in processes they do not really understand, and sensing that these things are beyond their control. The more information people have of their world, said Mills, the more powerless they often feel, and the less they can sense the meaning of their times for their own lives and wellbeing and how they "fit into" the world of their times. This widespread experience, Mills argued, can be seen as a result of people lacking sociological imagination.

For Mills, sociological imagination involves understanding "biography" and "history," and being able to grasp their relatedness within social life. Biography is our own private experience of life: what life is, or is like, for us. History refers to social structures and processes, and to changes that occur within them. The point is that biography and history are intimately, and intricately, connected, but we often have a poor understanding of how they are connected. Unemployed youth who cannot fathom their inability to obtain paid work despite having done courses and gone through work experience schemes are a case in point, as are those who explain such cases in terms of laziness, apathy, or lack of ability.

Being able to relate biography and history through sociological imagination enables us to make sense of our lived experiences, and of how and where we fit into our times. It also makes possible an informed basis from which to enter history in an active way, by throwing weight behind movements, causes, actions, and institutions with a view to enhancing one's own and other people's prospects.

These days, of course, we talk more in terms of subject identities being constituted, and human subjectivities constructed, in and through Discourse, than in terms of a dialectic between the biography of more or less unified subjects and the history that is created in and through more or less impersonal structures. Even allowing for Mills's undoubted sophistication among sociologists of his day, Hall's (1991) observation that, in New Times, "we cannot settle for a language . . . which respects the old distinction between objective and subjective dimensions of change" (p. 59), applies with some force to talk of sociological imagination. Accordingly, we recommend a modified view of sociological imagination, tailored to take account of insights opened up by Hall and Kalantzis and others in relation to demands for civic participation along the lines advanced by Bellah. For New Times, sociological imagination should be seen to comprise at least institutional imagination, political imagination, moral imagination, and cultural imagination.

Through institutional imagination we understand the extent to which humans are what we are as a consequence of participating in Discourses within primary and secondary institutions (Gee, 1991); and relate our own identities and subjectivities to our distinctive discursive histories within the institutions we have lived in and through; and can envisage alternative ways of (personal and collective) being in the world potentially available to us through participation in different Discourses grounded in different institutions, *including Discourses and institutions as yet inchoate or incipient*. Institutional imagination, then, presupposes what Gee called "meta-level knowledge" of institutions and their Discourses and associated discourses (Gee, 1990, 1991, see chap. 14, this volume). Meta-level knowledge permits analysis and critique of Discourses and their institutional settings, providing a basis from which either to participate in them more fully and satisfyingly or to seek to transform them as necessary for promoting the common good. If citizens are to live productively with diversity, to recognize "the multiple layers of their identities and political loyalties" and those of other people, and to negotiate across boundaries, they need specifically "to know the processes of their moral and political becoming . . . and to . . . [understand their] location in the world as cultural" (Kalantzis, 1992/1993, p. 31).

Through political imagination we understand our own ways of political being, our political identities and subjectivities, and those of others by reference to the discursive orderings and representations of structured power that we and they have experienced. Through political imagination we can envisage alternative actual and potential ways of political being from those we enact. In some cases this may involve understanding how people may be constituted as apolitical or anti-political. This is the deeper point lying behind the Senate Committee's recognition that some migrants to Australia retreat from involvement in any kind of formal politics because, for example, they have endured political tyranny and have no trust of politics. At a more subtle level it calls for appreciating how the aestheticisation of politics, or the cumulative effect of media emphasis on image and/or personality, have acted to depoliticize people. In other cases we relate, through political imagination, our own and others' political identities as socialists, liberals, feminists, gay activists, Greens, Democrats, Republicans, monarchists, and so on, to varying discursive histories. In a parallel way, through moral imagination we relate actual and possible beliefs, values, and behaviors pertaining to constructions of "the Good Life" and "human well-being" to actual and possible discursive histories.

Cultural imagination can refer to linking "cultural ways of being"—in the sense of cultural that is commonly linked to trappings of ethnicity, race, or even class—to their respective discursive genealogies. Alternatively, it can be given a more generic meaning. In this sense, to understand location in the world as being cultural is to recognize that people's identities and loyalties, beliefs and values, conceptions and practices are always historically shaped and contingent, rather than natural, transcendent, and necessary. Seen this way, cultural imagination informs us that we fit into the world on the same terms and in the same way as Others do: as beings constituted discursively, and having the same rights to recognition and correlative duties of recognition as Others.

We are suggesting, then, that a sociological imagination is integral to the way of life of an active citizen, and that in New Times sociological imagination should be seen to comprise at least institutional, political, moral, and cultural aspects. These are interrelated dimensions of human subjectivity and identity: places from which we make and live meanings that are fundamental to the active quest of citizens in pursuit of the common good. But, how might we work with texts in classrooms to promote the kinds of imaginations integral to active citizenship?

CRITICAL LITERACY FOR ACTIVE CITIZENSHIP

The practical suggestions offered below are constrained by space as well as by our own finite conceptions. We hope to have marked out an area for fruitful development. What follows should be seen as an initial exploratory foray to be elaborated and improved by anyone who finds our ideas helpful. The following scheme has been confined to written texts, and even within this limited scope is at best indicative and suggestive. The activities should not be seen as a discrete unit of work, nor as a bag of tricks. They are merely typical examples of the kinds of activities possible with forethought and planning among a team of participating subject teachers who seek to "orient, enhance, and synthesise" (language) learning in a unit with a citizenship focus (Queensland Department of Education, 1991, p. 39). Although our particular examples apply to secondary school level, the general approach may be adapted to primary and tertiary levels as well.

Clearly, teachers need institutional, political, moral, and cultural imagination themselves if they are to understand the sorts of activities we propose for what they are and to be able to make them work with students. The approach we advance here embodies the kinds of logics and learning processes that are the stuff of mastering sociological imagination in the sense we have outlined. As indicated, our scheme presupposes a context where teachers across several subjects (e.g., English, geography, modern history, social education, environmental studies) agree to work cooperatively and in an integrated way to explore aspects of citizenship through their disciplines. Our approach has two cornerstones: the English teacher and the teacher librarian.

The English teacher helps students "break texts open" by using available procedures for critical study of texts as described and modeled by Fairclough (1989, 1992), Kress (1985), and Gilbert (1993). In English, then, texts will be broken open in ways that require three kinds of resources to inform alternative "readings":

- information associated with other disciplines or subject areas;
- texts grounded in a range of theoretical-ideological perspectives;
- texts that cross historico-cultural time and space.

The English teacher, then, creates a need for exploration of issues traversing a range of subjects and from different standpoints. The teacher librarian, in collaboration with subject teachers, coordinates resources across the subject areas. He or she locates and assembles—for each subject area involved—texts conveying information that reflects different theoretical, ideological, and cultural perspectives pertaining to issues and themes that have been identified by breaking texts open linguistically and subsequently allocated to particular subject areas.

The starting place is an everyday text—a media story—that is rich in thematic possibilities for enhancing social imagination and understanding citizenship—as it has been constructed discursively, and how it might need reconstructing. Our text is a front page story from a major Australian daily (minus its accompanying photograph).

The face of starving Africa
AFRICA today. A starving child waits to die in the dust of Somalia
Hundreds of Somalis collapse every day, unwilling and unable to
live any longer in the worst drought to grip their continent for 100
years.
More than 30 million Africans, from Ethiopia to Mozambique, have
left their villages in search of food and water.
This photograph was taken by Care Australia's program officer, Ms
Phoebe Fraser, the daughter of former prime minister Mr Malcolm
Fraser, who is president of Care. "Somalia is desperate," she says.
"In a country where hundreds of bodies line streets, most of them
children, you can only hope the world is watching."
Yesterday, the United Nations said it would send 500 armed soldiers
to protect aid supplies to Somalia, which has been ravaged by
drought and civil war, following agreement by warring factions to
allow the safe delivery of aid.
The Australian's readers have helped raise thousands of dollars to
buy food and medicine by sending donations to the address of aid
agencies alongside articles on Africa's heartbreaking story.
Aid should be sent to: Care Australia, GPO Box 9977, in your capital
city; World Vision, GPO Box 9944, in you capital city; Save the
Children's Fund, GPO Box 9912, in your capital city; Austcare Africa
Appeal, PO Locked Bag 15, Camperdown, NSW 2050; Community
Aid Abroad, GPO Box 9920, in your capital city.

The Australian, Friday, 14 August 1992, p. 1

IN THE BEGINNING: CRITICAL LANGUAGE ANALYSIS IN THE ENGLISH CLASS

Drawing on work by linguists and literacy scholars, A. Luke (1992) advanced some very effective means for undertaking critical language analysis across a range of text types, including media stories. These can be used productively with a text like "The Face of Starving Africa" to explore how it constructs reality textually and positions readers. A preliminary "opening up" of the text provides a basis for exploring its practical and ideological implications for citizenship and for enhancing sociological imagination, through wider subject study that is integrated with more specialized language study in English.

Activity: Preliminary Critical Language Analysis of the Text

A. Luke noted that texts employ devices of various kinds to construct reality textually, and to position readers. For example, there are multiple and diverse ways in which the reality in Somalia might be represented or constructed textually. A given text, such as "The Face of Starving Africa," will represent it one way (a "possible world") rather than others. At the same time, the text will, by various means, position readers to make meaning from it in a particular way. It "positions readers in relation to a particular worldview or ideology" (A. Luke, 1992)—which in this case has implications for citizenship.

Text Analysis Exercise

Read "The Face of Starving Africa" and explore the following questions.

1. What version of events/reality is foregrounded here?
2. Whose version is this? From whose perspective is it constructed?
3. What other (possible) versions are excluded?
4. Whose/what interests are served by this representation?
5. By what means—lexical, syntactic, etc.—does this text construct (its) reality?
6. How does this text position the reader? What assumptions about readers are reflected in the text? What beliefs, assumptions, expectations (ideological baggage) do readers have to entertain in order to make meaning from the text? (adapted from A. Luke, 1992; Fairclough, 1989).

Objective and Rationale

As we see things, an important part of the English teacher's job is to enable students to understand what these questions (and similar ones) are asking, and to acquire a relevant meta-language of linguistic and semantic concepts and tools by which to break the text open through such questions. Such understandings are best acquired in contexts that incorporate precisely the kinds of text and activities in question here. We should note, however, that much of what is needed in order to identify versions that have been excluded, the interests served by a particular representation, and so on, is best pursued in wider subject settings. Thus, the English class breaks the text open in ways that call for elaboration from other subject areas, from whence further inquiry and critique can proceed in the English class. At this point in the inquiry, the English class might only get as far as addressing the construction of reality and aspects of reader positioning.

A Possible (Sample) Response to Text Analysis Exercise

A. Construction of Reality

1. Those people starving in Somalia—and, indeed, the 30 million Africans from Ethiopia to Mozambique—are suffering from the effects of drought.

2. This drought is the worst in 100 years.
3. Somalia is also ravaged by civil war, which contributes to starvation.
4. The situation is so desperate the only hope is international sympathy and goodwill (aid).
5. Readers have contributed money to aid agencies.
6. Aid agencies address the situation in Somalia.
7. Six agencies are named, to whom donations should be sent.

Putting these together, we find a construction of the Somalia reality in terms of a extreme drought happening in a setting where there is also a war happening. In such circumstances, aid agencies coordinate relief. The role for ordinary people is to donate aid. The action is undertaken by the aid agencies, with assistance from some (special) history-making individuals like the Frasers. Aid agencies exist to respond to calamitous happenings like droughts.

B. Reader Position

1. The reader is positioned to make meaning from an emotive rather than a rational or informed standpoint. The text conveys virtually no factual detail of consequence. (In terms of the matters we address later, it should be added that the page 7 stories, like most reporting in the mass media of the famine Somalia, construct essentially the same reality.) Wordings like "Africa's heartbreaking story," "desperate," "hope," "starving child," "collapse,"and so on, set the tone.
2. Outside of an emotive basis for making meaning, the reader is presumed to respond to a propaganda device that we here term *testimonial*. A former prime minister and his daughter are invoked here as authoritative support for the particular construction of reality, as well as for constructing the reader-citizen as donor.
3. To make meaning, the reader is required to operate from the following sorts of assumptions and beliefs that, it will become apparent, are profoundly ideological: "(natural) disasters happen"; "disasters are addressed by money, converted to aid or relief"; "aid and relief agencies are the officially valid mediums of action"; "some causes are genuine (hence worthy of our generosity)"; "children are always innocent victims"; "we can extend generosity by donating—their circumstances are unrelated to us"; "extending charity freely is a virtue—a human act," and so on.

Some Implications of This Analysis for Other Subject Studies

Let us assume that something like the above response might emerge from a careful probing of the text given a reasonably typical range of (English) teacher and secondary student understandings. To go further, however, and envisage other possible versions of reality, ideological and interest serving aspects, and implications for citizenship, calls for a wider curriculum base. References in the original text to drought, civil war, the creation of a continent wide refugee population, and the operation of aid agencies, create openings for further exploration across several subject areas.

ACTIVITY: Subject Teachers With Teacher Librarian

1. Locate for each subject area a range of texts relevant to situations like that in Somalia (*viz.* disasters).
2. Ensure that among them the texts reflect different perspectives.
3. Identify and describe key differences in the perspectives—in terms of their underlying theories, the questions or issues with which they are most concerned, their key assumptions, whose standpoint they most reflect, where you would locate them on a continuum.

Four Possible Sample Texts

1. . . . a whole variety of things [makes] people susceptible to drought. [A] factor that contributes to vulnerability is history. Many developing countries have inherited inappropriate economic structures and relatively weak positions in the global economy. In particular, colonization fostered the orientation of whole national economies towards exportation of one or a few products. . . . Such exclusive focus on one or two sources of export revenue increases vulnerability in many respects. Notably, it deprives the country of food crops for domestic consumption and leaves it at the mercy of international markets. Also, due to scarce resources, only enough staple crop is grown to satisfy immediate needs, leaving the population without a buffer of stored grain to carry it through periods of drought. (Castellino, 1992, pp. 8-9)
2. "The extensive plunder-culture [of plantations under colonization] meant not only the death of the forest but also, in the long run, of . . . fertility. With forests surrendered to the flames, erosion soon did its work on the defenceless soil and thousands of streams dried up."
   This process is continuing in many parts of the world. The desert in West Africa is spreading. With the growth of

refrigeration the number of food crops that can be exported for luxury consumption in the developed countries has increased. In Upper Volta peasants . . . organized themselves into unions to demand the right to grow crops for themselves rather than vegetables to export to France. (Hayter, 1982, p. 54; The quotation is from Galeano, 1973)

3. The fundamental causes [of Africa's food crisis] are varied and complex. . . . The cumulative effects over many years have resulted in decrease in per capita food production, deforestation, desertification, increasing reliance on imported foodstuffs, and a mounting foreign debt. Such consequences are rooted, however, not in impersonal "market forces" or climactic conditions, but in political decisions involving the allocation of resources . . . [For example] when resources were allocated to infrastructure and extension services in the agrarian sector, the bias was toward revenue-generating export crops, rather than food production.

. . . African states were colonial creations with a fragile history of internal cohesion. That which existed has been rent by harsh economic realities. . . . These divisions have been played upon by outside interests for their own ends. In Angola the CIA-backed UNITA rebels fought a protracted civil war against the Marxist government. The South African government gave military support to RENAMO bandits in an effort to destabilise Mozambique. . . . The militarisation of Africa, frequently funded by loans under the guise of development aid is yet another drain on scarce resources. The ending of the Cold War threatens to release even greater quantities of surplus arms onto Third World markets. (Dorward, 1992, pp. 5-10)

4. [In Ethiopia] massive deforestation contributed to a decline in precipitation, which . . . with other factors has been responsible for the country losing 1 bn tons of topsoil a year.

Apart from adverse environmental factors, existing social institutions combined with inappropriate government policies were also instrumental in engendering famine. During Haile Selassie's reign, large segments of the agricultural sector were under the tutelage of the royal household, the military, feudal lords, or the church. Heavily taxed peasants lacked motives to innovate and increase production. . . . Ethiopian food production was among the world's lowest.

. . . Following . . . the 1975 land reform program [of the new Marxist government] production began to fall markedly [and] the government arrogated to itself exclusive rights to market peasant produce, for which it paid little, on occasion less than cost. Coffee was so heavily taxed that . . . production halved. With steady rises in prices and limited availabilities of consumer goods, farmers scaled down food deliveries . . . the government . . . countered by requisitioning crops. Immediately prior to the 1984 famine, soldiers . . . confiscated surplus grain at gunpoint, and in so doing deprived peasants of the very reserves needed to ride out the drought. (Stein, 1988)

An Authorial Intrusion: What These Texts Suggest

We see such texts suggesting a number of things that relate back to the construction of reality in "The Face of Starving Africa" and help focus possible activities in other subject areas. They suggest, for example:

- Droughts are often not purely natural disasters.
- Droughts do not "act on their own" to cause famines and death by starvation.
- Famines are to an important extent created socially.
- Certain policies and institutions have contributed to causing starvation.
- Some people/countries benefit from activities that contribute to causing droughts, floods, famines, and so forth.
- People and countries across the entire world are implicated directly and indirectly in processes, relationships, and structures that contribute to famine.
- These same processes, structures, and relationships are integral to the social construction of refugees.

Activity: Subject Teachers Working as a Team

Around the texts located, develop complementary exercises in each subject area to reveal aspects that may have been left out or distorted in the original media story and initial (orienting) exercises. (Space limits us to considering just a few of the potential subject areas here, and a limited range of orienting exercises.)

Geography Exercise 1

1. In which countries do famines mainly occur?
2. Which social groups do they affect most?
3. Are famines natural disasters?
4. Find texts that provide significantly different accounts of particular famines.

Environmental Studies Exercise 1

1. Identify ecological variables (e.g., precipitation, soil) that are important to food production.
2. In what ways have human activities impacted on ecological variables?
3. What consequences can this impact have on food production?
4. Are there different views about the nature and the extent of human impact on ecology? If so, how do they differ?

Modern History Exercise 1

1. Identify some countries that have been badly affected by famine.
2. In which cases was "political instability" a factor?
3. In those instances where it was a factor, what different accounts are provided of the causes of the "instability".
4. In the different accounts, who is seen to "be behind," or benefit from, the factors causing instability? How do these interests differ according to the accounts provided?

Back to English

In the light of work done around the exercises in other subject areas, students can return to questions posed at the outset, and elaborations of them.

1. From whose perspective is "The Face of Starving Africa" presented?
2. What other possible (and actual) versions have been excluded or elided here?
3. Whose interests are served (and whose undermined) by the original representation?
4. Comment on the effect of the reader position evident in "The Face of Starving Africa." What other reader positions do you now see as possible for different texts on the same subject?
5. Analyze linguistically the role played by the references to "drought" and "civil war" in the original text. Note: For example, they might be investigated as possible instances of the syntactic device of *transformation* (Clark, 1992, p. 121; Fowler, Hodge, Kress, & Trew, 1979) e.g., nominalizations or some other kind of passivization (as described by Fairclough, 1989).

WHERE TO NOW?

At this point the ideological and practical implications for citizenship specifically can be explored. If there is a curriculum slot for social education, this might be the place to do it. Otherwise, the investigation could proceed in geography, history, or even in English. We cannot address these implications here in the detail they merit. Our thinking, however, is as follows, and we invite readers to consider what kind of activities and exercises might be appropriate. We envisage four main activities. These are related, and each comprises structured exercises or questions.

The first activity would explore Aid as Discourse (although it might be easier to construct the activity minus the jargon!). Within this, aid agencies could be investigated as a type of institution belonging to a particular *type* of Discourse. Structuring questions here might address such matters as:

1. What is the operating logic behind the aid approach to disasters, development, and so on (e.g., mopping up serves powerful interests better than preventing the spill)?
2. What roles do the various participants in the aid discourse play? How are they constructed? What are they constructed as?
3. What are they *not* constructed as? Insofar as aid activity is an example of activity (in the public sphere) intended to enhance the common good—albeit by merely ameliorating the worst harms—we are partially constituted as (global) citizens by the aid discourse. But as *active* citizens?

The second activity we envisage investigates local aid as Discourse, and its implications for citizenship construction on the home front. We might consider the extent to which local homelessness and hunger are symptoms of the same processes of power that elsewhere, and more dramatically, issue in famine. And is the approach to amelioration through appeals and charities simply a local extension of the larger logic we have observed? Who benefits from our construction as passive citizens within the local sphere? (Anyone with a markedly better than average income and standard of living?)

The third activity addresses the issue of whether the local and international aid discourses, and their discursive construction of (passive) citizens, are symptomatic of a larger Discoursal logic. To precis what we have in mind here, try this exercise.

Reader Exercise. Read the following public notice, which appeared in a New Zealand newspaper, and consider the extent to which it intimates a Discourse that channels power, maintains institutional models, and constructs citizens in ways that serve particular interests. Which interests might be thus served? And how? How does this (intimated) Discourse compare with the aid discourse? More generally, might representative parliamentary democracy provide a further parallel?; another insistence of the same 'logic'? In what respects?

OFFICE OF THE OMBUDSMAN
PROBLEMS WITH BUREAUCRACY?
TUESDAY, March 30, 1993, 11.30 a.m. - 3.30 p.m., REAP Centre, 61 Peel Street, WESTPORT. Ph. 789-7659.
Wednesday, March 31, 1993, 9 a.m. - 5 p.m. REAP Centre, 17 Sewell Street, HOKITIKA. Ph. 755-8700.
THURSDAY, April 1, 1993, 8.30 a.m. - 3.30 p.m., Community Law Centre, Waterfront Building, Richmond Quay, GREYMONTH. Ph. 768-0584.
The Ombudsmen may be able to help you if you are having problems with a government department, organisation or board, whether central or local. This includes local councils and boards, such as school boards of trustees, also state owned enterprises and some national boards as well as government departments.
If you think that one of these have behaved unfairly or unreasonably towards you, whether by doing something or by failing to do something, or you are having difficulty in getting information from them and would like to discuss the problem, you are welcome to call on my offices at the times and places mentioned. An appointment is not essential, but appointments may be made by telephoning my officers, either on the days of their visit at the above telephone numbers, or in advance by telephoning my Christchurch Office (03) 366-8556. Collect calls will be accepted.
Sir Brian Elwood
OMBUDSMAN
The (Christchurch) Press, 29 March 1993.

Finally, students need exposure through texts (as well as in lived practice, although that is beyond us here) to alternative Discourses of citizenship and to exemplars of varying constructions of the active citizen. Examples that range across time and space are helpful because they reveal the historical contingency of discursive practices and forms. At the same time, by revealing the concerns and practical issues that shape specific constructions of the active citizen, such examples remind us that for all the due emphasis being given at present to "multiplicity," "difference," "flux," and the like, humans share in the final analysis a remarkably common set of needs. It is from these that the quest for the common good as the quest for the good in common necessarily proceeds.

Interesting and challenging counterpoints to prevailing conceptions of citizenship within countries like our own can readily be found in descriptions of community development and defense organisations in a number of revolutionary—frequently single party state—societies. As just one example of many that can be found, we offer this fragment from an account of community development committee during the Nicaraguan Revolution. (Note: CDSs were development and defense committees.)

Georgino Andrade in Managua is a community of factory workers, artisans, market and street vendors, domestics, and the unemployed. Located in the belt of neighborhoods, industries, and commercial centers that sprang up after the 1972 earthquake destroyed the city's center, it is a sprawling settlement of some six thousand people. Until 1981, the land on which the barrio is located was vacant. In May of that year a handful of families from a few of Managua's other overcrowded barrios decided to build homes there. News of the developing squatter's community spread by word of mouth, and within a month scores of other families joined the pioneers, . . .

The residents of Georgino Andrade began to construct a neighborhood preschool in 1984. The Ministry of Education pledged sufficient funds to cover most of the cost, but the intensification of the contra war prevented the ministry from paying for the full costs. Consequently, the Sandinista Barrio Committee launched a drive to secure foreign donations. In March the Committee sent [an appeal] letter to sympathetic groups and individuals in the United States . . .

The residents of Georgino Andrade continued their efforts to develop the neighborhood throughout the next year. The government installed an electric transformer and lights. The CDSs conducted successful inoculation campaigns against polio, measles, and tetanus, and completed the third year of adult education classes. With material assistance from CEPAD, a Protestant development agency, the neighborhood committee sponsored a sewing class for more than 25 neighborhood women. The neighborhood's major achievement of the year took place in November, when [following community representations] the Ministry of Housing delivered land titles to 70% of the barrio's residents.

In January 1986, activists in Georgino Andrade's CDSs participated in a reevaluation of their organization. The reevaluation resulted in the following recommendations. . .

Neighborhood committees should try to involve everyone in the problems of each block by encouraging residents to participate in the various CDS commissions.

CDS leaders should try to limit all meetings to 1 hour. Good records should be kept of all CDS meetings.

The CDSs must continue to act as an educational vehicle for barrio residents. "Our principal task is to educate ourselves to express what we feel, to encourage people to participate in debates in order to further enrich ourselves."

Georgino Andrade inaugurated its preschool in March 1986 and began to build a classroom for the neighborhood's first grade students. CDS leaders also planned the construction of a health center and a new communal house. (extracted from Ruchwarger, 1987, pp. 180–186)

APOLOGIA AND POSTSCRIPT

We concede that we have left much—too much—unsaid and untouched. Specifically, our scope has been too narrow to address adequately Kalantzis' important concern that we understand the processes of our moral and political formation such that we can "disentangle the multiple layers of our identities and political loyalties" and be able to negotiate across the increasingly diverse boundaries we encounter daily. A fuller treatment must await another occasion. Our hope, however, is that the approach we have taken here, although far from complete, represents at least a small step in the right direction.

Finally, in no way do we want to suggest that donating aid is a mistake. At present, for many circumstances, aid is the only discursive mechanism available. The point is to work at constructing more active Discourses that can address causes rather than deal with symptoms alone; discourses that address existing configurations of power and privilege, and make them over differently. This chapter has at most begun to explore what this might involve.

REFERENCES

Baudrillard, J. (1981). *For a critique of the political economy of the sign.* St Louis, MO: Telos Press.

Bellah, R., Madsen, R., Sullivan, W., Swidler, A., & Tipton, S. (1991). *The good society.* New York: Alfred Knopf.

Berman, M. (1982). *All that is solid melts into air: The experience of modernity.* New York: Simon & Schuster.

Castellino, R. (1992, September). Drought in Africa—again. *Red Cross Red Crescent,* pp. 8-10.

Clark, R. (1992). Principles and practice of CLA in the classroom. In N. Fairclough (Ed.), *Critical language awareness.* London: Longman.

Department of Employment, Education and Training/Senate Standing Committee on Employment, Education and Training (1989). *Active citizenship.* Canberra: Author.

Department of Employment, Education and Training /Senate Standing Committee on Employment, Education and Training(1991). *Active citizenship revisited.* Canberra: Author.

Dorward, D. (1991, December). Famine: The economics and politics of the food crisis in Africa. *Current Affairs Bulletin*, pp. 5-11.

Enzensberger, H. M. (1992, December 20). In defense of illiteracy. *The Australian*, p. 11.

The face of starving Africa. (1992, August 14). *The Australian*, p. 1.

Fairclough, N. (1989). *Language and power*. London: Longman.

Fairclough, N. (Ed.). (1992). *Critical language awareness*. London: Longman.

Fowler, R., Hodge, B., Kress, G., & Trew, T. (Eds.). (1979). *Language and control*. London: Routledge & Kegan Paul.

Galeano, E. (1973). *The open veins of Latin America*. New York: Monthly Review Press.

Gee, J. P. (1991). What is literacy? In C. Mitchell & K. Weiler (Eds.), *Rewriting literacy: Culture and the discourse of other*. New York: Bergin & Garvey.

Gee, J. P. (1992/1993). Tuning into forms of life. *Education Australia*, *19/20*, 13-14.

Gee, J. P. (1996) *Social linguistics and literacies: Ideology in discourses* (2nd ed.). London: Taylor & Francis.

Gilbert, P. (1993). (Sub)versions: Using sexist language practices to explore critical literacy. *Australian Journal of Language and Literacy*, *16*(4), 323-331.

Graff, H. (1979). *The literacy myth: Literacy and social structure in the nineteenth century city*. New York: Academic Press.

Graff, H. (Ed.). (1981). *Literacy and social development in the west*. Cambridge, UK: Cambridge University Press.

Hall, S. (1991). Brave new world. *Socialist Review*, *21*(1), 57-64.

Harvey, D. (1989). *The condition of postmodernity*. Oxford, UK: Basil Blackwell.

Hayter, T. (1982). *The creation of world poverty*. London: Pluto.

Heath, S. B. (1983). *Ways with words: Language, life and work in communities and classrooms*. Cambridge, UK: Cambridge University Press.

Hinkson, J. (1991). *Postmodernity: State and education*. Melbourne, Australia: Deakin University Press.

Kalantzis, M. (1992/1993). Citizenship education after the monarchy: Five questions for the future. *Education Australia*, *19/20*, 28-31.

Kellner, D. (1991). Reading images critically: Toward a postmodern pedagogy. In H. Giroux (Ed.), *Postmodernism, feminism and cultural politics: Redrawing educational boundaries*. Albany: State University of New York Press.

Kress, G. (1985). *Linguistic processes in sociocultural practice*. Geelong: Deakin University Press.

Lankshear, C. (1995). Afterword: Some reflections on empowerment. In P. McLaren & J. Giarelli (Eds.), *Critical theory and educational research*. Albany: State University of New York Press.

Lankshear, C., & Lawler, M. (1989). *Literacy, schooling and revolution*. London: Falmer Press.

Levett, A., & Lankshear, C. (1992) *Recent global social and economic trends relevant to education*. Wellington: New Zealand Qualifications Authority, mimeo.

Luke, A. (1988). *Literacies, textbooks and ideology*. London: Falmer Press.

Luke, A. (1992). *Conference workshop materials. In Working conference on critical literacy*. Brisbane: Griffith University, Faculty of Education, pp. 4-8.

Luke, A. (1995). Genres of power?: Literacy education and the production of capital. In R. Hasan & G. Williams (Eds.), *Literacy in society*. London: Longman.

Lyotard, J-F. (1984). *The postmodern condition: A report on knowledge*. Manchester, UK: Manchester University Press.

Mills, C. W. (1959). *The sociological imagination*. New York: Oxford University Press.

Postman, N. (1985). *Amusing ourselves to death*. New York: Viking.

Queensland Department of Education. (1991). *Draft Years 1 to 10 English Language Arts: Syllabus and guidelines*. Brisbane.

Ruchwarger, G. (1987). *People in power: Forging a grassroots democracy in Nicaragua*. South Hadley, MA: Bergin & Garvey.

Scribner, S., & Cole, M. (1981). *The psychology of literacy*. Cambridge, MA: Harvard University Press.

Slattery, L. (1993, May 15-16). I think therefore I think. *The Weekend Australian*, p. 20.

Stein, L. (1988). Famine in Ethiopia. *Quadrant, 32*(3), 8-13.

Street, B. (1984). *Literacy in theory and practice*. Cambridge, UK: Cambridge University Press.

Trinca, H. (1993, May 8-9). What is the alternative? *The Australian Magazine*, p. 20.

Willinsky, J. (1989). *The new literacy: Redefining reading and writing in the schools*. New York: Routledge.

Willinsky, J. (1993). Lessons from the literacy before schooling 1800-1850. In B. Green (Ed.), *The insistence of the letter: Literacy studies and curriculum theorising*. London: Falmer Press.

7

Critical Literacies for Informed Citizenship: Further Thoughts on Possible Actions Response to Colin Lankshear and Michele Knobel

M. Garbutcheon Singh
Pat Moran
Central Queensland University

The role of literacy education in developing the competencies of students, young and old alike, and the need for informed and active citizenship have been well established but need to be reiterated. Lankshear and Knobel (chap. 6) contest the view that "active citizenship" should be limited to understanding the workings of parliament per se arguing that in "New (Postmodern) Times" the Discourse of citizenship requires a major overhaul. What is required is a socially critical education that develops in students a willingness and ability, the "civic courage" (White, 1988), to translate the ideals of classical participatory democracy into informed action. They argue quite correctly that a plurality of critical literacies are among the key competencies needed for the preparation of informed, active citizens. The literacy classrooms of adult educators, school teachers, and university lecturers provide important sites where students can test the relation between participatory democratic ideals and social realities, including the realities of institutionalized education itself.

Building on Lankshear and Knobel's proposal, we argue for a view of "informed active citizenship" that is grounded in social movement theory (M. G. Singh, 1992). We seek to extend the framework they have provided into a discussion of social movements, expanding the line they have taken with the aim of enlarging the scope of the debate. Various social movements have and will continue to play a significant role in influencing change nationally and globally. Social movements, and the informed and active citizens who give them form and substance, provide perhaps the greatest hope for the future of the world's children. Hence, in this chapter, we describe Touraine's (1971, 1981, 1984, 1988) theory of social movements, detailing four of its key tendencies (Arnason, 1986; Kivisto, 1984).

As Lankshear and Knobel demonstrate, the prevailing Discourse on citizenship seeks to regulate people's civic work, language, and relationships by integrating us into the operations of the state. It constructs an impoverished image of citizenship, one that emphasizes understanding and engaging with the workings of government on its terms, often silencing any sense of informed critique or collective action. Lankshear and Knobel propose a re-reading and rewriting of citizenship, producing a Discourse that enables students to understand the connections between their identity formation and subjectivities and their positioning in sociohistorical discourses. Such an approach to critical literacy, they argue, would enable students, as "citizens-in-training," to make sense of their lived experiences and provide them with an informed basis for entering into history as active citizens, to consciously make and remake it. It is in these terms that we can think of those women in civil society who struggled against the patriarchal state for the right to vote as informed and active citizens.

Following the work of the French sociologist Touraine (1981), it may even be possible to say that informed and active citizenship involves participation in a social force, or a social movement that is engaged in "informed critique" and "collective action" in a "social struggle" over the "distribution of social goods." If anything, we argue that citizens' movements are the quintessential representation of informed, active citizenship (M. G. Singh, 1993). An appreciation of the basic operational units of citizens' movements may increase students' understandings of the workings of government but may also increase their motivation to become informed and active citizens, as opposed to existing approaches that reinforce ignorance, indifference, and apathy. The formation and development of citizens' movements is an historically significant process in which individual citizens may play small, but nonetheless important roles. Solidarity among supporters of citizens' movements finds meaning in each individual's practical contributions to the struggle for social change. The idea of citizens' movements provides a way of mediating the connections between localized contestation and the resources of broader social forces of collective citizen action.

Through social movements, active citizens are able to envisage and work toward preferred futures through their participation in constructing the different Discourses generated in different social movements. Those informed and active citizens who have and continue to participate in women's movements raise questions about the dominant representation of gender relations in "teen romance" novellas, the mode of social "use" or exploitation of women in advertisements, the control of cultural models for constructing images of the "female," and the power to allocate the resources of different literacies to women and girls. This citizens' movement has a tradition of contesting not only the social use of public facilities for the literacy education of females, but also the world view and the social norms of the dominant supraliterate "order," in particular, challenging ideologies of sexism and patriarchy represented in cultural media. Thus, we might profitably think of the existing social "order" as the practical, material achievement of conflicting social movements of collective actors—active citizens—struggling with dominant social interests for the control and direction of a major historical field of cultural reproduction and transformation (McLaren, 1993; Wexler, 1983). By studying the particular understandings and capacities of those informed and active citizens who participate in social movements, teachers may be in a better position to know the types of competencies to develop in our own students, the rising generation of citizens.

MAKING MEANING OF CITIZENS' MOVEMENTS

What are the main characteristics of citizens' movements engaged in struggles for justice, rationality, and an amicable life for all, and working against oppression irrationality and alienation? To paraphrase Touraine (1971, p. 180), a citizens' movement signifies the existence of a group of informed active citizens (the protagonists), which is defending its "interests" (understood as being nonunitary, dynamic, and contentious even among the protagonists themselves), in a fight against the existing social order (the adversary), with whom it is wrestling for the future direction of society (the stakes). These citizens need to have strategies with which to engage the dominant order so as to secure what is at stake. They must also have an informed understanding of their opponents, as well as ways of keeping themselves and those in solidarity with their struggles informed. There are three key elements whose interrelationship form the basis of a citizens' movement, namely the protagonists, their adversaries, and the stakes. Each of these elements, which combine to give authenticity to a citizens' movement, is briefly considered.

First, a citizens' movement works to promote a consciousness—conscientization (Findlay, 1994), among those active citizens who support it, of its own complex and multidimensional array of identities, work that requires the use of alphabetic and media literacies. In these "New Times," many citizens' movements transcend particular societies, crossing national boundaries, both by their social impetus and by fitting into international movements of global citizens; this requires literate competence in different languages. All citizens' movements are, of course, heterogeneous and diverse social forces, and do not have a single or unitary orientation but move in different directions at the same time. In part, this is because the struggles and learnings that change the protagonists who participate in these citizens' movements, also change the form and intentions of the movements themselves. It is also a matter of politics. These citizens' movements stretch from conservatism and liberalism, through social and cultural agendas to radical insurrection. Many people have discovered and affirmed themselves to be part of these mass citizens' movements. They have seized the opportunity to create a consciousness of both group solidarity and individual human agency in collaborative civic action. For instance, some people have come to an understanding of the women's movement by identifying themselves with it, by sharing what it rejects in their particular culture (e.g., certain historical forms of sexism), and by joining in its work for social change. They have identified themselves with a movement that describes itself as an agent working against the multiple dimensions of social injustice, and that appeals to the liberation of new social forces to replace the irrational prejudices and alienating practices of patriarchy. Those people who identify with this and similar citizens' movements, feel themselves borne along by it to change the established social "order."

Second, as noted previously, there are opponents to these citizens' movements. The women's movement, for instance, continues to engage in struggles against those adversaries who have a stake in reproducing sexist rigidity and patriarchal dominance (Faludi, 1992). A good deal of this work is undertaken by informed and active citizens who use the skills of critical literacy, and who see themselves as part of a citizens' movement or social force in conflict with adversaries whose power resides in the existing social "order". Sometimes the adversary's resistance unites the social forces that fight it. The women's movement has not set out to defeat or destroy their adversaries as much as to unmask—through word and deed—their sectional interests. They seek to proclaim a nonsexist society, one in which rationality, justice, and fulfillment can no longer be confused with patriarchal power. Critical reading and writing has been employed by women's movements to render visible their struggles against the subservient role of women in society and their opposition to sexism (Daniels, 1985; Lingard, Henry, & Taylor, 1987). The success of the women's movement is evident in the recognition of women as political actors, as active citizens, and by increased material benefits such as equal pay and funding for child-care services. The success of those opposed to the women's movement is evident in the withdrawal of these benefits, although the political activity of the women's movement is still recognized, at least by some governments. The strength of the reaction by those opposed to the women's movement suggests that such collective action by informed citizens does possess significant transformative potential (Felski, 1989).

Third, the principal stake in this struggle between protagonists and adversaries is the power to make decisions about the control and equitable redistribution of socioeconomic and cultural resources. Citizens' movements are working for qualitative, socioeconomic changes, seeking structural changes that are intended to profoundly modify existing power relations and authority, including those embodied in written language and visual images. The dominant cultural project of many societies is no longer, if ever it was, regarded as an uncontestable, immutable, seamless given, at least not by those active citizens who identify with these social movements. Rather, they recognize that the way a society produces its particular cultural orientations, for instance, religious tracts relating to the role of women in the church, involves both social conflict and social relations of domination (Cohen, 1985). The women's movement contests the control exercised by men over the shape and substance of textual representations of particular societies, which men have tried to shield from public scrutiny. Citizens' movements seek to redefine the boundaries enshrined in legal texts between public and private domains of civic life. Among notable recent examples involving a redefinition of the public/private relationship has been the rewriting of laws proclaiming the illegality of rape in marriage, and other forms of domestic violence. By contesting the cultural terrain of a particular society, these citizens' movements have opened up previously privatized domains of social life to the possibility of justice and democratization, as well as animating struggles to reproduce and transform dominating textual formations of gender and sexuality.

TENDENCIES EVIDENT IN CITIZENS' MOVEMENTS

Lankshear and Knobel correctly argue for an increased focus on the explicit teaching of critical literacy. Students need to be taught to critically re-read and rewrite a range of texts. One possible strategy they suggest is that students learn to re-examine texts, such as newspapers, television news reports, and textbooks, to reveal and make problematic the "hidden" stories they tell about citizenship. This strategy enables students to learn how to re-read and rewrite texts in a critical way. It involves explicitly teaching them how to read between the lines, to seek out themes that may not be explicitly stated, to read for absences as well as presences, to decode the textual so as to discover suppressed meanings (Morgan, 1992). Critical literacy is a complex social practice that varies according to whether students are engaged in re-reading and rewriting items from the mass media, speeches, fiction and nonfiction.

Informed and active citizenship is part of the often hidden story that these texts have to tell. The question is how can we teach students to read, re-read, and rewrite texts as if they were about issues of citizenship. It means teaching them to read texts in ways that develop the higher order skills of critical reading and writing. Any text being used for educational purposes requires a multiplicity of re-readings and rewritings by exploring how it speaks to different people at different times, and drawing attention to omissions. The point is not simply to highlight "blind spots" in a text, but to demonstrate that the inclusion of notions of informed and active citizenship, participatory democracy and citizens' movements into the analysis often affects the interpretation by providing new knowledge and insights. In carrying out re-readings informed by Touraine's social movement theory, students bring an alternative understanding of active citizenship to give a text meaning.

This strategy of *breaking open texts* as Lankshear and Knobel term it, involves four key steps (M. G. Singh, 1990). First, it means having students read a text reporting the work of citizens, and discussing the reality it constructs, its positioning of the reader, and the meaning the reader is expected to make of the text. The second step involves students acquiring a meta-language or a range of ideas and conceptual resources to inform alternative readings. This may be done by having students investigate the nature of citizens' movements, drawing on interview data, audio or video resources, and textual sources of evidence. Here they could study the key features of social movements as discussed earlier: the protagonists, the adversary and the stakes, and consider the silences and absences that distort the textual representation of reality. Third, the students could re-read the original text and discuss how it might be rewritten in the light of what they have learned about citizens' movements from reading other texts and discussions. Finally, they attempt to rewrite the original text, but this time as an account of informed and active citizenship, drawing on their new sources of ideas and evidence; the intention being to explore alternative constructions of "citizenship."

We focus on the curricular possibilities of the second step in this strategy more closely, that is, the need for a range of ideas and conceptual resources for telling about, in this case, citizenship. In what follows, we highlight what we take to be four major tendencies of citizens' movements: their centrality in society and globally; their simultaneous tendencies toward rejection and participation; the contradictions and contestations they reveal; and their tendency toward reproduction and transformation.

Centrality of Citizens' Movements

The struggles of citizens' movements are not at the periphery but rather at the center of society. For instance, the ethnic rights movement and the issues it raises about native land title, citizenship rights, and equal pay do not stand outside or at the margins the existing social "order" but at its very center. The issue here is about refusing marginality by moving consciously to put these struggles on the "centered" ground. The struggles by this movement of informed and active citizens for change are not addressed exclusively to those who have been marginalized but also to those at the very heart of society, those most clearly bound to institutionalized racism. Munoz (1989) explored the varying responses of authorities in the United States to the civil rights movement that arose in response to discrimination and structural exclusion. The civil rights movement, also referred to as the ethnic revitalization movement or the ethnic protest movement, challenged the denial to Black and Native Americans of the right to receive a good quality education, to vote, to obtain jobs, and to participate as active citizens in processes of government. This citizens' movement struggled for the legitimization, recognition, and incorporation of their cultural projects into the public arena while seeking to reconstitute it. They challenged the failure of governments to close the substantial gap between democratic ideals and social realities. It was, however, a movement that provided citizens with a renewed sense of communal hope that was denied to them by the modern nation-state.

Similar ethnic rights movements have emerged in those countries, such as Australia, where imperialism and colonialism are a central part of their history. These citizens' movements attempt to improve the conditions of these victimized people, usually by bringing to the fore what was not previously acknowledged, that racism is a central component of their society. At least these movements have forced dominant social interests to acknowledge the force of racism within society. Through their participation in social movements these citizens have shaped new identities and legitimized their histories and cultures. Citizens' movements have won a number of symbolic concessions from the state, including such things as Indigenous, Black, and Chicano studies and the establishment of affirmative action programs. They have also demanded changes to socioeconomic institutions to enable active citizenship participation and the exercise of power. Movements such as these have also exposed the role of bastions of the status quo in the reproduction of inequalities of ethnic minority groups. Ethnic groups have formed coalitions with other disadvantaged groups to articulate their grievances.

Rejection and Participation

Citizens' movements are a major source of social critique because they simultaneously mount a case against what they reject in the existing social order, and struggle for participation in changing it (Touraine, 1971). Thus, for instance, the women's movement is oriented not simply to rejecting the existing textual representations of the patriarchal "order" (the "malestream" as it is more appropriately termed), but must also participate in it, engage with it, in order to make meanings for effecting changes in it. This paradoxical tendency is a source of strength, more than it is a weakness. This movement of informed active citizens has demonstrated its rejection of the malestream way of life in many countries. The women's movement protests against and authors critiques of patriarchal domination and sexist alienation in all quarters of society; it rejects the concentration of masculine authority at the "top" of the political hierarchy and fights against the associated sexism. It uses what Lankshear and Knobel call *critical media literacy* to reject the commodification of human relations, feelings, and sexuality, and challenges the manipulation of needs and desires by commercial propaganda where women are frequently represented as sex objects. It rejects forms of participation that are based on the assumption that the existing patriarchal "order," the malestream, should be taken for granted or as "natural."

This citizens' movement is trying to create public spaces in which women can participate in decision making: often in the face of considerable adversity. Under participatory democracy, the active participation of citizens is preferred over the imposition of decisions made largely by men, and which are misrepresented as the expression of "universal" or "natural" or "scientific" necessity. The participatory actions of the women's movement have stimulated waves of reform in society (Dowse, 1982).

Contradictions and Contestation

Citizens' movements reveal and define significant contradictions in dominant cultural projects, expose ever present sources of social friction, point out previously obscured social problems, and provide a reaction to the crises of a particular society as well as global crises. A case in point is the antinuclear movement that has confronted the industrial–military complex and has tried to open it up to what the citizens in that movement reject, and tried to force military and industrial powers to deal with their contradictions. The antinuclear movement criticized governments for defining the "national interest" exclusively in terms of military growth, and for their failure to address the interconnection between social and economic dimensions. It pointed out that the expenditure on arms did not serve the "common good" but imposed domination. The formation of the antinuclear movement is a response to scandal and provocation that has exposed conflicts and prepared many citizens to engage in the struggle to change their children's futures by confronting issues that concern the whole of society. The active citizens who participate in a range of social movements reveal the friction present in society.

The antinuclear movement provides useful material for developing critical media literacy, through an exploration of fundamental questions about the contradictions between participatory and representative democracy. Woods (1985) argued that this citizens' movement that is opposed to the production, deployment and use of nuclear arms, provides a good example of active citizenship that is integral to participatory democracy. It presents possibilities for students to undertake critical literacy projects using media reports to identify the means used by the protagonists in their struggle to achieve a freeze on the use of nuclear weapons. Students can investigate the campaign by the movement's adversaries to discredit proponents of a nuclear freeze, and explore the articulation between the media and government officials in delegitimizing the movement and its goals. In the course of this investigation, students consider what is at stake in this struggle between the antinuclear movement and the existing industrial–military "order." For instance, the contestation associated with this socially significant issue may be viewed as an instance of protectionist governance confronting a participatory democratic heritage.

Reproduction and Transformation

Society is reproduced and transformed through the productive work, ideas, and relationships of citizens' movements opposed to the existing social order. Those who work to preserve the existing social order recognize that their cultural projects are never absolute or guaranteed. They accept that they are surrounded by innovation born of the refusal by racial minorities, women, and people with disabilities to be unquestioningly assimilated into the malestream. The peace movement is an example of a historical social force that constitutes the central terrain of social struggle for cultural reproduction and transformation. Although the peace movement seeks to make a break with the existing militaristic "order" by transforming it, the movement also stresses the reproduction of certain worthwhile aspects of the existing "order." Thus, reproduction and transformation are inherently joined together in the dialectical process of social change and stability.

As letters to the editor, rallies, petitions, and lobbying activities reveal, the conflict over wars in Indo-China, Nicaragua, and the Arab region divides many citizens from the existing military order. Some oppose war, arguing that there are alternative ways of redressing aggression. Some challenge institutionalized violence, seeing it as a threat to the national interest of meeting the needs of oppressed people at home and abroad, that is those who are deprived of funding otherwise devoted to high technology weapon systems. Some contest militarism because of their moral commitment to nonviolence. Clearly, the struggles for peace will reproduce or ensure the continuity of the nation; but just as clearly, the nation will be transformed as a result of this process (Gollan, 1986). The peace movement has been influential in stimulating debate, especially through the work of unions (Smith, 1986). Inevitably, those active citizens who have worked with the peace movement, have come under attack by the established militaristic order (Poynting, 1986). However, the current legitimacy of civic action for peace among many people represents an important achievement for participants in this citizens' movement (Hicks, 1988). On the one hand, citizens working for peace seek to develop the human capacity for inquiry, rational argument, justice, respect, and tolerance, and on the other hand, they seek to overcome the use of violence and war as means for resolving conflict. Through such efforts citizens develop familiarity with institutionalized aspects of parliamentary governance.

CONCLUSION

As we near the end of the 20th century, it is difficult to believe that starvation in Somalia is a structural product of global interests, or that there could be widespread structural problems in the economy, the environment, the culture, and society in general. Moreover, it is difficult to understand why there is also open contestation in societies where there is apparently significant material progress. With the rise of more technical, prosperous, and mobile societies, we were led to believe that age-old socioeconomic problems and conflicts would subside in the face of all that modernism promised. However, modernism, with its technical orientation to problem solving, has not delivered on its promises to end major social problems, nor has it ensured an orderly process of social change. Its failure to do so is a major cause of pessimism. What the struggles over the role of women in society, the abuse of the environment and opposition to warfare have achieved is the increased realization that modernism has not delivered on its promises, but has compounded many of the problems we face.

Those who reduce the solution of these problems to matters of technical adaptations and adjustments to restore the equilibrium of the existing social "order" are confronted by an array of informed and active citizens who have indicted that "order." They argue that some social norms, for example, "domestic violence," and some cultural values, such as patriarchy and militarism, should be changed. They are asking why "science" is used to legitimize policy decisions we all know to be the product of "politics," broadly understood. Such Discourse undermines social change by failing to develop in students the competencies needed for social critique active social investigation and active citizenship.

Critical literacy, as Lankshear and Knobel argue, presupposes a particular orientation and capacity for making meaning about informed and active citizenship. Critical literacy requires the self-conscious construction of a new vision of citizenship. It involves the production of a new Discourse on citizenship, one emphasizing critical "civic" literacy that involves students learning that they too can enter consciously into making and transforming the culture and history of society. Critical "civic" literacy involves a process of counterconstruction that expands the competencies of students to deconstruct texts, messages, images and spectacles, and to "write against the grain." It is aimed at arresting the decline in higher order literacy competencies associated with developing an informed opinion, rational arguments, conceptual analysis, and abilities in public debating. The acquisition of a relevant meta-level knowledge grounded in an understanding of social movements permits students a re-reading, a renewed analysis and critique of passive notions of citizenship.

REFERENCES

Arnason, J. (1986). Culture, historicity and power: Reflections on some themes in the work of Alain Touraine. *Theory, Culture and Society, 3*(3), 137-152.

Cohen, J. (1985). Strategy or identity: New theoretical paradigms and contemporary citizens' movements. *Social Research, 4,* 664-716.

Daniels, K. (1985). Feminism and social history. *Australian Feminist Studies, 1,* 27-40.

Dowse, S. (1982). The women's movement's Fandango with the state: Some thoughts on the movement's role in public policy since 1972. *The Australian Quarterly, 54*(4), 324-345.

Faludi, S. (1992). *Backlash: The undeclared war against women.* London: Vintage.

Felski, R. (1989). Feminist theory and social change. *Theory, Culture and Society, 6,* 219-240.

Findlay, P. (1994). Conscientization and social movements in Canada: The relevance of Paulo Freire's ideas in contemporary politics. In P. McLaren & C. Lankshear (Eds.), *The politics of liberation: Paths from Freire.* London: Routledge.

Gollan, B. (1986). The Australian peace movement: Its early years. *Australian Journal of Social Issues, 21*(4), 245-256.

Hicks, D. (1988). Peace and conflict. In B. Carrington & B. Troyna (Eds.), *Children and controversial issues: Strategies for the early and middle years of schooling*. London: Falmer Press.

Kivisto, P. (1984). Contemporary citizens' movements in advanced industrial societies and sociological intervention: An appraisal of Alain Touraine's practique. *Acta Sociologica, 27*(4), 355-366.

Lingard, R., Henry, M. & Taylor, S. (1987)."A girl in a militant pose": A chronology of struggle in girls' education in Queensland. *British Journal of Sociology of Education, 8*(2), 135-152.

McLaren, P. (1993). Multiculturalism and the postmodern critique: Towards a pedagogy of resistance and transformation. *Cultural Studies, 7*(1), 118-146.

Morgan, D. (1992). *Discovering men*. London: Routledge.

Munoz, C. (1989). *Youth, identity, power: The Chicano movement*. London: Verso.

Poynting, S. (1986). "The Bang" and SNAP: Controversial issues in schools. *Australian Journal of Social Issues, 21*(4), 257-269.

Singh, M. G. (1990). Curriculum knowledge and Aboriginality: "Conservative capitalistic and favourable to long continued paternalism". *Curriculum Perspectives, 10*(2), 10-15.

Singh M. G. (1992). Studying Asia from the standpoint of active women citizens. *Asian Studies Review, 15*(3), 95-106.

Singh M. G. (1993). Teaching social education from the standpoint of active citizens. In K. Kennedy, O. Watts & G. McDonald (Eds.), *Citizenship education for a new age*. Toowoomba, Australia: University of Southern Queensland Press.

Smith, T. (1986). Educational change and peace studies: A natural progression. *Curriculum Perspectives, 6*(1), 29-34.

Touraine, A. (1971). *The May Movement—Revolt and reform: May 1968— The student rebellion and workers' strikes—The birth of a citizens' movement*. New York: Random House.

Touraine, A. (1981). *The voice and the eye: An analysis of citizen's movements*. Cambridge, UK: Cambridge University Press.

Touraine, A. (1984). Citizens' movements: Special area or central problem in sociological analysis. *Thesis Eleven, 9*, 5-15.

Touraine, A. (1988). *Return of the actor: Social theory in postindustrial society*. Minneapolis: University of Minnesota Press.

Wexler, P. (1983). Movement, class and education. In L. Barton & S. Walker (Eds.), *Race, class and education*. London: Croom Helm.

White, P. (1988). Educating courageous citizens. *Journal of Philosophy of Education, 22*(1), 67-74.

Woods, G. (1985). Education for democratic participation: Democratic values and the nuclear freeze campaign. *Theory and Research in Social Education, 12*(4), 39-56.

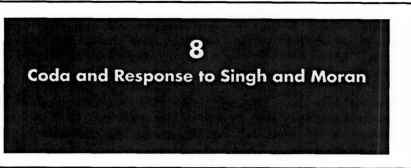

8
Coda and Response to Singh and Moran

Colin Lankshear
Michele Knobel
Queensland University of Technology

We welcome Singh and Moran's extension of our discussion of critical literacy into the terrain of social movements. Any viable praxis of critical literacy and active citizenship must carry into activity within public spheres, and social movements have a special place within the political order of New Times.

In contexts of active citizenship, critical literacy necessarily involves taking textual representations of social practices, processes, and their material outcomes, and subjecting them to critique in ways that promote embodied action for informed and responsible change within public spheres. More proactively, perhaps, critical literacy includes generating representations of social reality (possible worlds) with a view to mobilizing such activity. Of course, what counts as critical practice here is inseparable from how we construct "being informed," "responsible action," and "desirable change." Our preference is for critical readings and (re)writings that build solidarities across diversities, resist reducing "shared commitments" to totalizing or monolithic "visions," and seek productive interplays among local, regional, national, and global issues and concerns.

Our chapter and the response to it are, however, both constrained by an important omission, which has become increasingly evident to us during the 4 year "lead time" between the chapter's original production and its eventual publication. This is our failure to accommodate the rapid escalation of computer-mediated communications (CMC) technologies and their appropriation within educational settings. Any account of critical literacy, whether in relation to active citizenship or anything else, that does not take account of electronic texts and communications, and the burgeoning mode of information (Poster, 1990), is plainly incomplete. Writing in the *Arachnet Electronic Journal of Virtual Culture*, Lemke (1993) addressed the pressing need for educational theory to take account of ecosocial changes in the ways people interact with each other—and the scales on which they interact—and how these impact on teaching and learning, given contexts increasingly characterized by electronically mediated forms of social practice.

Many claims are made, and examples provided, for the active citizenship potential of CMC within so-called "virtual communities" of cyberspace. At one level, examples are provided of how routine democratic civic practices and procedures can be facilitated and enhanced electronically, such as where candidates running for local office post their policies on electronic bulletin boards, elicit comments and suggestions, and maintain their bulletin boards to continue communicating with constituents upon being elected.

At a different level, approximating to global social movements, we find examples like that cited by Rheingold (1994) of Aldo de Moor, a Dutch fourth-year information management student who created the Rainforest Network Bulletin on BITNET. The bulletin serves as an online think tank where ecological action plans are evaluated "from scientific and political perspectives" (p. 264). This initiative is but one of a much larger network wherein "ecologists, ethologists, biologists, anthropologists, activists around the world, have been using parts of the Net to coordinate scientific and political efforts" (p. 263).

Numerous issues—some of them by now quite familiar—arise here that have implications for our conceptions and practices of critical literacy. For example, critical literacy should address the questions of whether and how we might distinguish information from misinformation and dis-information, and how information is controlled and regulated within electronically mediated environments. In addition, critical literacy must extend into electronic realms its traditional interest in exploring cases where regulation and control of information results in people being served up mis-information and dis-information to the detriment of informed participation in public spheres.

Beyond this lies the concern expressed by Taylor and Saarinen (1994) as to how we might generate understanding in a world that desperately needs it, but where information and knowledge are out of control. According to Taylor and Saarinen, whereas understanding "presupposes information and knowledge," they "less and less lead to understanding." Extending critical literacy into the sphere of CMC can assist here by helping to transform "institutional technologies dedicated to the production of information that is not knowledge to the production of knowledge that advances understanding" (pp. 12 - 13).

This is an aspect of a much larger issue addressed by Taylor and Saarinen, who stressed that understanding is needed in order that knowledge be born and reborn as praxis, because "in the praxis-dominated world of ultra-tech the politics of critique must take a new form." Cyber-age citizens must become what they called "media philosophers," attempting "to move beyond existing institutions to imagine and *refashion* possibilities that might be" (pp. 17, 20; italics added). Rheingold's example (and like examples) of ecologists and others using the Internet to mobilize critique and appropriate action on scales equal to the challenges, is of people who are already active citizens; whose identities are constituted to this extent around focused civic concerns that bear upon the interests of human beings from local to global levels. Since practices of critical literacy are at least partly concerned with engendering this kind of commitment, the challenge of projecting critical literacy into electronic spheres includes finding ways of using CMC to promote communities of active civic practice.

With governments and education departments lining up to usher Internet access into classrooms, we must ponder the prospects for developing effective critical literacy practices within "wired" classrooms, given their relative underdevelopment to date within settings employing more conventional text types. We believe it is most important that in the charge to familiarize ourselves with the technical demands of electronic media we do not leave behind, or close ourselves off from, insights into critical practice generated around engagement with print and visual texts, and that we continue to build on these as appropriate. Although there is not total carryover from critical literacy in "bookspace" to critical literacy in "cyberspace"—and there are some important differences (Lankshear, Peters, & Knobel, 1996)—there is, nonetheless, much that can be transferred.

In this regard, we find online resources such as the recently terminated NOVAE user group (Teachers Networking for the Future) especially helpful. NOVAE provided teachers with information about resources available on the Internet, together with ideas as to where and how they might be used. Hence, an Internet resource like the Solar Cooking Archive (available at http://www.accessone.com/~sbcn/index.htm) could be integrated into a unit of work along similar lines to those we generated in our chapter around the Somalia text, without offending the integrity of either bookspace or cyberspace. On the contrary, such integrations bring these spaces together in ways that anticipate the future and actively implicate us in pursuing enhanced understandings of critical practices with texts. To be sure, had we known about, and had access to, the Internet Public Library (at http://ipl.sils.umich.edu/), and/or to the Web sites for worldwide newspaper access at the point of writing, we would have incorporated them within the original chapter. Fortunately, we have had the chance to acknowledge and briefly address this shortcoming.

REFERENCES

Lankshear, C., Peters, M., & Knobel, M. (1996). Critical pedagogy and cyberspace. In. H. Giroux, C. Lankshear, P. McLaren, & M. Peters, *Counternarratives: Cultural studies and critical pedagogies in postmodern spaces*. New York: Routledge.

Lemke, J. (1993). Education, cyberspace, and change. *The Arachnet Journal on Virtual Culture, 1*(1).

Poster, M. (1990). *The mode of information: Poststructuralism and social context*. Cambridge, UK: Polity Press.

Rheingold, H. (1994). *The virtual community: Finding connection in a computerized world*. London: Martin Secker & Warburg Ltd.

Taylor, M., & Saarinen, E. (1994). *Imagologies: Media philosophy*. London: Routledge.

9

Critical Literacy and Control in the New World Order

Nicholas Faraclas
University of Papua New Guinea

INDIGENOUS PEOPLES AND THE NEW ENCLOSURES

In this chapter, I trace the evolution of critical literacies in Papua New Guinea in order to draw attention to the potential contributions of indigenous peoples to global movements for critical literacy and social transformation. Before meaningful consideration can be given to the development of critical literacies in Papua New Guinea however, it is necessary to situate this development in its sociohistorical context.

Imagine a society where there is no hunger, homelessness, or unemployment and where, in times of need, individuals can rest assured that their community will make available to them every resource at its disposal. Imagine a society where decision makers rule only when the need arises, and then only by consultation, consensus, and the consent of the community. Imagine a society where women have control over their means of production and reproduction, where housework is minimal and child care is available 24 hours a day on demand. Imagine a society where there is little or no crime and where community conflicts are settled by sophisticated resolution procedures based on compensation to aggrieved parties for damages, with no recourse to concepts of guilt or punishment. Imagine a society that values human beings above all other things and in which the mere fact that a person exists is cause for celebration and a deep sense of responsibility to maintain and share that existence.

The first colonizers to the island of New Guinea did not find one society that exactly fitted the description just given. Instead they found more than 1,000 distinct language groups and many more distinct societies, the majority of which approximated closely this description, but each in its own particular way. These were not perfect societies. They had many problems. But when the colonialists arrived in the many parts of Africa and Melanesia where no absolute ruler existed, they promptly installed local males as "chiefs" and "big men" who were given the franchise, as the local agents of colonial domination, to exercise absolute rule. The breakdown of the collectively oriented extended family system and the installation of the father as the "absolute ruler" of the nuclear family has been encouraged for similar reasons, especially by the missions and the companies. The institutions of chieftaincy and male domination have now been elevated to the level of "tradition" in Nigeria and Papua New Guinea, whereas these institutions were in some cases first established and in the great majority of cases significantly strengthened and consolidated by the colonialists.

But after some 100 years of "Northern development" (I use the slightly more accurate term *Northern* to replace the term *Western* here), nearly all of the real developmental gains achieved over the past 40,000 years by indigenous peoples have been seriously eroded, whereas almost all of the original problems have worsened and have been added to a rapidly growing list of new imported problems.

Indigenous Peoples and Politics of Difference

The year 1993 was declared the UN Year of Indigenous Peoples. Rigoberta Menchu received the Nobel Peace Prize for her role in the struggle of the indigenous peoples of Guatemala against expropriation and genocide. Papua New Guinea is a nation of indigenous peoples. No single ethnic group is large enough to constitute more than 7% of the population, so there is no concentration of power in the hands of any particular group. With 97% of its land mass under the traditional control of its indigenous peoples, Papua New Guinea has provided a unique environment for the growth of truly indigenous critical literacies.

Was the UN Year of Indigenous Peoples less disappointing than the UN International Literacy Year that preceded it? It will be necessary for all of us to finally take seriously the struggles of indigenous peoples worldwide. Each of these struggles is unique and in each case the construction of politics and discourses of difference by indigenous peoples themselves needs the support of all who oppose any form of oppression (Nakata, 1993). In no way can the situation of one group be equated mechanically to the situation of another. However, there are threads of commonality (not universal absolutes) that bind these struggles together and provide fertile ground for collective and collaborative struggle by indigenous peoples. The work of identifying and tracing these threads is very important, and will best be done by the networks of indigenous peoples that are beginning to coalesce around the globe.

The struggles of indigenous peoples are distinct in nature, and cannot be subordinated to any other struggle. It has been common to lump together the politics of national liberation (so-called "third-world" struggles) with the politics of the emancipation of indigenous peoples (sometimes called "fourth-world" struggles) because of their common experiences under colonialism and neocolonialism. Although I do not fully subscribe to "many worlds" theories (in politics, in philosophy, or in physics), the general effect of the tendency to subsume indigenous peoples' problems and aspirations under the rubric of national liberation has been to silence indigenous voices and prevent the formation of networks of indigenous peoples across (or even within) national boundaries.

It is argued here that indigenous peoples have incredibly important experiences to share with those whose struggles are defined in other ways, such as class struggles, struggles against racism and ethnocentricity, patriarchy, and heterosexism, as well as national liberation struggles. It is the failure of those in other arenas to recognize the critical importance of indigenous peoples' struggles that has prevented us thus far from benefiting from the indispensable contributions that indigenous peoples have to make at the levels of the theory and praxis of social transformation.

If we come to terms with the struggles of indigenous peoples during the coming decade, it should be as unthinkable by the year 2000 for us to proceed in our work without the important discourses, knowledges, and praxis contributed by indigenous peoples—as it had become unthinkable for us to proceed without the contributions of the struggles of national liberation movements against imperialism after the 1950s, of the struggle against racism after the 1960s, of the struggle against patriarchy and heterosexism after the 1970s, or of the struggle against the enclosure of the global common (the "environment") after the 1980s. Each of these struggles was at first marginalized, trivialized, or discounted by those who felt that the class struggle, in the narrowest sense of the expression, was somehow more central, more strategically important. As each of these struggles became a broad social movement that could no longer be ignored, its contributions gradually have been integrated (sometimes not completely and at other times with great resistance) into all of those movements against oppression that have stood the test of time and survived into the 1990s.

Those who still pose the key struggle as a "class struggle" have so radically redefined the "working class" that it seems to have grown to include all peoples who, in one way or another, are struggling against oppression. An interesting example of this new expanded definition of the working class is provided by the Midnight Notes Collective (1992):

> Working class struggles are those that attempt to reduce the unpaid labour capital appropriates throughout the social circuit. Women's struggle against forced labour, . . . indigenous peoples' struggle against land appropriation are all working class struggles. . . . [R]egardless of one's gender, race, sexual preference, or feelings towards the earth, we all move through capitalist space; we live on capitalist soil, we eat capitalist bread, we expend our bodies on capitalist work. Everything is a commodity—the water, the land, even the air—and must be purchased through work. We experience capitalism in very different and at times apparently contradictory ways, but nonetheless the unity remains. A recategorisation of the working class allows us to see the diversity of agents behind a distinctly anti-capitalist project. If capitalism is all-pervasive, the struggle against it must operate on many fronts. (p. xii)

Marginalized groups are in the process of creating positive identities and voices for ourselves and learning to respect one another's identities and voices. This is a necessary, but not sufficient, condition for the elimination of our oppression. Another necessary condition is the identification and removal of the sources of our oppression. The dominant discourses of capital have warped the sociohistorical space–time within which we exist to such an extent that it is impossible to even contemplate the construction of discourses and politics of difference without attempting at the same time to deconstruct these dominant discourses and to actively struggle against the "social gravity" (Gee, 1992) that they wield. It is also necessary that the lessons learned and the experiences accumulated from each battle against each form of oppression be collectivized and become part of struggles in every arena. The extent to which this happens is a measure of our understanding of the common roots of all oppression and of our increasing sophistication in attacking and eradicating them.

The New Enclosures: Deconstructing "Post-Fordism"

According to Midnight Notes, what occurred in the 1960s and early 1970s was a prime example of the power that all oppressed peoples gain from respecting and learning from one another's viewpoints and experience. The workers', women's, and African Americans' struggles entered into just such a relationship at this time, with explosive consequences for capital. The 1960s and 1970s saw the beginnings of the demise of the Keynesian "deal" based on "a fair day's pay for a fair day's work" (with a "fair" profit for capital) that had been brokered with the largely White and male U.S. and West European assembly line workers during the inter war and post war periods. After the 1950s, the assembly line workforce was becoming less White and less male on one hand, and on the other, it was beginning to align its struggles with the "wages for housework" campaign led by feminists and the welfare and civil rights movements led by people of color. In this way, the ostensible link between work and wages was severed. The expanded demands of these new expanded "working classes" put capital into crisis. Although social services, unemployment insurance, wages, and benefits increased dramatically in the 1960s and early 1970s, profit margins plummeted.

It was therefore a collectivization of experience from different struggles that provoked the latest "world crisis" that has so thoroughly transformed our lives since the mid-1970s, and that has catapulted us into a post-Fordian era (Harvey, 1989). Many of us have felt a great sense of defeat as a result of the construction of the oil/energy/world "Crisis" discourse by capital and their largely successful use thus far of this discourse to deconstitute the (expanded) working classes and to extract unprecedented profits from them. But few of us have paid enough attention to the great successes of these same working classes that originally forced capital to rescind all of the "deals" that it had struck since World War II with "first-world" assembly line workers, "second world" socialist workers, and the nominally independent nations of the "third world."

Once the deals were off, capital could go on the offensive with a set of New Enclosures, which, like the Old Enclosures in the English countryside, involve a battery of expropriations by capital of land, jobs, homes, communities, social services, legal rights, and other assets that the working classes had previously struggled for and won, and that many had come to assume were inalienable. Thus far, capital has successfully transformed its own crisis into a crisis for all oppressed peoples, by means of a discourse of Crisis and the establishment of New Enclosures. The situation that we find ourselves in today is summed up by Midnight Notes (1992a) in this way:

> The Enclosures . . . are a regular return on the path of accumulation and a structural component of the class struggle. Any leap in proletarian power demands a dynamic capitalist response: both the expanded appropriation of new resources and new labour power and the extension of capitalist relations, or else capitalism is threatened with extinction. Thus . . . despite our differences, we have all entered capitalism through the same door; the loss of our land and the rights attached to it. . . . In the biggest diaspora of the century . . . millions are being uprooted from their land, their jobs, their homes, through wars, famines, plagues, and the International Monetary Fund . . . and scattered to the corners of the globe. . . . The "debt crisis," "homelessness," and the "collapse of socialism" are frequently treated as different phenomena by . . . the media. . . . For us . . . they but deceptively name aspects of a single unified process: the New Enclosures, which must operate throughout the planet in differing, divisive guises while being totally interdependent. (pp. 317-321)

The transparently global nature of the New Enclosures brings into relief the interconnectedness of the expropriations of indigenous peoples and the McDonaldization of work in postindustrial societies. If the conjunction of the class, race, and feminist struggles in the 1960s and 1970s led to the decoupling of wages from work, with all of its critical consequences, what will the addition of indigenous struggles contribute to this powerful constellation? If we define *indigenous peoples* as populations with a preEnclosures relationship to the land and each other, that is, whose relationship to their means of production and reproduction do not yet function within such fundamental capitalist discourses as "ownership," "science," "the nuclear family," and "control," the potential significance of the struggles of indigenous peoples begin to emerge. Once such basic discourses as "ownership" and "control" are called into question, deeper levels of oppression become vulnerable to critical analysis and creative struggle. In this way, indigenous peoples' struggles challenge us to reclaim our lives, our humanity, our loves, our communities, our land, our planet—things that most of us have forgotten are our birthrights.

RECOLONIZATION AND THE NEW ENCLOSURES IN PAPUA NEW GUINEA

The period of gradual decolonization that followed World War II has been succeeded by a period of rapid recolonization over the last decade (Federici, 1992). Papua New Guinea, like most of the countries that have experienced colonial underdevelopment, counts two dates among the most significant in its history: 1975, the year when it achieved political independence from Australia; and 1989, the year when it lost that independence, that is, the year when it was forced to accept a Structural Adjustment Programme (SAP) designed and implemented by advisers sent from the World Bank/International Monetary Fund (WB/IMF) joint headquarters in Washington, DC.

The WB/IMF SAP in Papua New Guinea

Papua New Guinean labor generates considerable wealth for the world economy every year, but most of this wealth is appropriated by international capital. The SAP was forced on Papua New Guinea ostensibly because it was unable to meet the payment schedule on its debts to the international banks in 1989. Most of these debts were accrued because of (a) the rapid rise in the cost of energy, food, and commodities imported from industrialized countries in the 1970s; (b) a series of "big project" loans, that have been aggressively "marketed" by the WB and other international banks since 1976; and (c) skyrocketing interest rates on loans and the simultaneous collapse of the prices of commodities produced by tropical countries in the 1980s. WB projects in Papua New Guinea have proved to be no more successful than in other countries, filling the pockets of consultants, contractors, and suppliers from the industrialized countries, and leaving behind little for the people of Papua New Guinea beside an ever growing debt burden. That burden became too great in 1989, and Papua New Guinea was forced to renegotiate its debts with the WB/IMF.

Before a nation is permitted to renegotiate its debt, it is forced by the WB/IMF to accept a SAP and a team of WB/IMF advisers to "manage" its economy and "get its house in order." However, Papua New Guinea's foreign debt has grown substantially since 1989, and with the active encouragement of the WB/IMF, the debt is likely to double over the next several years. The apparent intention of the SAPs is not debt reduction or economic recovery, but rather the consolidation of neocolonial power for a series of New Enclosures. It is not surprising then, that the goals of the Papua New Guinean SAP in 1989 are strikingly similar to the recommendations of the first WB mission to Papua New Guinea 25 years earlier in 1964 (World Bank, 1965), 11 years before Papua New Guinea achieved independence.

The 1964 WB report envisioned a cash crop export-led scenario for development in Papua New Guinea. Under the SAP, the "Expand to Export Campaign" was initiated in 1990, to promote the establishment and expansion of plantations in the country. This occurred at a time when the prices for cash crops were at all time lows, largely due to WB/IMF promotion of similar cash crop production campaigns in nearly every other tropical country where it "manages" the economy. Papua New Guinean cash crop producers are actually working harder and producing more than ever, but getting less and less for their efforts. To cushion the blow of low commodity prices, the government is now planning massive price support payments to cash crop producers. This constitutes a massive transfer of public funds to the plantation sector and public support for artificially low prices engineered by WB/IMF-induced market gluts and cartel busting.

Under the SAP, the currency was devalued by 10%, and there have been persistent rumors for further devaluation in the future. This amounts to pay cuts for all Papua New Guineans. In addition, the urban minimum wage (U.S. $36 per week) has been lowered to the level of the rural minimum (U.S. $16 per week), while some are talking of eliminating the minimum wage altogether. Pay raises, promotions, and new hiring have been frozen in the Civil Service, Papua New Guinea's largest employer. Traditional collective work practices were also targeted for criticism in 1964 and the "new wave" WB/IMF-designed plantations are based on the "block system," in which nuclear families are isolated on small lots of company land where they must tend cash crops without the help of extended family members.

Since the SAP was accepted in 1989, spending on social services has been slashed. Women's programs, youth programs, employment-generation programs, education, and health have been cut, whereas spending on the military, police, and prisons has increased substantially. These increases in funding for the SAP-sponsored "Law and Order Campaign" can be seen as part of the implementation of yet another of the WB's 1964 recommendations: the establishment of a "favorable investment climate" in Papua New Guinea. New legislation has been passed during the past 5 years, including the death penalty for certain crimes, a "Peace and Good Order Act" that carries a minimum 7-year sentence for obstructing the operations of a company, and new requirements for police clearance before staging public demonstrations.

The most salient recommendation of the 1964 WB mission to Papua New Guinea was to eliminate or radically modify traditional land tenure systems to make it possible for land to be owned individually and to be bought and sold. Since 1989, one of the flagship programs of the WB/IMF SAP in Papua New Guinea has been the Land Mobilization Programme (LMP). Although social services budgets are being cut under the SAP, the LMP is receiving more money than the average annual expenditure on health or education. Unlike most "developing" countries, Papua New Guinea has not yet had most of its land defined by the dominant discourse of ownership. In fact, 97% of the territory of Papua New Guinea is divided into customarily demarcated areas, each of which is collectively held by an extended family group. Virtually every Papua New Guinean (more than 95% of the population) enjoys this sort of collectively based land tenure today. Although 85% of the population live in rural areas and exercise their land tenure rights directly in their day-to-day lives, most of the 5% of the population that live in towns and the 10% that live in shanty settlements can also return at any time to their ancestral lands and claim their rights to use the land.

In the traditional discourse of land tenure, there is no concept of "owner." In most Papua New Guinean languages, people's relationship to land is not normally expressed in terms of alienable (commodifiable) possession, but rather in terms of an inalienable, that is, familial or even corporal association. Papua New Guineans traditionally refer to themselves as the children, siblings, or parents of the ground. In the customary conceptual framework, it is as impossible to envision the buying or selling of ground as a commodity as it is to envision the buying or selling of one's mother or child. Although many Papua New Guineans are referring to themselves as "landowners" these days, their uncritical acceptance of the name and the illusion of absolute control over land that it promotes, represent a major victory for the WB/IMF in its persistent drive to enclose the land of Papua New Guinea.

There are three stated aims of the WB/IMF LMP.

1. To mobilize land for "development." The assumptions here are that land in Papua New Guinea is not developed and that traditional land tenure is somehow preventing this development. If development means to improve the quality of life, it can be convincingly argued that the land of Papua New Guinea is some of the best developed land in the world. The accomplishments of this traditional form of development are impressive, and include techniques for conflict resolution and contraception that are unrivaled in their sophistication and the elimination of homelessness and hunger. In the growing number of instances where customary land tenure is breaking down in the name of development, the quality of life has depreciated. It is in areas of the country that have been developed by the WB and other capital-oriented projects that we are witnessing the first cases of homelessness, hunger, women forced to accept regular beatings and yearly pregnancies, serious alcoholism, violent crime, and so on.

2. Give landowners an opportunity to use their land as collateral to get loans from the banks. The assumptions here are that land is a commodity, that Papua New Guineans' greatest need is money, and that bank loans are designed to enhance the quality of life in Papua New Guinea.

3. Protect a particular group's traditional lands from encroachments by neighbors. The assumption here is that Papua New Guineans are their own worst enemies and that this WB program will "save Papua New Guineans from themselves and their traditions." This logic is typical of what critical literacy workers have named the Cargo discourse on development: the rejection by Papua New Guineans of themselves, their culture, and their resources as viable historical agents in the development process, accompanied by the uncritical acceptance of a version of "development" that is owned, operated, packaged, and imported into the country by capital.

The LMP is implemented through the various provincial Land Acts, which make provision for the registration of land. The registration procedures include the following:

1. The land is surveyed and boundaries delineated. Shared and contested lands may not be registered, leaving the way open for these to be declared state property and taken away from the people who traditionally used them.
2. The boundaries are then listed in the Land Register and one, or sometimes a few "landowners" or "trustees" sign the book. The registration process thus opens the way for the individuals whose names are listed in the Land Register to act "on behalf" of the rest of their extended family and to sell usage rights.
3. Once the land is registered, the "proud new owner(s)" can use it as collateral to take out loans from the Agriculture Bank, and almost invariably, they are obliged to use the money for cash crop projects. In the almost inevitable case of default, the bank is given control over the land for a specified number of years, to run as a plantation or for other uses.
4. Once the land is registered, it can be taxed. Under the SAP, a number of regressive taxes have been imposed on the people of Papua New Guinea. Without land registration, however, it is impossible to levy land taxes.
5. Land registration transfers control of land from the undetermined, decentered, orally transmitted authority of the elders to the absolute, centralized authority of the Land Register. According to at least one provincial Land Act, the Land Register is under the supervision of the Controller of Lands, who has discretionary power to change boundaries at any time.

Land tenure is at the very heart of the issue of control in Papua New Guinea. Control over the land gives Papua New Guineans economic independence. If a Papua New Guinean finds the minimum wage too low or working conditions unacceptable, she or he can always go back to the village, where most basic needs can be satisfied with little or no need for money. In the name of "economic recovery," the SAP both masks and implements the three main strategies for wrenching the land out from the control of Papua New Guineans. The short-term strategy is to forcibly evict communities from land targeted for key development projects, such as plantations and mines. The medium term strategy is to offer schemes such as the LMP to induce people to give up control over their land in exchange for promises of development. The long-term strategy involves the media, the schools, the churches, and other institutions that alienate youth from the attitudes and work practices that are necessary for maintenance of an economic base on the land. When these youths become adults, they will see little reason to hold onto their land, for they will no longer be interested or able to live a happy life there. Whenever the young people of Papua New Guinea are thus prepared to sell out, there is no doubt that agents of capital will be delighted to offer them a "fair market price" for their birthright.

Critical Literacy and Anticapitalist Struggles for Emancipation

Some readers will object to the fact that the versions of critical literacy described in this chapter elevate emancipation to a universal avocation. Still others will claim that they do not allow any space for Elites who could potentially become "border crossers" (Lankshear & McLaren, 1993). What gives the emancipatory the appearance of preeminence in this stage of human history is the oppression that presently devastates the lives of nearly everyone on the planet. Everyone, including those at the top, is oppressed by capital. The Elites in Papua New Guinea are, in the opinion of most Papua New Guineans, the unhappiest and most alienated people in the country. Emancipatory struggles do not by definition exclude Elites. In fact, it can be argued that the only option for the Elites to transform their reality is to join the emancipatory struggles of other oppressed peoples against capital. With limited resources at present, the movement for critical literacy in Papua New Guinea has consciously prioritized work with the rural villagers and urban shanty dwellers. As more resources become available, Elites too can be targeted by critical literacy programs.

Some will argue that to tie the movement for critical literacy in Papua New Guinea to the emancipatory struggles of oppressed peoples against capital is reductionist and totalizing. The ubiquity of the relations and discourses of capital make the struggle against it an urgent priority as well as a common point of reference and a common thread that binds together all struggles of oppressed peoples. It should be obvious to the reader by now that if Papua New Guineans do not actively engage in the deconstruction of the discourses that have allowed capital to implement the SAP in their country and in the construction of alternative discourses to those of capital, they will soon be landless. Will the next generation of Papua New Guinean parents be selling some of their children to the rich, in order to buy enough food for the others? In countries like the Philippines, the landlessness and misery caused by SAPs have given rise to the buying and selling of children. Are Papua New Guinean children to be butchered in cold blood for their organs? In Brazil, for instance, the expropriations and poverty brought about by SAPs have made possible a lively market in children's "spare parts" for export to the North. We cannot allow our justified critique of modernist absolutism to lead us into a postmodernist positions of ultra-relativism. Although we reject the disastrous totalitarianism of modernist struggles against capitalism (as in Stalinist policies), are we to replace them with a postmodernist abandonment of any struggle beyond an individualized and decentered search for meaningful subjecthood?

Yet, modernist struggles against capital, largely inspired by the work of Karl Marx, do not themselves have a very good record of support for the struggles of indigenous peoples. One of the major self-criticisms made by the Sandinista government in Nicaragua centered around its treatment of indigenous peoples and their concerns. The origin of this problem can be traced back to Marx's inability to critically analyze his own modernist notions of "progress," "civilization," and "universality."

Critical Literacy, Nongovernmental Organizations, and the New World Order

From World War II until the 1970s, newly independent governments and the socialist countries played a significant role in many struggles against the capitalist world order. But intimidation and direct intervention by capital via the WB/IMF SAPs and the collapse of socialism have silenced almost all of these governmental voices. In the 1980s and 1990s, a new set of voices have been raised to challenge this "New World Order": the nongovernmental organizations (NGOs).

NGOs have been the main critics of the WB/IMF worldwide and they have played a leading role in the organization of communities to resist the New Enclosures. Capital has also realized this, and there are now a set of well-financed international capital-oriented NGOs who are doing their best to prevent the development of strong movements of indigenous community-oriented NGOs in countries like Papua New Guinea. Those NGOs that have not reneged on their responsibility to vigorously confront the agents and discourses that directly threaten to destroy the lives of the majority of the people of Papua New Guinea realize that time is running out and that the stakes could not be higher. Community-oriented NGOs have found critical literacy to be an instrument with great potential for facilitating community-controlled social transformation. It is therefore no accident that the movement of NGOs in Papua New Guinea is inextricably linked with the movement for critical literacy. But as an instrument, critical literacy is still crude and blunt. Unfortunately, it seems that some Northern theorists may actually be rendering it less, rather than more effective. Back in the field however, Papua New Guinean NGOs are discovering that the best way to refine and sharpen critical literacy is to put it to the whetstone of praxis.

THE EVOLUTION OF CRITICAL LITERACIES IN PAPUA NEW GUINEA

If we are to define *critical literacy* as the process "reading and writing one's life" (see Lankshear & Knobel, chap. 6 , this volume), then it would be very difficult to cite a particular date for the advent of critical literacies in Papua New Guinea. In most Papua New Guinean traditions, every event in the life of an individual or a community is "read" for its underlying meaning. No event is considered to be unmotivated. The unquestioning acceptance with which most of the world's "literate" people face the often oppressive "facts" of their lives is something relatively new in Papua New Guinea. The scope for individual expression and voice in writing one's life, that is, in the determination of the general goals and the daily rhythms and activities of one's life, is much wider in "preliterate" Papua New Guinea than in the average print literate society. Here we are faced with a paradox: if anyone in the world today can be said to be practicing critical literacies in their daily lives, it is the most traditional and most print illiterate populace of a country like Papua New Guinea. The lives of these "illiterates" are relatively unaffected by the dominant discourses that "read and write" and discipline the lives of the majority of the print literate peoples of the world.

Colonialism, Cargo Cults, and Cargo Literacy

Print literacy began in Papua New Guinea with the arrival of the colonialists and slave traders in the mid-to late 1800s. Missionaries, whose god was presented to the people as the "only real god" and whose language and literacy were presented as the "only real language" and the "only real literacy," began classes in which Papua New Guineans were taught to decode the written text of the Bible. The missionaries' basic message to the people of Papua New Guinea was the message of Cargo: all that Papua New Guineans are, do, or have is evil and must be rejected, while the new imported Cargo (foreign commodities), its agents (the missionaries, colonial government, and companies), and their lifestyle (practices, knowledges, etc.) are good and must be acquired and emulated. Because the missionaries deemed all traditional practices to be the work of Satan, some Papua New Guineans started to reject their own customs. In the process of repudiating their traditions, Papua New Guineans have begun to lose the critical analysis and control that they have exercised over their lives for millennia.

The Cargo Cult is much more than a localized phenomenon, where an aberrant Papua New Guinean "holy man" establishes a religious sect around promises of the miraculous provision to the "true believers" of all of the trappings of the Northern consumer lifestyle. The

Cargo Cult is a discourse that has been promoted actively and systematically by missionaries, governments, and companies for more than a century, whose primary effect has been the accelerating abandonment of the discourses that govern traditional life in Papua New Guinea and the rapid growth in influence of the dominant discourses of capital in the country. The Cargo Cult and the dominant discourses it propagates play a role in the shaping of desires and identities (see C. Luke, chap. 2, this volume) of every individual and community in Papua New Guinea today.

It can be said that print literacy and its associated discourses and institutions (functional literacy, the mission and government education systems, etc.) have done more to destroy critical literacies in Papua New Guinea than any other force. In the process of learning to "read" the Bible, Papua New Guineans were taught by their missionary mentors that their traditions had to be rejected in favor of the ways of their new masters. When the colonial government established a system of primary education, reading and writing was taught exclusively in English from storybooks whose main characters were Australian (appropriately named Mr. and Mrs. White) with the typical Cargo lifestyle, complete with high covenant house, car, nuclear family, office job, meat pies, and so on. The only Papua New Guinean in the books was the houseboy.

Independence and the Cargo Discourse on Development

Since Independence, Mr. and Mrs. White have been replaced by the "Melanesian Series" whose main characters are Papua New Guineans, but whose lifestyle is nearly identical to that of the White family that they replaced. As this chapter is being written, Papua New Guinean children are still being punished for speaking their own languages in the English-only schools. Although the essential message of Cargo has been the same throughout the entire history of Northern style literacy and education in Papua New Guinea, the dispensers of Cargo have changed. Under the Australian administration, Papua New Guineans hoped to gain access to Cargo first through the missions, then gradually the schools became the gatekeepers. After Independence, the government was expected to deliver the goods. But now, in the New World Order, Cargo comes via the bank development programs and projects.

The effects of the Cargo Cult go far beyond the realm of literacy and education. Indeed, the dominant discourse on development in Papua New Guinea can quite appropriately be named the Cargo discourse on development. The WB/IMF and foreign companies are aggressively pushing Cargo development, with support from some sectors of the Papua New Guinean Elites. The message is basically the

Cargo Cult message, extended to the domain of control over labor and resources: Papua New Guinea has no "development" and no viable means to "develop" itself. If Papua New Guinea wants development, it will have to import it in the form of Cargo, owned and operated outside of Papua New Guinea. In this discourse, development is seen as a set of objects and projects such as plantations, mines, logging operations, big buildings, luxury cars, alcohol, plastic food, consumer goods, and so on. Questions about why these things are valued, how they are obtained, what they replace, and who controls and benefits from this type of development process are silenced within the Cargo discourse.

As a result of the Cargo discourse on development, most Papua New Guineans approach the whole question of improvement of the quality of their lives with a profound sense of powerlessness. Nearly all Papua New Guineans are incredibly powerful by world standards and have under their control and within their own communities excellent and abundant resources that could be used to improve their quality of life substantially. But because of the Cargo discourse on development, these community resources are usually discounted or completely ignored, in favor of inferior, and inappropriate resources from outside of the community. These, in turn, can only be obtained by relinquishing community and individual control over land, resources, and labor.

The products of the Papua New Guinea education system are designed to promote and perpetuate Cargo development in the country (Ahai & Faraclas, 1993). The 67% of children who begin school but are "pushed out" before Grade 10 acquire during their short academic careers a visceral distaste for life and work in their villages and a correspondingly strong appetite for the Cargo life of Mr. and Mrs. White. Although they learn few if any skills that will allow them to assume the types of employment that would give them access to the Cargo, they are also deprived of the traditional education that would have given them the skills to make use of the resources in their villages. Meanwhile, the 1% who attend university are trained from a very early age to live and love the Cargo life far away from their villages, in boarding schools (from Grade 7 on, students usually live on campus) and in Australia (the top percentiles of Papua New Guinean high school students are automatically given scholarships to complete their schooling abroad). With such training, it is not difficult to imagine why many of these Elites might be disinclined to oppose the WB/IMF programs to expropriate traditional land or to block the companies' efforts to make quick profits through grossly unfair resource extraction deals with local communities.

The 30% or so who never enter Grade 1 are arguably the happiest, and in many cases the most materially prosperous Papua New Guineans. The degree of control that they exercise over their lives and resources as well as the degree of critical discrimination with which they examine the events that constitute their daily existence are far superior to those of either the Pushouts or the Elites. These are the people who continue to practice the critical literacies that were bequeathed to them by their ancestors. These critical literacies represent an important developmental achievement whose significance extends far beyond the borders of Papua New Guinea.

The Revival of Critical Literacies in Papua New Guinea: The Movement for Local Language Literacy

The revival of critical literacies in Papua New Guinea began in the late 1980s as an attempt to move from a literacy defined as a set of word attack skills for reading the Bible to a literacy that included elements of experience, process, critical thinking, and creative self-expression (Stringer & Faraclas, 1987). The results of the introduction of a new pedagogy for literacy called the Multistrategy Method on the one hand, and the implementation of a new community-based methodology for starting and maintaining literacy programs called the Community Framework on the other, provided an important impetus for the birth of a significant grassroots movement for Local Language Literacy in Papua New Guinea by 1989.

What distinguished this movement from the literacy efforts that preceded it was that it was moving beyond prevailing models of print literacy and functional literacy. Beside advocating the initial teaching of reading and writing in a language familiar to the learner (rather than in English) for the obvious pedagogical reasons, the movement for Local Language Literacy was promoted as a process that could play a major part in the struggles of indigenous peoples to maintain their languages and cultures in the face of the onslaught of the languages and discourses of Cargo and capital. Local Language Literacy was also seen as a means to provide indigenous communities with the opportunity of establishing and maintaining literacy programs themselves, using their own ideas and locally available resources, thus challenging the Cargo notion that all development must be imported and controlled from outside of the community. Given its emphasis on the preservation and development of local languages and cultures, the focus of this movement was largely confined to local language literacy for preschool children.

The Multistrategy Method: Student-Controlled Learning

The most effective pedagogy for critical literacy in Papua New Guinea has proved to be the Multistrategy Method that was originally developed as part of the Local Language Literacy movement to reflect traditional Papua New Guinean teaching and learning styles (Stringer, 1988). The Multistrategy Method has as its goal the facilitation of a student-controlled learning process, with demystified and flexible procedures for teaching and materials production. The Multistrategy Method consists of two parallel tracks: the Story Track and the Workbook Track, each with its own separate teacher, lessons, time allotment, approach, and materials.

The Story Track is based on a Whole Language approach (Edelsky, 1991) where students are reading and writing their own stories from the very first day of classes. The Story Track is focused exclusively on reading and writing for meaning. Word attack skills are relegated entirely to the Workbook Track. The Story Track teacher acts as a model and never corrects students, stressing confidence and reading for meaning and enjoyment. All of the Story Track materials are composed and produced by the community or, whenever possible, by the students themselves. The Workbook Track uses a set of purely structurally oriented key word/syllable-based primers, that do not attempt to include any reading or writing for meaning. If a set of primers has already been designed and printed for the local language, these can be easily adapted and used as the Workbook Track primers. The Workbook Track teacher corrects students' mistakes and stresses accuracy.

There is no attempt to integrate the two tracks at the level of instruction. Each day, students participate in a rich variety of Whole Language experiences in the Story Track and are drilled in full range of word attack strategies in the Workbook Track. Students are left in control over the process of integration, putting it all together at their own pace, when they are ready.

The Community Framework: Community-Controlled Programs

Like the Multistrategy Method, the Community Framework was developed as part of the movement for Local Language Literacy in Papua New Guinea and has become an important element in the implementation of critical literacy programs. If a community opts for print literacy, it is expected to plan, finance, and manage its own program. A literacy committee is formed by the community to manage the program. About U.S. $150 must be raised by the community to buy the paper, ink, and silkscreens necessary for the community to write and print all of the local language storybooks and primers that will be used in their classes, as well as other items such as blackboard paint, chalk, and pencils. Communities themselves are responsible for locating a space to hold classes and for payment of teachers. Outside help is only needed for a few days to design a working alphabet and primers, if these are not already available and for a 4-week teacher training/materials production course, held in the village itself.

Critical Literacy, NGOs, and the Papua New Guinea Trust

As the movement for Local Language Literacy developed and more communities began to organize around literacy projects, it became apparent that even this expanded conception of literacy was still inadequate and naive. NGOs from around the country who had used the new framework and methodology to establish successful children's programs attempted to start adult literacy classes, but were finding this much more difficult. Meanwhile, women's organizations and other NGOs involved in programs for social transformation began to respond to a rapidly growing demand for literacy programs by the communities in which they were working.

The Local Language Literacy-oriented NGOs and the social transformation-oriented NGOs began to realize that they both shared a vision of community work as a process of community members taking control over their lives. In 1990, these two groups of NGOs formed a network called the Papua New Guinea Integral Human Development Trust (PNG Trust). The PNG Trust was partly inspired by the Solomon Islands Development Trust, which had been working successfully for social change at the community level in the Solomon Islands since the early 1980s.

The term *Integral Human Development* refers to the type of development that is prescribed for Papua New Guinea both by the National Constitution as well as by the National Philosophy of Education. Integral Human Development explicitly mandates human-centered political, social, economic, and spiritual development and education "for the liberation from all forms of oppression." It was felt that this vision of development was a basis on which an alternative discourse on development could be built for Papua New Guinea, to contest the prevailing Cargo discourse.

Many versions of critical literacy are developing in Papua New Guinea. There has been no attempt to impose a single model, but there is an active attempt to promote communication, dialogue, and exchange among PNG Trust member NGOs, so that one can benefit from the other's ideas and experiences. Some groups are expanding the scope of their work from print literacy to "literacy and awareness." Other groups that have been involved in movements for social change are incorporating print literacy training into their programs as well as using the framework provided by the critical literacy movement to reconceptualize how they might go about working with communities to bring about social transformation.

Community Dialogues

PNG Trust training for critical literacy workers focuses its attention not only on the Multistrategy Method and the Community Framework, but also on the community dialogue process. The PNG Trust trains members of village and settlement communities in the skills and techniques that they need to actively engage themselves in participatory dialogues with their communities around various issues. Teaching and preaching (the Cargo models for educational work) are discouraged at all costs. Instead, workers are trained to ask questions and to encourage community members to discuss and identify their own problems and goals for themselves and to devise their own plans for solving their problems and achieving their goals. These dialogues begin the process of community mobilization and the formulation by the community of its own vision of development. The community's vision of development is seen as a product of its analysis of its own local problems and goals in the context of its analysis of the problems and goals of the larger communities to which it belongs: Papua New Guinea and the world community.

Print literacy is only introduced when and where a community identifies it as an important element in the solution of a community problem or in the achievement of a community goal. The community dialogue process includes traditional forms of community discussion as well as Freirean codifications and questioning techniques. There is no need, however, for a team of literacy workers from outside to go into the community to identify "generative words." The Whole Language component of the Multistrategy Method makes it possible for community viewpoints and voices inspired by the dialogues to be transformed immediately into materials that the community can use to learn to read and write with, from the very first day of print literacy classes. In this way, community members can proceed immediately to Freire's "generative themes" stage, before actually mastering or even opting for print literacy. As much as possible, critical literacy in Papua New Guinea has rejected linear sequencing in favor of an inclusive holistic approach that approximates traditional patterns of organizing human activities.

Critical Literacy Workers and NGO Networks

Community members themselves have the best knowledge of their own problems and goals in life, as well as the greatest capacity to devise and implement equitable and sustainable strategies for solving those problems and for achieving those goals. Unfortunately, community members are often the last people to be consulted about what needs to be done in their communities and how to go about doing it. The PNG Trust training team works in close association with the grassroots NGOs who belong to the PNG Trust network to identify key community members who can be trained to involve their communities in the dialogue process. The PNG Trust trains community members who have an ongoing day-to-day relationship with the people to become critical literacy workers. Most of these critical literacy workers are Pushouts from Grade 6, 8, or 10. The NGO network members of the PNG Trust organize district-level follow-up training workshops to reinforce the skills gained by their critical literacy workers at PNG Trust courses, as well as to adapt these skills to the particularities of local conditions.

Materials for Critical Literacy

The PNG Trust has found that the most effective and well-received critical literacy materials are the ones that the community members design and produce themselves as a result of their discussions during the dialogue process. Locally produced materials allow the people to tell their own story with their own voice. Due to the fact that there is no single unifying national language in Papua New Guinea and because language and culture are inextricably bound together, it is important that critical literacy materials and messages be designed and produced in all of the country's 869 languages. Locally produced materials, designed and written by the people themselves and printed on their own low-cost silkscreen printers are maximally adapted to local cultural and linguistic sensitivities and cost much less than materials printed centrally in a single language.

The great majority of the population is print illiterate, so that it is essential that critical literacy materials and messages be designed for both print literate and print illiterate community members. During PNG Trust courses, participants are trained to facilitate the local writing and printing of literacy books, posters, and leaflets, to encourage the formation of local theater groups, and to work with community members to compose songs and dances. When the equipment is available, participants are also trained to use a set of awareness videos produced in Papua New Guinea and abroad.

CRITICAL LITERACY AND CONTROL

It is impossible to do critical literacy work without being immediately confronted by the question of control. In Papua New Guinea, the ultimate goal of critical literacy movement is to enable people to exert or reclaim control over their lives through the process of critically analyzing the realities that they are living (critical reading) as well as through the process of actively creating those realities (critical writing).

In accordance with Lankshear and Knobel's position (chap. 6, this volume), the critical literacy movement in Papua New Guinea has found that the contradiction around who controls critical literacy is one that cannot be resolved in theory, but it can be struggled with in practice. It is only through that struggle and the lessons learned from it that we can construct critical literacies that have power to transform society. The critical literacy movement in Papua New Guinea therefore adopts a constuctivist theory of knowledge (Lankshear & McLaren, 1993).

All meaningful praxis must be situated within some discourse. Critical literacy workers in Papua New Guinea are constructing alternative discourses for social change within which they can work with communities until such point as the communities themselves are able to deconstruct not only the dominant discourses but also these alternative discourses. The eventual goal is the construction by the communities themselves of their own discourses for the transformation of their own realities.

Critical Literacy and Control: Contested Ground

One of the major potential contributions of critical literacy at the level of praxis is the deconstruction of the literacy worker as "expert" or "professional." It was not until Freire that the locus of power in literacy programs began to shift from literacy professionals from outside of the community to the community members themselves. Freire has, however, been accused of not making this shift as completely as necessary. The internal problems experienced by the Nicaraguan program, for example, can be traced directly to issues of control over curriculum and content (Lankshear & McLaren, 1993). These weaknesses were admitted by Freire himself (Gee, 1992a) and they are understandable given the constraints under which Freire labored at the time. Building on the work of Freire, but incorporating traditional Papua New Guinean conceptions of literacy, praxis, and control, a more thoroughgoing critique of the role of the expert, and a Papua New Guinean version of the whole language approach—new critical literacies are taking shape in Papua New Guinea. As a result, Papua New Guineans are achieving previously unobtainable levels of community control over curriculum, content, teaching, training, and materials writing and production, as well as over the definition of literacy itself.

The NGOs and the communities with whom the PNG Trust works have made it clear that their attitudes will need to be radically different from those of the literacy workers that preceded them. This change in attitudes must be determined by the attitudes and demands of the communities themselves. There is no way to predict before entering a community what will be appropriate. All preconceived notions about how critical literacy should be done need to be critically analyzed and in no way should they be allowed to get in the way of the community taking control over the process. The typical attitudes of experts or professionals are not acceptable, and must be replaced by an unshaking commitment to the establishment between critical literacy workers and the community of relationships of equality, respect, trust, and engagement.

The Contested Ground of Content

Although the goal of critical literacy is community control, the critical literacy worker may not be able to avoid intervening in the community dialogue process, especially at the beginning. Community control has been interpreted by some literacy workers who have attempted to appropriate the movement for critical literacy in Papua New Guinea as an excuse to avoid active engagement in community work. Nothing could be farther from the truth. Working with community members to enable them to identify and solve a particular problem in their lives requires a tremendous amount of work and commitment, much more than that required of community workers who attempt themselves to "solve" the problem on behalf of the community.

The process of critical literacy does not occur in a vacuum. Dominant discourses will hold sway over people's minds wherever these discourses are not consciously and vigorously challenged and deconstructed. If the community are not accustomed to applying this type of critical analysis to dominant discourses, it is the task of the critical literacy worker to encourage this process. Critical literacy workers can stimulate the critical analysis and deconstruction of the Cargo discourse of development and other dominant discourses by juxtaposing to them alternative discourses, such traditional Papua New Guinean discourses on control, land tenure, and so on. This process of juxtaposition is discussed by Gee (see chap. 16, this volume).

Alternative discourses are not introduced to the community as 'the truth' but instead as a different way of looking at things. These alternative discourses are deliberately unfinished and open to community input so that, as much as possible, they pose questions rather than providing answers. Critical literacy workers present alternative discourses in a self-critical way, pointing out their own contradictions and deficiencies. Critical literacy workers must realize that the alternative discourses that they bring to the community reflect their own point of view, their own subjectivities. This helps to ensure that they continue to interact with communities as co-learners, rather than as teachers or preachers.

Communities cannot begin the process of finding solutions to problems until they have identified and understood the causes of these problems. Critical literacies use questioning techniques that can help community members to get to the root causes of their problems and to avoid the tendencies to passively accept problems as the "natural order of things," to mistakenly attribute blame to the wrong agent, or to blame themselves. Because many of the causes of community problems lie outside of the community, it is absolutely essential that critical literacy workers be familiar with global problems, issues, and trends and share these knowledges with community members in the course of the dialogues. There is no community in Papua New Guinea today that remains unaffected by events in the rest of the country and the rest of the world. Papua New Guinean critical literacy workers attempt to engage community members in discussions about models for development, women's issues, the debt crisis, the AIDS epidemic, environmental issues, and so forth. No one of these problems can be fully and meaningfully understood without some preliminary understanding of the others.

The Contested Ground of Methodology

The development of the Multistrategy Method illustrates how both traditional ways as well as a particular relationship of praxis to theory have contributed to the movement for critical literacy in Papua New Guinea. In traditional Papua New Guinean societies, the acquisition by children of skills such as gardening and fishing is mainly done by observation of and participation in the daily activities of their elders. There are, however, certain knowledges that are taught more formally, such as the boundary marks of traditional lands or the knowledges, languages, and songs learned in initiation ceremonies and on other special occasions. On these grounds, it could be said that there is a basis in traditional educational practice for both the observation/participation oriented whole language approach and the more structurally oriented word attack skills approach to learning print literacy.

In practice, many Papua New Guineans come to the print literacy process with existing notions about how literacy should be taught. The influence of the mission and governmental education systems, whose approach has been strongly biased toward word attack skills at the expense of reading and writing for meaning is still quite strong, especially among the members of communities who are likely to become involved in the administration and implementation of community-based literacy programs. A literacy methodology that excludes or trivializes a word attack skills component would not be readily accepted by most communities. Pressure from whole language theorists to do away completely with syllable-based primers has come up against pressure from Papua New Guinean communities to retain them.

As a test of the Multistrategy Method, Stringer and Faraclas (1987) set up three initial literacy classes for three groups of children who spoke the same Papua New Guinean language. Group 1 was taught with a whole language approach, Group 2 with a word attack skills-oriented approach, and Group 3 with a dual (multistrategy) approach. At the end of this experiment, Group 1 could look at the pictures in their books and improvise wonderful stories about them, but they had great difficulty decoding the graphemes on the page. Group 2 students could sound out the words on the page, syllable by syllable, but their reading was mechanical and comprehension was low. Only Group 3 members could both grasp the meanings of the passages and decipher the written code with competence. The most dramatic result from Group 3, however, was their capacity to write creatively. These findings show how a praxis that is controlled by community members themselves and informed by their traditions can help literacy workers to make better choices between the various alternatives made available to them by the methodologists and theorists. Community control can also provide literacy workers with the grounds to reject all of these ready made imported options and with the impetus to create new methodologies and theories.

In the case of the Multistrategy Method, several significant breakthroughs were made that challenged the existing assumptions about pedagogies for literacy. In the first place, the Multistrategy Method resists the pressure to choose sides in the great debate between the proponents of whole language and word attack skills-oriented approaches. It opts instead to give equal weight to both, and expose students to as many elements as possible of both approaches every day, thus attempting to provide a learning situation that is as rich and varied as the traditional one. If critical literacy is to be a community controlled enterprise, theoretical preferences will need to be balanced with community preferences. Critical literacy in Papua New Guinea is not a technicist quest for an ideal pedagogy (see Luke & Freebody, Chap. 10, this volume). It is rather a struggle to develop, together with the community, a set of work practices and styles that will allow community members to take as much control over the critical literacy process as possible.

The constraints of a community-based praxis were instrumental in the development of perhaps the most important theoretical contribution that the Multistrategy Method has made: its novel approach to the integration of reading and writing for meaning with word attack skills. Australian whole language teachers still find it difficult to integrate word attack skills into their teaching routines, even after extensive formal training and with the support of a battery of error analysis techniques and teaching aids designed to identify and solve particular problems experienced by individual students. If Papua New

Guinean communities are to be in control of the processes of teacher selection, training, and payment, it is necessary that the teaching method be demystified and straightforward to the point that an unpaid Grade 6 pushout would be able to master it during a 1-month training course and continue to teach it thereafter with minimal supervision and few if any teaching aids. The Multistrategy Method does just this, by separating the two approaches completely.

If it is not necessary for teachers to integrate the two approaches in the same lessons, the lessons become maximally easy to teach. Confusion is avoided by having separate teachers teach the separate approaches. An indication of the power unleashed by this process at the community level is the fact that over the past 4 years, more literacy programs have been started in Papua New Guinea than in the last 100 years. Thousands of pushouts have been trained to become successful Story Track and Workbook Track teachers in hundreds of critical literacy programs throughout the country, thus providing them with the incentive and opportunity to become productive and respected members of their home communities.

The Contested Ground of Orthography

The traditional role of missionary linguists in the control of the design of orthographies and of the writing and printing of literacy materials is a good example of the practices and attitudes that the critical literacy movement in Papua New Guinea has been struggling against. Many expatriate linguists have so idealized and mystified the process of designing alphabets for previously unwritten languages, that it takes them an average of 1 year just to complete the phonological analysis on which the alphabet will eventually be based. There also have been cases where linguists waste several years more arguing with community members about why the community's notions about how their language should be written do not match the linguist's scientific approaches. The technicist quest for "the perfect alphabet" both denies the community any significant voice in how their language will be written as well as delaying for years any practical action by the community to implement their literacy programs.

In the development of the movement for critical literacy in Papua New Guinea, the process of designing alphabets has been demystified. Now, a critical literacy worker can ascertain the major phonological contours of any language and choose the appropriate graphemes within just a few hours (Faraclas, 1987; Stringer & Faraclas, 1987). All decisions concerning which symbols are to be used are made by the community itself. If one of their decisions is pedagogically unsound, they soon become aware of it because the best test of a new orthography is its use in literacy materials. In any event, areas where an in-depth phonological study is necessary or where a community's preferences clash with a linguist's judgments constitute in almost every case a minute problem, calling into question the use of no more than two or three symbols. Imagine for a moment how much easier life would be for all of us if our orthographic headaches in English were confined to the erratic behavior of only two or three of its letters! As was the case in the area of methodology, an approach based on community control has had revolutionary consequences in the area of orthography design. Over the past 5 years, the critical literacy movement has created alphabets for more than 150 languages in Papua New Guinea, surpassing the number of alphabets created by an army of missionary linguists over the last 100 years.

The Contested Ground of Materials Writing and Production

Because they attempt to integrate some reading for meaning into what is essentially a word attack skills-oriented method, the average time that it takes missionary linguists to devise Gudschinsky style primers for a Papua New Guinean language is 3 to 5 years. The process is totally controlled by the linguists, and so complex as to make it necessary for them to call on the aid of consultants specialized in the task. There is no possibility for community members to take part in the process. All materials are formatted and printed professionally at the mission print shop.

The novel way that the Multistrategy Method treats the question of integration has revolutionized the materials production process, allowing any community to write and print a full set of literacy materials in their own language in a few weeks, with very little input from outside experts. Because the Story Track is completely meaning-oriented and ungraded, any community members who are print literate can compose and produce the stories that constitute the Story Track materials themselves, with a minimal amount of training. Because the Workbook Track is wholly oriented toward word attack skills and there is no attempt to integrate meaningful sentences into the Workbook Track primers, they are relatively easy to design. Papua New Guinean critical literacy workers now can design an alphabet and the full set of four primers for a new language in two days, with the help of a few native speakers.

The opportunities made available by these advances for an increase in community control over the content and production of materials are enormous. For the first time, it has become possible for community members themselves to incorporate their own stories, knowledges, identities, viewpoints, and voices directly and immediately into their literacy materials. Over the past 5 years, PNG Trust critical literacy workers have worked together with communities all over Papua New Guinea to produce full sets of literacy materials for more than 100 languages, proving in the process that local materials production in all 869 languages of Papua New Guinea is not only possible, but more feasible than centralized materials production in one or a few "national" languages.

The Contested Ground of Training

PNG Trust training courses place just as much emphasis on the reasons for doing critical literacy as on the procedures for carrying out critical literacy programs. It is only when people have an understanding not only of how to do something, but also why they are doing it that they can begin to take control over the process. The course content and daily schedule of activities are discussed and determined by the participants at the beginning of the course and renegotiated every morning before work starts. Although the process is a bit slow at the beginning, by the end of most courses the participants have accomplished much more than they would have at any preplanned course directed by experts. It is common for participants to work until after midnight for weeks on end to meet training and materials production goals that they have set for themselves.

The value placed on inclusivity and collective work in many Papua New Guinean societies has had a profound effect on how critical literacy training is carried out. In principle, there is absolutely no "streaming" or "tracking" at any level. Critical literacy trainers, program coordinators, supervisors, community dialogue animators, Story Track teachers, Workbook Track teachers, materials producers, and other critical literacy workers of all sorts attend the same courses. No one is excluded. The question of control is once again crucial here. Critical literacy workers cannot be expected to be able to make independent decisions about their work, unless they are familiar with the effects that these decisions will have on co-workers with different spheres or levels of responsibility. At every course, all of the participants are given the chance to observe and to participate in the training of every category of critical literacy worker as well as in the production of every type of critical literacy material. In this way, every participant has the opportunity to get an overview of the entire process and to attempt to master the skills necessary to control whatever parts of the process she or he chooses. Each local NGO organizes its critical literacy program in a different way, so that each participant is expected by his or her community to learn a slightly different set of skills at any given course.

Critical literacy workers are recycled through the same course as many times as they are willing and able to participate. Most critical literacy workers master the skills necessary to start the community dialogue process, to teach one of the literacy tracks, and to produce critical literacy materials by the end of the first course that they attend. Those who attend the course two or three times usually gain enough skills to supervise critical literacy workers in their districts. Critical literacy workers who attend more courses often become trainers or provincial coordinators. As the pool of critical literacy trainers has grown, the trainers themselves have demanded in-depth training to address the specific problems that they face in the field. In response to these demands, the PNG Trust held its first national courses specifically for critical literacy trainers in 1992.

Contesting the Definition of Literacy Itself

The ultimate contested ground is the notion that print literacy is a necessary component of any critical literacy program. Our experience in Papua New Guinea indicates that it is not. Critical literacy was arguably strongest in Papua New Guinea when print literacy was completely absent and many Melanesian communities are currently relearning to read and write their lives in critical literacy programs, without the aid of print literacy. This does not mean that most communities will not make print literacy an integral part of their critical literacy. Most will. But the way in which print literacy is implemented must not be counterproductive to the ultimate goal of critical literacy: the reclamation by the community and the individuals in it of some control over their destinies.

Modern, Postmodern, and Traditional Discourses of Control

In the modernist universe, the literacy worker is "enlightened" and in possession of the absolute truth. The literacy worker thus has a franchise to exert control, not as an individual, but as a dispenser of Cargo. For absolute truth is the ultimate Cargo: the imported prepackaged solution par excellence. In the postmodern world, there is no absolute truth, and therefore no absolute control. Control thus becomes a very complex local and global phenomenon, from which too many postmodernist literacy theorists seem to have retreated.

But if one seeks to change relations of control, these relations must be confronted head on. To pretend that they do not exist is to endorse the status quo by default. Our tools of confrontation, however, cannot be totalizing, absolute truths about the "nature of things" but instead they must be unabashedly relative, incomplete, and self-critical assertions of discourses that challenge the dominant discourses that (universal or not) presently allow capital to exercise brutal and anonymous control over vast portions of our world.

One of the ironies associated with control is the fact that once we free ourselves from the illusion of absolute control, we begin to reclaim a degree of real control over our lives. When we reject the idea of absolute control, those who exert control over our lives lose control over our minds, for we realize that their power is constrained and vulnerable. At the same time, we can begin to reclaim powers that, following the last round of Enclosures, we had either forgotten about or had given up hope of resuscitating in our lives.

In traditional Papua New Guinean cultures, the control that an individual exercises over her or his life and surroundings is substantial, but it is relative, always balanced by a corresponding degree of community control. Absolute control is not part of the conceptual universe, from religion to science. Although most Papua New Guinean religions include a deity who underlies and permeates creation, there is no paternal, exclusive, and tyrannical Jehovah in the pantheon. Traditional science is not afraid or ashamed of what it cannot fully control or understand. For this fearlessness, it is branded primitive, supernatural, and subjective by Northern science, which presumes itself to be all powerful, omniscient, sophisticated, natural, and objective.

Instead of following the North in its search for streamlined, neatly packaged answers to the problems of life and shunning loose ends and rough edges, Papua New Guineans often consciously cultivate indeterminacy, incompleteness, and "messy" solutions. Although Northerners are constantly struggling to relieve themselves of the ties of obligation and responsibility that bind them to other human beings, Papua New Guineans actively seek out such ties. These differences are not just a peculiarity of the Melanesian "temperament." They highlight major differences between pre-Enclosures and post-Enclosures relationships to control. The average Papua New Guinean has not yet experienced the bite of Enclosures and retains the inalienable control over the considerable surplus that all human beings once enjoyed. For an individual in such a position, relations with other human beings are potentially enriching, rather than threatening or exploitative. There is no great desire to dominate, because a measure of control over resources sufficient to one's survival and happiness has always been guaranteed.

Although it is true that traditionally Papua New Guineans do not seek relationships of dominance, neither do they accept relationships of subservience. By custom, more prosperous community members regularly distribute surplus wealth to the less prosperous. Failure to do so would provoke severe criticism and hostility from the entire community. Just as the enclosures of land are yet to occur in Papua New Guinea, so are the concomitant enclosures of consciousness. In the industrialized countries, people have for centuries accepted as "natural" the "fact" that a few people have tremendous wealth and power, while the majority of people have barely enough to survive. Papua New Guineans are yet to have their sense of justice and equality enclosed to the point that they can be convinced that this is an acceptable state of affairs. Papua New Guineans have not yet been defeated.

In other parts of the world, the landless face scarcity all the days of their lives. Although some of the landless (especially in the industrialized countries) have great illusions of control, they are arguably the most powerless and controlled people on the planet. Control becomes their obsession because most never enjoy enough of it to relax and overcome the basic insecurities resulting from their expropriation. In such an environment the idea that absolute control is possible becomes part of the world view. Human relationships become either threats to one's limited control over one's circumstances or opportunities to gain a bit more control at someone else's expense.

The present contention between the modern and postmodern in Northern academic circles underscores the limitations of science in a culture obsessed with control. Whereas modernists insist on absolute control, postmodernists reject absolutes and control absolutely. Like children who refuse to play a game if they are not allowed to have their way, Northern academicians and scientists must either be in full control over the object of their study or they reject it categorically. Postmodernists are completely justified in criticizing the simplistic absolutist and totalizing tendencies of modernism. But their retreat into extreme relativism and particularism is just as simplistic.

In the science of many indigenous peoples in Papua New Guinea, absolutes are rejected, but the threads of commonality that hold the world together are explored and exploited. Although traditional Papua New Guinean science and epistemology have no problem in coming to terms with a relativistic universe or with the indeterminate and paradoxical behavior of subatomic particles, postmodern theories of knowledge for the first time allow us to begin to come to grips with some of the phenomena that have been described and observed by physicists for more than century. The real advance that this represents for Northern epistemology is evidenced by the revolutions that postmodernism is inspiring within a wide range of disciplines, including literacy theory. Postmodernism will ultimately fail in this enterprise, however, if it continues to reject generality and integrity as vehemently as modernism worshiped them (Lankshear & McLaren, 1993). Here we witness the unending tendency for Northern academia to swing from one extreme to the other; from the illusion of absolute power over the world to the illusion of total powerlessness. Either extreme cedes real control to capital, which proceeds to enclose and to appropriate knowledges and consciousness as it sees fit. If postmodernists continue to drown themselves in a sea of debilitating ultraparticularism, they will be tolerated and used by capital, until the next wave of frustrated intellectuals espouses a revolutionary "neo-modernist" absolutism.

Feminism especially has challenged the basic assumptions on which Northern academia is constructed. The feminist critique of Northern science has in many ways provoked the modern–postmodern conflict. But at present this conflict seems to be irresolvable. Perhaps indigenous peoples' struggles can help to lead us out of this impasse by finishing some of the job that feminism started, that is by liberating us from more of the shackles of an outmoded paradigm that still determines the very manner in which the modernist–postmodernist debate is framed.

POSTSCRIPT: IS TRADITION THE SOLUTION?

There can be no one answer to the questions raised in this chapter. The traditions of indigenous peoples, however, must play an integral part in the construction of viable strategies for the solution of the problems discussed here. Invoking tradition does not mean advocating an about-face return to an idealized past by Papua New Guineans or by any other people on the planet. Tradition is a human creation and must evolve and change constantly if it is to survive. In the critical literacy process, the focus cannot be on traditions themselves, but rather on the role of tradition in the struggles of indigenous and other peoples to maintain and expand control over their lives and destinies in the face of ever expanding control by capital. When tradition is used as an alternative discourse that can be juxtaposed with and used to deconstruct dominant discourses, it is emancipatory. When tradition serves as a foundation for the reclamation, establishment, or consolidation of community control, it is empowering. But when tradition is idealized and appropriated by dominant groups (including literacy workers), it becomes a disciplinary tool for the oppression of indigenous peoples (Nakata, 1993).

Tradition can be seen as the product of thousands of years of struggle. Struggle does not happen in a vacuum, and those who have struggled before us have left us a rich legacy that capital and its Cargo cults have tried to make us reject. Although many modernists and Marxists have been quick to discount the potential of tradition for use as a collective space and a base for struggle and many postmodernists have shied away from tradition as a totalizing concept, capital has taken advantage of every opportunity to appropriate tradition and twist it to its own ends. The enclosure of traditions, land, good jobs, individual power, community control, civil rights, and critical literacies go hand in hand. To deliberately trivialize or avoid the struggle against any one of these enclosures, constitutes nothing short of a betrayal of the struggles against the others.

REFERENCES

Ahai, N., & Faraclas, N. (1993). Rights and expectations in an age of 'debt crisis': Literacy and integral human development in Papua New Guinea. In P. Freebody & A. Welch (Eds.), *Culture and power: International perspectives on literacy policy and practice.* London: Falmer Press.

Edelsky, C. (1991). *With literacy and justice for all.* London: Falmer Press.

Faraclas, N. (1987). Developing or revising alphabets. In S. Malone (Ed.), *Developing Tokples education programs in Papua New Guinea.* Ukarumpa, Papua New Guinea: Summer Institute of Linguistics.

Federici, S. (1992). The debt crisis, Africa, and the new enclosures. In Midnight Notes Collective (Eds.), *Midnight oil: Work, energy, war 1973-1992.* New York: Autonomedia.

Gee, J. P. (1992, February). *Social gravity, discourses, and education.* Paper presented to the Department of Curriculum and Instruction. Louisiana State University, Baton Rouge, LA.

Harvey, D. (1989). *The condition of postmodernity.* Cambridge, UK: Polity Press.

Lankshear, C., & McLaren, P. (1993). Introduction. In C. Lankshear & P. McLaren (Eds.), *Critical literacy: Politics, praxis, and the postmodern.* Albany: State University of New York Press.

Midnight Notes Collective (1992a). The new enclosures. In Midnight Notes Collective (Eds.), *Midnight oil: Work, energy, war 1973-1992.* New York: Autonomedia.

Midnight Notes Collective. (1992b). Oil, guns, and money. In Midnight Notes Collective (Eds.), *Midnight oil: Work, energy, war 1973-1992.* New York: Autonomedia.

Nakata, M. (1993). An Islander's story of struggles for "better" education. *Ngoonjook: Journal of Australian Indigenous Issues, 9*(1), 53-67.

Stringer, M. (1988). Can adults learn to read using the Multi-Strategy Method? *Read Magazine, 23,* 10-18.

Stringer, M., & Faraclas, N. (1987). *Working together for literacy.* Wewak, Papua New Guinea: Christian Books Melanesia.

World Bank. (1965). *Report of the International Bank for Reconstruction and Development mission to the Territory of Papua and New Guinea, 1964.* Washington, DC: Author.

10
Tradition, Colonialism, and Critical Literacy
Response to Nicholas Faraclas

Fazal Rizvi
Monash University

In recent years, it has become something of a cliché to say that we are living through New Times. But clichés have a way of revealing something that is basically true. It is certainly true that recent economic reconfigurations have changed our social and cultural landscapes; that our cultural and political lives are now differently organized; and that new technologies have linked us inextricably to cultural formations that are truly international. At the same time, however, cliches can be misleading. The phrase *New Times*, for example, obscures the importance that most of us continue to attach to our most cherished cultural practices and institutions—our traditions. We want to preserve many of the cultural symbols and customs that make us culturally distinctive—that define our cultural identities.

Lehman and Moore (1992) suggested that for all of us:

> social landscapes are being transformed in a variety of uneven and chaotic ways: commodities and communications offer new possibilities yet threaten indigenous diversities; multilateral agreements may help to dismantle trade barriers yet foster domestic elites; transnational companies fragment production across national boundaries yet intensify relations of dependency. (p. xi)

We live in an era that is characterized by a fundamental contradiction between globalization, nationalization and localization. Responses to this contradiction vary markedly. Some theorists view globalization as inevitable and positive, leading to greater economic growth, secularization and cosmopolitization, representing a desired evolutionary stage. Others argue that the global economic and cultural

173

intervention into national lives is potentially alienating and psychologically degrading, exploitative of national cultures and indigenous social movements.

Faraclas belongs to this latter category of thinkers. In his view, although recent changes in the way global capitalism operates might open up new opportunities for those living in wealthy first-world nations, to the people of the third world it appears simply as another form of colonization. He points out, rightly, that the processes of globalization are not neutral; and that they favor the West (or *the North* as Faraclas calls it in an effort to avoid the ethnocentrism implicit in that term), and in particular, the United States. It is the West that has the power to define the terms of the globalized cultural economies that affect us all. For a country like Papua New Guinea (PNG), globalization effectively represents yet another way in which the power of international capital manifests itself, making its people even more dependent on commodities produced elsewhere. It constitutes a set of New Enclosures with which the cultural and political autonomy of its people is diminished. Owing a large debt to international banking organizations, PNG finds itself unable to access the goods that the global economy makes available to its citizens. Alienation results as Papua New Guineans increasingly lose the capacity to define their own future.

According to Faraclas, new forms of literacies are required in Papua New Guinea to combat the destructive effects of the New Enclosures. His chapter discusses a range of programs in critical literacies that indigenous educators and Nongovernmental Organizations (NGOs) are trialing in the villages where more than 80% of the Papua New Guinea population still lives. Faraclas describes the evolution of these programs, claiming that they have achieved a remarkable degree of success. These programs are based on many of the Freirean principles of participatory research and critical social praxis. Faraclas is of course aware of many of the criticisms that have been leveled against the idea of praxis but insists that the initiatives in Papua New Guinea show that it still has practical relevance. Give praxis a chance is the main message. He suggests moreover that the PNG programs in critical literacy have the potential to make a significant contribution to the "global movement for critical literacy and social transformation."

Faraclas' discussion of the impact of the New Enclosures on Papua New Guinea is both useful and instructive. Never one to mince words, Faraclas remains highly suspicious of the "gleaming ideals of globalism," preferring to refer to their impact on Papua New Guinea as part of a "global wave of recolonization." Also, inappropriate for Faraclas is the politically docile language of postcolonialism, tied as it is to the assumptions of textualism and devoid of political content. He insists that what Papua New Guinea is experiencing cannot be called anything but "a new expression of colonialism," although this time it is not any one nation that has sought to subjugate the people of PNG but a conglomeration of international organizations, such as the World Bank (WB) and the International Monetary Fund (IMF). These organizations have been attempting to expropriate the rights of the indigenous people by insisting on a set of new conditions that define the policy parameters within which the government of Papua New Guinea can pursue radical reform.

According to Faraclas, the New Enclosures are best viewed as a dynamic response by capitalism to recover the ground it had lost to marginalized people, through the successes of the women's and civil rights movements in the first world and the nationalist struggles in the third. Thus, over the past two decades, we have witnessed an unprecedented movement of capital to places where labor is both cheap and unregulated; the promulgation of a market ideology that benefits some more than others; the environmental exploitation of indigenous lands; the development of a language of management that renders people powerless; and the emergence of a borderless media culture the impact of which has been to silence many marginalized and oppressed voices. Each of these developments has served to extend capitalist relations globally, bringing into relief the interconnectedness of the expropriations of indigenous peoples and the McDonaldization of work in postindustrial societies.

Of course, to maintain that the New Enclosures have a global character is not to suggest that they work in the same way everywhere. Faraclas recognizes that in order to understand the manner in which the New Enclosures function in Papua New Guinea, we have to consider the relationship between the global and the local—the universal and the particular. Disappointingly, however, Faraclas does not follow through this advice. In his chapter, the blame for much of Papua New Guinea's current economic difficulty is laid squarely at the feet of the international banks. But in doing this, he risks portraying the activities of the international banks in Papua New Guinea as somehow independent of a whole range of local factors that are also relevant to an understanding of Papua New Guinea's political economy. To overlook these local factors is to present an analysis that is functionalist and unidimensional in that it does not take into account the way the processes of globalization relate to the particulars of Papua New Guinea's colonial history, the problems associated with the constitution of its politics, the organization of its bureaucracy, and the way its cultural diversity has always made it difficult to keep the nation together as a single unified entity.

A major difficulty I have with Faraclas' analysis is that it accepts somewhat uncritically the account of recolonization of the third world provided by *Midnight Notes*, an unreconstructed Marxist account that is, in my view, insufficiently sensitive to historical differences and specificities, and also to the factors that are not reducible to class. Social life in Papua New Guinea is clearly constituted by a number of other dimensions not directly linked to economic issues, and to fail to recognize this simple fact is to exclude the possibility that critical literacy programs might not only be concerned with matters economic but also with matters that are concerned with such issues as gender inequality, regional politics, and cultural diversity in Papua New Guinea.

Faraclas argues that the problems that Papua New Guinea currently confronts can be traced back to the big project loans the Papua New Guinea government accepted in the late 1970s from the international monetary organizations. These loans now have to be repaid, in a climate of ever increasing interest rates and unpredictably fluctuating commodity prices. Unable to service the loans, in 1989, Papua New Guinea was forced to renegotiate its debts that involved among other things accepting a Structural Adjustment Program (SAP). The program has not only meant slashing expenditure on welfare, health and educational programs but it has also created a more regulative state that has had to pass legislations designed to create social conditions more conducive to overseas investment in the country. As part of SAP, a Land Mobilization Program (LMP) has been introduced, which has had the impact of overturning many of the traditional customs that defined the way people related to the land. There has now emerged a new discourse of land ownership, mobilization, and use that is linked to a capitalist notion of "development"—to what critical literacy workers in Papua New Guinea call "the Cargo discourse on development." The Cargo discourse suggests that the Papua New Guineans are not capable of defining what "development" might mean. As Faraclas puts it, the assumption underlying both SAP and LMP is that Papua New Guineans need to be "saved from themselves and their traditions." Thus, for the WB and IMF, the explanation of Papua New Guinea's current economic difficulties lie in the cultural pathologies that are assumed to characterize Papua New Guinea society.

In the main, I concur with this account of the economic difficulties facing Papua New Guinea. However, in my view, it is too general and needs to be articulated with the specificities of Papua New Guinea's colonial history, and to the legacy of this history. It should be remembered that the national entity that we now refer to "Papua New Guinea" is a Western colonial construct. Papua New Guinea was forged into one nation-state out of diverse ethnic groups by the colonial powers that ruled over it before 1975. There are some 1,000 language and tribal groups that still survive in Papua New Guinea. But, as Kulwaum (1994) pointed out, it was colonialism that provided the binding force for these different tribal groups to come together as one nation. With the creation of the colonial state, the smallest groups were made part of a larger unit that had its own structures that cut across the traditional tribal patterns. This was a forced amalgamation; and not surprisingly, therefore, it has not only been pressures from the outside, but also pressures within the nation that have challenged its cohesion and integrity. No account of Papua New Guinea is possible without an adequate treatment of the political pressures created by its diversity. To the people in Papua New Guinea villages, their colonization has many forms; and that colonialism has not come to an end simply because independence has been declared on a construct that was never of their own making in the first place.

It is much too easy to represent the colonized in Papua New Guinea as the passive victims of outside aggression, and colonization as a monolithic hegemonic project. But as Bhabha (1994) argued, an ambivalence lies at the heart of the colonial project: for the colonizer "the other" is at once an object of desire and derision, and as such the colonial discourse is founded on an anxiety. The colonized on the other hand is not entirely powerless, and is indeed sometimes complicit in the project of colonialism itself. Bhabha's insights are valuable in revealing the complexities of the issues in relation to the New Enclosures that the *Midnight Notes* fail to pick up. These insights suggest that the activities of the international banks cannot succeed without the complicity of the new Papua New Guinea Elite that plays a significant role in the nation's public life and enjoy considerable prestige and power. This power articulates with global capitalism in a range of historically specific ways that clearly need to be taken into account in thinking about the possibilities and potential of critical literacy in Papua New Guinea.

The way people in Papua New Guinea villages are subjected to the New Enclosures is thus mediated by the country's political and administrative structures. As part of its colonial inheritance, Papua New Guinea maintains a system of strong centralized government supported by an administrative structure with national and provincial departments which relate to each other in an hierarchical manner. Kulwaum (1994) argued that the attempts to introduce policies of devolution and decentralization have largely been successful because of the reluctance of the Elite—the "big men"—to share power. The manner in which the Elite exercise influence is relevant to an understanding of the way public policies are formulated and the way such policies as devolution are implemented. Many of these big men have played an important role in the construction of Papua New Guinea as a nation-state by being compliant with the colonial authorities, and their power has not diminished. Many of them have been educated in an administrative rationality that bears no resemblance to the traditional ways in which social relations were organized.

Not surprisingly, therefore, the political and administrative Elite finds nothing wrong with the Western concepts of "development," tacitly accepting the basic assumptions of capitalism, which in Papua New Guinea implies the need to establish a flourishing cash economy, replacing the traditional modes of exchange. It is important to note also that the big men have, to a certain extent, replaced the authority once held by the chiefs. They relate to the people in an entirely different way, exercising their power through the new bureaucratic institutions of the administrative state. The authority that the big men enjoy is legal-rational, having become assimilated within the Western system of governance. The traditional authority of the chiefs in relation to stories, customs, moralities, and knowledges has become weakened, relegated increasingly to the status a unrecoverable past.

Yet Faraclas' view of critical literacy is based partly on the premise that these indigenous traditions "must play an integral part in the construction of viable strategies for the solution of the problems discussed above [of recolonization and the New Enclosure]" (chap. 9). It is only in his Postscript that Faraclas acknowledges that traditions are human creations, dynamic, and are constantly changing. In my view, it is this observation that poses the central question that all literacy workers in Papua New Guinea must confront: that is, how should traditions be invoked in constructing a cultural politics that is responsive in a dynamic manner both to the dominant cultural economies, increasingly tied to Western institutions, and to the indigenous cultural practices that still survive?

Recovery of a romantic idealized tradition is neither possible nor desirable. It is not possible because even the most remote villages are subjected to the imperatives of a modern administrative state constituted by a colonial history and to the requirements of a global economy to which every nation is now connected. As new information technologies reach the farthermost points of the globe, they increasingly acquire the power to shape people's interests and aspirations. Nor is the idealization of tradition desirable because, when appropriated by dominant groups, it becomes, as Faraclas points out, a disciplinary tool of oppression.

Spivak (1988) has argued that it is easy for the radical critic of colonialism to be drawn into a nativist position. She suggested that such a position produces the double bind of "considering the 'native' as object for enthusiastic information-retrieval and thus denying its own 'worlding' " (p. 245). If the focus of critical literacy is simply on the recovery of the lost traditions then the risk of nostalgia for a lost or repressed culture is considerable, idealizing:

the possibility of that lost origin being recoverable in all its plenitude without allowing for the fact that the figure of the lost origin, that the "other" that the coloniser has repressed, has itself been constructed in terms of the coloniser's own self-image. (p. 245)

Spivak argued that the nativist position simply reproduces a Western fantasy about its own society onto the lost society of the colonized other. In light of Spivak's argument, the enthusiasm that many NGO officers and expatriate educators in Papua New Guinea display for literacy programs designed to enable the villagers to recover their lost traditions runs the risk of appearing patronizing.

However, these critical remarks should not be taken to suggest that traditions are unimportant in literacy programs. Quite the contrary: they form the basis on which our cultural identities are formed. But the relationship of contemporary cultural politics to the past—to traditions—in Papua New Guinea, as elsewhere, is complex. Such a relationship cannot be simple; or unmediated either by the experiences of colonialism or by the global cultural economies that shape our practical options. As Hall (1992) puts it, there is:

no simple "return" or "recovery" of the ancestral past which is not re-experienced through the categories of the present: no base for critical enunciation in a simple reproduction of traditional forms which are not transformed by the technologies and the identities of the present. (p. 258)

Of course, literacy workers must teach their students to honor their traditions but in ways that are both critical and creative. The students must be encouraged to develop skills that help them to make sound judgments on which of the traditions and which of the new knowledges are relevant to the solutions to their practical and political problems. Programs in critical literacy must not assume a simple dichotomy between resistance and accommodation, but must work creatively through those aspects of the dominant cultures that need to be resisted and those to which accommodation is necessary. They must aim for the development of not only cultural and aesthetic sensitivities but also social criticism, critical imagination, and political creativity.

REFERENCES

Bhabha, H. (1994). *The location of culture*. London: Routledge.

Hall, S. (1992). New ethnicities. In J. Donald & A. Rattansi (Eds.), *"Race," culture and difference*. London: Sage

Kulwaum, G. (1994). *Problems of devolution in PNG educational administration.* Paper presented at the Graduate School of Education, The University of Queensland, Brisbane.

Lehman, C., & Moore, C. (Eds.). (1992). *Multinational culture: Social impact of global economy.* Westport, CT.: Greenwood Press.

Spivak, G. C. (1988). *In other worlds: Essays in cultural politics.* London: Routledge.

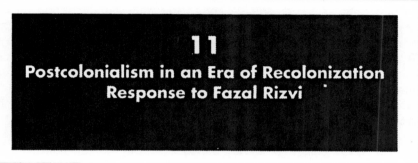

11

Postcolonialism in an Era of Recolonization
Response to Fazal Rizvi

Nicholas Faraclas
University of Papua New Guinea

In a world where the limited sovereignty that the colonized nations of the South won at independence has been appropriated, reconstructed, and deployed by international capital, principally through such agents as local Elites, the World Bank, the International Monetary Fund, and the World Trade Organization/General Agreement on Tariff and Trade, to speak of postcolonialism is meaningless. For this and other reasons, I heartily agree with Rizvi that "to the people in Papua New Guinea villages, their colonialism has many forms; and that colonialism has not come to an end simply because independence has been declared on a construct that was never of their own making in the first place."

Although this mode of operation has been modified somewhat, the basic aims of colonialism remain the same and the power relationships deployed and exploited by the colonial enterprise are still intact and propagating themselves ever more widely and deeply into the lives of everyone on the planet. The contradictions between globalization and localization that Rizvi identifies as characteristic of the times in which we are living may be an important one, but it still has not replaced the more fundamental and persistent contradiction that centers around the question: "Who will control our lives, our bodies, our minds, our land, and our labor?"

Because they have at worst tended to negotiate away the existence of this fundamental contradiction and at best distracted attention from it, discourses of postcolonialism and globalism have for the most part represented an impediment to the exploration of the power relations that underlie colonialism as well as a hindrance to the eventual transformation or eradication of those relations. I am surprised that after reading my contribution to this volume (especially the passages regarding global recomposition of the working classes) Rizvi has drawn the conclusion that I am anti-globalist (and therefore "pro-localist"?) or that I somehow harbor an attachment to the nation state! In any case, I believe that the more important question is: On whose terms and in whose interests will any globalization or localization take place? What in fact has emerged thus far from community level praxis around such questions in Papua New Guinea has been a rejection of binary choices such as "globalization versus localization" in favor of much more creative solutions that simultaneously involve elements of the global and the local.

Rizvi is troubled that I might be portraying Papua New Guineans as "passive victims" of colonization. To the contrary, the critical literacy project in Papua New Guinea has as its primary goal the recognition, celebration, and cultivation of the countless ways the Papua New Guineans have successfully maintained their posture as historical agents and retained control over their land, labor, and lives. The Enlightenment Project not only enclosed the land of the North, it also enclosed the Northern mind in such a way that it tends to think of the binary choices that capital presents to it as the *only possible choices*. Because the land, the labor, and the consciousness of Papua New Guineans are yet to be completely enclosed, I contend that traditional systems for analyzing and solving problems represent a solid foundation for the construction of new ways of creating meaning and acting on it that do not limit us to binary choices, but instead open us up to the infinity of possible choices available to us in any given situation. In response to this, Rizvi warns of a "patronizing" search for the "recovery of a romantic idealized tradition." But in Papua New Guinea unenclosed ways of understanding and acting in the world are not some figment of a romantic imagination. They are still very much a part of day-to-day life.

Contrary to the stereotypical Enlightenment view of tradition as backward and stagnant, tradition in Papua New Guinea is an extremely mutable, adaptable, and creative instrument that has proved to be incredibly open to influences and innovations from outside of the community whose needs it was developed to serve. Rizvi must certainly realize that colonialism is not the only force that has bound the peoples of Papua New Guinea together. The peoples of Papua New Guinea had extensive contacts with one another long before the period of colonization. For thousands of years, Melanesians have exchanged goods, dances, songs, marriage partners, gods, languages, and technologies over distances that stretch far beyond the present day borders of Papua New Guinea. It can be easily shown that Northern or Northern-influenced governments, churches, schools, languages, technologies (including communications technologies), and companies have done more to divide Papua New Guineans (Catholic vs. "mainstream" Protestant vs. Fundamentalist, Elites vs. "grassroots", "literate" vs. "illiterate," Papua New Guinean vs. West Papuan, rich vs. poor, English-speaking vs. "uneducated," "on line" vs. "snail mail" vs. "inaccessible,"etc.) than to unite them.

It can also be argued that the Enlightenment conception of progress and science, economics, and social practices that underpin it rely on the most conservative, conformist, fossilized, and repressive set of beliefs ever inflicted on our species. For the past few centuries, the world has been told that liberal or neo-liberal economics, Newtonian–Cartesian science, the nuclear family, and vast inequalities in power and wealth are the "natural order of things." But millions of years of human existence on the Earth without these "natural" disasters and the living evidence of 869 indigenous sciences, economies, and social systems in Papua New Guinea that have not yet been swept away by the Enlightenment tidal wave show that we do not have to accept the choices that capital makes available to us as the only choices and in fact, the choices and possibilities are infinite.

Rizvi is troubled by the fact that I invoke the work of the Midnight Notes Collective, which he characterizes as a group of "unreconstructed Marxists" and that in reducing the scope for political action to the "simple dichotomy" of resistance/accommodation, I discount the possibility of accommodation at any level. Given the critique of Marx put forward by myself and in the passages from Midnight Notes that I quoted in my contribution to this volume, I can only be amazed by the knee-jerk anti-Marxism that has infected post-ist academic discourse. If Rizvi would examine my work and the source materials more closely, he would find that I and my Midnight Notes colleagues, rather than being fixated on either resistance or accommodation as the only possible ways forward, have spent the past years rejecting the binary choice between resistance and accommodation. Capital may prefer accommodation, but it can deal with and even thrive on many forms of resistance, too. The only thing that capital cannot sanction is its loss of control over minds, bodies, land, and labor. Whether people resist, accommodate, or do something else is a secondary matter. What is important is that we get beyond resistance/accommodation to begin addressing the question that this and the other binarisms constructed by capital so effectively silence: Who will decide that accommodation, resistance, both, or neither is the way forward and in whose interest will this decision be made?

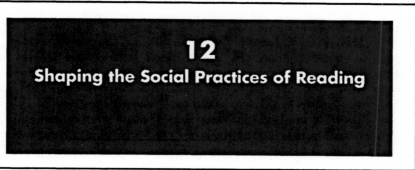

12
Shaping the Social Practices of Reading

Allan Luke
University of Queensland
Peter Freebody
Griffith University

READING AND COLONIZATION

What is the nature of reading? What are its social functions and effects?
How is it learned? And how is it best taught? These questions have been
at the center of continuous and often acrimonious debate in many
countries over the last 100 years, at least since the commencement of
legally mandated state schooling. In this chapter we explore the
development of current answers to these questions. We argue that
reading is a social practice using written text as a means for the
construction and reconstruction of statements, messages, and meanings.
Reading is actually "done" in the public and private spaces of everyday
community, occupational and academic institutions. Reading is tied up
in the politics and power relations of everyday life in literate cultures.

To begin, we consider the reading materials that were used in
previous eras. Most children attending school in the 19th century in
Australia, for instance, were taught with materials such as the Royal
Readers. These largely contained short pieces of literature and "moral
tales" that were British in origin, but that often depicted aspects of life in
the colonies with a strongly European version of everyday culture and
morality. As in England, Canada, the United States, and other English-
speaking countries, such introductory reading materials were meant to
afford the learning of the alphabet, the rehearsal and practice of
sound–letter correspondences, and the recitation of key words to be

learned eventually by sight. The programs progressed typically toward the oral reading of poetry and short literary stories. The writing associated with these readers consisted principally of the copying of words and sentences through dictation. A sample from the Royal Readers is shown in figure 10.1.

This is an illustration of the kinds of lessons for which the readers were tailor-made. The lessons begin with review lessons from previous stories, rehearsals of syllables, and of the writing of words that may be taken to be rare and, as we would now define them, literary uses of English. The story is also preceded by some indications of key and possibly difficult terms in the story with a guide to their meaning and pronunciation. In considering the story itself it is informative to keep in mind that these colonialist narratives were for young Australian readers. As an instance of the cultural location of this story, it is left implicit in the first sentence which country is being referred to in the term *our country*. The story goes on to talk about England and about the production of tea in Chinese villages. Clearly, the cultural center of the passage is England; and the depiction of Chinese tea production, ostensibly for information on life in a colonial diaspora, is presented from a Eurocentric view that might now be considered quaint. The inclusion of the picture demonstrates the exoticism with which the piece is meant to be affiliated.

The central question that this chapter deals with is "What kinds of readers are and can be produced by contemporary reading materials and the lessons for which they are purpose-built?" In colonial education, the goal of literacy education was the successful introduction of the student into a canon of classical English literature. In fact, this goal was achieved only for a minority of predominantly urban middle-class or affluent children who progressed through a grammar school education and then on to professional, business, or government positions. This progress was achieved at the highest levels largely by men. Females who demonstrated capabilities at school were generally excluded from university training for most of the 19th century and were often streamed into various forms of education where they might have been trained to be teachers, governesses, or "gentlewomen."

The literacy education that was available in the 19th century and the early part of the 20th century was based on a two-stage model: "the basics," entailing word recognition, hand writing, spelling, and reading aloud, followed by "the classics," entailing exposure to a canon of valued literature. These versions of reading education related directly and sequentially to the production of two kinds of literate students: One group who managed the first stage of reading development, and the other group who managed both stages. This was regarded as legitimate, did she get her answer? What were Jim's last words? What did his father do when he came in? What did both father and mother then do?

PRONOUNCE in syllables:—

cot-tage	col-lier	an'-swer	ut'-tered	coup-le
ev-er-y-thing	hur-ry-ing	trem-bling	nei'-ther	up-lift-ed
storm-y	pray-er	dy-ing	hum-bly	an-gels

WRITE:—

patient   *uttered*   *couple*
moisten   *neither*   *stricken*
hurrying   *trembling*   *quivering*

THE TEA-FARMER.

Bam-boo', the stem of a tall, strong reed | Mer-chant, one who buys and sells.
Coins, pieces of stamped metal, money. | Plen-ti-ful-ly, in great abundance.
Mead, a sweet kind of wine, made of | Strewed, spread, or scattered loosely.
honey and water. | Tank-ard, a large drinking-can.

ONCE upon a time there was no tea at all in our country. In England, in the olden time, people used to drink ale, and a sweet kind of wine called mead.' Great tankards' of ale stood on the breakfast table. Now we use tea and coffee.

When tea was first brought to England, an old man and woman had some sent to them as a great treat. But when they got it, they did not know how it ought to be used. At length they boiled the leaves, and strewed' them on a piece of bacon which they were going to have for dinner. They ate the leaves, and threw the tea away!

In those days, a pound of tea cost so much money that only the rich could buy it. Now it is so cheap that even the poorest can enjoy it.

Tea is the leaf of a plant which grows plentifully' in China, Japan, and other Eastern lands. The

Chinese drink their tea without either milk or sugar. Whenever a visitor comes into a house, a servant always brings him a cup of tea.

Every cottager in China has his little tea-garden. He sells what he does not use, and can thus buy food and clothing for his family.

When a man has a large piece of ground, and grows a great many tea-plants, he is called a tea-farmer. When the tea-leaves are ready to be gathered, the farmer and his family are very busy. They pull off the leaves and throw them into baskets. When the baskets are full, they are carried into the house. The leaves are dried in iron pans over a fire. While they are drying, men and women keep turn-

Figure 12.1. Text from The Royal Readers: No. 3 (1883). Edinburgh: T. Nelson and Sons, pp. 12-13

and patterns of differential school success and failure between urban and rural students or, in Australia between Anglo Protestant and Irish Catholic students, for example, were not viewed by educational authorities or by the community at large as principally educational problems. In light of Australia's cultural composition, these differentials were even less visible and problematic to educational administration of the day. The substantial Aboriginal, Islander, and Asian populations that existed in Australia in the 19th century were effectively not even recognized as Australian citizens, let alone legally entitled to state schooling, and least of all entitled to successful school achievement.

In this way, reading instruction was exclusionary both in practice and content. As this sample narrative indicates, instruction involved colonialist literature par excellance, setting out who and what was to count as diasporic, exotic, and indeed Oriental in relation to a European cultural and textual center. The act of reading was crucial to the reproduction of allegiance to and legitimation of the center.

The basics plus classics model of literacy education began to change with certain demographic and socioeconomic developments in the first quarter of the 20th century. These changes were contemporaneous with the impact of educational psychology on educational practice, a move that began in the United States and spread across Western countries. Educators there debated the question of the optimal ages of "readiness" for reading and how best to teach reading. One critical move at this point was the de-emphasis of oral reading practices and their replacement by methods that stressed silent reading and the individuated experience of the reader. Another important development was the gradual replacement of versions of Protestant moralistic reading materials such as those exemplified by what were considered to be more scientifically based materials and curriculum methods. In Australia, for example, the last remnant of the colonial basal reader, the Queensland Readers (a direct relative of the Royal Readers), was replaced as late as the 1950s by Dick-and-Jane-style standardized reading materials. Stories of idyllic postwar suburban life came, with comparative rapidity, to replace the moral tales, informational tracts about various forms of citizenship, and explicitly moralist poems in this period. Word recognition, sound–letter correspondences, and spelling were still addressed in these materials, but they were addressed in ways that were at least designed to be incremental and systematic. More importantly, the content of the material began to be less explicitly about colonial moralities and more evidently about everyday "western" suburban and urban experience and citizenship, as it was defined through standardized curriculum packages.

So reading had come to be seen primarily as a set of skills that were transportable and were developed within an apparently value-neutral pedagogical and curriculum environment. These skills were taken to be transportable from context to context as part of the moral, psychological, and economic capital of the citizen of an industrialized urban culture. No longer was the primary definition of reading concerned centrally with moral and citizenship training that was fitted to a Eurocentric view of cultural experience. What was now taken to be of primary interest and significance with respect to reading was a matter of psychology and not a matter of morality or citizenship. The reader came to be seen not primarily as a citizen with normative responsibilities, but as a psychological entity with a set of (nonetheless normative and "western") mental capabilities.

This is a reader not well fitted to a rural economic or colonial experience but rather to a more urban industrialized experience, and an experience by which the standardization of apparently everyday suburban life is the core of what would emerge later as a globalized set of cultural patterns. The new mythical heroes of the reading schemes, Dick, Dora, Peter, Jane, Nip, and Fluff, were the artifacts of inter- and postwar Western cultures: They were gendered and covertly (by exclusion) racialized identities constructed through optimistic narratives of urbanization, industrialization, and democratization (A. Luke, 1988).

Since the 1960s, debates among reading educators have been concerned with the movement away from skills-based approaches toward what have been described as experiential or "whole language" approaches. This is paralleled by a shift in educational psychology from behaviorist models of reading, as the connections between stimuluses and responses, to those founded on more humanistic and cognitive models of reading as ways of processing information or ways of accessing and practicing deep linguistic structures. In secondary English education, this shift has been matched by a move from a more strictly canonical model of the literary heritage, with the reader being enculturated to the great classics of literature, toward a model of reading that has stressed personal, genuine, and emotional responses to literary works. What became canonical were ways of showing motivation to be a reader and particular displays of "authenticity," "voice," and "response."

Another way of considering this shift is to view it as a movement away from an emphasis on the code patterns of written English, that is, sound–letter correspondences and individual word meanings, toward a concern with reading as the construction of meaning in the internal cognitive space of the reader. What this has meant in many classrooms is that there has been a shift away from the passive reception of information and skills as the core of the reading classroom experience toward an apparently more active and oral construction of ideas that relate to a text, and pedagogies that aim to develop the individual's meaning making capabilities through talk, and to allow the individual to respond to works of literature at a personal level. These pedagogies, which have been termed *progressivist*, have emphasized immersion in language and print materials, the need for instruction to center always on the meaning of texts and on readers' responses to literature, and the appropriateness of more qualitative and observation-based assessment procedures. It is notable that direct instruction in the code aspects of reading has often been relegated to readers who appear to be demonstrating "special needs" and to the introduction of more specialized content-area discipline texts in the upper primary and secondary years.

Research programs in psycholinguistics and cognitive psychology developed partly in support of these pedagogical developments have in turn themselves come to be used retrospectively as support for those research initiatives. This attendant theoretical, empirical, and pedagogical work defined and enacted reading as an orchestrated set of psychological processes, highlighting internal mental operations acquired in childhood and later transferred to applications across various educational, community, and occupational contexts (Stanovich, 1991). Furthermore, many psychological models tended to view the contents of the texts students read as either not pertinent to learning reading, ideologically neutral, or benign, in the same way as the more traditional skills-based pedagogies and materials common earlier in this century neutralized the content and the pedagogies of reading.

The ascendancy of an emphasis on personal response to literature was in part a product of the liberalization of public life in Western countries that began very visibly in the late 1960s. Across many counties, this liberalization found its way into reading lessons in the form of child-centered progressivist pedagogy and alternative models of education. In Australia, for example, the 1970s witnessed an apparent globalization of culture through television popular culture, coverage of the Vietnam War, continued and expanded immigration programs, and other social and technical developments that generated a more outward looking cultural and economic orientation. Although the movement from traditional, skills-based pedagogies and materials toward these progressivist ways of teaching was surrounded by often heated and lengthy debates, it is constructive to consider the ways in which both of these approaches entail comparable assumptions about the nature of reading, what is and is not to be read, and how reading is best learned and taught. Unlike the oral reading emphasis of 19th-century programs, both skills-based and meaning-based pedagogies view the activity of reading as essentially an internal, individual, and silent practice. Both view the key processes for acquisition to be portable and to be associated with individual ownership. Both foreground and, in an important sense, culturally isolate the individual, and can be viewed as an articulation of the rise of a self-interested individual as the central platform for effective action in late capitalist society (Apple, 1982). So we can view developments from the early part of this century to the present time in reading education as being directly associated with the construction of a particular kind of worker and community member, a citizen whose moral, economic, and political interests were essentially focused on the self, and whose capabilities were resolutely defined as individual possessions.

Many readers of this book, particularly those who have lived through these periods, will cite different accounts of the historical developments that we have sketched above. Ours is clearly an interpretation located in our historical place and time, and these changes have been inflected in different ways in different countries, states, and schools. Nonetheless it is arguable that remnants from all of these models are sustained in most contemporary classrooms and lessons.

However we tell this story, and however the story may vary across nation-states and communities, the means and practices of reading have changed significantly in important ways in relation to cultural, economic, and social developments. Models of reading have been based on models of the social order and how the literate person can and should fit into that order. Ways of reading are not neutral but are indeed correlated with issues of identity and cultural and political power, access to capital, and contemporary configurations of gender, ethnicity, class, and citizenship in late-capitalist societies. One question we can now ask is: What are the models of reading currently practiced and enacted in primary and secondary schools? The question to which that leads is: How well are these models suited to the demands and imperatives of citizenship in postmodern conditions and fast-capitalist contexts.

Recently, a distinctive approach to reading pedagogy has emerged that defines reading as a critical social practice. It draws variously from critical language studies (e.g., Gee, 1996; Halliday & Martin, 1993), educational sociology (e.g., Baker & Luke, 1991), social anthropology and ethnography (e.g., Street, 1984, 1995), feminisms (e.g., Lee, 1996; Luke & Gore, 1994) and poststructuralism (e.g., Kamler, 1994; Lemke, 1995). This diverse corpus of work begins from two related assumptions: First, reading practices that are developed in schooling contexts constitute selections of practices, and these selections are not accidental, random, or idiosyncratic. Rather they are supportive of the organizational needs of the institutions of schooling and the stratified interests within social organizations. So it should not be surprising that a good deal of institutional effort is put into making these materials and activities appear "natural" and "essential" characteristics of literacy. In that sense at least, literacy education and research about it can be viewed as "political," in that each entails choices among theories and methodologies that afford or reinforce radically differing competencies and ways of engaging in social experience, all of which have significant material consequences for learners, communities, and institutions. In another sense, the materials and interactive practices of reading education are best seen as key sites where cultural discourses, political ideologies and economic interests are transmitted, transformed, and can be contested.

The exercise of cultural and political regulation has always been implicated in research and practice in reading education just as surely as in those fields we might consider explicitly political—minority education, the economics of education, or comparative education—even if that implication has not been acknowledged by researchers who study how, why, and what people read and write (Edelsky, 1996). If for no other reason, in an era of postcolonialism and global capitalism, marginalized, minority, and indigenous communities have an urgent stake in the nature and efficacy of literacy education efforts, and, importantly, in the dominant theories and methodologies used to legitimate those efforts. The decisions facing teachers of reading are decisions about how and to what end they should shape literacy in contemporary fast-capitalist culture, and how and to what end they can influence the development of literate citizens and workers.

READING AND SOCIAL EPISTEMOLOGIES

The core shift represented by this family of approaches is in the redefinition of reading toward the view that it is about engaging with, transforming, and critiquing a particular culture or subculture's ways of seeing the world, its ways of valuing, weighing, and understanding the world. This approach challenges both traditional and progressivist approaches not only in their claims for effective teaching. It is based on assumptions about a series of contrasts and relationships: between oral and written language; between personal and cultural resources; between mind and society; and among the various ideological practices of schooling outlined earlier in this chapter. Furthermore, it holds contrasting implications about what teachers can and need to know to be effective teachers of literacy practices. We can make a beginning list of core propositions that distinguish critical approaches to literacy education.

1. Reading and writing are social activities. That is, we are always reading something written by someone or writing something for someone. These others are always in some relationship to us—often materially and symbolically unequal relationships of power but always relationships in which versions of "ourselves" and "others" are implicated and constructed. Even those texts we read or write that come from or are intended for people we do not know assemble versions of our identities and positions as readers—as men and women, students and teachers, taxpayers and newspaper readers, and so forth. These versions of our identities we can think of as the reading and writing positions that are available to us in various circumstances as readers and writers. When we adopt these, or try to, we call upon resources that we are not born with - they are cultural products. We learn and practice them as natural, even though we may not feel that we explicitly know much about them. Our lack of explicit knowledge about them is a direct reflection of the ideological work achieved through our histories as readers.

2. All texts are motivated—there is no neutral position from which a text can be read or written. All language, all text, all discourse thus "refracts" the world; bending, shaping, constructing particular versions and visions of the social and natural world that act in the interests of particular class, gender, and cultural groups (Voloshinov, 1986). Both discipline-based and common sense knowledge are recontextualized in and by schooling. Schools, as social organizations, are premised on certain notions of orderliness, regulation, and surveillance, and these are constitutive of ways of knowing. These particular ways of knowing and their attendant contrasting forms of capabilities are not equally or randomly distributed by schools, but are constructed and distributed as part of a social division of textual work and discourse.

    Literacy practices are primarily courses of social action, so a key question is "What form of 'the capable literate citizen' is afforded by our literacy pedagogies, materials, policies?" Much of the important work that is accomplished or attempted in a society is conducted with or at least with the help of written texts. On the surface, some of that work is about informing us, and some of it is about persuading, regulating, or controlling us. As well, some of it is potentially about offering ways of resisting persuasion, regulation, or control.

3. We learn about appropriate reading and writing positions within the relationships that take responsibility for our

learning—often parents, teachers, perhaps the media, and certainly the writers of the texts we learn to read with, and the readers of the texts we write. Therefore, it may well be a mixed blessing for a person or a community to become readers. To start with, many of the texts that accomplish important work in a society may not be written in the same language, dialect, or style of communication that is used by many of the members of a particular community. Consider the varieties of English spoken in the country in which we live, and as well of the comparatively narrow range of acceptability of public, political, educational, and civil service language use. It is clearly the case in countries with many languages that the choice of which of those languages is used in schools and for literacy education is partly political—serving the interests of some groups against those of other groups. However, equating nationhood and nationality with monolingualism is empirically and culturally untenable, an artefact of the imperialist equation of nation with single language and race. In this context, ideas about literacy and literacy education are always subject to contestation. This is particularly the case where the learning and display of official reading or writing positions requires that student to "write over" her or his fundamental ways of communicating in the world with the ways of others, disguised as Standard or Official or Literate Language.

At the same time, many of the texts that accomplish important work in a culture may not be based on the unstated systems of ideas or beliefs shared by a person or community within that society. So, to adopt officially recognized reading or writing positions may require that a person write over his or her fundamental ways of thinking about the world, while dominant ideology and practice may be disguised as Common-Sense or Scientific Thinking or Reasoned Logic or even Morality.

4. Institutionally purpose-built repertoires of "selves" are represented to us either explicitly or otherwise in all of the texts we read and write. In these ways, various identities are textually connected to cultural and political interests. However, the institutional structuring of literacy education described here tends toward homogenizing significant differences; and this "writing over" leads to the re-production of the unequal material and symbolic conditions that formed literacy-for-school in the first place.

So the contemporary literate nation-state is a place where dynamic interests and positions are at work to shape the distribution of material wealth, symbolic values, and textual resources. Reading practices are implicated not only in competition for jobs and wealth, but also in contestation over symbols, images, and texts. These fundamentally entail disputes over the kinds of consciousness and identity produced by differing reading and writing programs. Our point here is that the teaching of reading is in fact the teaching of cultural ways of looking, describing, and explaining (Gee, 1996), and ways of knowing what is so preconditional to a reading activity that it does not attract notice, description, or explanation. In this respect, the teaching of reading is a way of enculturating people into the significance of "skills" or "reader responses" or "cognitive processes" or "love of quality literature." It is important to note that the perspective outlined here asserts that these glosses are the products rather than the means or motivations of some kind of culturally neutral or technical activity called *reading education.* However noticed, they constitute selective traditions of consciousness, serving particular interests and groups within societies, and they build up and service particular versions of the social, cultural, and moral order.

In this light, the question of how we should teach reading becomes more than determining the best or latest "state of the art" way of transmitting reading "skills" or "abilities." There is no such thing as reading per se. One never just (generically) reads. Readers always read something, a textual representation, and readers always take up an epistemological standpoint, stance, and relationship to the values and ideologies, discourses and world views in the text. Teaching involves making decisions about how and in which directions to shape a social practice and students' social identities as readers and writers in a literate culture. Teaching, then, requires an understanding of how those resources and practices that children bring to classrooms are cultural resources, and not idiosyncratic individual differences, learning styles, skill deficits, or innate abilities. The critical consequence here is that these cultural resources, including forms of consciousness, are connected to and transformed by political and economic outcomes, ranging from access to jobs and further training and education, to religious and political participation.

CROSS-CULTURAL AND HISTORICAL EXAMPLES OF READING

Different cultures and subcultures frame up who, what, and when people read for particular social purposes. In contemporary Islamic cultures, reading in Classical Arabic consists of learning and reciting from memory long passage of the Koran, the sacred book. There reading is a gendered practice, principally undertaken by men. Furthermore, there is little "lay" debate over meaning. In the West African tribal culture of the Vai, reading in Vai is not learned until young adulthood, it is taught by tribal elders (Scribner & Cole, 1981). Only certain text types are read and written in Vai: specifically mercantile and personal transactions. In many South Pacific cultures, reading is tied up closely with religious practice propagated by Missionaries, and it entails reading hymns, scripture, and praises and learning to discuss in groups the meaning and significance of scriptures (Mangubhai, 1987). In contemporary religious school training, differing religious denominations—whether Protestants or Catholics, Amish or Adventists—train youth in the kinds of interpretations and talk around scriptural text that are required for membership in a church (Kapitzke, 1995).

In bilingual and multilingual communities, reading and writing in different languages is also used for distinctive social purposes. For instance, in contemporary Navajo community life in the U.S. southwest, writing in Navajo is used for religious purposes, personal letters and notes, ceremonial journals, and for school signs, diplomas, and graffiti (McLaughlin, 1989). School letters, notes, and diaries are written bilingually in both English and Navajo, with English-only writing becoming more significant in secondary schools. The formal teaching of Navajo literacy is a relatively recent "invention," introduced through bilingual and English-as-a-Second Language (ESL) programs in the 1960s. But, McLaughlin (1989) argued, it has flourished and expanded in various areas of everyday life, as part of a larger agenda for Navajo political control and cultural power within and over institutions. Which literacies are used thus is tied closely to how social and cultural identity is shaped, and to how economic and political power is established and distributed in institutions.

Similar issues have arisen in Aboriginal communities in the Northern Territory, where new domains of reading and writing in Australian languages have developed as a result of early and mid-century missionary translations and education, and more recent bilingual education programs and publishing projects in state schools (Walton, 1993). The issues that arise are complex when vernacular languages like Burada or Walpiri are written down and brought into schools as languages of instruction, recast to the purposes and methods of schooling. In communities in the Central Desert and Arnhem Land, fluency in writing in more than one language and fluency in two or three spoken languages are common. As in Navajo, Vai, and other multilingual communities, who reads and writes which languages, in which domains are matters tied directly to the balance of power, gender, culture, and age relations in communities, and to issues of the balance of power and knowledge between Aboriginal peoples and mainstream White Australians. At the same time, the melding and blending of cultures, languages, and literacies has produced new hybrid cultural forms (e.g., bilingual blues rock music written by Maningrida's Sunriz Band in Burada; dot paintings that meld western and Aboriginal motifs produced in the community of Utopia) and indeed new relations of power between political elements in communities.

These cases illustrate how different cultures and communities prescribe and direct who can read, what texts people can read, how reading should occur, when, where and under what institutional conditions and controls people should read and should learn to read, and, significantly, what reading entails practically for different categories of persons. We exemplify these cultural constraints and how they are tied to larger political imperatives in the sections to follow here.

WHO CAN READ?

We can start by asking an apparently simple question about reading: How many adults in the world do not yet "have" reading? Where are these people, and why might they not yet have been successfully encultured as readers? Table 12.1 shows the numbers of illiterate people in various parts of the world, as assembled by UNESCO in 1990, and including UNESCO's predictions for the next 5 years (cf. Freebody, 1995). To be classified as *illiterate* and a *nonreader* by UNESCO's definition, the person

Table 12.1. Estimated Nonreaders among Adults (15 Years and Over) in Millions.

	1985	1990	2000 (predicted)
World total	965	963	942
"Developing" countries (total)	908	920	919
Sub-Saharan Africa	134	139	141
Arab States	58	61	66
Latin America/Caribbean	44	44	41
Eastern Asia	297	281	234
Southern Asia	374	397	437
"Developed" countries (total)	57	42	24

Source. UNESCO Office of Statistics (1990) Compendium of statistics on illiteracy. Paris: UNESCO.

showed no beginning knowledge of how to read in the written script of his or her community or the official script and language of their country. We pick up in later discussion the methodological problem of "naming the illiterate" in survey research such as this.

In the context of mass international and national campaigns for schooling and literacy in many parts of the world, there are large numbers of people who appear to have had no exposure to or no opportunity to develop capabilities in reading. Even in those countries that are more fully industrialized and that have had at least three generations of compulsory mass schooling, *illiteracy* is a label that is still applicable to large numbers of people.

But even though there are apparently more people in the year 2000 predicted to be without exposure to reading practices in sub-Saharan Africa, the Arab states, and Southern Asia, for example, the estimated population growth rates are such that those people will represent a smaller proportion of the population of those regions. That is, the numbers of people shown in Table 12.1 should not deflect our attention away from the enormous progress of reading education in proportional terms. Achieving 12% increased access to basic reading skills by the year 2000 in Southern Asia, for instance, would represent a significant educational effort by institutions and communities, particularly given the challenges of population growth.

In the late 1960s and early 1970s, UNESCO sponsored the "Experimental World Program" in literacy education, a mass campaign to eradicate illiteracy especially in Southern hemisphere ("developing") countries among adults from 15 years onward. This program, aimed at developing "functional" everyday literacy capabilities, has since been acknowledged to have failed. The inferences to be drawn from this failure are crucial for our discussion of the politics of literacy. The current director of UNESCO's literacy section, Limage (1993), outlined several messages from the widespread failure of these programs and experiments: (a) literacy is an important concern for communities and for nation-states, including the noneducation and nonpublic sector members of those communities; (b) literacy, as a complex set of social practices, is always part of other everyday ways of communicating, in different ways in different cultures; and (c) therefore, plans for enhancing literacy levels need to take this seriously into account if they are to have any chance of affecting the everyday lives of their clients.

This last point is an intriguing one, when we consider that Limage's own final pronouncement on the reasons for the failure of these campaigns was not to do with the "delivery" of a "commodity," but rather with how full or how limited were the ways in which the capabilities that were taught fitted into the everyday beliefs and activities of the "illiterate" people themselves. At issue here are: What are the competing uses and values for reading and writing? We might even reflect on whose ways of talking, thinking, feeling, and judging are being written down, and thus being taught and learned, and whose are not. As a dramatic but simple example, we could ask which of the 869 languages spoken in Papua New Guinea are being privileged in that country's growing literacy education campaigns, and what a parent in a community that speaks a minority language in that country would say about the local school's efforts to pass on the wisdoms and ways of the outside.

We might then examine patterns of inclusions and exclusions in the distribution of literate capability within and across localities and nation-states. Are there certain kinds of people who seem to be systematically included and excluded from the growing, if patchy, story of the success of modern reading education? What might we suspect about what kinds of people in any particular society these might be—particular ethnic and cultural groups? Language groups? Economic elites? Consider, as an example, the issue of gender and reading. Table 12.2 shows the percentages of men, women, and total adults in a selection of countries who are literate by UNESCO's definition.

Clearly, the distribution of reading capability is not evenly administered among men and women in countries such as these. From one perspective this may seem intriguing because, compared to cross-race and cross-economic class contact, the contact between men and women is comprehensive, their lives typically intertwined in more ubiquitous ways than the lives of people from different races or classes. The percentage differences shown in Table 12.2 represent vast numbers of people—in the

Table 12.2. Estimated Male and Female Literates in Selected Countries in 1990 (in percentages).

Country	Men (%)	Women (%)	Total (%)
Sudan	33	15	23
Afghanistan	39	8	24
Liberia	47	23	35
Mozambique	55	22	39
India	57	29	43
Saudi Arabia	71	31	51
P. R. of China	82	56	69
Hong Kong	95	81	88

Source: United Nations Development Program (1990). Human development report 1990. Oxford/New York: UN.

case of India, about 65 million fewer women than men are literate, and in the case of China, about 100 million fewer. However we might care to explain these differences, the categories of people we might expect to have the least access to literacy are among the least politically powerful participants in public, economic, and social life in these nation states. But there are clear cautions against falling into the causal arguments of a new literacy myth. Are they less powerful because they are less literate, or less literate because they are less powerful? If we prefer the first explanation, then we are open to the charge of "blaming the victims." We are in fact accepting that, in the example from Table 12.2, each and every one of these tens of millions of women happens to be individually less capable of learning to read and write than her male counterpart—a hypothesis that is, in a statistical sense, preposterous, even though it could be a direct consequence of the strong form of the psychological model of reading. What is clear here is that who gets to be a reader is not simply a matter of pedagogical efficacy—it depends in large part on patterns of the distribution of power and knowledge in a society.

WHAT TEXTS CAN PEOPLE READ?

There is another sense in which reading might be thought of as political, a sense that challenges the figures in Table 12.2, and that opens up a further critique of psychological models of reading: How was the reading of these men and women assessed? What particular reading texts and tasks were taken to be important and central enough to find their way into the literacy tests? With respect to gender differences, for example, we know that, to differing degrees in different societies, there are divisions of discursive and social labor in public and private life. We also know from studies of reading and writing in everyday life (e.g., Barton & Ivanic, 1991) that these divisions of labor involve many different reading tasks for men and women, as well as certain common tasks. If we were to think of how we would validly test the reading capabilities of men and women in our society, we might conclude that many of the materials and purposes we would select in our first efforts would already be gendered—not equally the typical communicative province for both men and women. Whose reading practices are assessed? Whose reading and writing practices are used as benchmarks against which functional literacy is evaluated? It may be, for example, that many of the 100 million Chinese women who fail to appear as literate as their male counterparts indeed possess reading capabilities—understanding written lists, understanding and sharing instructions for domestic practices, reading personal communications—but that these tasks failed to appear on the reading assessments, because as gendered labor they are not valued activities in the worlds of schooling and public employment.

Importantly, gender is not operating in any of these contexts as a stand-alone variable influencing distribution. Rather, it is by definition tied closely to the distribution of wealth, the stratification of domestic and waged work, and distinctive cultural and religious practices that are expected of and available to men and women of particular communities and subcultures. The connectedness of these categorizations is demonstrated in work on standardized reading testing. A recent example is a national study of reading in Canada reported in Montigny, Kelly, and Jones (1991). As summarized by Jones (1993), these researchers defined *everyday reading* as requiring the reader "to use a text to find information that will then be used as part of some larger task" (p. 7). Six categories of reading tasks were used to operationalize this definition. These were described as blueprints or charts; reports, articles, or books; catalogues and lists; manuals and instructions; letters, memos, and notes; and notices, labels, and forms. Placement on the four levels of reading attainment developed in this project was strongly correlated with educational attainment, age (with older individuals predominating in the lower attainment levels), current employment status, and socioeconomic status as assessed by occupational level. The modal high-attaining Canadian reader as judged by this survey is university educated, 25 to 34 years of age, currently employed in a "management" occupation, and, but only for those born outside Canada, male.

In considering whether this modal set of categories contains "the best readers," we need to reflect critically on the list of tasks presented that were used to come to these rankings, and to reconsider who has access to and practice in the everyday tasks in the survey. The study by Montigny et al. (1991) contains some of the answers to these issues as well. They reported a strong correlation between the levels of reading they determined and people's exposure to the various tasks in the survey. The people designated as "higher" level readers reported greater exposure to the particular demands of the survey test and more diverse demands at work with respect to those tasks.

So there are at least two aspects to the question of what the reading tasks are for schooling and assessment: The first concerns what texts are chosen and the second concerns what reading event or task is put in place. The second of these aspects itself is associated with the question of the reader's familiarity with the textual and functional features of the task and with the reader's familiarity and acceptance of particular discourses and ideologies that make the text and task sensible. Reading is about reading cultures and worlds. There is a long tradition of research and theorizing about the discursive and ideological contents of materials used in reading lessons and tests. Critiques have been developed by educators examining reading materials with respect to gender (e.g., Poynton, 1985; Sheridan, 1983; White, 1990), ethnicity and nationality (e.g., Carlson, 1989; Cope & Kalantzis, 1993), and generation (e.g., Baker & Freebody, 1989). These critiques point to a number of generalizations about reading, which specify some of the basic assumptions about reading listed earlier in the chapter. The first is that texts are in important ways purpose-built for instructional use and thus reflect a particular institutional view of their readership and a particular set of disciplinary "truths" about what kinds of pedagogies are appropriate or possible. Therefore, books, as objects, afford an implicit notion of what categories of readers will have differential access to various kinds of knowledges and values. A second general observation is that readers are positioned ideologically by the patterns and assumptions of the texts themselves and that becoming a successful reader of a particular text entails, among other things, the mimicry of its ideological propositions and preconditions, however temporarily. When these texts call upon, either explicitly or by comparison or analogy, domains of experience with which the readership is familiar, this sharing amounts to a recasting of experience and the representation of that experience in official instructional language, but, resolutely, in the institution's image both in terms of the shapes and artifacts of the practice, and ideologies.

As an example, we show here a selection from an Australian high school Geography textbook, available as a reference text for high schools, in which the notion of "the third world" is discussed (described more fully in Freebody, 1991). The fundamental questions for our purposes here are: What does the successful reading of this text install and/or rebuild in the readers' ideological resources? That is, in this case, what might the reader learn and, in the effort to make the text sensible, what does the reader need to assume about poverty, nationhood, literacy, and the production of poverty through historical and political processes? More strongly, what does learning to read with these texts prescribe about what we should "learn" and "know" about the political, economic, and social power of literacy?

1. The bulk of third world lands have in the past been European
2. colonies. During the twenty years after World War II, when most
3. of them obtained their independence, the ex-colonial powers tried
4. to encourage democratic, parliamentary forms of government in
5. them. But western-style parliamentary government has failed to
6. take root and flourish in countries were there is widespread
7. illiteracy: where there is no real national feeling, but a collection
8. of tribes or groups who owe their common nationality to the mere
9. accident that they were once ruled over by the same colonial
10. power; where there are enormous social and economic problems to

11. be faced. Small wonder, then, that many more or less
12. authoritarian regimes have come to power, or that there is a
13. temptation to experiment with communism as a way of providing a
14. better life for the masses.
    (Raufer, Thompson, Sturtz, & Brown, 1977, p. 5)

For our purposes, we would put aside for a moment whether this text, in some final or transparent sense, "tells the truth." More significantly, we can note first some features that mark this text as a reference text for doing geography in school (Lee, 1996): the location of the discussion in the concept of "lands"; the chronological information; and the presentation of key explanations in a list formation, for ease of "studying" and "summarizing." So, in certain ways the text casts its database into the format of school activities, connecting with a particular school subject, and projecting notions of what the student may do with "the information." These features, however, are not independent of the issue of what may be learned from the text, or how it might be read. The calling up of geographical concerns, the dating of the events under discussion, and the provision of a list all serve to isolate the events from surrounding forces, and to stabilize and legitimate the narrative by which the events are reconstructed.

In addition, we can note some of the features of the text that can serve to position the reader and recast some common-sensical ideas about, for example, "nations" and "illiteracy":

- The text is based on a self-evident distinction between "third-world" and "European" communities; furthermore, the text characterizes these two groups differentially, the one being mature and the other less so, set up by the "encouragement" motif, and enacted partly through the use of metaphors that are based on a stage-of-life device: "take root and flourish," "accidents" of communal birth, and "temptation to experiment."
- The text is grounded in historical statements about the past, seen in Lines 1–4 in which the past definite tense is used, but shifts, unannounced in Lines 5 and 6, into evaluative statements about the present, given in the past continuous "has failed" and immediately following in the present "there is." Of interest to us is that this transition occurs in the statement about illiteracy as the first in the list that provides a causal account for the failure of democracy in "third-world lands."
- Groups of people are described in strikingly different and oppositional ways, depending on who they are. The Europeans are described as "colonial powers" (Lines 3 and 9). The third-world communities start off as "lands," become "countries," then

"nations" artificially composed of "tribes or groups." The contemporary notion of the nation-state is thus given its origin in land formations (a most "natural" basis), but becomes undermined by the "tribalism" of the inhabitants, whose premodern status (as "tribes") was temporarily domesticated by colonial rule.

- We can consider the first listing of illiteracy in the causes of the failure of "third world lands" to become democracies. In fact, the following elements in the list can be viewed as an elaboration of the core problem of illiteracy. The text calls upon assumptions about the moral, cultural, and political centrality of literacy in the formation of the modern nation-state. Literacy is presented as a self-evident marker and precondition of modernity, as defined by European democracy and the economics of "development."

- Finally, the failure of "democratic, parliamentary government," which is immediately recharacterized as "western-style," is explained solely in terms of "lack," absence, and problems in the communities under discussion.

So in reading this passage, we are asked, among other things, to implicate our everyday knowledge of reading and writing in the political experiences of communities that are culturally affected by communal poverty and authoritarian governance, and in our judgments about those communities. The text shows a relationship between reading as a set of practical and sited procedures and the political structures and potentials of nation-states. Thus, our reading of this text must locate that relationship within the self-serving accounts offered by "developed" industrial societies of, first, their role in the production of other communities' economies, and, second, the degree of legitimacy of their account that is directly and unquestionably substantiated *by their being literate.* That is, the reader, in the very act of reading, is positioned as a sympathetic, "encouraging," but nonetheless judgmental and centered participant (as already a "reader" in a "developed" country) in the narrative of the text— and this is in a text on the discipline and science of "geography."

In these ways, it has been argued that the materials used in reading for school necessarily reinforce the school's "conservative force" in society (Bourdieu, 1974), not only in the selective content and narratives of history and daily domestic and public experience, but moreover in constructing and practicing versions of the (neocolonial) self as a certain kind of successful reader. These versions of the self can and need to recognize and come to display, as educationally marketable attributes, the "rarefied" cognitive and moral categories that official instructional texts use in recasting history and daily domestic and public experience.

But it might be argued that our assertions here about the significance of what is read rely on a passive view of the reader or at least a view that the reader interacts with the text in social and interactional isolation: Textual ideologies and practices are made and remade in classroom talk. Many teachers of senior geography would critically analyze the text just quoted by drawing out some of the ideological suppositions of the text. Yet instructional texts themselves afford and presume some pedagogies and make less likely some others. A critical treatment of the text above would posit and help produce a different kind of reader from that produced by a read-and-summarize approach, much less for a "answer the questions at the end of the chapter" lesson with minimal teacher mediation of the text.

For a contrasting example, consider how the following text from a social studies resource book for school might be treated in an upper primary classroom. It addresses the issue of the first White settlement in Australia:

> The Destruction of a Culture
>
> Prior to the arrival of Europeans in Australia, the Aborigines lived orderly and socially stable lives based on values of co-operation and sharing. They had adapted and survived for at least 30,000 years in a continent with a diverse and harsh climate. This lifestyle changed with the arrival of the Europeans.
>
> When different cultural groups who have different values and beliefs interact and meet, the smaller group often suffers from "culture shock". Its members become confused and bewildered about what is expected of them. This is what happened with the Aborigines. The European culture demanded certain things such as land-ownership, keeping domestic animals and private ownership which were in conflict with traditional Aboriginal beliefs. The Europeans had the military might and strength of numbers to support their viewpoint. (Hardie, Rutherford, & Walsh, 1987, p. 58)

What reading practices might accompany the use of this text? We can imagine that in some classrooms this piece might be read aloud "round robin" style, in which the students' attention is drawn to the accuracy of the oral rendering of the text. Perhaps we can imagine small groups working with this text, discussing its meaning, so that students can re-inflect the text into material useable for a school project on "aboriginal culture," in which the meanings of the text may be clarified and paraphrased. Or a comprehension focus might generate a graphic overview of the sequencing of propositions or foreground new and difficult vocabulary.

But these and other typical uses of this text in a "reading" or "social studies" lesson risk making invisible the ideas that underlie the text, their questionability, and their ideological outcomes. It is the enactments of the educational productivity that this text affords that will relate to the question of what kind of reader it helps to produce. For example, there are certain features of this text that might easily remain beyond the reach of some instructional approaches. For instance, the text is factually wrong: When the Whites first landed in Australia, the Aborigines were not the "smaller group"; the suggestion that the Whites "demanded" that the Aborigines demonstrate "land-ownership" is laughable almost to the point of cruelty; the claims that there was a singular Aboriginal lifestyle and that it changed, in terms of its cooperative and adaptive basis, when the whites arrived are again, demonstrably misleading, unless it is also explicated that Anglo colonialism rendered Aborigines incapable or uninterested in cooperativeness or adaptation.

In this section we claimed that the selective process that leads some texts to be used in instruction and others not to be is necessarily a process of ideological selection, regardless of any other criteria that might explicitly come into play when materials are chosen. We have also tried to show how the question of "what is read?" is necessarily conflated with the learning and teaching activities that render the text educationally productive on any given occasion—that is, with the question of "how do we read?". Educationally, the text is most often taken as a material, purpose-built adjunct to a particular selection of pedagogical and assessment imperatives; but the text must also be seen as a cultural, moral, and ideological adjunct, again purpose-built to support particular forms of organization of schools and societies.

An important procedure in our social repertoire is to infer the psychological from the social signs of speech, writing, gesture, and other forms of expression. Educators spend a lot of classroom time observing, themselves "reading" social interaction, language, and bodily movement around texts, and then predicting psychological processes or states (e.g., comprehension or miscomprehension, appropriate background knowledge, word attack skills) from these social observations. Our argument here is not that these observations and inferences are somehow finally invalid, but rather that, like the geography text about "less developed countries," in taking reading to be fundamentally a problem internal to individuals, these processes systematically write out the social nature of reading and thus produce readers who are vulnerable to and collusive in ideological forms of regulation.

REDEFINING READING: FROM PSYCHOLOGICAL TO SOCIOLOGICAL MODELS

We now turn to formalizing and summarizing the contrast between psychological and sociological perspective on reading. Table 12.3 is

Table 12.3. Psychological and Sociological Models of Reading.[a]

Feature	Model	
	Psychological Model	Sociological Model
Definition	Natural processes	Cultural practices
Reader Background	Cognitive schemata	Discursive/ intertextual resources
Reader Perspective	Individual point of view, knowledges and feelings	Social epistemologies
Text Attributes	Neutral informational and affective content	Ideological reading and writing positions
Reader/Text Relationship	Response/meaning	Power/knowledge
Instructional Emphasis	Activity/task/process	Social event/practices
Goals	Decoding/comprehension/personal growth	Pragmatics/critique/ cultural action/ social identity
Explanations of Success/Failure	Individual difference	Available social and cultural resources and institutional practices
Research Agenda	Experimental description of the reading process	Contextual description of cultural practice and social interaction

[a]The models provided here are not mutually exclusive, and may overlap in some significant ways (Gee, chap. 16, this volume). Our aim here is to "change the subject," to provoke an alternative vocabulary for talking about the teaching and learning of reading.

presented as deliberately polemical, a heuristic to challenge everyday common sense assumptions about reading. It presents as stark and simple what for many practitioners and theorists of reading are a blurred and complex set of dimensions. But why go to all the work of changing the way we talk about reading? Our principal purpose here is to disrupt contemporary common sense notions about reading. Here, the products of 50 years of reading instruction informed by psychology are provided in the left column. An alternative vocabulary for reading as a social practice is listed in the right column. Our aim here is to ask the polemical question: Why not start from a social perspective on reading, rather than treat it as an "add on" to individualist models of competence? The challenge here is to shift our own "ways of seeing" and talking about reading from psychological towards sociological models.

Table 12.3 describes the possibilities for shifting from psychological models that describe reading as a "natural" psychological process to those that view reading as a social and cultural practice. Although psychological models define reader background in terms of an individual's cognitive schema and background knowledge, sociological models emphasize the cultural resources, discourses, and practices children acquire in community language socialization. These resources are not natural or idiosyncratic, but are built through cultural and subcultural "ways of taking" from the community environment and texts to which the student has access to (Heath, 1982). The shift here, then, is from viewing that which students bring to schools and classrooms in terms of individual differences, knowledges, skills, and backgrounds—to a view that students bring to classrooms available cultural, community and social resources, texts, and discourses. These are intertextual resources that can be traced back to the other texts of everyday life that children have experienced.

This move is significant in terms of how we see difference and diversity in the classroom. Instead of seeing individual skill deficits or gaps, we can begin to identify different cultural and linguistic resources that children bring to classrooms. In so far as we view literacy as a psychological phenomenon, we will tend to define classroom problems in terms of student lack (in their heads). Instead, a sociological approach focuses on the kinds of discourses, language, and practices that students have had access to and practice with. These are the products of participation and membership in particular interpretive communities, not of simple individual difference. They are the resources of cultural practice, not of innate intelligence, natural ability, or developmental stages.

Finally, this model calls for a different vision of the purposes and goals of reading education. Psychological and personal growth models have tended to define the aims and outcomes of our instructional work in terms of student skills, knowledges, and development—in terms of student personal choice, growth, self-esteem and, more recently, "individual empowerment." A sociological focus would stress the social concomitants and consequences of literacy. It shifts our classroom focus to the particular texts, discourses, and practices to which students have access to and to the different kinds of social activities and cultural action that instruction can shape, encourage and yield. To circle back to our claims about social epistemology, teaching and learning to read is about teaching and learning standpoints, cultural expectations, norms of social actions and consequences.[1]

One interesting way of showing these two models at work is to undertake contrasting interpretations of the same section of talk from a reading lesson. The following year three primary school lesson shows a teacher using the pictures and writing from a big print book to build a discussion from which the students will go on to write stories of their own:

1.   T Have another look at that picture.
2.   Ss ((laughter))
3.   T What I said to you yesterday was I was going to get you to write, at each stage, as Jacob said, what old Tom was thinking. Now if he's just been kicked, what do you think he might be thinking there?
4.   S He's smiling//
5.   T   //Hands up. Put your hand up Dwayne. You've just been kicked, pretend that you're old Tom who's gone over to the cow to milk it and all of a sudden she's given one almighty..?
6.   Ss ((most students)) Kick ((some students)) splat/crash
7.   T No, we haven't landed in the mud yet. We've just been kicked so what do you think you'd be thinking?
8.   S You'd think um, like um, instead of you were going upward, you'd just fall and hit yourself with a rock?
9.   T So what do you think you might be thinking in your head though? I hope I don't fall?..on a rock or something like that? All right. Good. What do you think, James?
10.   J Um ouch?
11.   Ss ((laugh))
12.   T Right, you might, do you think it might have hurt?

***

---

[1]The pragmatics of "doing" reading in public life require an instructional model that shifts between "doing" and "analysis," between actually reading texts and developing a critical "metalanguage" for talking about these texts, between what Gee (1991) called acquisition and learning. Such lessons, then, might shift back and forth between filling out job application forms, and talking about their language characteristics and their social agendas, or, to take another example, between reading and using classified advertisements, and talking about their euphemisms, pitches, and lexicogrammatical techniques.

22.	T	So what, all right, he might have thought "ouch that hurt". What else do you think? Do you have one Caroline?
23.	C	Why did she do that?
24.	T	Why did she do that. I wonder why? He might be thinking, you know he always gets milk, why did she do that?/
25.	S	Ouch-i-wah-wah
26.	Ss	Ouch-i-wah-wah ((laughter))
27.	T	All right. He might have been thinking all those things. Let's do the last one. HE LANDED WITH A..?
28.	Ss	((unison)) THUD IN THE MUD
29.	T	What do you think he would have been thinking there? Pretend you're old Tom, you've just landed in a whole big lot of mud.

***

33.	T	... I'd like everyone to have a little think. Sam what do you think? What would you think if you landed in the big pile of mud?
34.	Sm	I don't know
35.	S	I know!
36.	S	I know!
37.	T	((to Sam)) You wouldn't think anything at all? Gee whiz, I know what I'd be thinking. Bella?
38.	B	Yuck?
39.	T	Yuck? All right. Another good idea. Amy?
40.	A	Yuck I'm all dirty?
41.	T	Good. I like those longer sentences. They tell me a little bit more information. Good.
42.	S	Yuck I wish Bessie was here?
43.	S	No //
44.	T	//who's Bessie
45.	Ss	His wife
46.	T	Oh, I thought some people might have forgotten. Good one. Yes?
47.	S	I'd feel like throwing up?
48.	T	Do you would've felt physically sick? Maybe?
49.	S	Cause his head (..)
50.	T	Well it didn't say where he got hit, did it? All right, I'm not going to ask any more because other people might steal your ideas. ((lesson continues))

To read this classroom event, it is important to put aside for the moment whether we might think this is particularly "good" or "bad" reading instruction. Here we want to use it to test the different lenses that we might use to study the teaching of reading. What is significant is that most reading educators familiar with primary school reading lessons would recognize the pedagogical routines exemplified here.

We might first develop a plausible psychological account of this stretch of talk. This lesson could be viewed as an "immersion" in literature, that develops "reading processes." It is about teaching "inferences" from pictures and text, and we could maintain that the teacher is displaying to the students how to draw productive inferences from the particular parts of the story or details of the pictures, considered by some psychologists an important part of meaning construction. Furthermore, we could argue that the teacher is displaying the importance of thinking about characters' motivations and internal states, as well as causes and consequences from textual information. Notice also that the teacher is foregrounding particular textual and pictorial features (turns 7, 22), focusing the students' perception on particular information. She also models the need for students to imagine themselves in the fictive scene (turns 5–10, 29 ff) and works hard to display this as a strategy for reading with a view to the internal feelings and thoughts of the characters.

From a psychological perspective as described in Table 12.3, then, we could view this as an activity where children are (more or less successfully) being skilled in particular kinds of information and text processing, involving background knowledge and their capacity to display a particular kind of comprehension of the text. The teacher displays, helps to coproduce, and thus foregrounds as significant the making of inferences about characters' internal processes. The teacher makes judgments (e.g., turns 9, 33, 39, 41) about the students' individual reading processes. By interpreting students' responses, most teachers would come to conclusions about which students were developing "reading processes" (e.g., student taking turn 8, Bella, Amy) and which were not (e.g., Sam).

Consider how we could talk about reading if we looked to the right-hand column in Table 12.3. Taken from a sociological perspective, a different set of interests emerges. In this social event, students and teachers are engaged in doing the practices of school reading (Baker, 1991). That procedure entails taking a particular standpoint toward the ideological content of the text. With the exception of Sam, the students apparently know the rules of the game: provide a short word, phrase, or sentence that best approximates how the teacher is reading the text. Furthermore, the repeated question–response–evaluation sequence of the lesson supports and validates those students whose cultural resources best match those of the text. In this way, the social interaction of the lesson generates an alignment between the world view of the text, the preferred interpretation of the teacher, and the standpoint of the child reader. The child reader here learns that reading as a cultural action involves, quite literally, using the text and lesson as a platform to give voice to the preferred social epistemology, the ideology of the teacher. The variation and possible divergence of her or his cultural resources is not really called into play in the discussion—only convergent statements of agreement are accepted—but it might account for the difficulties that Sam appears to have encountered: What does it signify for him "not to know what he would think?" We might also draw attention to the fact that the information modeled by the teacher and re-presented by the students is also named as private property with potential market value in this event (turn 50). Through the teacher's questioning and selective rewarding, the students are shown how to participate successfully in what counts as a reading lesson. The interpretive processes she models, and the managerial norms she applies for the acceptance of answers (turns 5, 37, 50) amount to the conflation of her interpretive and interactive preferences, both constructing a version of the ideal student reader, and shaping norms for the ideological display of cognitions.

Our first analysis, the psychological interpretation, suggests that teachers can decide whether this lesson is effectively teaching a certain skill, or encouraging a certain process. Certainly, most of us would have different views of how well and to what end this lesson is proceeding. But from a sociological perspective, the issue is not how well or poorly this lesson is being taught. This latter perspective focuses on how our texts and teaching shape what counts as reading: What standpoints, views of the text are being stressed? What actual practices with texts are being rewarded and valued? What kinds of statements by students of their cultural resources are being highlighted, supported, and foregrounded? The displays of what kinds of subjectivities are named as having market value at this site and in a larger political economy of reading practices?

Psychological approaches to reading entail varied claims about developmental contingency: that if one learns basic decoding then comprehension will follow; that if one learns how to infer and predict, that comprehension will follow; and that if one can display empathy, critical analysis of cultural texts and ideologies will follow. We argue instead for a social practice hypothesis: that one learns to do with reading what one is taught to do and what is valued and encouraged and useful in cultural, interpretive communities, and sites. Reading requires institutional supports, and social institutions set out sites and procedures for practice, and metalanguages for practices, ways of talking about and around texts (Heath, 1986).

THE ELEMENTS OF READING AS A SOCIAL PRACTICE

We have claimed that reading is a variable social practice, that can be shaped, used, applied to various social purposes. If this is the case, it presents a new question for teachers. The historical question of the great debate—What is the best way of teaching reading?—becomes obsolete and downright misleading. Instead, the issue is: What kinds of reading practices and positions should schools value, encourage, and propagate? In order to answer this question, we need to have a better description of how people use reading in their everyday lives, and a prescription for the kinds of reading required in a multimediated, fast-capitalist, late 20th-century culture. Since the early 1980s, studies of what people do with reading and writing show variations across regions, between men and women, rural and urban, migrant and indigenous peoples (e.g., Barton & Ivanic, 1990; Street, 1993). A great deal of everyday reading practice for people is what has typically been referred to as *documentary literacy* (as in the examples from Jones, 1993), tied to everyday responsibilities of citizenship in the industrial workplace, family, and everyday life (cf. Hull, 1993). The extent to which people read signs, forms, memos, newspapers, and other material everyday cannot be underestimated.

Each approach to reading is based, whether explicitly or not, on a vision of an idealized literate society where reading is done, and a vision of what the reader should do in that utopia (or, to use Foucault's term, *heterotopias*, communities of discourse where difference and diversity are valued rather than shunned). We here review a four-tiered model (Table 12.4) for thinking about the literate demands of postmodern culture, work and community, which stresses coding, meaning, pragmatic and critical practices. Our vision is of a 'heteroglossic democracy', where in principle all voices and texts of difference have a right to be heard, critiqued, analyzed and constructed in the public forums of governments and schools, workplaces and community meetings, churches and corporations (Mouffe, 1993; Yeatman, 1993). In Table 12.4 we have recast some of the terms to better fit the sociological vocabulary for reading described above.

Reading and writing are practices with and around material codes for recreating a sequence of sounds. As such, the resources for developing those practices that beginning readers—both children and adults—bring to classrooms will be diverse and various. In some cases, the focus of the task of acquisition will center around different representational codes of writing systems, between for instance, logographic systems like Chinese, to English—as any English speaker learning to read and write Chinese or Japanese would know. In other cases, this issue may not be the focus of the task because of a beginner's prior experience with an alphabetic system. For instance, many Hmong

Table 12.4. Elements of Reading as a Social Practice.

Coding Practices	Text-Meaning Practices	Pragmatic Practices	Critical Practices
Developing your resources as code breaker:	Developing your resources as text participant:	Developing your resources as text user:	Developing your resources as text analyst and critic:
•How do I crack this text? •How does it work?	•How do the ideas represented in the text string together?	•How do the uses of this text shape its composition?	•What kind of person, with what interests and values, could both write and read this naively and unproblematically?
•What are its patterns and conventions?	•What cultural resources can be brought to bear on this text?	•What do I do with this text, here and now? What will others do with it?	•What is this text trying to do to me? In whose interest?
•How do the sounds and the marks relate, singly and in combinations?	•What are the cultural meanings and possible readings that can be constructed from this text?	•What are my options and alternatives?	•Which positions, voices, and interests are at play? •Which are silent and absent?

Note. Based on Freebody and Luke (1990).

immigrants from Laos have entered ESL programs in the United States, Australia, and Canada. The Hmong language was only recently written down through a Romanized Popular Alphabet by missionaries in the 1950s (Weinstein-Shr, 1993). Hence, the move from reading and writing (Romanized) Hmong to English might be less of a sharp transition than, say, the move from a logographic to an alphabetic system.

Reading entails other forms of agency and action on the part of the reader, an agency based on available cultural resources. In this sense, readers are active social "participants" in the building of cultural meanings. To the extent that readers are able to draw upon and use relevant resources, they are able to construct a relationship with the available statements and discourses of the text, and they are able to construct and reconstruct these statements and discourses in different inflections and patterns. Here we can consider discourse, following Foucault (1972), as a chain of recurring statements in which certain compatibilities and contradictions are highlighted from occurrence to occurrence, and by omission others are silenced. In this respect, reading entails the practice of drawing into play previous experiences with statements to recognize recurrence, similarity, and difference in the text. Importantly, it also entails an enculturation into procedures of omission— knowing what not to pursue empirically, inferentially, and evaluatively.

The 1980s push for meaning-centered teaching, for content-area reading and comprehension illustrates how teachers can build readers' resources for constructing analyses and interpretations of texts. But like code-breaking, constructing meanings—however conventional and unconventional—is yet another necessary but not sufficient element of literacy as a critical social practice.

To reiterate: All texts represent cultural positions, ideologies, and discourses. All readers construct readings from particular epistemological standpoints. Both writers' and readers' resources are cultural resources; they are not about representing and accessing neutral information structures. Many psychological models of reading have failed to take up the question of "whose meanings" will count in private and public forums. Where these questions are not raised, classrooms run the risk of a reproductive model of meaning, where teaching comprehension is about cultural assimilation and colonization, about bringing readers' social epistemologies into acritical alignment with those of a canonical corpus of texts. Furthermore, what is left out of an account, in this case of reading, may be deemed to be uninteresting and insignificant.

The perennial stress on individual, silent reading as meaning construction is very much modeled on a 19th-century model of the solitary literary reader: the reader envisioned by Wordsworth and Coleridge in *Preface to Lyrical Ballads*, a reader for whom the power of the text is private and personal. But reading literature privately, both for leisure and work and religious purposes, is but a minor part of many people's everyday lives. Reading practices generally entail pragmatic activities conducted in literacy events, instances of face-to-face oral interaction, negotiation around written texts. In workplaces, service encounters in offices, banks, corporations, government agencies—people engage in various kinds of talk around text to achieve particular social goals (e.g., financial exchange, workplace production, consensus and agreement, identity statements).

Gray's (1987) work on concentrated language encounters addressed the need for pragmatic practices explicitly. Gray realized that many of his Alice Springs Aboriginal students had difficulty seeing the relationship between texts and the actual cultural contexts where they were used. Hence, he developed an instructional model that moved students back and forth from studying texts to actually modeling and doing the texts in contexts. His task was to build up the students' cultural and linguistic repertoires for participating in, for instance, service encounters at the local store. An equally important part of his task was to build up a familiarity with the routinized cultural contexts that required people to do reading, writing, listening, and speaking.

To see an (almost) literacy event at work, consider an everyday occurrence, recorded in a home (Freebody, Ludwig, & Gunn, 1995), in which mum (m), dad (d), and a 5-year-old child, here called Cherry (Ch), are having a discussion over breakfast. Cherry, who is near the end of her first year of formal schooling, has been saving up for something that costs $100:

1.   d How much have you got there?
2.   Ch I've got thirty-two dollars mummy. I've never had thirty-two dollars.
3.   d What's thirty-two from a hundred? What's thirty-two from a hundred?
4.   Ch No, but daddy. Daddy //
5.   d   //Work it out this way, come on.
6.   Ch No I got (this much) in the bank at the moment, I'll have it in next year.
7.   m No, but how much have you got to save up?
8.   d You've already got thirty-two. How much (to make) a hundred?
9.   m One hundred take thirty-two?
10. Ch No, but mummy, I'm learning how to (take away) next week. I only got//
11. m   //What thirty-two, you wont have thirty-two 'till next week?

12. Ch Next time we (get)//
13. m   //Well okay, we'll just take a hundred dollars, and thirty-two.
14. Ch ( )
15. m One hundred dollars take away thirty-two dollars, what have you got left?
16. Ch I don't know, why?
17. d You should know.
18. Ch Why?
19. m Can't you work it out in your head?
20. d What's two from zero?
21. Ch No.
22. d What's two from zero?
23. m Never mind, never mind. Okay here they ((other children)) come.
24. d Write it down. Write it down. A hundred take away thirty-two.
25. Ch I don't know. ( )
26. d Hey, get a piece of paper.
27. Ch No.
28. d (get some) paper and write it *down*.
29. Ch No. ((pause)) If you'll be *quiet* I might be able to.

This is a complex event: There are coding issues at work (e.g., trying to get Cherry to write numbers, in turns 15–22); meaning issues (e.g., that the amount yet to be saved can be expressed as an algorithm, turns 6–9); issues of age, and authority relations and regulatory practices (e.g., Cherry's resistances in turns 4, 6, 10, 21, and 27, and her defense that she has not covered this topic in school yet, in turn 10). As well, a set of pragmatic demands are also in play. This event requires a set of staged compliances with and challenges to a complex set of conventions about who can speak, when, and how, about what (Cherry's "why" questions are not answered as "why" questions), and who can determine the very nature of what kind of interchange this is (e.g., Cherry's questions as to "why" she can know and should know, as in turns 16 and 18). There are forms of address used by Cherry when she wishes to resist the other speakers' courses of action (turns 4 and 10) as a polite softener when the event still seems negotiable (up to the unsuccessful recourse to the sequence of the school curriculum in 10). Turn-taking rights are enacted (e.g., only parents interrupt, in 5, 11, and 13). As in many interactive events, these conventions are not static or predetermined: The event may or may not have ended up with a written "take-away" procedure; and the relationships are also fluidly constructed, most dramatically evident in Cherry's admonition to her parents to be quiet in the final turn quoted. (Cherry went on to bring off a topic shift later, the time of her tennis lesson that afternoon, and the take-away was not completed.)

Consider another example of pragmatic practices at work. In a case study of a reading and writing in a US community credit union, Keller-Cohen (1987) found that people rarely read verbatim loan applications and other legal documents. Instead, the event pivoted on the verbal interaction between the loans officers and the applicants. The actual reading was secondary to the verbal explanations and details provided by the loans officers. Like lawyers, the loans officers acted as specialized readers and interpreters. To make decisions, clients at the credit union relied on signals and interactions in the literacy event more than they did on the text per se.

Critical literacy practices include an awareness of how, why, and in whose interests particular texts might work. To teach critical literacy thus encourages the development of alternative reading positions and practices for questioning and critiquing texts and their affiliated social formations and cultural assumptions. It also entails developing strategies for talking about, rewriting, and contesting the texts of everyday life. Classroom frameworks and practices developed for discourse-analytic approaches to critical reading include the reading of multiple texts and conflicting discourses against each other within single lessons; the encouragement of alternative readings and writings that attempt to bring community and familiar discourses to bear on those represented in texts; and, the foregrounding of the histories and cultural contexts of texts and discourses under study. These pedagogical routines are based on several guiding principles. First, the emphasis on juxtaposing texts and discourses to be "read against each other" (Freebody, Luke, & Gilbert, 1991) aims to generate difference, conflict, and debate, focal points for teaching critical reading. This might involve, for example, reading two versions of the same historical event and comparing lexicogrammatical choice in the texts. Or it might involve contrasting differing generic treatments of the same themes (e.g., representations of Asia and Asians in tourist and current affairs magazines).

Second, classroom debates can be informed by teaching that makes explicit and foregrounds how texts work ideologically. Instruction based on text and discourse analysis aims to give students insights into how texts work, and more specifically, how texts situate and manipulate readers. Kress (1985) outlined how texts construct "subject positions" and "reading positions." That is, texts both represent and construct "subjects" in the social and natural world, and they position and construct a model reader. The lexical, syntactic, and semantic devices of texts thus portray a "possible world," and they position the reader to read or interpret that possible world in particular ways. Accordingly, a discourse-analytic approach to critical reading might include, for instance, an understanding of how words and grammatical structures shape up portrayals of the world, human agency, cause and effect, and so forth. It would also point out many of the linguistic techniques that texts use to define and manipulate readers (e.g., imperatives, pronominalization). For example, Kamler (1994) recently described classroom approaches where students compared lexical choice in gender portrayal of athletes to show how texts construct and manipulate patriarchal "common sense."

Critical reading, then, need not be some kind of esoteric linguistic "deconstruction" or political "ideology critique" divorced from everyday life. It is not an add on. It is essential for dealing with apparently quite straightforward and innocent community texts like job applications, credit forms, and loan applications. These have powerful positioning devices that bear discussion and debate, careful consideration before signing on the dotted line. Consider the following text, an extract from the current *Real Estate Institute of Queensland Agreement for Tenancy Residential Premises*:

> The Tenant hereby covenants and agrees with the Landlord . . .
>
> (e) Damage by the Tenant—To repair at the Tenant's expense within a reasonable time damage to the premises [sic] furniture, fixtures and fittings caused by the wilful or negligent conduct of the Tenant or persons coming into or upon the premises with his [sic] consent.
>
> (f) Nuisance—To conduct himself [sic] and to ensure that other persons in the premises conduct themselves in a manner that will not cause disturbance or be a nuisance or an annoyance to adjoining or neighbouring occupiers.

This text constructs an ideal world of male tenants, a set of moral codes governing renters' behavior and so forth. But there is more to this than just a set of legal sanctions. The moral description here is ambiguous, subject to interpretation. To read and sign this, and to put down your first and last months' rents and deposit, is to effectively open yourself up to someone's (the landlord's? the magistrate's? your solicitor's?) interpretation and "reading" of your behavior. The positioning of the reader/tenant is obvious. You are "the tenant" and you are, more or less, instructed to comply and sign this lease: the verbs "to repair" and "to conduct" are about the renter/tenant. But your fate pivots on the ambiguity of the terms *reasonable, willful, negligent, nuisance* and *annoyance*. Teachers and students might be well advised to consider and clarify these reading and subject positions, these meanings and implications before signing and paying. In this way, critical reading is not about "cognitive processing," "affective or personal response," "deconstruction" or "linguistic analysis". It is about developing ways of seeing through texts, their descriptions of cultures and worlds, and how they are trying to position you to be part of these cultures and worlds.

Two points of clarification are in order in considering the four resources model of reading in Table 12.4: First, each element—coding, text-meaning, pragmatic, and critical—is necessary but not sufficient for reading in contemporary culture. Just as stressing the "code" at the expense of "meaning" will not suffice as a comprehensive approach to literacy education, doing critical analysis and not attending to issues of students' intertextual resources or "cracking the code" in, for example, an early childhood or ESL class may present problems. Second, this is not a developmental sequence or cycle or taxonomy. These resources should not be construed as stages or levels to be dealt with in turn: There is no natural or necessary movement from coding to semantic to pragmatic to critical in an age/grade/program sequence. In the study of all texts at all stages in our programs, we can ask ourselves: "What kinds of code, meaning, pragmatic and critical demands and possibilities are in play?" Citizenship in postmodern literate society requires flexible practices that enable critical engagement with new and innovative texts on a daily basis. These elements of practice, then, offer a template for questioning and revising reading programs. Each is necessary but not in and of itself sufficient for literate practice in "new times."

There are a range of implications of such an approach for everyday pedagogic work of reading education. For example, the notion of four resources may encourage lessons built around multiple instructional passes through texts. In such pedagogical patterns, teachers and students conjointly undertake several readings of the text, each time foregrounding different elements of reading as a social practice. The purpose of this approach to reading as a social practice is not to advocate a new method or technical solution to the instructional problem of reading. Rather, its aim is to provide a prescriptive framework for looking at how teachers and students, lessons and programs are shaping reading as a social practice. The four elements of reading as a social practice should provide categories for reframing practices in use, for reviewing how they generate a selective tradition, and for moving in new and innovative practical directions.

We have here argued for a sociological model of reading that is based on a normative analysis of the requirements of what have been called "new times" in countries like Australia and the United States. As in all technologically advanced nation states, this linguistically and culturally hybrid population must face the prospect of structural unemployment and a fluid and rapidly changing job market. There, reading and writing practices continue to be focal elements for doing the work of producing goods, services, and texts in economic life, and for consumption and leisure. In an economic climate that, rightly or wrongly, equates literacy with economic productivity and in a cultural climate that equates literacy with moral virtue—economically and culturally marginal groups are all too easily written off in terms of literacy "deficits" and "lacks." This can be part of a blame-the-victim strategy and is particularly dangerous. Those who are cast as "deficit" will be seen as a drag on a productive economy, and simple measures of literacy may provide schools, employers, and governments attractive, if misleading, systems for identifying and classifying those with "deficit." The need here is for a richer understanding of literacy that recognizes and builds on students' prior cultural resources, experiences, and knowledges in all instruction and programs.

At the same time, for much of the last 40 years the debate over language and literacy in Australia and other "western" nations has been waged under the assumption of a principally monolingual, male monocultural populace. This assumption of a monocultural, gender-free literate populace has also persisted even in those educational systems that officially encourage bilingual training for their scientific and technical elite, in educational systems as diverse as those of Western Europe and Japan. But since the demise of the so-called "White Australia" policy in the early 1970s, the legal recognition of Aboriginal and Islander Australians and the educational recognition of migrant Australians has accelerated (Kalantzis, Cope, & Slade, 1989). At present, almost 30% of Australian school students come from non-English-speaking backgrounds, and it has been estimated that by the year 2000 only about one third of the population will be of Anglo/Australian background (e.g., Ozolins, 1993). Educators at all levels must take seriously the knowledge and identity claims of Aborigines, Torres Strait Islanders, and migrants, and those of women.

Given cultural resources, institutional access, and support, entire populations can learn to read. To reshape that selective tradition, there are several imperatives:

1. That we attend to critical, pragmatic, text-meaning, and coding elements of reading at all stages and levels, including critical practices even at the earliest stages of reading instruction.
2. That we move away from a focus on psychological skills models that identify deficit and lack, toward those sociological models that recognize and capitalize on the varied and hybrid cultural and discourse resources that students bring to classrooms.

3. That we integrate the analysis and study of new text forms of multimediated postmodern culture, and continually reappraise the cultural form and content of literary canons.
4. That we focus instruction on how community, workplace, and everyday cultural texts and discourses work, linguistically and politically.

As for questions of how to teach, we have here argued that these are not matters of finding the truth about reading once and for all, or finding the right method to prevent reading failure. The issue is how we want to shape reading, how we want to form a selective tradition of materials and practices. That shaping and building of reading needs to be done in relation to an analysis of the demands of social and cultural, economic and political change. We began with these questions: What is the nature of reading? What are its personal and social functions and effects? How is it learned? And how is it best taught? These appear to be straightforward empirical questions. But in this century, philosophers have argued compellingly that paradigms are partly matters of choice and ideology, guided by empirical considerations, but also by what practitioners in a discipline regard as the most profitable orders of interest.

We have here made the case that traditional, skills-based, psychological, and progressivist approaches to reading have more in common with one another than might first appear and certainly than is evident from the perennial debates among their advocates. What they have in common are certain central conservative propositions—about the neutral or self-evidently proper contents of reading materials, the private and portable capabilities of reading as an industrial and moral commodity, and the assumption that full enculturation as a reader is a natural extension of the educative process. These propositions, we suggest, deal the educator out of the most interesting and salient aspects of enculturating readers. A social view of reading education not only deals the educator back in, but also foregrounds the rightful significance of sociopolitical contexts and issues in reading instruction.

ACKNOWLEDGMENTS

Carolyn Baker's collegial support has strongly influenced this article and its perspective on reading. Thanks also to Malcolm Vick for the Royal Readers.

REFERENCES

Apple, M. W. (1982). *Education and power*. London: Routledge & Kegan Paul.

Baker, C. D. (1991). Reading the texts of reading lessons. *Australian Journal of Reading, 14*(1), 5-20.

Baker, C. D., & Freebody, P. (1989). *Children's first schoolbooks: Introductions to the culture of literacy*. Oxford, UK: Blackwell.

Baker, C. D., & Luke, A. (Eds.). (1991). *Towards a critical sociology of reading pedagogy*. Amsterdam: John Benjamins.

Barton, D., & Ivanic, R. (Eds.). (1990). *Writing in the community*. London: Sage.

Bourdieu, P. (1974). The school as a conservative force: Scholastic and cultural inequalities. In J. Eggleston (Ed.), *Contemporary research in the sociology of education*. London: Methuen.

Carlson, D. (1989). Legitimation and delegitimation: American history textbooks and the cold war. In S. de Castell, A. Luke, & C. Luke (Eds.), *Language, authority and criticism: Readings on the school textbook*. London: Falmer Press.

Cope, B., & Kalantzis, M. (1993). *The powers of literacy: A genre approach to teaching writing*. London: Falmer Press.

Edelsky, C. (1996). *With literacy and justice for all* (2nd ed.). London: Taylor & Francis.

Foucault, M. (1972). *The archaeology of knowledge* (A. M. Sheridan Smith, Trans.). New York: Harper & Row.

Freebody, P. (1991). *Language and ideology*. Paper presented to the Language and Education Workshop, Brisbane.

Freebody, P. (1995). The status of reading in adult education. *Prospect: A Journal of Australian TESOL, 16*, 2-18.

Freebody, P., Ludwig, C., & Gunn, S. (1995). *Everyday literacy practices in and out of school in low socio-economic urban communities*. Report to the Department of Employment, Education and Training, Canberra.

Freebody, P., & Luke, A. (1990). Literacies' programmes: Debates and demands in cultural context. *Prospect: A Journal of Australian TESOL, 11*, 7-16.

Freebody, P., Luke, A., & Gilbert, P. (1991). Reading positions and practices in the classroom. *Curriculum Inquiry, 21*(4), 435-57.

Gee, J. P. (1996). *Social linguistics and literacies: Ideology in discourse* (2nd ed.). London: Taylor and Francis.

Gray, B. (1987). Natural language learning in Aboriginal classrooms: Reflections on teaching and learning style for empowerment in English. In C. Walton & W. Eggington (Eds.), *Language: Maintenance, power and education in Australian Aboriginal contexts*. Darwin, Australia: Northern Territory University Press.

Halliday, M. A. K., & Martin, J. (1993). *Writing science: Literacy and discursive power.* London: Falmer Press.

Hardie, N., Rutherford, M., & Walsh, A. (1987). *Enquiry about society: Book 2.* Melbourne, Australia: Longman Cheshire.

Heath, S. B. (1982). What no bedtime story means: Narrative skills at home and at school. *Language in Society, 11*(1), 49-76.

Heath, S. B. (1986). Critical factors in literacy development. In S. de Castell, A. Luke, & K. Egan (Eds.), *Literacy, society and schooling.* Cambridge, UK: Cambridge University Press.

Hull, G. (1993). Hearing other voices: A critical assessment of popular view on literacy and work. *Harvard Educational Review, 63*(1), 20-49.

Jones, S. (1993). *Reading but not reading well. Report from the survey of literacy skills used in daily activities.* Ottawa, Canada: National Literacy Secretariat.

Kalantzis, M., Cope, W., & Slade, D. (1989). *Minority languages and dominant culture.* London: Falmer Press.

Kamler, B. (1994). Lessons in language and gender. *Australian Journal of Language and Literacy, 17*(2), 56-71.

Kapitzke, C. (1995). *Literacy and religion: The textual politics and practice of Seventh-day Adventism.* Amsterdam: John Benjamins.

Keller-Cohen, D. (1987). Literate practices in the modern credit union. *Language in Society, 16*(1), 7-24.

Kress, G. (1985). *Linguistic processes in sociocultural practices.* Geelong/Oxford, UK: Deakin University Press & Oxford University Press.

Lee, A. (1996). *Gender, literacy and curriculum.* London: Taylor & Francis.

Lemke, J. (1995). *Textual politics: Discourse and social dynamics.* London: Taylor & Francis.

Limage, L. (1993). Literacy strategies: A view from the International Literacy Year Secretariat of UNESCO. In P. Freebody & A. Welch (Eds.), *Knowledge, culture and power: International perspectives on literacy as policy and practice.* London: Falmer Press.

Luke, A. (1988). *Literacy, textbooks and ideology.* London: Falmer Press.

Luke, C., & Gore J. (Eds.). (1994). *Feminism and critical pedagogy.* London: Routledge.

Mangubhai, F. (1987). Literacy in Fiji: Its origins and its development. *Interchange, 18*(1/2), 124-135.

McLaughlin, D. (1989). The sociolinguistics of Navajo literacy. *Anthropology and Education Quarterly, 20*(4), 275-290.

Montigny, G., Kelly, K., & Jones, S. (1991). *Adult literacy in Canada: Results of a National Study (part 1).* Ottawa: Statistics Canada.

Mouffe, C. (1993). *The return of the political.* London: Verso.

Ozolins, U. (1993). *The politics of language in Australia*. Melbourne, Australia: Cambridge University Press.

Poynton, C. (1985). *Language and gender: Making the difference*. London: Virago Press.

Raufer, B., Thompson, B. K., Sturtz, H., & Brown, H. (1977) *Three worlds: Man and his world, Book 5*. Artamon, NSW: Macmillan Australia.

Scribner, S., & Cole, M. (1981). *The psychology of literacy*. Cambridge, MA: Harvard University Press.

Sheridan, E. M. (Ed.). (1983). *Sex stereotypes and reading*. Newark, DE: International Reading Association.

Stanovich, K. E. 1991. The psychology of reading: Evolutionary and revolutionary developments. *Annual Review of Applied Linguistics, 12*, 3-30.

Street, B.V. (1984). *Literacy in theory and practice*. Cambridge, UK: Cambridge University Press.

Street, B. V. (Ed.). (1993). *Cross-cultural approaches to literacy*. Cambridge, UK: Cambridge University Press

UNESCO Office of Statistics. (1990). *Compendium of statistics on literacy, 1990 edition*. Paris: UNESCO

United Nations Development Program. (1990). *Human development report, 1990*. Oxford/New York: UN.

Voloshinov, V. N. (1986). *Marxism and the philosophy of language* (L. Matejka & I. R. Titunik, Trans.). Cambridge, MA: Harvard University Press.

Walton, C. (1993). Aboriginal education in northern Australia: A case study of literacy policies and practices. In P. Freebody & A. Welch (Eds.), *Knowledge, culture and power: International perspectives on literacy as policy and practice*. London: Falmer Press.

Weinstein-Shr, G. (1993). Literacy and social process: A community in transition. In B. V. Street (Ed.), *Cross-cultural approaches to literacy*. Cambridge, UK: Cambridge University Press.

White, J. (1990). On literacy and gender. In F. Christie (Ed.), *Literacy for a changing world*. Hawthorn, Vic: Australian Council of Educational Research.

Yeatman, A. (1993). *Postmodern revisionings of the political*. New York: Routledge.

13

Reading with an Attitude; or, Deconstructing "Critical Literacies" Response to Alan Luke and Peter Freebody

Bill Green
Deakin University, Geelong

Let me take as my starting-off point what may seem like a casual, throw-away gesture. Certain gestures, that is, or what might be characteristic, even stereotypical moves in a game of claiming and naming, of positioning and partitioning on the part of the "critical literacies"[1] movement—like:

> Critical reading . . . is not some kind of esoteric linguistic "deconstruction" or political "ideology critique" divorced from everyday life. It is not an add on. (Luke & Freebody, chap. 12, p. 219)

Or this:

> [C]ritical reading is not about "higher cognitive processing," "affective or personal response," "deconstruction" or "linguistic analysis". It is about developing ways of seeing through texts, their descriptions of cultures and worlds, and how they are trying to position you to be part of these cultures and worlds. (chap. 12, p. 219)

Elsewhere, a discourse-analytic approach to "critical reading" ("drawn from poststructuralist discourse theory, functional linguistics, and neo-marxian cultural studies"; Luke & Walton,1994) is described thus:

> [It] does not aim for effective "comprehension," the valorization of the "power" of literature, the "liberation" of "voice" or, for that matter, the development of esoteric skills of "deconstruction".

---

[1]Henceforth simply *critical literacy*, for rhetorical reasons as indicated in what follows.

Rather, it sets out to teach critical reading as "an understanding of how texts are public artefacts available to critique, contestation and dispute." (Freebody, Luke, & Gilbert, 1991, p. 453)

It is not something limited to this (con)text, moreover. For instance, elsewhere another well-known proponent of "critical literacy" refers in an interview to the "risk [of] of putting our energies into endless cutesy bourgeois deconstruction: a politics of the salon" (Lankshear, cited in Peters, 1995, p. 110).

Something is going on here that intrigues me. Partly it has to do with constructing an agenda, and moreover, this evidently is something that is very serious business indeed. There is no room or occasion, or excuse, for frivolity here. This is work—not play. Being the sort of (il)literate subject I am, however, I can't help wondering: Are there any other binaries lurking in the wings, like characters in a well-known and well-rehearsed drama? What is being staged here?

So "critical reading" is neither "esoteric"—like "deconstruction"—nor simply "an add on." Rather: "It is essential for dealing with apparently quite straightforward and innocent community texts like job applications, credit forms and loan applications. These have powerful positioning devices which bear discussion and debate, careful consideration before signing on the dotted line" (chap. 12, p. 219).

Signing what, though? One's signature, of course. And here, all at once, we are swept into what would seem, on this evidence and this testimony, the very territory we are most warned about. Care is needed, clearly. But already things have become much more complex than might have been expected, in seeking to account thus for critical literacy. Too much is being excluded here, too insistently; there is a powerful, insistent logic of classification working through this no doubt equally "innocent" text; something is at stake, or at risk. But what, and so what? In the text that follows, I explore what might be involved in questions such as these, by way of an erratic commentary on literacy's *raison d'etre*: the changing New Times matrix of textuality, time and Being.

Luke and Freebody's argument can, perhaps rather too neatly, be summarized thus:

1. Reading, and hence reading pedagogy, is never a neutral activity, or even necessarily a benign one, as generations of scholarship and praxis have at least implied; rather, it is fundamentally implicated in, and complicit with, structures of power and social relations in what is manifestly an unjust world.

2. Reading *is* literacy, further; or rather, that aspect of literacy that counts most, in practice, perhaps because it would seem simply

self-evident that more people read or "consume" texts than write or "produce" them, in the usual sense of these activities.

3. Moreover, with the transition of society from an "industrial," print-oriented order to one that is "post-industrial" and oriented more to information and the image, new challenges and problematics are emerging for literacy pedagogy, requiring concomitant changes in the concept and practice of "critical literacy."

These, for me, are crucially important theses. In themselves, they might well form the basis of an extended study of literacy and schooling in critical–historical perspective. Certainly, they need to be taken actively into account in developing policies and programmes in and for literacy education and, in particular, reading pedagogy. In that regard, the work begun in an earlier volume (Baker & Luke, 1991) is hereby consolidated and refocused, as a further stage (or at least a distinctive moment) in what is arguably a paradigm shift in the field. The case is made convincingly for a reconceptualization of "reading as a critical social practice," and there is a clear mandate for linking research in literacy and citizenship: "The decisions facing teachers of reading are decisions about how and to what end we should shape literacy in contemporary "fast-capitalist" culture, and how and to what end we can influence the development of literate citizens and workers" (chap. 12, p. 192). That is, the project that is at issue here is one that is unabashedly *normative*. It is also, emphatically and avowedly, a *social* project, understood in these terms:

> (R)eading is a social practice using written texts as a means for the construction and reconstruction of statements, messages, and meanings. Reading is actually "done" in the public and private spaces of everyday community, occupational and academic institutions. Reading is tied up in the politics and power relations of everyday life in literate culture. (chap. 12, p. 185)

Later, the assertion is made that "[n]one of us would dispute that reading is necessary for participation in the text-drenched version of 'fast-capitalist' society we find ourselves in". This is used to make the point that not all contexts for reading are of this kind—characteristic, that is, of the technologically advanced societies, such as feature either implicitly or explicitly in most accounts of the so-called "postmodern condition"; a point that itself prepares the ground for the assertion of *difference* as a fundamental principle in and for reading pedagogy. This, it must be stressed, is not so much a philosophical matter as it is "anthropological" in character, with direct reference to cultural diversity (notwithstanding the New World Order) and the multicultural cast of nation-states such as Australia. It is also, of course, predicated on the value and necessity of historical imagination, given that the archive indicates very clearly that what counts as literacy and as reading has changed considerably over time, and hence that what goes around comes around—witness the recurrent manifestations of "the literacy debate" in Australia and elsewhere, and the triumphalist tone of recent newspaper headlines such as "Grammar Comes Back in Fashion."[2]

Everything here is on the surface, if not altogether on the level. This is to refer both to the object of analysis here—the social diversity of reading practices—and to the manner in which that analysis is conducted: a seemingly scrupulous attention to what can be "read" from the *public* activity of reading, in all its complex visibility. Part of what is at issue in understanding reading as a practice is that reading is necessarily transitive: "There is no such thing as reading per se." That is, "One never just (generically) reads. Readers always read something, a textual representation, and readers always take up an epistemological standpoint, stance and relationship to the values and ideologies, discourses and worldviews in the text" (chap. 12, p. 195).

Hence, "Reading is about reading cultures and worlds" (chap. 12, p. 201). Drawing partly from the Freirian insight that one is always, in reading, necessarily reading the wor(l)d—the world and the word, bound together in a "dynamically intertwined" relationship—this statement is at once strikingly programmatic and deceptively straightforward. Elsewhere (Green, 1991), I have developed this point in my own way, in referring to reading in terms of the strategic interplay of "text" and "context" as semiotic categories, emphasizing their dynamic undecidability. That remains for me a compelling thesis, if a nagging one, because I am very much sensitive to the need for rendering it less abstract than it currently is and has been for some time now. Accounts such as that provided by Luke and Freebody certainly offer possibilities in this regard. However, "context" is too easily jettisoned, it seems to me, as here, although the argument against its (realist) formulation remains formidable. Equally problematical is their common sense usage of "text," as here, to denote the "hinge" on which world and word turn, as a tangible expression of the significant materiality of cultural practice. What does it mean, for instance, to refer to "values and ideologies, discourses and world views *in* the text" (chap. 12, p. 195, emphasis added)?

At this point it becomes appropriate to draw in more formal accounts of textuality and politics, and more specifically the relation between "problems of textuality and the field of politics" (Spivak, 1990, p. 1) because that would seem the crucial referent for "critical literacy"

---

[2]I take up some of these issues, including this particular headline, elsewhere (Green, 1997).

in this instance. This means engaging, or confronting, the spectre of *deconstruction*. To do this is also to suggest the value of philosophy in and to debates such as this, notwithstanding the fact that philosophy as such is unfashionable today, and effectively marginalized. Two points can be made here, at the outset: First, deconstruction *is* reading, and second, it is best understood and practiced as a distinctive species of textual politics. Hence, part of what is at issue is precisely the significance of the work of Derrida in and for literacy pedagogy, conceived explicitly as a political project. This is not the place to explore that thesis in the manner it requires and deserves; suffice it, rather, to indicate something of what might be involved in such a venture.

Above all else, then, deconstruction is to be reckoned as *reading*, as a specific mode of reading practice. As such, it encompasses both a politics and an ethics, understood not so much in terms of a "method" or a "program" as of a distinctive, and distinctively worldly, *attitude*. That is to say, deconstruction is to be grasped as a strategy, an attitude, a stance toward texts, institutions, the social world and Being itself. Derrida (1988) himself has always been very clear about this: "Deconstruction is not a method and cannot be transformed into one" (p. 3). Importantly, his concern in this regard is directed not simply at reading but also at politics, and hence the relationship between reading and politics. Spivak (1990) wrote thus of "Derrida's articulation of a new politics of reading: that you do not excuse a text for its historical aberrations, you admit that there is something in the text that produces these readings. . . . But then making the protocols of the text your own, you tease out the critical moments in the text and work at useful readings—readings that are scrupulous re-writings"(p. 107). Texts are always already implicated in history, including the history of their own régimes and practices of production and reception. Reading texts is therefore always necessarily a reading of history, which might be seen also as the complex conjoining of "word" and "world," "text," and "context." As Derrida glossed the notion of *deconstruction*: "it's a matter of gaining access to the mode in which a system or structure, or ensemble, is constructed or constituted, historically speaking. Not to destroy it, or demolish it, nor to purify it, but in order to accede to its possibilities and its meaning; to its construction and history" (Mortley, 1991, p. 97). At issue here is the vexed and contentious issue of "textuality," to be conceived above all else as a matter of *worldliness*. Spivak, again:

> I think the notion of textuality was broached precisely to question the kind of thing it is today seen to be—that is, the verbal text, a preoccupation with being in the library rather than being on the street. As far as I understand it, the notion of textuality should be related to the notion of a worlding of the world on a supposedly uninscribed territory. (p. 1)

Moreover, "this worlding is also a texting, a textualising, making into art, a making into an object to be understood" (Spivak, 1990, p. 1). She cited the example of imperialism, and all the dangers of "textuality" or "textualism" might be evoked at this point, in her own forms of expression ("art," "object," or even "worlding") as much as in the example itself, as an always already textualized reference point. What might it mean to understand "poverty" in these terms, or "disadvantage"—clearly key words in the lexicon of "critical literacy?" How is it possible to write about, for instance, "poverty?" Who is it that writes thus? For what reason(s)? What counts as "poverty?" In short, how is "poverty" constituted as "an object to be understood?" And then again, what might "understanding" mean in this context, and why does "understanding" matter, if indeed it does? These are questions at the very heart of the deconstructionist project.

But what does all this mean from the point of view of politics, and even or especially a provisional, pragmatic politics in and for postmodern conditions (A. Luke, 1995), where things need to get done—and are done—regardless of theoretical subtleties and scruples, like the mundane necessities of housework or the practices of everyday life and global postmodern-capitalist culture alike? Here it is becomes imperative to confront head-on the single most dangerous "myth" concerning Derrida's work, what Brunette and Wills (1989) described as "the supposed apolitical and ahistorical nature of deconstruction" (p. 21). Their refutation of this "misreading"—like that of figures such as Ryan (1982) and Spivak, and many others, to say nothing of Derrida himself—represents a powerful and convincing counter construction. What emerges very clearly is that politics and history are immanent in deconstructionist readings and writings, with a necessary relation proposed and generated between the "local" and the "global" dimensions of (con)textuality, the "inside" and the "outside" of textual practice. As much and often at the same time—although not necessarily so—as a political intervention "out there," in the world, deconstruction compels attention to the local politics of reading and teaching, "in here," in the classroom and the text. It encourages a relentless vigilance, including a self-regard that is always poised between introspection and interrogation. Hence:

> Deconstruction cannot found a political program of any kind. Deconstruction points out that in constructing any kind of an argument we must move from implied premises, that must necessarily obliterate or finesse certain possibilities that question the availability of these premises in an absolutely justifiable way. Deconstruction teaches us to look at these limits and questions. It is a corrective and critical movement. It seems to me, also, that because of this, deconstruction suggests that there is no absolute justification of *any* position. (Spivak, 1990, p. 104)

Or as Johnson (1981) put it, in describing deconstruction as "a form of what has long been called a *critique*":

> A critique of any theoretical system is not an examination of its flaws or imperfections. It is not a set of criticisms designed to make the system better. It is an analysis that focuses on the grounds of that system's possibility. The critique reads backwards from what seems natural, obvious, self-evident, or universal, in order to show that these things have their history, their reasons for being what they are, their effects on what follows from them, and that the starting point is not a (natural) given but a (cultural) construct, *usually blind to itself*. (p. xv; italics added)

As she continued: "Every theory starts somewhere; every critique exposes what that starting point conceals, and thereby displaces all the ideas that follow" (p. xv). Importantly, deconstruction as a mode of reading and textual politics is reflexive, or self-disclosing, never taking for granted its right to read thus, and in this event; always problematizing its own speaking position and its own enunciative practice, as always already implicated in the metaphysics of power and the power of metaphysics.[3] In Johnson's (cited in Salusinszki, 1987a) terms:

> In order to be truly deconstructive, you would have constantly to move the locus of your questions, not just to move on to another text. You'd have to say: "What am I doing, sitting and talking like this, in this institution?" And: "Why am I reading this text?" Instead of just, "This text is a given, now let me read it." (p. 158)

What is contested and challenged in this way is the claim to take up any position *outside* power and metaphysics in any absolute sense, and to seek to occupy accordingly the privileged, pristine space of commentary. Not that commentary or even advocacy are denied altogether, or discounted as strategy; rather, the emphasis and the injunction is on taking *care*.

Noting the "Leftist" identifications of those critical of deconstruction's supposed apoliticism, Brunette and Wills (1989) observed that "the stumbling block that will always remain for Marxists" (p. 21) and similarly oriented critics is that

---

[3]For instance, rather more prosaically perhaps, the "context" here might well explicitly be drawn into a reading of the "text"—the book itself, a worldly intervention into the field of literacy pedagogy and education studies; the chapter, written and authorized by two of the editors, both key players in the debate and the scene; the history of its production, including its originating conference event; reputations, constituencies, and agendas; the whole question of positioning within a competitive academic-intellectual market, and so on.

deconstruction does not allow *any* text to remove itself from the play of difference, including even those political texts that may 'use' deconstructive techniques to analyze culture but that then characteristically want to privilege their own discourse. What deconstructionists have always insisted upon, to the understandable dismay of some, is that political texts as well are written in language and not in some unmediated metalanguage far above the fray. (pp. 21-22)

No text is "innocent," or disengaged from the arenas and forums, praxis traps and problematics that it purports to represent, however complex or sophisticated its understanding of representation, power, and textuality. Indeed, such texts might well be most dangerous of all, because they are so clearly on the side of the Angels, and seemingly so complicit with our own investments and desires.

A further aspect of why deconstruction, and Derrida generally, are viewed with such suspicion or disdain, or dismissed as irrelevant to practical fields such as literacy pedagogy, is the perception of their characteristic "difficulty." Why is reading deconstruction so difficult? Isn't it, at best, esoteric and avant-gardist, and at worst, elitist and exclusionary? This is an important point, and quite fundamental to any political assessment of deconstruction and reading pedagogy. There are various rejoinders to this kind of criticism. One concerns the very question of linguistic or textual "difficulty," and involves the manner in which Derrida's writings strategically play with *form*, the form of the question and philosophy and the form of the text, foregrounding rhetoric as the counterpoint to logic and thus staging the play of knowledge, argument and textuality. "Style" matters, literally. The very resistance to the idea(l) of "clarity" that Derrida's work characteristically performs, and that deconstructionist readings often exhibit, serves to highlight the problematic nature of logocentric rationality: the desire for transparency and simplicity, to "see through"—unimpeded, unmediated—the complex materiality of meaning-making and institutional practice. Rather than nihilism or decadence ("art for art's sake"), then, deconstruction can be seen as exploring and thematizing the limits of reading, as intrinsic to reading. Consequently one well-known formulation of deconstruction goes as follows:

Deconstruction is not a form of textual vandalism designed to prove that meaning is impossible. . . . The deconstruction of a text does not proceed by random doubt or generalised scepticism, but by the careful teasing out of warring forces of signification *within the text itself.* (Johnson, 1981, p. xiv)

Again, vigilance is the key, and scrupulous attention to the *practice* of close reading and to the interrogation of text , or rather, to the intricate interplay of "text" and "context," bearing in mind always that this is more than a matter simply of "the verbal text," as Spivak indicated. Moreover, it is important that reading is thus estranged, defamiliarized—the familiar act(s) of reading made strange, or denatured, and the desire for information-as-exchange thwarted accordingly, or at least delayed. From a pedagogical point of view, of course, this assumes that reading as such *has* become naturalized, and hence could be seen as dependent on established reading capacities and competencies: a second-order operation, parasitic with regard to the first-order business of "learning-to-read." Again the question of systematization emerges, or "institutionalization," and the production and deployment of identities and places, demarcations and relationalities ("reading" is here and not there, is this and not that; one is ready now and not then, or not yet, and so on). Yet this raises precisely the (im)possibility of pedagogy, and what can be seen as a fateful aporia at the very heart of literacy itself, an unresolvable paradox. As Derrida himself argued, "deconstruction, to the extent that it's of some interest, must first insinuate itself everywhere, but not become a method or a school." Moreover, "if deconstruction is of some interest, it must have effects on teaching at all levels" (Salusinszki, 1987b, p. 14). What can this mean, however, in "practice"?

A critical-poststructuralist discourse-analytic view of reading pedagogy that seeks to bring together the "political" and the "practical": that is the promise of Luke and Freebody's essay into "critical literacy." Duly acknowledging its value and achievement, then, I want now to tease out some of its "warring significations," and in this way indicate (affirmatively) some of the complexities of the concept and the project that it seeks both to introduce and to represent. Clearly this will require a cool hand.

'Reading' is (re)defined at the outset as "a critical social practice," with reading pedagogy accordingly to be understood from an expressly social perspective. This argument is organized essentially in a "from . . . to . . ." structure: "Why not start from a social perspective on reading?" (chap. 12, p. 208). The challenge here is to shift our own ways of seeing and talking about reading from psychological to sociological models of reading? Although psychology is not dismissed out of hand (along with "50 years of reading instruction informed by psychology," p. 207), there is little doubt that it is presented as at least of limited and dubious value, along with so-called "personal growth"-oriented versions of literacy pedagogy and English teaching. The pedagogical consequences of these latter frameworks and discourses are described thus:

Psychological and personal growth models have tended to define the aims and outcomes of our instructional work in terms of student skills, knowledges and development—in terms of student personal choice, growth, self-esteem and, more recently, "individual empowerment." A sociological focus would stress the social concomitants and consequences of literacy. It shifts our classroom focus to the particular texts, discourses and practices that students have access to and to the different kinds of social activities and cultural action that instruction can shape, encourage and yield. (chap. 12, p. 208)

This is illustrated by a table setting one "model" up against the other, the "psychological" and the "sociological" ("On the left . . ."). All this is, itself, eminently "teachable": "Consider how we could talk about reading if we looked to the right-hand column." Overall, the table (as "text") is presented as indicating "the possibilities for shifting from psychological models that view reading as a 'natural' psychological process to those that view reading as a social and cultural practice."

Staged in this fashion—repeated, or quoted thus—what can be said about these formulations? The first thing to note is the orchestration of particular binaries, and a binary structure of argument, of a kind and to a degree that immediately invites a Derridean deconstructionist reading. It is not simply that the disciplines of sociology and psychology are hereby counterposed, and re-valued and evaluated accordingly, nor is it simply a matter of drawing out the ironically "sinister" evocations of all that is consigned here to the "left"—although a powerful case can and must be marshaled regarding the manner in which "inside" and "outside" are so easily and unproblematically (uncritically?) organized into distinct, highly classified ontological territories. This is because a series of slippages can be seen as activated, discursively, between "what happens invisibly in people's heads" and what is "in the text," and all that belongs properly speaking to the "outside," the "visible," the "public," the "social." "[W]hat reading *really* is" goes hand-in-hand with what the social *really* is—which means that what is at issue here, as much as anything else, is what counts as the social. Rather, the point is to indicate the manner and extent to which nothing can be taken-for-granted any more, in which everything is dangerous, including that which speaks for "us." A text such as this one, for all its virtues, has particular designs on "us," some of which it cannot and will not either recognize or acknowledge. Its "insights" are strategically, necessarily related to its "blindnesses." And hence the most appropriate reading is one that (also) goes against the grain, as it were, that is suspicious and skeptical *without* succumbing to the too-easy option of simply dismissing the argument, or of stopping reading; that reckons into calculation the full measure of complexity that attends all such exercises in rhetoric and textuality.

In grand philosophical terms, this means acknowledging complicity in Western metaphysics. The temptation, of course, is to say "So what?" Certainly this might well be the response of the practitioner, and perhaps understandably so. Indeed Luke and Freebody here avowedly seek to speak to and for the "practitioner," in setting out a comprehensive "prescriptive framework for looking at how teachers and students, lessons and programs are shaping reading as a social practice" (p. 200). Yet notions such as metaphysics and logocentric rationality, although not usually part of the lexicon of schooling or reading pedagogy, are not at all necessarily either abstruse or abstract, nor are they lacking in relevance; rather, they are *different*. Not only is there arguably a close relation between "ideology," however this is understood, and metaphysics, as Ryan (1982, p. 117) proposed ("metaphysics [as] the infrastructure of ideology"), but metaphysics itself might be better understood as a practical resource for living and learning, or rather, a resource for *practice*. This includes the practice of critique:

> [T]he aim of Derrida's critique is to work through, to unpack the operations of logocentrism, the functions by which Western thinking has assured its sameness and repressed its otherness, but in such a way as to avoid falling back into a system of analysis that does nothing but repeat, in practice, those very same pitfalls. (Brunette & Wills, 1989, p. 12)

In this regard, then, the pervasive binary logic that structures Luke and Freebody's account of reading pedagogy is neither incidental or accidental. Why for instance is there so much energy devoted, here and elsewhere in the discourse of "critical literacy," to expelling all traces of interiority, including presumably those associated with psychoanalysis? The very insistence here with which the classical relations of "inside" and "outside" are reorganized and reversed is symptomatic: *from* "psychology" *to* "sociology." Yet it is always a simple reversal, from one to the other (from "voice" to "text"), rather than a displacement of the system altogether, and the flip into another, now dynamic and undecidable space marked by complexity, chaos, and risk: the "real" order of things. Instead, what happens here is, in effect, a re-play of the same metaphysical game, which cannot do anything other than "repeat, in practice, those very same pitfalls" that characterize its expelled Other. Hence, identities are assigned, hierarchies established, textualities domesticated: business as usual.

This may seem, itself, too esoteric and abstract: too "impractical." After all, what is needed, surely, is a way of making complexity manageable, and classrooms and schools are perhaps above all else exemplary sites of social complexity. The virtue of Luke and Freebody's project in this instance, and that of "critical literacy" more generally, is that it is deliberately made *programmatic;* that is, it is realized as a program for pragmatic-intellectual work in educational sites. As such, it risks Error and metaphysics, and the praxis traps of various "isms" (reformism, pragmatism, opportunism . . .). It willingly takes on the obligation of "getting [its] hands dirty," in the interests of "everyday pedagogic work" (A. Luke, 1995). That is its supreme virtue, yes; but there are costs and limits, and these must also be drawn into calculation. In response to the request for "a lay-person's definition of deconstruction" (when it gets down to the "bottom line"), Johnson made the following point: "What deconstruction does is teach you to ask: 'What does the construction of the bottom line leave out? What does it suppress? What does it disregard? What does it consider unimportant? What does it put in the margins?' " (Salusinszki, 1987a, p. 164). These are crucial questions that need to be put to "critical literacy," and to Luke and Freebody. It would be possible to indicate ways in which the now ritualistic, doctrinal reading of progressivism can be understand in these terms, *without denying either the value of or necessity for critique in this instance.* But I want to take a somewhat different tack here. I want, instead, to draw attention to some of the consequences and implications of the shift to "sociology" as a preferred frame for rethinking reading pedagogy.

In particular, the question of *framing* becomes pertinent. In arguing for a social perspective, Luke and Freebody's preferred emphasis on economics and political economy is made very clear. A crucial link is thus constructed between "literacy" and "economics," within a "critical sociology" that foregrounds and forges a close and necessary relation between "reading pedagogy" (in this instance) and "political economy"—the project is ultimately addressed to formulating "a theoretical *and* practical framework" for operationalizing a political economy of reading pedagogy. Bringing this to earth, grounding it, making it "worldly" and now conceivably part of "everyday pedagogic work": there is no doubt about the value of such a project. A political economy perspective is indeed much needed in and for the task of "constructing critical literacies." But what is excluded, or glossed over, or marginalized, or simply unseen or unthinkable in such arguments and orientations? What is at issue here is a particular formulation of politics, which is arguably as constricting and constrictive as it is "constructive." Is *power* exhausted in its intimate exchanges with *economy*? Is there anything else? Anything left over, excessive? In short, political economy, made "practical," is the dominant framing for critical literacy, privileging therefore the economic dimensions of social life and human existence. But at what cost, especially when (or if) it becomes Law? What is kept at bay, what might be the other side of this "critical distance?" Can this be seen as a register of the characteristic "distancing" effect associated with intellectual practice and the intellectually trained?

In this spirit, consider the possibilities of drawing in a Heideggerian concern for Being, temporality, care and death, not so much as an alternative framing but as something in the order of a supplement-complement. What might this yield? What lies behind, or beyond, the necessary "abstractions" of economics and political economy, of sociological-existential categories such as "poverty" and "disadvantage?" In essence, literally, life and death. This means taking on board notions such *as* "Being-in-the-World" *as* "Being-toward-Death," in Heidegger's terms, and grasping the fact that, philosophically, literacy is to be understood as a quintessential human gesture *against* the awe-full fact of death, linked directly to "the fate of the earth": Death, therefore, as a limit condition of language and learning, and an aporia at the very heart of literacy pedagogy. Are such notions as poverty and disadvantage to be necessarily apostrophized ("poverty," "disadvantage"), in order to be understood, and revealed in all their unconcealing? How are they to be cited? Can they *be*? How re-cited, and by whom, and why? What story matters? Understanding poverty and disadvantage in these terms re-frames the accounting that can and must be made of the *project* of "critical literacy," as a political–philosophical matter of enormous moment. It is not enough, then, to talk about "reading" and "writing" the "word-world," not any more. Rather, we need to draw into our project the notion and the necessity of caring for the "word-world," of *care*; of attending to, engaging with, intervening on behalf of, and looking after what might now perhaps be better described simply as the Wor(l)d. Literacy and Care, then. Literacy and Death. "In the long run, we are all dead": a formulation, attributed to Keynes, which may serve here, however apocryphal, as a final telling aphorism, or an epitaph. "Being in the world is essentially care" (Heidegger, 1973, p. 237).

A question of Identity, then, of Being here and there and everywhere, of being in the library and on the street alike. Given this, how is the project of "critical literacy"[4] gathered in and brought together, as evidenced here? Crucially, the positive thesis is the provision of a distinctive "model" of reading, understood as a "critical social practice," and arguably fitted to the demands of "fast-capitalist late 20th-century society." The first thing that must be said is that this is

---

[4]Even if *literacy* is pluralized (literacies), could it be that the qualifying term *critical* arguably remains firmly, obdurately singular *in effect*, suggesting the persistence of a logic of "presence" or "identity" that, conceivably, contaminates the text more generally?

an avowedly prescriptive, normative account, writing, constructing, and claiming an agenda. It is therefore a matter of and for *representation*, and participates accordingly in what must be grasped from the outset as a politics of representation. Reading *is* this and not that. Secondly, what it specifically proposes is "a four-tiered model for thinking about literate demands of postmodern culture, work, and community, which stresses coding, semantic, pragmatic, and critical practice." What can be said about this, succinctly? One thing, certainly, is that, for all its "practical" heuristic and explanatory value, this is a statement fraught with metaphysical complexity and hazard. That wouldn't matter, of course, if it didn't have "worldly" consequences: in this case, the wager of an incoherence at its very heart, which threatens to bring the whole House of Cards tumbling down, or at least to generate a disturbance, a "noise" in the classroom. For one thing, there is the not-so-implicit metaphor organizing it: "a four-*tiered* model." Elsewhere, the point is made most emphatically that this is not intended as "a developmental sequence or cycle or taxonomy," and that "there is no 'natural' or necessary movement from coding to semantic to pragmatic to critical in an age/grade/program sequence," and hence by implication no hierarchy of emphasis and value in what is presented, diagrammatically, as "elements of reading as a social practice" (see Table 10.4). Yet clearly, even unavoidably the *effect* is to suggest that there is—not just in the way the argument is marshalled but also in the semiotic organization of the (printed) text. Perhaps it can be argued that the choice of "tier" in this instance is incidental and accidental, and at any rate picked up in a possibly wilful misreading. But Derrida, and Derrida's example, makes it impossible to console ourselves with this easy way out. The dictionary definition is unequivocal: "row or rank, esp. one of several placed one above the other as in a theatre; one of several units in a structure placed one above another" (*Aust. Concise OED*). "But you know what we *mean*." "What is always involved here, interminably and interminably paradoxically, is the question of reading" (Brunette & Wills, 1989, p. 5).

We must ask, finally, again and again: What is the status of the *critical* in the concept and the project of "critical literacy?" As the disciples begin to gather around, it becomes all the more imperative to question the "critical," to open up the debate, and to admit that nothing is certain or safe, and that this too after all is just a Fiction, albeit one that can and does have effects in the world. The risk, always, is that what we have here, in the end, is simply of an adjectival status, something that qualifies, or is added on to suit the moment or the cause. Might it not be the case, instead, that the necessary effort must now go into reclaiming literacy as, *from the outset*, always already political? That is, is the "critical" simply an "add on?" Or is it, rather, what Derrida (1976) described as a "necessary supplement"? If this latter is the case, then it throws the very project of "critical literacy" into disarray, or at least into history, because it means now that we can work, strategically, from the outset with a politicized understanding of literacy, with the view that any literacy worth the name (and worth working with and struggling for—worth spending time on . . .) is always already political, and moreover, an instrument and a resource for *change*, for challenging and changing the Wor(l)d.

Two points, in closing. One concerns the status and value of this present work towards the formation of a praxis-oriented socially critical agenda for curriculum and literacy. Nothing I have said and done here is possible, or at all intelligible, outside of its context of provocation and ('critical') dialogue: reading and writing and reading. . . . As Derrida insisted, deconstruction is *affirmative*. The other is offered here in the interests of continuing the debate and the interminable, pleasurable, (im)possible work of literacy and teaching. What haunts the discourse of "critical literacy," increasingly as it matures and enters into the institution, is the logic of *supplementarity*. There is, for me, some irony then in contemplating the manner in which the culture and metaphysics of print function as an implicit organizing principle in accounts such as these, even those that are clearly enlightened in this regard, as this undoubtedly is. Which leaves us with the enigma of the last section, addressed to the textual dynamics of "multimediated postmodern culture," curiously, awkwardly motivated, and, in an extraordinarily resonant sense, itself something of a final, compelling "add on."

REFERENCES

Baker, C. D., & Luke, A. (Eds.). (1991). *Towards a critical sociology of reading pedagogy*. Amsterdam/Philadelphia: John Benjamins.

Brunette, P., & Wills, D. (1989). *Screen/play: Derrida and film theory*. Princeton, NJ: Princeton University Press.

Derrida, J. (1976). *Of grammatology* (G. C. Spivak, Trans.). Baltimore/London: Johns Hopkins Press.

Derrida, J. (1988). Letter to a Japanese friend. In D. Wood & R. Bernasconi (Eds.), *Derrida and différance*. Evanston, IL: Northwestern University Press.

Freebody, P. Luke, A., & Gilbert, P. (1991). Reading positions and practices in the classroom. *Curriculum Inquiry, 21*, 435-458.

Green, B. (1991). Reading "readings": Towards a postmodernist reading pedagogy. In C. D. Baker & A. Luke (Eds.), *Towards a critical sociology of reading pedagogy*. Amsterdam/Philadelphia: John Benjamins.

Green, B. (1997). Born again teaching? Governmentality, "grammar" and public schooling. In T. S. Popkewitz & M. Brennan (Eds.), *Governmentality through education: Foucault's challenge to the institutional production and study of knowledge.* New York: Teachers College Press.

Heidegger, M. (1973). *Being and time* (J. Macquarie & E. Robinson, Trans.). Oxford, U.K.: Basil Blackwell.

Johnson, B. (1981). Translator's introduction. In J. Derrida, *Dissemination* (B. Johnson, Trans.). Chicago: The University of Chicago Press.

Luke, A. (1995). Getting our hands dirty: Provisional politics in postmodern Conditions. In P. Wexler & R. Smith (Eds.), *After postmodernism: Education, politics and identity.* London: The Falmer Press.

Luke, A., & Walton, C. (1994). Teaching and assessing critical reading. In T. Husen & T. Postlethwaite (Eds.), *International encyclopedia of education* (2nd ed.). London: Pergamon Press.

Mortley, R. (Ed.). (1991). Jacques Derrida [an interview]. In *French philosophers in conversation.* London/New York: Routledge.

Peters, M. (1995). Literacy, philosophy and postmodernism: An interview with Colin Lankshear. *The Australian Educational Researcher, 21*(3), 97-113.

Ryan, M. (1982). *Marxism and deconstruction.* Baltimore: Johns Hopkins University Press.

Salusinszki, I. (Ed.). (1987a). Barbara Johnson [an interview]. *Criticism in society: Interviews.* New York/London: Methuen.

Salusinszki, I. (Ed). (1987b). Jacques Derrida (an interview). *Criticism in society: Interviews.* New York/London: Methuen.

Spivak, G. C. (1990). *The post-colonial critic: Interviews, strategies, dialogues* (S. Harasym, Ed.). New York/London: Routledge.

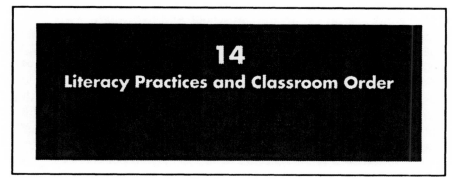

14
Literacy Practices and Classroom Order

Carolyn D. Baker
University of Queensland

CONSTRUCTING AND RECONSTRUCTING CLASSROOM LITERACIES

The project of remaking classroom literacies in the direction of producing new kinds of work with texts is the implicit if not explicit point of much recent theorizing about literacy practices in school. What is involved is the production of new literacies as new kinds of textual practice. Such a project goes well beyond changing formal aims and materials and methods in literacy curricula or changing surface features of language and literacy instruction. It extends to remaking classroom rules and relationships that are assembled through textual practice. As this chapter shows, classroom work with text is intimately tied to the construction of classroom order. The construction of classroom literacies involves organizing the production of classroom knowledge and assembling classroom relations in some way. As an account of how classroom literacies are constructed, the chapter gives an indication of what kind of work may be involved in reconstructing literacies.

The chapter is based on examples of how teachers and students construct classroom literacies through their talk and interaction around story texts. These illustrations are drawn from audiotapes of reading lessons in the first years of school. With these examples it is possible to observe connections between "the space of the classroom" and "the space of the textual practices that occur there" (McHoul, 1991, p. 201), and to consider ways in which changes to classroom literacies amount to remaking the classroom as a social and moral space, a theme taken up in several chapters in this volume (see chapters by Luke & Freebody, Hunter, Lee, and Threadgold, this volume).

LITERACY TALK AND CLASSROOM ORDER

Among the observations that can be drawn from studies of classroom literacy talk are: (a) that reading in school, and particularly early school reading, is a distinctive kind of reading (cf. Baker & Freebody, 1989a, 1989b; McHoul, 1991); and (b) that learning to read and write and talk in school is a special kind of learning (cf. Gee, 1996; A. Luke, 1992, 1993; Michaels, 1981, 1987). Early literacy events can be analyzed to show the pedagogical, institutional, and sociological work that is accomplished in the course of talk about texts. They can be analyzed to show how students are introduced to the practices and procedures that assemble the conventions of school reading and writing.

Studies of literacy events in the early years of schooling have been particularly informative for appreciating how students are made into members of a school-literate culture, or how they are excluded from membership. Studies of classroom literacy events have described how institutional relations, particularly relations of age and authority, are organized through classroom talk about text. Together, such studies show close connections between school-based literacies, pedagogies, and classroom order. These interconnections are produced as part of the texture of action and accomplishment in classroom talk.

One aim in this chapter is to elaborate these connections by analyzing instances of story talk in early schooling. The materials as well as the methods of literacy pedagogy are central to the social organization of classroom knowledge in the early years of school. The literacy events described here are all instances of classroom work with stories in books and were audiotaped in kindergarten and first-grade classrooms in New South Wales, Australia.

Storytelling and story reading sessions are prevalent features of early schooling. As introductions to school literature and as introductions to school literacy, stories are treated in various ways as texts to enjoy and/or texts to reason about and/or texts from which to learn information. The use of fictional texts can be seen as part of the constitution of childhood in early schooling (Baker & Freebody, 1987, 1989b). Such texts provide characterizations of the (child) readership that are in line with the ideologies surrounding early reading instruction and early schooling (A. Luke, 1988). Such texts also support particular textual practices, such as methods of "reading for character" (cf. Mellor & Patterson, 1991) and, closely associated, reading for storyline or plot. The selection of fictional texts and the reading practices that follow that selection are consequential for what counts as reading in schools. Gender and generational relations also enter into literacy pedagogy and into the social and moral organization of the classroom through the use of story texts (cf. Baker & Davies, 1993). As this chapter shows, the classroom "story" is more than (and other than) the narrative found in a book. In several ways, the "story" stands at the center of early literacy pedagogies based on fictional texts written for children.

Another aim of this chapter is to present analyses of classroom storytalk that show how classroom order is achieved through the reasoning practices and reference to rules that are used in the course of these literacy events. Studying methods of reasoning about texts and culture, including classroom culture, draws attention to the importance of "cultural logic" in making sense of texts in classrooms (cf. Heap, 1985). The codes of classroom life are also found in the work that classroom members do in reference to rules of participation and of reading.

This work with rules is introduced through the metaphor of ceremony and game in reading events. Reading events are shown to be situated within classroom ceremonies. The story in the text is read from within, and as part of, the ongoing assembling of classroom order. As participants reason about texts and their relation to culture, they make and sustain reference to rules for relating in the classroom. These rules for relating are textually mediated (Smith, 1988); talk about specific stories grounds the institutional relations being organized in the classroom talk.

These analyses are brought together to show how the social order of the classroom—its coherence as a social and moral space—is an effect of literacy practices and an effect of pedagogy. This interest in classroom order as an effect of literacy practices is turned toward a consideration of the possibilities and limits of introducing substantially different reading practices in early schooling.

LEARNING TO READ AND LEARNING TO RELATE IN SCHOOL

Literacy lessons in early schooling show the various practices that teachers and students use to relate to text and to relate to each other. These practices include references to rules of participation and procedure in reading events and methods of reasoning about story content. These practices are powerful in assembling the social and moral order of the classroom. An example of the beginning moments of a reading session in a first-grade classroom shows this work being done:

1. T It could well be just like last week's story couldn't it? What was our story last week?
2. S One Cold Wet=
3. T =Oh, someone put (up) their hand up. They
4. S Uhh!

5.   T   They might've even had the right answer. Helen.
6.   H   One Cold Wet Night.
7.   T   One Cold Wet Night. (From) the look of the outside I think it might be a cold wet day. (2.5) And perhaps a cold wet night. Alright well our story this week is, Yes Ma'am. Yes Ma'am. . . .

Classroom order is assembled by teachers and students as a framework of rules of participation and procedure (see Davies, 1983). This framework includes preferred methods for working with text, as well as methods for interacting. In this first illustration, the rules for talking in class overlap with the methods used for the production of a correct answer and of the grounds for excluding or including ideas in the storytalk. Rules are invoked—they are made, and made relevant—in the course of working out what should happen in the reading of a story. These references to rules underlie the moral order that is being described and achieved in the course of classroom reading.

CEREMONY AND GAME IN READING EVENTS

The analogies of *ceremony* and *game* can be used to describe the ways in which classroom literacy has been organized, routinized, conventionalized, and naturalized. Research on classroom talk has shown some of the procedural routines and games that defer achieving some knowledge or insight or, more to the point, crediting it, until the pedagogic hoops have been gone through (see, e.g., Baker & Freebody, 1989b, 1993; Cazden, 1981; Hammersley, 1977). Further to this, classroom reading and writing can be seen to have their own ceremonial order that is ultimately a moral order linking (adult) teachers, (child) students, and (school) texts in systematic relations.

McHoul (1991), drawing on the work of Freadman (1987/1994), considered the relation of ceremony and game in connection to classroom reading. Referring to tennis, Freadman (1987/1994) commented that:

> Ceremonies are games that situate other games; they are the rules for the setting of a game, for constituting participants as players in the game, for placing and timing it in relation to other places and times. They are the rules for the playing of a game, but they are not the rules of the game. (pp. 46-47)

McHoul's interest was in the ceremonies of classroom reading, the conventions and traditions of reading in a classroom. As he put it, "The category of ceremony, in effect, subsumes the game" (pp. 197–198). Where does ceremony end and game begin? Reading pedagogy can be equated with achieving the ceremonial order of the classroom in that whatever text is read, whoever is present or not on the day, there will be ceremonies for the setting up and rules for the "playing" of the reading. These ceremonies and games are sites where students are being shown how to organize talk in these literacy sessions. These ceremonies and games are central to the moral order of the classroom, as just described. Aspects of this are developed with further extracts from early literacy lessons.

In the analysis of the next transcript, taken from a first-grade reading lesson, attention is given to the students' work in finding the rules of the game embedded in the ceremony that precedes and subsumes it, and finding them, in this case, problematic.

1.   T (It's a) story about Arthur.
2.   Ss ((giggles, comments))
3.   T Let's have a look at the picture
4.   S ( ) my brother has this
         ((faint whistling))
5.   T What do you think this story's going to be about
         ((whistling))
6.   T Mike?
7.   S [Um I was just going-to s//
         [((whistling))
8.   T //You've read the story have you ['cause your brother's got it
9.   S   [yeah
10.   T well if you haven't read it, now [if you keep making
                                          [((whistling))
      that noise I think (you're going to spoil our story). Have a look
      at the picture and tell me [what the story is about. Brett?
                                  [((whistling))
11.   B It's about this [dog called Arthur
                         [((whistling))
12.   T Yes about a dog called Arthur. 'N if you look closely, he's a
      [bit of a strange dog.
      [((whistling))
      He's doing some funny things there.
13.   Ss ((laugh))
14.   T Let's find out what [happens about Arthur
15.   S   [different
      Ss ((whispering 4 seconds))
16.   S I think we've had this before
17.   T Have you [well you haven't had it our class=
18.   S   [yes
19.   S =in this class
20.   T [maybe you had it in library or something like that
21.   S [in this class

22. S [in kindy
23. T Oh well, let's see, [I'm sure it's a story
24. S 　　　　　　　　[have we?
25. S 　　　　　　　　[( ) long time ago
26. T that you've enjoyed if you have had it. ((reads)) ARTHUR WAS
　　　A VERY ORDINARY DOG. HE LIVED...

In this extract, the issue is how the story is to be read. The teacher begins with the proclamation that it is a story about Arthur (line 1), then asks the students to look at the picture (line 3), then asks them what they *think* the story is going to be about (line 5), repeats the instruction to look, and repeats the question (line 10), and acknowledges the answer (line 12) that the story is about a dog called Arthur. Across this sequence some whistling can be heard and in line 10 the teacher attempts to stop the student(s) "making that noise" and "spoiling our story." This is a best hearing of the latter phrase, which is unclear on the tape. If it is "spoiling our story," it can only be heard as "spoiling this *reading* of the story." "Our story" becomes not what is in the text, but in the collective reading of the text. The "story," then, is a *course of classroom action*.

In lines 4, and 6 to 10, we hear a side sequence involving, at best guess, one student and the teacher. Assuming it is the same student speaking and being addressed in lines 4, 7, 8, and 9, the teacher's comment in line 10 can be heard as disqualifying Mike from participating in answering the questions because he has presumably read the story before or knows it because his brother has it. Line 10 serves as an announcement for how students may participate in the story reading ("well if you haven't read it"). This observation is presented in an earlier analysis of this segment (Baker & Freebody, 1989b). The teacher's comment could also be heard as holding out to Mike as well the possibility that although his brother has the story, he might not have read it, so, he could participate as if he has not read it. We cannot be certain exactly what agreement was reached between the teacher and Mike in respect of his previous knowledge of the story, but whichever way we take this, the issue of having read it before or not is certainly on the table.

Turning attention to the students' work, it is possible that Mike, or someone, as early as line 4, only seconds into the teacher's reading of the story, signaled the issue. The teacher seems to have heard this signal across all the whistling:

4. 　S ( ) my brother has this
　　　((faint whistling))

5.   T What do you think this story's going to be about
          ((whistling))
6.   T Mike?
7.   S [Um I was just going-to s//
         [((whistling))
8.   T //You've read the story have you ['cause your brother's got it
9.   S   [yeah
10.   T well if you haven't read it, now if you keep making

Here the force of the *students'* appreciation of ceremony and game, of how ceremony shades into and subsumes the game, can be observed. What Mike (or whoever) could have or must have heard in the teacher's opening turns was an invitation to participate as if they had not had this story before. It is possible that Mike wanted to convey to the teacher that he had knowledge that could be helpful to her reading of the story, but in any case, the teacher in line 10 resolves in favor of talking as if the story is new. The ceremonial order of the classroom that Mike is concerned about is not the whistling but the clarification of how his previous knowledge of the story is to be handled. He had something to say of sufficient importance that he produced an unusual interjection: "Um I was just going to say." What he presumably heard in the teacher's opening to the story reading was an appeal to students to hear and enjoy the story in a way that matched her telling of it. This is continued in her appeal for them not to "spoil our story."

An analogy can be drawn between sorting out the rules for the playing of this game (reading this text) and the pre-game ceremonies in tennis matches: tossing of coins, choosing of sides, and so on, occur while the excited crowd is still waiting for the game proper to begin. But as indicated before, ceremony subsumes game in the classroom analogy. It takes a little time for the whistling to die down, as the game proceeds:

10.   T well if you haven't read it, now [if you keep making
                                          [((whistling))
         that noise I think (you're going to spoil our story). Have a look
         at the picture and tell me [what the story is about. Brett?
                                    [((whistling))
11.   B It's about this [dog called Arthur
                         [((whistling))
12.   T Yes about a dog called Arthur. 'N if you look closely, he's a
         [bit of a strange dog.
         [((whistling))
         He's doing some funny things there.

13. Ss ((laugh))
14. T   Let's find out what [happens about Arthur
15. S   [different
     Ss ((whispering 4 seconds))

In lines 12 to 14, the crowd seems to have settled. The teacher serves once, the students return, the teacher serves again, but then there is an interruption to the play. What follows is quite faint on the audiotape. It is again a commentary on the rules for the playing of the game; more students appear to notice a problem.

      Ss ((whispering 4 seconds))
16. S   I think we've had this before
17. T   Have you [well you haven't had it our class=
18. S   [yes
19. S   =in this class
20. T   [maybe you had it in library or something like that
21. S   [in this class
22. S   [in kindy
23. T   Oh well, let's see, [I'm sure it's a story]
24. S   [have we?
25. S   [( )long time ago]
26. T   that you've enjoyed if you have had it. ((reads)) ARTHUR WAS
         A VERY ORDINARY DOG. HE LIVED...

It is an unusual move for students to question the terms of the pedagogy in this way. This move is done delicately, following some whispering that may or may not be related to the pronouncements that follow. It is possible that some other students had heard and noted the earlier exchange with Mike, and the teacher's concern that "our story" not be spoiled (if these words have been heard correctly). This is being done "to" a teacher who is obviously trying to make the story something for them to enjoy. The teacher's position is recognizably one of resistance to the students' insistence that the story is not new and is an appeal that the students should hear and accept her terms for their engagement with the "story" as a course of classroom action.

It appears that the students' decision to comment is done in consultation with each other. They do it collectively, even talking, possibly, with each other (see lines 24–25) to sort out the problem (see also Baker, 1992). That this is "bad news" is found not only in the students' comments, but in the teacher's repeated appeals for reversing their decision. One student at least maintains that they have had this story in this class. The teacher's appeals are finally accepted and the story reading proceeds in the teacher's terms, and the students "enjoy" it with and for the teacher. In the rest of the audiotape, we hear much laughter, cheering, and applauding as demonstrations of that enjoyment. With the ceremonial order sorted out, the classroom game can proceed.

The ceremonial order of the classroom is one that assembles and celebrates some version of the "teacher–student couple" that Hunter (1991) identified as an ideological formation in modern schooling. In early literacy talk, the student is constituted as a learner, and further to this as a "child" learner, theorized and realized in and for the pedagogy (cf. Jenks, 1982). The teacher is the benevolent and necessary complement to this theorized learner. The classroom, in this formation, is not only a physical and social space, but also a morally organized course of action. This is seen in how the students question the presumptions of the teacher's work (i.e., her deployment of a pedagogy that involves their agreement to being positioned by her teaching practice). But also, it is evident in how they hear her need and desire for them to enjoy the story with her and for her (and possibly the researchers who had asked for the recording to be made). The teacher's appeals to other places they might have had this story are attempts to remedy their shared problem, invoking a rule that the reading that counts is this one, with her. In these very appeals, the teacher is invoking the foundation of their relationship as members of the same social and moral space, their class.

LEARNING TO READ AND LEARNING TO REASON

The force of the ceremony–game metaphor in classroom practice, with ceremony surrounding and subsuming the game, is that "the rules for the playing of the game" are the rules that are used to assemble the classroom as an ongoing course of action. The occasioning of these rules provides continuity. Whatever the specific game (e.g., text being read), the organizational work preceding, surrounding, and subsuming the game calls on a history of other games, and situates and naturalizes every new game. As Freadman (1987/1994) stated, these are rules "for constituting participants as players in the game, for placing and timing it in relation to other places and times" (p. 47). This can be seen in the organization of the brief sequence presented earlier:

1.   T It could well be just like last week's story couldn't it? What was our story last week?
2.   S One Cold Wet=
3.   T =Oh, someone put (up) their hand up. They
4.   S Uhh!

5.   T They might've even had the right answer. Helen.
6.   H One Cold Wet Night.
7.   T One Cold Wet Night. (From) the look of the outside I think it might be a cold wet day. (2.5) And perhaps a cold wet night. Alright well our story this week is, Yes Ma'am. Yes Ma'am. ...

In this transcript, the teacher makes reference to two (and only two) stories, last week's and this week's. No matter how many other stories the students could have heard, read, told, watched on television, and so on, there are only two that count as "our" stories. These are the story that was read collectively with the teacher "last week" and the one to be read with the teacher "this week" (a history of other games). The grammar here is that "weeks" have "stories." Students are asked to orient to the *school* week (their time with this teacher) as the relevant time frame, and to select from that frame, one event. The event that counts as "our story" appears to be a specific, ceremonial classroom event: a book read in a particular way, the way that "this week's" is going to be read, a story reading in which *the teacher* was included ("our story last week").

It is improbable that over the course of a school week only one story is encountered or referred to or read or written by any or all of the students or the teacher. The students can find which story the teacher is referring to with their knowledge of the rules for the playing of this game, including who the players are. First, they may be assembled physically in a special way, for example in a reading circle that is part of "the week's story" ceremony. This could be enough, just as hearing the microphone tested on a sports field tells us that the game is about to begin. But even so assembled, they can find *which story* at the intersection of two categorization devices (cf. Sacks, 1974): "stories last week" and "stories read in this way with this teacher" (for example, seated like this). Categorization devices are made up of collections of categories and of rules for their application. Teacher reference to "last week's story" is not unique to this lesson. Retrieving what "we" did or covered or talked about last lesson, last week, last term, last year is a routine opening to many lessons and students have to select, given sometimes relatively few or oblique clues to the categorization devices in play, what it is that "we" did. And that is most usually what "we" as this class did with this teacher, or, more specifically, what it could be that the teacher presumes "we" did. On each such occasion, the classroom is constituted as an ongoing cast of players and an ongoing course of action.

READING AS A DISPLAY OF REASONING

What we observe in these examples of early introductions to classroom literacy practices can be seen as moral–organizational work in the sense of achieving the rule-governedness of their action and interaction. That is, rather than viewing the teacher and students as "following" rules, we can view them as positing rules, referring to rules, constructing and reconstructing rules: finding the order in their talk and interaction. The interactive process of finding the rules that could govern their actions and interactions is part of the work of moral organization. We can think of these as rules of participation, rules of category membership and relationship, and rules of textual practice. Furthermore, because rules are invoked in accounting for their actions and interactions, we can see teacher and students audibly finding their interactions in relation to text and to each other as rule-governed, rule-oriented, and principled. This perspective again leads us to see how closely related are the institutional, social, and moral orders of the classroom.

In another first-grade story-reading session it is possible to see the organization of a page-by-page, question-by-question, naturalized, normalized and routinized relationship. In this case, the teacher's interest in the students' reading is organized around how they achieve displays of reasoning:

19. T ... okay. Have a look at the next page. What do we see him in here, Tammy?
20. Ta He's flying a racing airplane with a dog in the back that doesn't like it up in the air.
21. T He doesn't, h- how do you know he doesn't like being up in the air?
22. Ta Because he's ( ) he doesn't look like, he's doesn't the puppy isn't looking very uh sa- isn't very happy.
23. T He's looking rather pale to me. He's sort of thinking "we're a bit far up in the air. I don't like this very much!" How do you think the, Smarty Pants feels, Chris? Is he quite happy?=

The task for the participants in this reading lesson appears to be to interpret illustrations as a means of "reading" the story. This task is produced and led by the teacher through questioning and through reformulation of the students' answers. The questions are organized around two sets of teacher concerns that are available in the teacher's talk: What is going on with the text characters? and How do you know? The first concern, with the actions and motives of text characters, is hearable as a concern with the fictional truth of the story, and as an early introduction to "reading for character" which is prevalent in the teaching of literature. This concern is made possible by the selection of a fictional text, a "story." "What is going on here?" is the same kind of question that anyone could ask in trying to follow a narrative.

The second concern—how do you know?—signals a specialist, pedagogic, interest. It calls on students to describe their reasoning practices in work with text, and the talk amounts to a running demonstration of the "rationality" of their collective story reading. There is a repeated request in this teacher's talk to make explicit how we/you can know these things, how we can interpret the characters' actions and motives. When these ways are found, they are made collective solutions to puzzles the teacher has found in the text. This talk could be viewed as a clear case in point of Heap's (1985) observation that reading comprehension is "comprehension of culture and the logic of its organisation and possibilities" (p. 247) and that literacy teaching is acculturation. What this teacher can be seen to be doing is to call for displays of reasoning practices employed in looking at illustrations. This second interest of the teacher is a specifically pedagogic interest, asking the students to show how they are reasoning, asking them to match their reasoning practices to hers. In addition to being expected to read the story line from the illustrations, students are being expected to provide accounts of how they or anyone would and could arrive at correct answers.

23.   T He's looking rather pale to me. He's sort of thinking "we're a bit far up in the air. I don't like this very much!" How do you think the, Smarty Pants feels, Chris? Is he quite happy?=
24.   C [Yep!
25.   T =[Yes, I think he's [enjoying himself. Beg your pardon?
26.   S   [going sideways to:o
27.   S He's going sideways, too.
       T Right, he is too. Yes he's doing some tricks. ((turns page)) Oh, what's happening here?
28.   S ((giggles))
29.   T What's happening what's happening here, Mandy? What's he got in his mouth?
30.   M He's blowing a trumpet and the dog doesn't like it, 'cause I think it's going in his, in the dog's ear.
31.   T Right. He's blowing a trumpet. But how could we tell that the dog doesn't like it? ((sternly:)) Emily! ((back to usual voice:)) How could we tell, Helen, that the dog doesn't like it?

The participants' orientation to the two-part sequence ("what is happening?" and "how do we know?") as a template for this literacy talk is shown in Mandy's provision in turn 30 with more than "what is happening?" She adds a "because" clause. The teacher accepts her "what is happening?" answer but issues part two again: "how could we tell?" Helen finds a clue, which the teacher endorses.

32.   H   'Cause he's um looking a little bit pale.
33.   T   He's looking a little bit pale, and he's got his hand up to his *what*. He's saying "oh this is just a bit much for me." Cindy he's got his hand up to his?
34.   C   Ears. So he can't hear it.
35.   T   (answer.) Mrs Jamison might like to have a couple of people in her office Emily! Right, what's happening here? Donna?
36.   D   He's swimming in the, he's swimming in the pool.
37.   T   Right, he's swimming in the pool! (3.0) Is he enjoying that? Is he having a lot of fun doing that? Simone Enn?
38.   S   Um the dog doesn't like water because um because, because it's more deeper.
39.   T   Right, good girl. Good answer the dog doesn't like the water very much, we can tell by the look on his face. Right, he's a little bit afraid p'haps perhaps he thinks it's just a little bit deep for him. What about Smarty Pants, is he frightened? Is he frightened of that water Emily?

There is much more than filling in the blanks of the teacher's guided tour of the story available in this transcript. The students could take it that they are being asked to find answers to questions, and that their reading consists of that activity, at least for this lesson. Their reading can, however, be seen to involve also some other kinds of cultural work.

Question-asking and answering are methods in the description of competent reasoning practices: What is there to say about a text like this, and how are these things sensibly said? What are the contours of plausibility—rationality—as expressible through a reading of this story in this site? What is a warranted interpretation of an illustration? This appreciation and reproduction of the "local rationality" (cf. Heap, 1990) of the story reading is a form of intellectual work, and equally a significant form of cultural work. What is also produced through this talk is a description of the social and moral order of the classroom in which this talk is taking place.

The talk takes as its topic the possibilities and facts of the story in the book. The talk is also situated within the classroom as a social space. The local rationality of story reading is therefore found to be part of the local rationality of the classroom as a site for doing literacy talk. The story, again, becomes not the words and illustrations in a book, but an ongoing course of classroom action in relation to the book.

How things are competently done is presented as how things should be done. Thus, the social facts of the story and classroom become moral facts. The story reading is collective work that organizes a trajectory of practice through the story reading. This is a trajectory that becomes oriented to, as rule-governed and principled, and that connects characters' actions (what are they doing) with readers' actions (how do you know).

39. T Right, good girl. Good answer the dog doesn't like the water very much, we can tell by the look on his face. Right, he's a little bit afraid p'haps perhaps he thinks it's just a little bit deep for him. What about Smarty Pants, is he frightened? Is he frightened of that water Emily?
40. E No
41. T How can you tell?
42. E Because he's smiling.
43. T Right, he's smiling he thinks that's a lot of fun, he's really enjoying that. ((page turning)) Right, goodness me! Isn't he a clever person he can do lots and lots of things. What's he doing here? Somebody who hasn't talked to me? Susie Tee?

This twin interest in what is going on, and how can you/we tell, in this case of story reading, looks to be a teacher's way of making particular ways of looking, thinking and reasoning intelligible and valid. The teacher is supplying a "canon of procedure," "rules of grammar" (McHugh, 1974, p. 332) that can govern story-reading.

44. S He's skiing.
45. T Right. Is he enjoying that?
46. S [No
47. T [What sort of skiing is he doing, Chris?
48. S (Snow).
49. T What sort of skiing is it? Is he water skiing?
50. S Snow [skiing
51. T   [He's snow skiing. How do we know he's snow skiing. How do we know he's snow skiing, Heidi?
52. H Because um you can see the snow.
53. T Right we can see the snow and he's got these special snow skis. And what are these things for? What do you think these things are for, Nicole? Why is he holding these things?

The working out of "rules for reading" and particularly of rules for accounting for one's reading as illustrated here shows that classroom readings are ultimately consensual practices that affirm membership of a moral community. However, although correct method should lead to correct knowledge, it does not guarantee it.

53.	T	Right we can see the snow and he's got these special snow skis. And what are these things for? What do you think these things are for, Nicole? Why is he holding these things?
54.	N	To help him go.
55.	T	Right, to help push him along. But what about the poor old dog. What does he think about it all, Bradley?
56.	B	He thinks (1.8) um (2.0) he fell off his skis and um (2.3) Smarty Pants uh um (3.0) ( ) pushed him the dog over.
57.	T	*Right.* Do you think that's what's happened? Smarty Pants has pushed him over or he's just fallen over? What do you think, has happened. Do you think that he's not such a good snow skier and he's *fall*en over? Sit down please.
58.	S	He's fallen over.
59.	T	Beg your pardon?
60.	S	I think he's probably has fallen over.
61.	T	You think he's fallen over. Okay, let's have a look at the next page. Oh! Goodness me from snow skiing to where? Where has he found himself here, Erica? (2.7) Erica Baker?

The student's proposal in line 56 that Smarty Pants had "pushed the dog over" as a way of accounting for the illustration is corrected by the teacher and student in lines 57 to 61. Here they agree that it was a case of the dog falling over because he is not a good skier, rather than a case of his being pushed over. This preferred interpretation is provided in the teacher's questions (57) that propose an alternative account of how it could have happened and that seek agreement to this alternative. This is an interpretation that withdraws responsibility from Smarty Pants, that deems him innocent of wrong-doing. It is an intervention in the story telling that suggests that the student made a mistake in reading character. This is a clear-cut moral lesson in how to "read for character," and a demonstration of how reading for character is a moral activity. The "subjectivity" of Smarty Pants and the learning-to-read subjectivity of the students are aligned in the work of description and the work of accounting throughout the story reading.

These instances of story reading could be examined in more detail for the methods the teacher and students use to invoke rules of participation, rules of category membership and relationship, and rules of textual practice. The achievement of orderliness in the talk is simultaneously the achievement of rationality (and morality) in the story text, and in the course of the here-and-now story reading.

The social relations, reasoning practices, and rule-referential work described here are organized around talk about character and storyline in fictional texts. In the course of reading these stories in school, an ongoing narrative of the classroom, with its own cast of characters, is produced. Students read themselves into membership of the classroom by reading themselves into the characters and plots of these stories under instruction from the teacher's questions.

GENERATIONAL RELATIONS

It can be seen in the transcripts presented here that the teachers are working from texts designed for reading with and by "children." A generational relationship between teacher and students is implied in the selection of texts and in methods of reading them. This is part of what makes books "appropriate" for children at school. The texts are selected to provide for particular textual practices, and to enable and not to interrupt or confound the production of classroom order. The texts used often in early reading instruction are "stories," works of fiction, that sustain talk about improbable events that can be made "fictionally true." The "space of the story" fits nicely into the "space of the classroom" and the "space of the reading practices that occur there" (cf. McHoul, 1991, p. 201), in part because "stories" provide for the teacher's continuing recognition and achievement of what children need or want, and therefore her own work as a teacher of children. The provision of early schooling through stories is part of the assembling of childhood (Baker & Freebody, 1989a). It is also part of the assembling of a teacher who complements the children for whom the stories are selected.

These generational relations are continuously recoded and reachieved in classroom ceremonies and games, in how teachers assemble students both literally and verbally through the questions they ask, so that the space of the texts (their characters' courses of actions) and the space of the classroom (its characters' courses of action) secure each other. These overlapping courses of action are shown in the talk presented here.

Different pedagogies fill in and fill out what kind of child/learner and what kind of adult/teacher are connected through the pedagogy. The teacher is the complement of whatever learner the pedagogy posits. Or, from the other direction, the learner is the recipient and beneficiary of the teacher's work, however that is described. These two central categories of classroom member are outlined and colored-in over the course of turns at talk. The moral–organizational work described here assembles and connects the subjects and agents of pedagogy.

TEXTS, TALK, AND CLASSROOM ORDER

The kinds of texts that are routinely worked with in some sites are consequential for the assembling of social and moral order in that site because these texts become parts of the courses of action and interaction that go on in the site. The classroom practice with story texts described here is one case of what Smith (1988) calls "textually mediated social organisation". The work that is done with texts is bound up with the contents and properties of the texts—in these cases specifically the characters and storylines—to produce connections between (in this case) the interiors of the stories to the interiors (feelings, reasoning) of the students. How different kinds of texts might work in organizing connections among literacy, pedagogy, and classroom order is an open question. "Critical" literacies would be part of a different texture of classroom order organized around some other forms of textual practice.

The invention and adoption of new ways with text entails an associated transformation of the category memberships and attributes and the social relations that obtain in the classroom. Talk about text assembles who the teacher and students are to each other, practically and morally. What a "teacher" says and does describes what kind of school-relevant category "teacher" is, what kind of character in what kind of classroom space. Similarly, the kind of work a student does in text reading defines what a student is (and should be). Thus, "teachers" and "students" are effects of classroom practice, not preexisting or fixed categories. These core practices—assembling classroom-relevant categories and the relations between them, and filling out the social and moral attributes of each—are at the center of classroom order.

Different literacies and pedagogies cannot be substituted for each other while holding constant the classroom order, because every classroom order is built through some combination of textual and social practice. The specific texts and practices drawn on here have been used to illustrate these observations. Analyses of classroom literacies built on different kinds of texts and talk would show differently how these combine in the construction of classroom order. Observing the close relation between the "space of the classroom" and the "space of the textual practices that occur there" indicates the depth and subtlety of changes that would accompany new kinds of work with text.

REFERENCES

Baker, C. D. (1992). Description and analysis in classroom talk and interaction. *Journal of Classroom Interaction, 27*(2), 9-14.

Baker, C. D., & Davies, B. (1993). Literacy and gender in early childhood. In A. Luke & P. Gilbert (Eds.), *Literacy in contexts: Australian perspectives and issues.* Sydney, Australia: Allen & Unwin.

Baker, C. D., & Freebody, P. (1987). "Constituting the child" in beginning school reading books. *British Journal of Sociology of Education, 8,* 55-76.

Baker, C.D., & Freebody, P. (1989a). *Children's first school books: Introductions to the culture of literacy.* Oxford, UK: Basil Blackwell.

Baker, C. D., & Freebody, P. (1989b). Talk around text: The construction of textual and teacher authority in classroom discourse. In S. De Castell, A. Luke, & C. Luke (Eds.), *Language, authority and criticism: Readings on the school textbook.* London: Falmer Press.

Baker, C. D., & Freebody, P. (1993). The crediting of literate competence in classroom talk. *Australian Journal of Language and Literacy, 16*(4), 279-294.

Cazden, C. (1981). Social context of learning to read. In J. T. Guthrie (Ed.), *Comprehension and teaching: Research reviews.* Newark, DE.: International Reading Association.

Davies, B. (1983). The role pupils play in the social construction of classroom order. *British Journal of Sociology of Education, 4,* 55-69

Freadman, A. (1987/1994). Anyone for tennis? In I. Reid (Ed.), *The place of genre in learning.* Geelong, Deakin University Centre for Studies in Literacy Education. Reprinted in A. Freadman & P. Medway (Eds.), *Genre and the new rhetoric.* London: Taylor & Francis.

Gee, J. P. (1996). Social linguistics and literacies: Ideology in discourses (2nd ed). London: Taylor & Francis.

Hammersley, M. (1977). School learning: The cultural resources required by pupils to answer a teacher's question. In P. Woods & M. Hammersely (Eds.), *School experience.* New York: St Martin's Press.

Heap, J. L. (1985). Discourse in the production of classroom knowledge: Reading lessons. *Curriculum Inquiry, 15*(3), 245-279.

Heap, J. L. (1990). Applied methodology: Looking for the local rationality of reading activities. *Human Studies, 13,* 49-72

Hunter, I. (1991). Learning the literature lesson: The limits of the aesthetic personality. In C. D. Baker & A. Luke (Eds.), *Towards a critical sociology of reading pedagogy.* Amsterdam/Philadelphia: John Benjamins.

Jenks, C. (1982). Introduction: Constituting the child. In C. Jenks (Ed.), *The sociology of childhood: Essential readings.* London: Batsford.

Luke, A. (1988). *Literacy, textbooks and ideology*. London: Falmer Press.

Luke, A. (1992). The body literate: Discourse and inscription in early literacy training. *Linguistics and Education, 4*, 107-129.

Luke, A. (1993). Stories of social regulation: The micropolitics of classroom narrative. In B. Green (Ed.), *The insistence of the letter: Literacy studies and curriculum theorizing*. London: Falmer Press.

McHoul, A. (1991). Readings. In C. D. Baker & A. Luke (Eds.), *Towards a critical sociology of reading pedagogy*. Amsterdam/Philadelphia: John Benjamins.

McHugh, P. (1974). On the failure of positivism. In J. Douglas (Ed.), *Understanding everyday life*. London: Routledge.

Mellor, B., & Patterson, A. (1991). Reading character: Reading gender. *English in Australia, 95*, 4-23.

Michaels, S. (1981). Sharing time: Children's narrative styles and differential access to literacy. *Language in Society, 10*, 423-442.

Michaels, S. (1987). Text and context: A new approach to the study of classroom writing. *Discourse Processes, 10*, 341-326.

Sacks, H. (1974). On the analyzability of stories by children. In R. Turner (Ed.), *Ethnomethodology*. London: Penguin.

Smith, D. E. (1988). *The everyday world as problematic: A feminist sociology*. Milton Keynes: Open University Press.

Jill Freiberg
Griffith University
Peter Freebody
Griffith University

This response explores some of the points made in the previous chapter by Baker. Our comments on various aspects of Baker's chapter center on the advisability, for theorizing and for changing practice, of conflating versus separating different kinds of "orderliness." Baker's proposition about the connections between literacy practices and classroom order in the achievement of critical literacies in the classroom is discussed. Furthermore, we question possible readings of the ceremony–game metaphor and the suggestion that when a change is attempted in pedagogy and/or practices (the games), the change might not be effective because every new game is situated in and naturalized by the classroom's "ceremonial order that is ultimately a moral order linking (adult) teachers, (child) students, and (school) texts in some way" (p. 246). In Baker's view, pedagogies and practices, critical or noncritical, become effects of the ceremonial order of the classroom. This conclusion is based on analyses of classroom ordering through practices that are clearly non-critical searches for meaning in texts, and in which literacy becomes largely or solely the ability to read particular cultural meanings into texts. This chapter focuses, finally, on Baker's conclusion that "Critical literacies would be part of a different texture of classroom order organized around some other forms of textual practice"(chap. 14, p. 259).

So what are the textual practices that might produce critical literacies and what is the kind of classroom orderliness they might require and produce? The use of the umbrella term, *classroom order*, does not discriminate among managerial, social, moral, and cultural orders, making it difficult to consider constructively possible changes in textual practice that might make for a more critical literacy within the context of the classroom. Also explored is Baker's suggestion that the very existence of a managerial order in the classroom that maintains conventional teacher–student and generational relationships will make impossible the achievement of some form of critical literacy, oriented to textual crafting, and not so "bound up with the contents and properties of the texts—in these cases specifically the characters and storylines—to produce connections between . . . the interiors of the stories to the interiors (feelings, reasoning) of the students" (chap. 14, p. 259).

Some preliminary outline is in order to describe what we take to be the main points made by Baker and what we believe they offer as valuable observations about classroom life and literacy learning. First, we take the interrelatedness of pedagogical organization and literacy practices in the classroom as an important starting point for any account of the nature and acquisition of school literacy. In the history of mass education, the use of physical means of coercion and the symbols of that potential have only recently been abandoned and only in a few places in the world. In the classrooms instanced in Baker's chapter, the work of organizational coherence—attention, diligence, cooperation, and so on— is conducted and effected through talk that is at the one time able to be heard as instructional and managerial. The placement, distribution, timing, and content of teachers' questions, for example, can be heard as being as much about the maintenance of attention and focus and the avoidance of distraction and fragmentation of the topic of attention as they are about a sequenced, orderly, learning-driven progression through the topic. So documenting the strong relationship between what is displayed and accountably learned and what are moves toward discipline by teachers and students affords a significant advance on approaches to classroom life that view everyday classroom activity as either uninteresting or as at least as displaying features unrelated to learning.

Equally valuable is the way in which Baker has drawn connections between classroom organization and pedagogy on the one hand, and social and moral order in, and projected out of, the classroom. A local moral order is enacted through the moral ordering of commentaries on story contents. This in turn opens up many avenues of interest in the exploration of the everyday ideological work performed in classrooms dedicated to noncritical searches for meaning in texts. This gives important substance to Heap's (1985) notion that learning how to do "reading comprehension" is learning about preferred forms of cultural logic. It denaturalizes what are often taken to be neutral practices of talk management in the classroom.

Baker also illuminated the important role that narrative can play when treated uncritically in early literacy learning as the unnoticed platform for displays of out-of-classroom moral and cultural norms. This connection goes some way to accounting for the heavy reliance on the story as a vehicle for early school literacy teaching, usually explained by appeals to the apparent naturalness of the story for young children as opposed to the apparent unnaturalness of other textual forms that are important in later schooling. Teachers often call upon and reward displays of the everyday cognitive, emotional, and moral knowledge of young students as they read characters in apparently everyday stories. Baker has expanded our understanding of school literacy by exemplifying this feature of early literacy learning and its connection with the orderliness of the classroom brought off by teachers and students. As a central example, she has further shown how the discourses surrounding the child–adult polarity inform the selection of reading and writing materials, the kinds of work that goes on around those texts, and the relation of both of these to the in- and out-of-school moral orders that these discourses both reflect and build. Clearly, these factors can constrain the degree of critical work available. It is worth noting, however, they may, at the same time, provide the context for productive critical practice if the fundamental relational practices are treated as topic rather than taken for granted.

THE "OPEN QUESTION" OF TEXTS, LITERACY, AND ORDER

The major conclusions of Baker's chapter are to challenge the intersubstitutability of literacy practices in classrooms, and thereby to introduce new aspects of both interest and caution in considerations about the possibilities for introducing critical literacies in conventional classrooms. These conclusions are based on the careful documentation and interpretation of segments of lesson transcripts as demonstrating the connectedness of reading practices, pedagogy, and aspects of managerial order, the latter being related to moral orderliness in and out of classrooms. This connectedness is read by Baker as entailment, a move of logic that allows the conclusion that the "classroom order" and the teacher's apparent ongoing work toward the ordering of the classroom in a particular way presents a barrier to the achievement of some form of critical literacy in classrooms that are so ordered. It is the nature of these connections that needs some initial explication. We examine briefly the notion that the term *classroom order* in Baker's formulation subsumes practices related to local managerial order, social orderliness, the moral order, and cultural orders of practice, and we question whether or not these conflations are useful theoretically and pedagogically.

In her chapter, Baker employs about 20 different terms to describe the relationship between literacy practices, pedagogy, and classroom/moral order. These can be grouped, in order of the degree of entailment, under five possible meanings:

1. *accompaniment* (e.g., "fits nicely," "overlap with").
2. *connectedness* (e.g., "intimately tied," "interconnected").
3. *mutual support* (e.g., "built through").
4. *cause–effect* (e.g., "organized though," "effect of," "enable").
5. *equation* (e.g., "amount to," "are part of").

Clearly, the highest order of entailment carries with it the other four meanings. Only Meanings 4 and 5 clinch the conclusion that, for any to change, all must change. If these connected features are seen as, at best, only mutually supportive, then the conclusion drawn is speculative. The possibility that different textual forms or different literacy practices around texts could bring with them "organically grown" pedagogies and orders is left open up to and including entailment Meaning 3.

There is no doubt that the transcripts and commentaries provided by Baker substantiate the mutual supportiveness (and selectiveness) of literacy practices, pedagogy, and classroom order. Two questions remain: Do these data sources and analyses actually substantiate the larger and more telling levels of entailment among the various factors at work? Are particular types of managerial order always (and already) tied to or implicative of particular social, moral, or cultural normative practices or disciplinary orientations?

On the matter of the first question, the higher levels of entailment can be substantiated, we suggest, only by studies of change or attempted change in varying classroom circumstances. The data and commentaries provided by Baker fully allow the possibility that the impetus for change could come from an effected change in textual practices, pedagogical practices, or the in- or out-of-school moral order developed and critiqued in the classroom. What has yet to be established, however, is that all would need to be simultaneously changed for any productive outcomes in the achievement of a form of critical literacy. To speculate about some of these possibilities, we focus a little more closely on whether or not classroom order is well described by the ceremony–game metaphor and on critical literacy.

NORMS, AGENCY, AND RESISTANCE

We query the appropriateness of the ceremony–game metaphor used by Baker. It seems that the meaning games in which these words typically play may not afford the work that Baker asks of them. Baker proposes that, rather than viewing the teacher and students as following rules, we can view them as positing rules, referring to rules, constructing and reconstructing rules: finding the order in their talk and interaction. In games and ceremonies, as those terms are readily understood, the processes of reconstruction are not only not in operation, but, if they appear, they are heavily sanctioned. The account preferred by ethnomethodology can be drawn from one of that discipline's central operating principles (see Heritage, 1984, p. 23ff), the principle of *reflexivity*: that people have insight into the normative "shouldness" of their actions and act on others' similar insights.

   This principle draws our attention to participants' awareness of norms of expectation and their moral value, and to the notion that people act with, by, and around that awareness as they interact in concrete circumstances. This awareness of and reference to norms is consonant in its outline with Baker's description of the work done by the classroom members in constructing and reconstructing the codes of classroom life, but not with the positing of rules as the focus of reference, and not with the use of games and ceremonies as a template for understanding everyday interactive practices.

   The point is not just about shades of meaning; it is consequential for critical literacy educators. A characterization of social activity as rule-governed "rules out" agency and resources drawn from out-of-the-classroom sites, and thus "rules out" multiplicity of interpretive moves, resistance, and challenge as possible methods and positions for reading, writing, and being a student. It posits in the end a source of rules rather than a source of situated authoritativeness; it makes at least secondary, and possibly irrelevant, explicit, and purposive principles for exchanging critiques of interpretations and representations. In these ways, at least, it falls short of Baker's accounts of classrooms practices:

> It appears that the students' decision to comment is done in consultation with each other. They do it collectively, even talking, possibly, with each other (see lines 24–25) to sort out the problem. . . . That this is "bad news" is found not only in the students' comments, but in the teacher's repeated appeals for reversing their decision. One student at least maintains that they have had this story in this class. The teacher's appeals are finally accepted and the story reading proceeds in the teacher's terms, and the students "enjoy" it with and for the teacher. (chap. 14, p. 250)

Authoritative agency is afforded here to the students so that although the "story reading proceeds in the teacher's terms" it is only because the students "finally accept" her repeated appeals for reversing their decision. A rules account is also not compatible with or productive of critical educational practices, or reflective of the moral orders outside of the classroom that those practices seek to reveal and challenge. So it need not play even a metaphorical part in answers to the question of critical literacy practice, however open that question may remain.

The goal of critical, or indeed any other, literacy education is not, in either the teacher's or demonstrably the students' accounts, the order of the classroom. That order is rather a lived aspect of the literacy activities. Clearly, the "codes of classroom life" are in a sympathetic relationship to these activities, and are at the one time productive of moral orders beyond the classroom. But, by Baker's account, "the social order of the classroom—its coherence as a social and moral space—is an effect of literacy practices and an effect of pedagogy" and the accomplishment of this order is the underlying motive of pedagogy and practice.

Although changing the literacy activities with the pedagogy could be assumed to lead to variations in the classroom order, resistance to this latter process derives from a view of the classroom orders documented in Baker's transcripts as visibly and, according to her account, independently supporting the teacher as teacher, rather than as teacher of literacy. If this is the "bottom line" of Baker's argument and commentaries—that the students' answers are always already provisional in this order and dependent on the teacher's authority for their status as accountable knowledge and practice, and it is this recalcitrant dependence that will resist or undermine attempts toward more critical practice—then it follows that an effective critical literacy approach would need to assume the legitimacy of students' responses to literacy tasks as the organizing principle of the pedagogy. We would be left with the celebration of students' textual and ideological common sense.

Another possibility, however, is that a teacher's commitment to a position as teacher in the classroom, as teacher of literacy practices, or as deployer of effective pedagogical strategies, need not simultaneously be readable as a commitment to the role of arbiter of cultural order. This, among other things, permits of the possibility, yet to be given empirical substance, that pedagogy and/or literacy practices may be able to be changed to achieve critical literacy while the managerial and social order of the classroom remains the same or at least recognizable.

That is, we are suggesting that theory and practice may well benefit from at least a discursive separation of the various dimensions of managerial, social, moral, and cultural orderliness, no matter how simultaneous their interactive embodiments. So, a classroom in which orientations to hierarchical placements such as adult–child, and student–teacher couplets are evident may not necessarily be a learning environment that excludes critical literacy practices—that is, practices that work against common sense to make problematic the textual orderings of social, moral, and cultural patterns of orderliness beyond the classroom.

"ORDERLINESS" IN THE CRITICAL LITERACY CLASSROOM

We can illustrate the issues raised here by exploring answers to the second question of whether particular types of managerial order are always (and already) tied to or implicative of particular social, moral, or cultural normative practices or orientations. To do this we ask what some of the features of pedagogy and classroom order might be that would support a form of early literacy education that might be called *critical*. First, Baker's documentations add to the long tradition of research into classrooms that shows the primacy of teachers' questioning. They show again that teachers claim and are accorded the right to ask questions, and that these questions serve as displayed guides to what is important and to what counts as appropriate understanding in a reading lesson. The particular inflection placed by Baker on this claiming and according of questioning rights to the teacher is that, for the purposes of the classroom, students do not need to develop or practice questioning. They learn the habitus of the answerer, the moral position of the respondent to the teacher's or other authority's properly motivated questions. This learning has clear implications, not only for educational practices, notably assessment practices, that visibly persist well beyond beginning schooling, but also for the learning and practicing of reading positions out of school. Such a distribution of rights posits a potential passivity in those positions, and a disposition to attend to aspects of texts about which the reader may be questioned. In these ways, perhaps the most striking and empirically robust feature of classroom activity (teacher asks questions—students attempt answers) can be seen to support, most obviously, noncritical literacy practices.

But there is another reading of the "teacher asks questions–students attempt answers" order that may have more substantial implications for a critical approach to literacy teaching and learning. To explore this, we need to outline briefly one of the ideas central to such an approach (described more fully in Freebody, Luke, & Gilbert, 1991) and to its contrast with progressivist educational practices. Tenets of progressivist education include that teachers' questioning can educe relevant knowledge about reading and writing; that the teachers' role is largely to construct the conditions in which students can share and become aware and in control of their own growing knowledge; that, following these, students should select their own reading and writing topics, and teachers should not provide explicit, "transmissionist" teaching, but should, by artful questioning, draw out and elaborate students' background knowledge. Michaels (1987) showed the limits and contradictions involved in such practices. More significantly for our purposes, researchers such as Martin (1985, 1991) and Gilbert (1988, 1991) showed, in the case of students' writing, that such practices set unsatisfactory limits on the forms of writing and inquiry made available to students, and the immediate "this-text" dependency of those limitations, and celebrate a deeply ideological common sense as valued school knowledge. Gilbert's dramatic examples of young male students' violently antifemale writing, and the teacher's entrapment in the logic of her accepting pedagogy, demonstrate that progressivist approaches, for all their strengths, have defined the student romantically on at least two counts—as intrinsically and broadly textually competent, and as a member of an ideologically innocent subculture. The assumption of textual competence allows the literacy curriculum to ignore the craftedness of texts and to focus instead on their meaning(s).

In our view, one crucial feature that pervades early literacy and later "English" lessons, and that does need critical exploration, is the relentless focus on "meaning." This seems to be an undue focus among many teachers as much as among many researchers and theoreticians who study their practices. Debates often dissolve into contests about, on the one hand, whether there is one meaning of a text, whether there is a technical or meta-language that can exhaustively address and clarify that meaning, and thus whether the teacher should work, however covertly, toward that meaning, or, on the other hand, whether a text has multiple meanings, and if therefore the classroom should be a place in which this multiplicity is encouraged and used as the central resource for learning to be a reader and writer. Regardless of how much explicit substantiation from the text is modeled or called for, this central focus on accomplishment of meaning/s produces a teacher or researcher whose role becomes one of thinly disguised amateur moral technician— whether authoritarian or liberal.

It is our view that learning to be critically literate is not about the accomplishment of meaning or meanings. It is about learning how the material and ideological sources of a text shape the way that text is crafted and how in turn that crafting positions the writer and reader. Through the examination of supporting and contesting texts, critical literacy practices are aimed at developing understandings of how readerships are written into existence and into silence. In pursuing how such practices can be developed and the features of orderliness that might enact them, the multitudinous forms of hunting for and authorizing the meaning/s are less than uninteresting. They are downright distracting.

CONCLUSION

A disposition, almost an instinct, of a critical approach is to query what appears natural and common sensical, and to inquire instead about the processes by which any sign (in our case a text) can come to be accorded status as natural or common sensical. The resources a critical educator may draw upon in that inquiry typically include attending to the craftedness of the text in its time and place and the discourses and assumptions that are called on to make the text "sensible": What kind of person could write, in good faith and without any problems, like this? What kind of reader does the reader need to be in order to read it, again, in good faith and without any problems?

There are two general polar extremes of orderliness that proponents of critical reading and writing have typically adopted. On the one hand, an orderliness might be built that encourages and celebrates differences of reading and writing resources. Pedagogical strategies might be deployed that stimulate an acceptance of diversity of interpretation and representation. The central goal of such strategies, for the local site of the classroom and for learning more broadly, is an instinct and a growing capability for production and acceptance of the "plays of difference."

Without some systematizing of the forms, sources, and implications of difference, however, such a pedagogy might lead to the textually and ideologically romantic outcomes critiqued by, for example, Martin and Gilbert. It is arguable, indeed, that a classroom order dedicated to the legitimate hearing of these playing differences might be more explicit and necessarily more authoritatively orderly than is shown in the transcripts documented by Baker.

From the viewpoint of a contrary position, a critical approach to literacy would be more explicitly orderly, according the teacher the authoritative role in the disturbing and bracketing of students' common sense. That is, in an important sense, this form of critical literacy is against common sense, and thus against pedagogies that connote the disorderly play of common sense-based differences. These critical literacy educators would provide displays and practice of de-naturalizing interrogations of a text and its claims to both a single and a common sensical interpretation. They would not imagine that their student readers can already deploy the resources for such interrogations, and they would certainly not build implicit, apparently natural or conversational participation structures in which to conduct those interrogations. Therefore, if these assumptions governed the pedagogy, they might run the risk of claiming exhaustive knowledge of powerful, culturally located interpretations and representations, and thus of overwriting different reading and writing positions.

It is appropriate to suggest that the managerial and social orderliness of a critical literacy classroom looks very much like the orderliness that would obtain in effective classrooms generally, with cycles of modeling, direct instruction, student-led input, and ways of talking guided by explicated principles of acceptance and interrogation. Such a form of orderliness would be no more guided by a single instructional strategy than would conventionally effective phonics, comprehension, or composing lessons, but would be characterized by cycles of sequentially appropriate and explicitly understood changes of order based on both the teacher's and the students' different and shifting moments of authoritativeness over the topic and the text.

REFERENCES

Freebody, P., Luke, A., & Gilbert, P. (1991). Reading instruction and discourse critique: Rethinking the politics of literacy. *Curriculum Inquiry, 21,* 235-257.

Gilbert, P. (1988). Stoning the romance: Girls as resistant readers and writers. *Curriculum Perspectives, 8,* 13-19.

Gilbert, P. (1991). Shifting the parameters of writing research: Writing as social practice. *Australian Journal of Reading, 14,* 96-102.

Heap, J. (1985). Discourse in the production of classroom knowledge: Reading lessons. *Curriculum Inquiry, 15,* 245-270.

Heritage, J. (1984). *Garfinkel and ethnomethodology.* Cambridge, UK: Polity Press.

Martin, J. R. (1985). *Factual writing: Exploring and challenging social reality.* Geelong, Victoria: Deakin University Press.

Martin, J. R. (1991). Critical literacy: The role of a functional model of language. *Australian Journal of Reading, 14,* 117-132.

Michaels, S. (1987). Text and context: A new approach to the study of classroom writing. *Discourse Processes, 10,* 321-346.

16
Meanings in Discourses: Coordinating and Being Coordinated

James Paul Gee
Clark University

There is an intimate connection between how we view minds and how we view schools, because schools are ostensibly about transmitting mind-stuff (knowledge). The current, but threatened, cognitivist perspective on the mind views it as a "place" where "representations" of the world and rules are "stored," representations and rules that underlie talking, listening, writing, reading, and acting (Barsalou, 1992). On this view, education is about placing "correct" ("expert-like") representations and rules in the mind (Gardner, 1991; Perkins, 1992). In this chapter, I argue that a new view of the mind is emerging, both in psychology and sociocultural approaches to education, a view that unsettles the boundaries between the mind, the world, and society (and culture). This view also has deep implications for how we view schools and schooling, implications that unsettle the dichotomy between progressive (immersion) pedagogies focused on process and traditional (explicit instruction) pedagogies focused on product, as well as the dichotomy between "diversity" and "commonwealth." I believe we are converging on a view of mind, meaning, and society that sees critical thinking as not just higher order thinking, but a language of critique (appreciation and assessment) of the socioculturally and sociohistorically situated workings of mind-in-society.

In this chapter, then, I argue that a sociocultural and critical approach to language and literacy follows not just from our politics, but from emerging theories of mind, society, and education that can be rendered plausible even to those who do not share our politics. This does not render political struggle to eradicate social injustice any less important, but it may indicate that political alignments of the past will be resituated as the social, economic, political, and cognitive landscape changes all around us. As this landscape changes, it will be become crucial that we delineate the foundations, in theory and practice, of a postprogressive pedagogy, one that will rewrite, in multiple ways, some of the distinctions between the margin and the center that we have heretofore drawn in the struggle to establish the distinction and dignity of multiple language and literacy practices against the hegemony of "essayist literacy" (Scollon & Scollon, 1981). This chapter is but a bare beginning of this project. It is meant to be suggestive, rather than definitive.

The layout of this chapter is as follows: The first section offers an argument that meaning is not in the head, but in social practices, and that in acquiring social practices one gets "deep" meanings "free." The second section argues that meaning does not travel well, in that the social practices that give rise to meaning are not abstract systems, but networks of situated material objects and concrete actions tied to specific times and places. The next section takes up the issue of what is in human heads, if meaning is not, and argues that the insides of heads point us right back out to social practices. The fourth section looks more closely at just how social practices operate so as to render the insides of our heads less essential than we might otherwise have thought. The fifth section argues that meaning and knowing, even in science, are sociohistorically situated and go well beyond the boundaries not only of scientists' heads, but of their contemporary practices. The conclusion develops some implications of the preceding sections for a notion of liberation from the inherent limitations of social practices.

IS MEANING IN THE HEAD?

Initially trained as a (U.S.-style theoretical) linguist, I worked in that tradition for some years, before realizing that a very basic assumption of my (sub)discipline was wrong. Theoretical linguists, like cognitive scientists more generally, believe that "meaning is in the head" (in the form of representations and mappings among them; see Sterelny, 1990, for an overview of the issues). That meaning is not in the head dawned on me when I was confronted with several narratives by quite young children. One of these, a story told by a 5-year-old Anglo-American middle-class girl, whom I call "Jennie," is reprinted here (see also, Gee, 1996). Jennie was holding a book and pretending to read it to her mother and older sister.

I print the story broken into lines and stanzas, which makes it easier to understand the story's structure:

JENNIE'S STORY

STANZA 1 (Introduction)
1. This is a story
2. About some kids who were once friends
3. But got into a big fight
4. And were not

STANZA 2 (Frame: Signaling of Genre)
5. You can read along in your story book
6. I'm gonna read aloud
   [story-reading prosody from now on]

STANZA 3 (Title)
7. "How the Friends Got Unfriend"

STANZA 4 (Setting: Introduction of Characters)
8. Once upon a time there was three boys 'n three girls
9. They were named Betty Lou, Pallis, and Parshin, were the girls
10. And Michael, Jason, and Aaron were the boys
11. They were friends

STANZA 5 (Problem: Sex Differences)
12. The boys would play Transformers
13. And the girls would play Cabbage Patches

STANZA 6 (Crisis: Fight)
14. But then one day they got into a fight on who would be which team
15. It was a very bad fight
16. They were punching
17. And they were pulling
18. And they were banging

STANZA 7 (Resolution 1: Storm)
19. Then all of a sudden the sky turned dark
20. The rain began to fall
21. There was lightning going on
22. And they were not friends

STANZA 8 (Resolution 2: Mothers punish)
23. Then um the mothers came shooting out 'n saying
24. "What are you punching for?
25. You are going to be punished for a whole year"

STANZA 9 (Frame)
26. The end
27. Wasn't it fun reading together?

28. Let's do it again
29. Real soon !

The story has obvious linguistic markers of the genre of *storybook reading*, a genre connected to both children's literature and high literature. Within this genre, certain literary devices are relevant. One of these, which this text draws on, is the *sympathetic fallacy*, a device in which nature, or the cosmos, is treated as if it is "in step with" (in sync with, coordinated with) human affairs (e.g., the beauty and peace of a sunset matches the inner peace of the elderly poet resigned to the approach of the end of life).

In Jennie's story, the sympathetic fallacy is a central organizing device. The fight between the girls and boys in Stanza 6 is immediately followed in Stanza 7 by the sky turning dark, with lightning flashing, and thence in line 22: "and they were not friends." Finally, in Stanza 8, the mothers come on the scene to punish the children for their transgression. The sky is "in tune" or "step" with human happenings.

The sympathetic fallacy functions in Jennie's story in much the same way as it does in high literature. The story suggests that gender differences (Stanza 4: boy vs. girl) are associated with different interests (Stanza 5: Transformers vs. Cabbage Patches), and that these different interests inevitably lead to conflict when male and female try to be equal or sort themselves on other grounds than gender (Stanza 6: "a fight on who would be which team"—the fight had been about mixing genders on the teams). The children are punished for transgressing gender lines (Stanza 8), but only after the use of the sympathetic fallacy (the storm in Stanza 7) has suggested that division by gender, and the conflicts that transgressing this division lead to, are sanctioned by nature, are "natural" and "inevitable," not merely conventional or constructed in the very act of play itself.

It was clear to me, at least, that this story was in no sense "naive" in its "meaning potential"; rather, it carried a tremendous amount of ideological force. Confronted with such texts, I asked myself: "How can a 5-year-old *mean* anything this sophisticated? How can it be that this little girl appears to *mean* beyond her own 'private' resources?" The answer seemed to be that if you place the sort of allusion to nature this little girl has used at just the sort of textual location she has, then you get these sorts of meanings "free," because to do this "resonates" with particular historically derived interpretive practices "owned and operated" by certain groups of people (Hodge, 1990; Leitch, 1992). And you get them free not just in the sense that others can use these meanings, but in the sense that you, too, even if a child, can use them, and in a variety of ways: to internalize ideological themes as senseful and natural perspectives on the world; to interactively reproduce with others cultural practices that you can participate in without full understanding; and to achieve a "social language" that characterizes your group and its perspectives on the world.

But, then, I faced an obvious objection, one that might run something like this: What does it matter that this text potentially has the sorts of sophisticated meanings you have pointed out? If it is not in the little girl's head, what good does it do *her*, how can it be *her* meaning? At the time I knew nothing about education and educational systems, but after learning something about them, it became clear that such potential-meanings-in-practice do, indeed, do this little girl a lot of good and a lot of harm, and are, indeed, her meanings in a way that they are not available to other children who cannot place cues that resonate with such interpretive practices in their preliteracy texts.

To see this, consider how the text came about. This girl's mother regularly read storybooks to her two young daughters. Her 5-year-old had had a birthday party, where there were some problems. In the next few days the 5-year-old told several relatives about the birthday party, presumably reporting the events as a chronologically sequenced set of events in the nature of a report, without the literary trappings shown earlier. A few days later, when the mother was reading a storybook to her other daughter, the 5-year-old said she wanted to "read" (she could not yet decode print), and pretended to be reading a book, while telling what happened at her birthday party. Her original attempt at this was not very good, but eventually after a few tries, interspersed with the mother reading to the other girl, the 5-year-old produced the story just presented.

Supported by her mother and sister, the 5-year-old is apprenticing herself to a specific social practice, namely (mainstream, school-based) storybook reading. But this social practice is itself an aspect of apprenticeship in another, more mature social practice, namely literature. Both these practices are integrally connected to certain interpretive practices. This child, when she goes to school to begin her more public apprenticeship into the social practice of literature (or "essayist literacy," for that matter) will look like a quick study indeed.

This home-based social practice, with its ways of interacting, talking, thinking, valuing, and reading, and its books and other physical props, enables this little girl to form a text of a certain type. And that form invites the operation of the interpretive practices that are part of literary (and school-based) social practices. The little girl gets this meaning free so to speak—being that it is in the world, it need not be (fully) in her head.

Does it do her any good? Indeed, it does: We know that such practices are one of the foundations of the disproportionate success such children have in school in comparison to many "nonmainstream" children from poorer homes (Adams, 1990; Chall, Jacobs, & Baldwin, 1990). Is it her meaning? Yes: There is a real sense in which she and the other members of her group come to own such meanings by controlling such social practices and the social institutions (e.g., schools) that they are embedded in (Bourdieu, 1977; Bourdieu & Passeron, 1977; Gee, 1991). She is open to attributions of literary meaning, as well as attributions of intelligence, without our needing to ask what is going on in her head.

However, the meanings her text generates as potential grist for interpretive mills do her some harm as well. The sympathetic fallacy is a double-edged sword. On the one hand, it has been used, from time immemorial, to suggest a deep commonalty between human beings and nature; on the other hand, it has also been used to suggest that Nature underwrites the hierarchies of power, status, and prestige found at particular times and places within particular cultures.

The little girl's text resonates with a particular ideological message about the distribution of gender roles, a message that may well be against her own self-interest as she grows older and desires to see herself as the equal of men. She is already becoming at home in certain social practices—in the way in which certain people are quite at home in a certain city—which will make her a bearer of meanings in conflict with her own interests within other social practices (e.g., women's groups).

My argument here is, by no means, a deterministic one that this little girl now has to grow up a victim of the gender ideology that helps to structure her meaning-making. Rather, the argument is that just as her textual practice, even as a 5-year-old, will bring her attributions of intelligence and "giftedness" from mainstream and powerful institutions, so, too, her own texts and the institutions that so validate them (and her through them) naturalize female as other and different, to be assigned value and identity in terms of a binary contrast with male, a binary contrast that it is dangerous to broach. The little girl's own meaning-making (and it is hers in several individual and social senses), then, defines the work, the project, that she will later have to engage in—and the forces (some of them her own) that she will be up against—should she wish to acquire new social languages and new perspectives on her self and world. It is no easy matter to return gifts (or give up giftedness).

MEANING DOES NOT TRAVEL WELL: MEANING IS IN MATERIALLY SITUATED SOCIAL PRACTICES

Meaning is not in the head, but in social practices. But social practices are not abstract things, like Saussure's *langue*, rather they are embedded in material objects (such as bodies, places, objects, institutions, and texts) and concrete actions. This fact raises some important paradoxes. To see this, consider another story told by a young child. The story printed here was told at sharing time (show-and-tell) in school by a 7-year-old African-American girl, whom I call "Leona" (see Gee, 1992, for a fuller discussion of this text):

CAKES

FRAME

STANZA 1

1. Today
2. it's Friday the 13th
3. an' it's bad luck day
4. an' my grandmother's birthday is on bad luck day

PART 1: MAKING CAKES

STANZA 2

5. an' my mother's bakin' a cake
6. an' I went up my grandmother's house while my mother's bakin' a cake
7. an' my mother was bakin' a cheese cake
8. my grandmother was bakin' a whipped cream cupcakes

STANZA 3

9. an' we bof went over my mother's house
10. an' then my grandmother had made a chocolate cake
11. an' then we went over my aunt's house
12. an' she had make a cake

STANZA 4

13. an' everybody had made a cake for nana
14. so we came out with six cakes

PART 2: GRANDMOTHER EATS CAKES

STANZA 5

15. last night
16. my grandmother snuck out
17. an' she ate all the cake
18. an' we hadda make more

STANZA 6

(she knew we was makin' cakes)

19. an' we was sleepin'
20. an' she went in the room
21. an' gobbled em up
22. an' we hadda bake a whole bunch more

STANZA 7
23. she said mmmm
24. she had all chocolate on her face, cream, strawberries
25. she said mmmm
26. that was good

STANZA 8
27. an' then an' then all came out
28. an' my grandmother had ate all of it
29. she said "what's this cheesecake doin here"—she didn't like cheesecakes
30. an' she told everybody that she didn't like cheesecakes

STANZA 9
31. an' we kept makin' cakes
32. an' she kept eatin' 'em
33. an' we finally got tired of makin' cakes
34. an' so we all ate 'em

PART 3: GRANDMOTHER GOES OUTSIDE THE HOME
NONNARRATIVE SECTION (35–41)
STANZA 10
35. an' now
36. today's my grandmother's birthday
37. an' a lot o'people's makin' a cake again
38. but my grandmother is goin' t'get her own cake at her bakery
39. an' she's gonna come out with a cake
40. that we didn't make
41. cause she likes chocolate cream

STANZA 11
42. an' I went t'the bakery with her
43. an' my grandmother ate cupcakes
44. an' an' she finally got sick on today
45. an' she was growling like a dog cause she ate so many cakes

FRAME
STANZA 12
46. an' I finally told her that it was
47. it was Friday the thirteenth bad luck day

The language of this text is recognizably part of an African-American cultural tradition that has now been fairly well studied and documented (Abrahams, 1964, 1970, 1976; Baugh, 1983; Finnegan, 1970, 1988; Kochman, 1972, 1981; Smitherman, 1977; Stucky, 1987). The child uses language in a poetic, rather than a prosaic way; she tries to "involve" the audience, rather than just to "'inform" them (Nichols, 1989). She uses a good deal of syntactic and semantic parallelism, repetition, and sound devices (phonological sequences, intonation, and rate changes) to set up rhythmic and poetic patterning within and across her stanzas, just as do Biblical poetry (e.g., in the Psalms), the narratives of many oral cultures (e.g., Homer), and much "free verse" (e.g., the poetry of Walt Whitman).

And, like Jennie, Leona means far beyond her private resources. To see this, consider what this story might mean. The non-narrative "evaluative" (Labov, 1972) section in Stanza 10 suggests that there is something significant in the fact that the grandmother is going to get a cake at the bakery and thus "come out with a cake that we [the family] didn't make." And indeed, the story as a whole places a great deal of emphasis on the production of cakes within the family, a production that does not cease even when the grandmother keeps eating them. The grandmother, the matriarch and repository of the culture's norms, is behaving like a child, sneaking out and eating the cakes and rudely announcing that she does not like "cheesecake" even though the cake has been made by her relatives for her birthday. The story, in fact, contains a humorous paradox about cakes: The grandmother eats innumerable cakes (big and small) at home, made by her relatives, and never gets sick. Then she goes outside the home, buys little cakes ("cupcakes") at the bakery, and, not only does she get sick, she "growls like a dog," that is, loses her human status and turns into an animal. Why?

What I would argue is this: The grandmother is learning, and the child narrator is enacting, a lesson about signs or symbols. A birthday cake is a material object, but it is also an immaterial sign or symbol of kinship, when made within the family—a celebration of birth and family membership. The cake at the bakery looks the same, but it is a duplicitous symbol—it is not actually a sign of kinship, rather it is a commodity that non-kin have made to sell, not to celebrate the birth of someone they care about. To mistake the baker's cake as a true symbol of birth and kin is to think, mistakenly, that signs have meaning outside the contexts that give them meaning (Birch, 1989; Hodge & Kress, 1988; Stahl, 1989). In the context of the family, the cake means kinship and celebration; in the context of the bakery and market society, it signals exchange and commodities. The grandmother, in her greed, overvalues the material base of the sign (its cakehood) and misses its meaning, undervaluing the network of kin that gives meaning to the cakes. This is particularly dangerous when we consider that the grandmother is a senior representative of the family and culture. Her penalty is to momentarily lose her human status, that is, the status of a giver and taker of symbolic meaning—she becomes an animal, merely an eater. We may remember Levi-Strauss' (1966) claim that to many cultures, the material world is not only "good to eat," but "good to think with."

Here, again, we face the paradox of how such a young child can mean so much; but here we do have something of an understanding (rough as it is) of how Leona manages to mean beyond her private resources. Leona belongs to a sociocultural group that still has ties to a rich oral tradition (this is not true of all African Americans, but of African Americans who still have, as one of their identities, at least, allegiance to specific sociohistorical practices of the sort I am talking about here). Leona's performance is part of a very long tradition of oral storytelling, not because she and her family are not literate (they are), but because her culture has retained a high regard for face-to-face, interactive, participatory, storytelling as a way of making deep sense of life and the experience of being human.

Leona's apprenticeship in the language practices of her community has given her certain forms of language, ranging from devices at the word and clause level, through the stanza level, to the story level as a whole, forms of language that are intimately connected to "forms of life" (Wittgenstein, 1958; see also Gee, 1992/1993; Malcolm, 1989). These forms of language are not merely structural, rather they encapsulate and carry through time and space meanings shared by and lived out in a variety of (creative) ways by Leona's social group.

It is interesting to note that the sorts of literary devices that occur in Leona's story due to her culture's retaining rich ties to the values of orality, show up in another form in the 5-year-old's story. This is because the 5-year-old is participating in an aspect of our print-based high culture literary tradition, a tradition that, of course, has its origins in oral-culture practices (think of the line running from Homer to Hesiod to Chaucer to Shakespeare, and beyond).

But Leona's sharing time stories did not go over at all well in school. The teacher felt that her stories, and others like them told by other African-American children, "rambled on," were disorganized, and that Leona had nothing much to say, but just wanted to keep the floor. In other words, a story that has a deep meaning when Leona tells it in her own community or when we situate it the interpretive setting of poetics and linguistic stylistics, has no very deep meaning when it is situated in school at sharing time (Cazden, 1988; Gee, 1996; Michaels, 1981).

The same thing is true of Jennie's story. It has a deep meaning at home (her mother, a graduate student of mine, had, in fact, brought it to me to show me what a wonderful and literary story her daughter had created "on the spot") and would have a deep meaning at school when "creative writing" or "literature" is being done. But Jennie would never have tried such a literary story at the sort of sharing time Leona was involved in. Sharing time in that class was early "essayist (reportive, linear, 'the facts') literacy" training (Michaels, 1981, 1985). Neither Leona's nor Jennie's text resonate well with that practice, whereas other sorts of texts do.

The paradox is, of course, why Leona was tempted to transport her text to sharing time and Jennie would not be. And, why does the school construct a practice where certain sorts of perfectly creative texts are excluded without overt warning and certain sorts of children are tempted (even encouraged, in a sense) to transport their creative masterpieces only to have them devalued? In fact, this is but a part of a much larger picture and history: African-American creativity has continually been "debased" by the power that mainstream institutions (from schools to entertainment) have had to "resituate" it within a "White" perspective, rather than allow it as a resource for resituating the perspectives and values of these institutions themselves (Watkins, 1994). And similar things can be said in regard to a number of other minority groups.

Knowing little about education, I found this was deeply mysterious. Now that I know more about education, it is still deeply mysterious. Nonetheless, what it taught me was that one gets meanings "free" by being in a specific social practice, but these meanings are set off, like a chain reaction, only if one is at the right time and place (and, as is seen here) resonating with the right history, where "right" here is an inherently political notion.

KNOWING AND HEADS

Because meaning is not in the head, it is worth asking what is in there, because, it turns out, that when we find out what is in heads—at least, in regard to what human heads are particularly good at—we are basically just led right back out to social practices. However, this detour through heads has the value that it suggests a number of important implications for educational theory and practice.

A still quite strong view in "standard" cognitive science holds that to learn and know something, like physics, is to have in one's head lots of sentence-like things about physics. These sentence-like things are encoded, not in English, but in a language of thought—let's call it *mentalese* (Fodor, 1975, 1983; Fodor & Pylyshyn, 1988). Mentalese, in turn, can be, at least potentially, translated into English. On this model of the mind, education becomes a matter of using English, or some other natural language, to transfer the mental sentences in a teacher's head to a learner's head, where, it is hoped, they will lodge. Such a view of mind stresses the encoding of generalizations over specifics as the basis of knowledge. Because a single generalization covers a wealth of specific cases, one can always deduce the specific cases from the generalization by the rules of logic, which are themselves general sentences in mentalese.

This older view of the mind is currently being challenged by a variety of new viewpoints that share the idea that the mind is made up, in some significant part, of *networks of associations* (Allman, 1989; Bechtel & Abrahamsen, 1991; P. M. Churchland, 1989; P. S. Churchland, 1986; Churchland & Sejnowski, 1992; Clark, 1989, 1993; Gee, 1992). This newer conception—the *network view*—suggests that what is in our heads is, not a set of mentalese sentences, but rather rich networks of associations among experiences we have had—verbal and nonverbal experiences. Furthermore, this network model suggests that we do not store generalizations, but rather that we store specifics, from which useful generalizations emerge, provided we have experienced enough specifics and organized them in fruitful ways. Thus, this view of the mind places the emphasis on situated experiences, the contextualized nature of meaning and knowledge, and multiple associations. This is, of course, quite the opposite of the sorts of decontextualization, broad generalizations, single perspectives, and distancing from experience that has characterized the mainstream literacy practices of our schools.

Let me briefly show you how this works. Imagine you have had a good deal of experience with two street gangs, named the "Jets" and "Sharks" (the example is from McClelland, Rumelhart, & Hinton, 1986; see also Gee, 1992). One way to encode information of this kind would be to just list the information as a set of sentences—for efficiency's sake, listing generalizations whenever we can (e.g., "Most Jets are not married"). Another way to encode such information is in terms of an associative network, which may be represented as in Figure 16.1.

Figure 16.1 works this way: each name (e.g., "Lance") is connected via lines to all the properties of that person (e.g., "being in one's 20s" or "being a Jet," or "having only a junior high school education") through the solid black dots in the center. Note, for example, that the name "Lance" is connected to the solid black dot labeled #1, and that, in turn, this dot is connected to the properties "being in one's 20s," "being a burglar," "being single," "being a Jet," and "having only a junior high school education."

Imagine that you "activate" the name "Lance" (e.g., imagine the little circle containing Lance's name being a light bulb that you have just lit up). Then, thanks to the lines connecting the name "Lance" to the solid black dot #1, the activation (energy) you have given "Lance" will also be passed along to dot #1. So, now "Lance" and dot #1 are activated

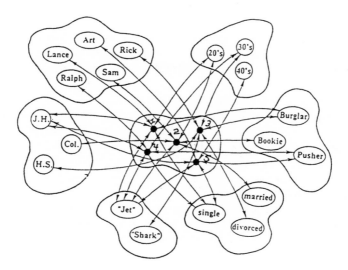

Figure 16.1. A connectionist network (adapted from J. McClelland, D. Rumelhart, & G. Hinton, "The Appeal of PDP," in D. Rumelhart, J. McClelland, and the PDP Research Group, Parallel Distributed Processing: Explorations in the Microstructure of Cognition, Vol. I. Cambridge, MA: MIT Press, 1986, p. 28, Fig. 11)

(lit up, let us say). In turn, thanks to the fact that dot # 1 is connected by lines to various properties, the activation that dot #1 has received will also be passed along to these properties. Therefore, now "Lance," dot #1, and (what happen to be) Lance's properties are all activated (lit up). Thus, if you activate "Lance," then eventually, as activation is passed along the lines, all of Lance's properties will be activated (lit up), representing what you know about Lance.

Of course, it works in any direction. Imagine, instead of lighting up "Lance," you activated the property "single." This would pass activation along its lines to everything it is connected to via the black dots in the center. Thus, activating "single" will eventually activate the black dots labeled #1, #4, and #5, to which "single" is connected. These, in turn, will pass activation to the properties to which they are connected. For example, considering just the names, these dots will pass activation to "Lance," "Ralph," and "Art." As these names light up, we will represent the fact that you know that Lance, Ralph, and Art are single.

There is one thing about Figure 16.1 you do not yet know. There are actually inhibitory lines among all the items within one irregular cloud, but I have not shown them, because they would clutter up the figure. Thus, there are actually inhibitory lines between 20s, 30s, and 40s because these items are all within one irregular cloud. This means that when any one of these properties (e.g., "being in one's 20s,") is activated (either directly or by being passed activation) it not only lights up, but it sends signals to its cloudmates inhibiting them from activating (lighting up). This, of course, captures the fact that if someone is in their 20s, he or she can not then also be in his or her 30s or 40s.

Now you know enough about such associative networks to see one very important property they have—one that I want to suggest people have, too. The network in Figure 16.1 knows things that are not actually anywhere encoded in it. Only specific experiences of actual people and their properties are encoded in the network in Figure 16.1. Nonetheless, thanks to the way these specific experiences are organized and associated, flexible generalizations emerge out of the network, generalizations nowhere stored in it. Such emergent properties are a hallmark of connectionist approaches to the mind, as, indeed, they are also of contemporary approaches to complexity and chaos, whether these are studied in social, economic, cultural, or physical systems (Briggs & Peat, 1989; Lorenz, 1993; Waldrop, 1992).

Here is how it works: Suppose we wanted the typical Jet. The network can tell us this, even though it stores no typical (general) Jets, just specific Jets. All the network directly knows about are individuals, none of whom need to be perfectly typical. But, suppose we now seek a sketch of the typical Jet. It turns out that there are patterns in Jet membership, although no individual Jet is a perfect example of all these patterns at once. Thus, three of the four Jets are single; three of the four are educated only to the junior high school level; two of the four Jets are in their 20s (one other is in his 30s, the other in his 40s); and two are pushers (one other is a burglar, the other a bookie).

If the system is given "Jet" as input, the black dots #1, #2, #4, and #5 will also be activated, because "Jet" is connected to these. In turn, three of these dots (namely #1, #4, and #5) will pass activation to the units for "being single" and "being educated to junior high school level" (because three of the dots are connected to each of these properties). Thus, these two properties will show significant activity, with three doses of activation each (one each from dot #1, #4, and #5). Furthermore, each of these properties will dampen (through inhibition) the other members of its cloud, even if one of its fellow units does get a dose of activation from the fourth Jet.

The units "pusher" and "20s" will each get two doses, because each of them are connected to two of the black dots that were activated by the unit "Jet" ("pusher" is connected to dot #4 and #5; and "20s" is connected to dots #1 and #4). They are, thus, somewhat more weakly activated than the units "single" and "junior high school educated." However, their two doses will dampen the single dose each of their cloudmates happens to get (one Jet is a burglar and one is a bookie, so each of these gets one dose, whereas "pusher" gets two and wins; one Jet is in his 30s and another in his 40s, so each of these gets one dose, whereas "20s" gets two and wins).

In this way, the network effectively generalizes to the nature of the typical Jet, that is, someone who is single and junior high school educated, and, with a little less confidence, a pusher and in his 20s. No single Jet actually meets this description, nonetheless the network can give it. And note that nowhere does the network actually store this generalization as a separate piece of information—all it contains is information about actual individuals and their properties.

Here we see a quite different view of the mind. In this case, the mind is held to store specific experiences and to associate and organize them in various ways. These specifics are not deduced from general sentences, rather generalizations (e.g., the typical Jet) emerge from the specifics—they come along "free" (and flexibly) so to speak. This sort of account can help us to see how, in considering the 5-year-old's story about her birthday party, "ideologies" (value-laden sociopolitical meanings) about gender, nature, and the organization of society can emerge from her texts, experiences, and the associations formed among them without ever being overtly formulated as a set of rules or generalizations. They are, in this sense, all the harder to critically confront and all the more effective in guiding situated practice (in which they, in fact, have their roots).

This model also suggest that the debates between "progressives" (e.g., "process approaches," "whole language," and so forth) and "postprogressives" are centered around a false dichotomy. The progressives are right in claiming that learning does require lots of rich experience and practice, not direct generalizations; the postprogressives (Delpit, 1988; Martin, 1991) are right in claiming that although lots of experience will give you rich networks out of which generalizations will emerge, unless you have had some direct focusing early on about how to set up relations between your experiences and what sorts of generalizations count, you will never be able successfully to coordinate with others in a specific social practice.

The necessary balance between "immersion" (what in Gee, 1996, I called *acquisition*) and "explicit focusing and instruction" (what in Gee, 1996, I called *learning*) will be a concern of much of the rest of this chapter. But the basic point here is this: if knowledge (including knowing that, knowing how, and the situated knowing by which we conduct our verbal and nonverbal interactions, see Shotter, 1993) is a matter of generalizations emerging out of our experiences and the multiple links we have formed among their features, then, for each of us, these experiences and links are quite different, because our situated experiences have been quite different. Furthermore, the features of our experiences and the links among them that we could pay attention to are infinite. Therefore, there has to be something to knowing beyond these experiences, associations, and their emergent properties, something beyond the mind, namely, what gives us common experiences and what focuses us on the relevant features. And this something beyond the mind is the work accomplished by the sociocultural groups and social institutions to which we belong.

These groups and institutions constitute what is common and relevant through work that is quite inherently political and ideological, because constitutive (with and out of our uniqueness) of our minds and worlds. And it cannot be otherwise: If there is no formation, there is a formless self, what the ancient Greeks called an *idiot*, a private person; if there is no unique experience and associations, there is nothing to form. One of the virtues of the connectionist approach, as is seen later, is that it can show us how the sociocultural work of formation still leaves us quite variable "selves."

Thus, knowing is irredeemably an inextricable product of mind–world–culture, and pedagogies that work (for good or bad) must be "explicitly focused immersions." Traditional pedagogies worked because some children got immersed elsewhere; progressive pedagogies worked because some children got explicit focusing elsewhere. Postprogressive pedagogies should give all children both. If one thinks that explicit focusing is violence, then let us acknowledge that education that works is violent and acknowledge, too, that immersion without some outside socioculturally defined focus is a form of exclusion.

BIRDS

Now I want to argue that, given what I have just said heads are best at—storing rich associations among specific experiences—if we are interested in learning and knowing, we need to focus not on minds, but on social practices. That is, contemporary discussions of mind, I believe, actually very quickly return us right back where we started, namely to social practices. Here is why.

Let me use as a specific example here, learning and knowing in a domain that is "strange" enough to most of us for matters normally hidden to become clear, namely what is sometimes called in the United States *birding* ("bird watching," see also Gee, 1992). Good birders acquire a "sixth sense" about what kinds of birds and how many different kinds will be found in a given sort of habitat. Thus, they see many birds, many more than you and I when we go out hiking. But birders cannot explain how they know this. This is not to say that they will not try: But what they will offer as an explanation is their "folk theory" about what determines the diversity of bird species in a given area, what Holland and Quinn (1987) called a *cultural model*. This cultural model need not be correct for the bird watchers' practices to work successfully because the practices do not in actuality (completely) follow the cultural model. This is certainly not to say that the bird watcher's cultural model of bird watching is not important. It may be very important, indeed. Bird watchers may very well judge other bird watchers on whether they have allegiance to the cultural model, and bird watchers organize large parts of their social practice (clubs, newsletters, trips, etc.) around it.

In addition to their (at least partially conscious) cultural models, birders also have in their heads a great many (unconscious) associations among various features of objects and events that they have experienced, along the lines I have suggested in Figure 16.1 above. Thus, we all recognize birds because a great many features—feathers, flying, beaks, certain ways of perching and walking, and so on—are variously associated with each other to various degrees of strength. They are associated in such a way that seeing or thinking about one or more such features brings to mind—more or less strongly—all the others. Of course, the networks of associations in birders' heads are much richer, more detailed, and more complex (e.g., a white rump is associated with birds of type X, Y, and Z, and no others).

However, there is something above and beyond these mental associations and cultural models. There is also the social practice of bird watching. Bird watching (in the sense of "birding") is certainly not in peoples' heads, nor is it in their acts of looking at birds in fields and woods. It is a set of on-going activities and interactions among birders in certain places and at certain times—ways of talking, acting, watching, interacting, reading, writing, with associated meetings, written materials, bird reserves, associations, and physical settings for meetings and materials.

Such a material social practice with its associated people and things is, what I call, a *Discourse* (Gee, 1992, 1996, see also, of course, for a somewhat different but related, notion of "discourse," Foucault, 1972, 1973, 1977, 1980, 1985). I use the term *Discourse* (with a capital D) to make clear that I am talking about something that *means* (*discourses*), although it is not in any one person's head, and is not "just language," but rather an amalgam of language, bodies, heads, and various props in the world (like birds and books).

The Discourse of bird watching has several functions, among which are the following: (a) it serves to apprentice new birders; (b) it helps people form cultural models about birds, habitats, and bird watching, which need never reside totally in their heads because it is inscribed in the books, journals, newsletters, as well as the social practices, organizational structures, institutions, and conversations of the Discourse; and (c) it keeps everyone's mental networks of associations in regard to birds, habitats, and bird watching "pretty much" alike by ensuring that they hold relatively similar folk theories, have many experiences of relevantly similar sorts, and focus on the "right" parts of that experience. If your mental network of associations (which is never identical to anyone else's and doesn't ever need to be) gets too much "out of line," or your cultural model deviates too far from that of others, your practice will begin to render you marginal to the Discourse and the Discourse will "discipline" you and put you back in line, or you will cease to be a birder.

This discipline can, of course, take a great many forms, including diverse interactions with other birders, references in conversations and publications, and the workings of the physical world, which is, of course, part of the Discourse. In fact, aspects of the social practice and the physical world often play a more important role in birders' sightings than anything going on in their brains or eyes. If a birder has not followed the "rules" for ethical claims in having sighted a rare bird, the bird has not ("officially") been "seen" and it cannot go on the birder's list. And the presence or absence (e.g., through extinction) of rare birds in the world has a great deal to do with what birders can claim to have sighted or not, certainly more (or, at least, not less) than any chemical reaction going on in their brains (claims to have sighted extinct birds are disciplined severely by the Discourse). The social practice and the physical world structure the activity of bird watching as much as or more than the nature of the human brain. To study only the latter and ignore the former would leave one with a quite silly view of the nature of bird watching.

What I have said about birding as a Discourse can be said about any other Discourse, for example, being (enacting) a type of American or African-American, man or woman, factory worker or executive, doctor, lawyer, or hospital patient, teacher, administrator, or student, student of physics or literature, physicist or literary critic, gang member or regular at the local bar (pub). Discourses are always embedded in a medley of social institutions, and often involve various props like books and magazines of various sorts, laboratories, classrooms, buildings of various sorts, various technologies, and a myriad of other objects from sewing needles (for sewing circles) through birds (for bird watchers) to basketball courts and basketballs (for basketball players). It is an interesting fact about the human condition that we can actually be members of two conflicting Discourses, thus living out internally and in the world the opposition between our Discourses.

KNOWING IN DISCOURSES

In light of our discussion about mental networks, birds and Discourses, let us reformulate the point we reached in regard to Jennie and Leona: Jennie's and Leona's mastery—even at their young ages—consists in their abilities, in mind and body, to coordinate and be coordinated by the resources—other people, types of language, objects (e.g., books and cakes) and spaces—of specific Discourses (different ones in each case). When we look at things this way, Jennie and Leona become simultaneously agents (coordinating) and patients (being coordinated by). Furthermore, they become agent-patients "in sync with," "linked with," "in association with," "in coordination with," however we want to put it, other *actants* (adapting a term from Latour, see Callon & Latour, 1992; Latour 1987), like particular forms of language, other people, objects (e.g., books and cakes), places (e.g., livingroom, street, or classroom), and nonverbal practices (e.g., holding up a book or encouraging and responding to audience participation)—note that not all actants are human.

Yet another way to put the matter: Meaning is not in mental networks like those in Fig. 16.1, rather meaning emerges out of the changing and ever "newly" produced links among such networks, the bodies they are in, other minds and bodies, objects, places, practices, and linguistic and other sorts of symbols systems (Knorr-Cetina, 1981, 1992, Latour, 1987; Latour & Woolgar, 1979). This is to take a "connectionist" view of society. Just as flexible generalizations emerge out of mental networks like that in Fig. 16.1, so flexible, changing, adapting Discourses—always and only "more or less stable," always and only "on the edge of chaos" (Waldrop, 1992)—emerge out these wider, sociocultural and sociohistorical links.

I want now to develop a particular example of what I am talking about here by taking one sentence uttered by a scientist, showing how the scientist is an agent-patient, coordinating and being coordinated by other actants in her Discourse. The same sort of thing could have been developed for Jennie and Leona, but this example has the advantage of showing that the claims I have been making are true for learning, knowing, and meaning in prestigious realms like science, as well. I also want to stress here the inherently *historical* nature of Discourses, and the ways in which they hide their ideological effects by effacing their historicity.

The sentence I consider was uttered during an undergraduate classroom presentation on the neuroanatomy of finches presented by an outstanding biologist. In finches, only males sing. The scientist was interested in the way in which the development, perception, and production of the male's song relates to the structure and functioning of its brain. In the course of her presentation, the scientist drew a diagram of the male finch's brain on the board (note, this is an actant in the Discourse, a thing she is coordinating and being coordinated by). The diagram was a large circle, representing the bird's brain, with three smaller circles inside it, marked "A," "B," and "C," representing discrete localized regions of neurons that function as units in the learning and production of the male's song. When the young bird hears its song (in the wild or on tape), it tries to produce the various parts of the song (engages in something like "babbling"). As the young bird's own productions get better and better, the neurons in Region A are "tuned" and eventually respond selectively to aspects of the song the young bird was exposed to and not other songs. The regions marked "B" and "C" also play a role in the development of the song and in its production.

The scientist also discussed the relationship between the male's brain and the hormones produced in the bird's gonads (more actants). The A, B, and C regions each have many cells in them that respond to testosterone, a hormone plentifully produced by the testes of the male bird. If these cells do not get sufficient testosterone, the development of the male bird's song is disrupted. If a male finch is deprived of testosterone altogether, Regions A, B, and C will not develop, and the bird will not sing. On the other hand, if a female bird is artificially treated with testosterone from birth, she develops Areas A, B, and C along the lines of the male, and eventually sings.

The scientist described the intricate methodological and experimental techniques that have been developed to isolate and describe discrete localized regions of the brain, like Regions A, B, and C in the male finch brain. These included intricate microscopic electrical probes (yet more actants) that measure the activities of small groups of neurons within regions like A, B, or C. She, thus, described a whole research area, its central questions and concerns, as well as its methodological and experimental techniques.

In this context, the scientist uttered the following sentence: "If you look in the brain [of the finch] you see high sexual dimorphism—A/B/C regions are robust in males and atrophied or nonexistent in females." The word *atrophied* in this sentence is a technical term—the correct term required by the current Discourse of biology. Note that one could have viewed the male brain as containing "monstrous growths" and thus as having deviated from the "normal" female brain. Instead, however, the terminology requires us to see the male brain as having developed fully ("robust") and the female brain as having either "atrophied" or failed to develop ("nonexistent").

Here, I briefly discuss two important moments in the history of the Discourse of biology and its interactions with other Discourses that have helped to shape our scientist's sentence in the present. It is, of course, not an historical accident that *atrophied* has ended up a technical term for the female finch brain (and other similar cases), although this brain is simply less "localized" in terms of discrete regions like A, B, and C. To see why, we need to talk both about females and brains.

First, females: In the West, for thousands of years, females have been viewed as either inferior to males or, at the least, deviant from the male as the "norm" or "fully developed" exemplar of the species (Fausto-Sterling, 1985; Laqueur, 1990; Schiebinger, 1993). Rather than retrace this immense history, consider one very salient moment of it in regard to the sentence previously quoted: Darwinian biology was based on the assumption that behavior and body shape go hand in hand. For example, the environment of a certain species of grain-eating birds changes—say, grain disappears—and they must crack nuts in order to eat; eventually the bodies of birds of this species become shaped to this task, because only birds with the thickest and hardest beaks survive and pass on their genes. Analogously, the argument goes (Degler, 1991), throughout history, women's environment has been the home, while men's environment has been out in the world competing with other men and animals (hunting). These different environments have differently shaped the bodies and minds (brains) of men and women. Hence, to quote Darwin (1859) himself:

> It is generally admitted that with woman the powers of intuition, of rapid perception, and perhaps of imitation, are more strongly marked than in man; but some, at least, of these faculties are characteristic of the lower races, and therefore of a past and lower state of civilisation. The chief distinction in the intellectual powers of the two sexes is shown by man's attaining to a higher eminence, in whatever he takes up, than can woman—whether requiring deep thought, reason, or imagination, or merely the use of senses and hands. (p. 873)

Although Darwin usually did not himself interpret "evolution" as linear development upward to "better things," many of his followers did (Bowler, 1990). The competition men have faced in their environments has caused their bodies and brains to "develop" further than those of woman, so that it is a commonplace by the 19th century and in the early decades of the 20th that "anthropologists regard women intermediate in development between the child and the man" (Thomas, 1897, cited in Degler, 1991, p. 29). This logic, of course, leads us to see the whole woman, in body and brain, as an "atrophied" man (exactly as Aristotle and Galen did), less developed because she is less challenged by her environment.

Now, one may object at this point: "All right, it is no historical accident that 'atrophied' has ended up getting attached as a technical term to the female finch's brain. Still the brain *is* localised into discrete regions, isn't it? And, thus, the male finch's brain *just* is the *right* thing to take as the 'norm' or 'standard' here." But, it turns out, that even the choice to see the male's brain as the obvious and worthy thing to study (and around which to develop intricate methodologies) was formed in and through history. Such a choice is not by any means "natural" or "obvious." Things could have turned out differently. This brings us to brains.

In the 19th century there was a raging debate over whether the brain is "localized" (i.e., composed of distinct parts, such as the "speech area" or "motor area," each with its own unique function) or "diffuse," operating holistically, without, "separation of parts or a pointillist division of labor" (Star, 1989, p. 4). This debate was eventually settled in favor of the localized position, although not (initially, at least) on the basis of "objective" evidence (there was about equal evidence for both sides), but as part of the emergence of the modern medical profession in 19th-century England (Desmond, 1989; cf. Haraway, 1989). Again, I point to but one moment in this history.

As modern "professional" medicine emerged out of an earlier system tied to aristocratic patronage and an education in the classics, there was a significant "collusion" (coordination) between surgeons and those medical researchers who believed in the localized view of the brain. Based on the symptoms displayed by neurological patients (e.g., people suffering from aphasia or epilepsy), these researchers claimed to be able to identify the location in the brain that was diseased (something the diffusionists denied could be done). Given this information, the surgeons claimed to be able to excise the offending tumor or abscess and cure the patient.

In actual fact, even after the development of relatively sophisticated surgical techniques for brain surgery, there was still no one-to-one correlation between symptoms thought to point to a tumor or abscess in a certain area ("localizing signs") and the actual location of such a tumor. Nonetheless, surgeons and researchers cited exemplary, but exceptional, cases in which the two matched as "proof" of localization of function. These claims benefited both surgery and those researchers devoted to the localizationist position, making the latter look like they had "special" knowledge that enabled them to find what the former, with their "special" skills, could cure. Evidence for localization was collected from both surgery and neurological research. Each field tended to attribute certainty to the other: Researchers pointed to medical evidence when their own results were anomalous or uncertain; doctors pointed to physiological research of the localizationist sort when they could not find clear postmortem evidence for discrete functional regions.

The emerging professional medical schools demanded unambiguous pictures of typical brains to put in their textbooks (what student wants to be told that things are complex and messy?). The researchers on the localizationist side offered unambiguous functional anatomical maps (e.g., maps that could indicate the anatomical point in the brain that was the source of loss of speech), something the diffusionists could not do. These maps "hid" irregular or anomalous findings from theoretical sight. The demand for such maps in medical education, diagnosis, and texts "represented a market intolerant of ambiguity and of individual differences"; the localizationist theory became unambiguously packaged in the map of *"the* brain, not *a* brain" (Star, 1989, p. 90). The localizationist view of the brain has, in important respects, won out in contemporary neurological studies. Far more research and effort has been devoted to it than to more holistic aspects of the brain's functioning, although this is now beginning to change with the development of new models of the mind/brain (Kosslyn & Koenig, 1992), including the connectionist views discussed earlier. Localizationist views have, however, directed both the procedures and goals of research for some time now.

From the perspective of the historical Discourses on females and brains I sketched previously, the male finch's brain, with its clear localized sites, looks to be a particularly natural and obvious research site, reflecting not an anomaly, but a particular clear example of what is normal. Furthermore, from this perspective, the female's brain does, indeed, look to be "undeveloped" and "abnormal," to deserve its classification as "atrophied."

Now, my point here is not that the science our scientist is doing, with its theories, technical vocabulary, and intricate methodologies and experimental procedures is "wrong." Nor do I want to claim that she and her peers have not discovered important "facts." Rather, imagine that the two moments I described earlier (i.e., the Darwinian "logic" on women and the collusion between surgeons and researchers around localizationist theories of the brain) had not occurred. Imagine further that different moments had occurred, moments in which women and holistic approaches to the brain had been advantaged. Then our scientist's presentation would have been different—her words and her science would have been shaped differently. And that science may very well have also not been "wrong" and may very well have discovered important "facts" too, they simply would have been different facts. In that science, the male finch's brain might have been seen as overly specialized and monstrous, and may, in fact, have not been a particularly worthy research site, at least for the purposes of developing initial theories in neurobiology. There may have been intricate techniques to measure diverse parts of the brain operating in tandem, and not tiny probes narrowing in on a small set of neurons. The technical term *atrophied* would not have existed for the female finch's brain.

The scientist, in uttering her sentence, just like Jennie and Leona, coordinates and is coordinated by the resources of sociohistorical Discourses, and, in the act, gets lots and lots of meaning "free." What is in her head does not matter much. She and her sentence resonate with other actants now and throughout history. Of course, this resonance is most certainly not entirely accidental (although chance and accident do play an important role in history and other complex systems, see Briggs & Peat, 1989; Waldrop, 1992), but is tuned to the frequencies of human desires and interests, politics and ideologies, as these are woven into Discourses and their relationships.

CONCLUSION

Meaning, learning, and knowing are matters of coordinating and being coordinated with self and others and things (actants) within sociohistorically situated Discourses. But, a problem arises when we realize that the meanings that Discourses give us "free" are, sometimes, gifts we do not or should not want. They can be gifts that, in certain respects, are against our interests as defined within other Discourses or gifts that hurt others (see Gee, 1996). In any case, because any Discourse always excludes certain meanings and knowings that other Discourses include, Discourses are inherently oppositional and limited.

We cannot liberate ourselves from the ideological effects of Discourses by standing outside all of them. There is no such place to stand, because meaning exists only within specific Discourses. However, there is one act that, in general, Discourses do not encourage. This is the act of juxtaposing texts from different Discourses (which we did in the case of Jennie and Leona) or juxtaposing texts from different historical stages of a Discourse (as we did in the case of the scientist). Such juxtapositions expose the limitations on meaning that all Discourses effect and open out new meanings, because the very act of juxtaposition always requires a meta-language, with accompanying meta-practices within an emerging meta-Discourse, to enclose both texts in a more encompassing system.

Such juxtapositional practices, of course, must be done within a Discourse, and, indeed, emerging work on sociocultural and sociohistorical literacies, being done by people from a great variety of fields, and at all different levels of the educational system, is creating just such a new Discourse (see, for a small, and somewhat random, sample: Baker, 1991; Bloome & Green, 1991; Cazden, 1988; Cook-

Gumperz, 1986; Edelsky, 1991; Gilbert, 1989; Green, 1990; Heath, 1983; Lemke, 1989; A. Luke, 1988, 1993;. Luke & Luke, 1990; C. Luke, 1989, 1991; Scollon & Scollon, 1981; Street, 1984; Stuckey, 1991; Walkerdine, 1986, 1988). Of course, this Discourse, too, will attempt to oppose juxtaposition applied to itself and to efface its history, but, we can hope, that, being based on just such juxtaposition, it will never completely succeed at this. Hence, the value of the oppositions and juxtapositions that are emerging across this book.

I am arguing, then, that the basis of responsible pedagogy, both from a cognitive and a cultural perspective, is juxtaposition of differences in such a way that commonness can emerge (variable and changing patterns, associations, or generalizations) without obliterating the differences as lived and situated realities. Let us view each child as a network of associations formed by his or her sociocultural experiences, a network from which specific ways of knowing the world emerge. Then, a classroom should be a network of such networks from which new, ever variable, and "meta-level" forms of knowing emerge, forms that emerge from and transcend diversity without effacing it in any way, because each child's own continuing experiences contribute to the transformation of that common knowledge. A new Discourse is formed in the classroom. Looked at in this way, a classroom with too narrow a spectrum of diversity is cognitively impoverished, whatever else we may want to say about its ethics. The "generalizations" that can emerge from such a classroom are too narrow to "make history" rather than to replicate it.

Furthermore, a classroom using the diversity of its students to make connections, uses the same tactic of patterns emerging from diversity in its curriculum. For example, to see the poetic orality in the Discourse of African Americans as associated with the still oral-aural-rooted literariness of canonical literature is not merely to understand both Discourses anew, but to achieve a meta-understanding of the multiple, dynamic interrelations of speaking and writing, listening and reading, as well as their very nature as companions and competitors in history. Or, to juxtapose popular science, journal science, and earlier instantiations of scientific writing and practice, and all of these with nonscientific practices, is to cause the meaning-making of scientists to emerge in clear relief, in all its cognitive, social, cultural, and political complexity. But such juxtapositions must always be made with texts and practices fully embedded in their Discourses as historically unfolding coordinations of resources centered around values, interests, and desires, and perspectives on other Discourses.

Of course, such juxtaposition has not merely theoretical consequences, it has practical ones as well. Having done it myself, I could no longer be coordinated by the Discourse of theoretical linguistics, and, thus, ceased to get those meanings free. I can only hope that the meanings I get and have gotten free within the emerging Discourse of sociohistorical and sociocultural literacies are more liberating.

REFERENCES

Abrahams, R. D. (1964). *Deep down in the jungle: Negro narrative folklore from the streets of Philadelphia*. Hatboro, PA: Folklore Associates.

Abrahams, R. D. (1970). *Positively black*. Englewood Cliffs, NJ: Prentice-Hall

Abrahams, R. D. (1976). *Talking black*. Rowley, MA: Newbury House.

Adams, M. J. (1990). *Beginning to read: Thinking and learning about print*. Cambridge, MA: MIT Press.

Allman, W. F. (1989). *Apprentices of wonder: Inside the neural network revolution*. New York: Bantam.

Baker, C. D. (1991). Literacy practices and social relations in classroom reading events. In C. D. Baker & A. Luke (Eds.), *Towards a critical sociology of reading pedagogy* Amsterdam: John Benjamins.

Barsalou, L. W. (1992). *Cognitive psychology: An overview for cognitive scientists*. Hillsdale, NJ: Lawrence Erlbaum Associates.

Baugh, J. (1983). *Black street speech: Its history, structure and survival*. Austin: University of Texas Press.

Bechtel, W., & Abrahamsen, A. (1991). *Connectionism and the mind: An introduction to parallel processing in networks*. Oxford, UK: Basil Blackwell.

Birch, D. (1989). *Language, literature and critical practice: Ways of analyzing texts*. London: Routledge.

Bloome, D., & Green, J. (1991). Educational contexts of literacy. *Annual Review of Applied Linguistics, 12*, 49-70.

Bourdieu, P. (1977). *Outline of a theory of practice* (R. Nice, Trans.). Cambridge, UK: Cambridge University Press.

Bourdieu, P., & Passeron, J. C. (1977). *Reproduction in education, society and culture* (R. Nice, Trans.). London: Sage.

Bowler, P. J. (1990). *Charles Darwin: The man and his influence*. Oxford, UK: Basil Blackwell.

Briggs, J., & Peat, F. D. (1989). *Turbulent mirror: An illustrated guide to chaos theory and the sciences of wholeness*. New York: Harper & Row.

Callon, M., & Latour, B. (1992). Don't throw the baby out with the Bath school! A reply to Collins and Yearley. In A. Pickering (Ed.), *Science as practice and culture*. Chicago: University of Chicago Press.

Cazden, C. (1988). *Classroom discourse: The language of teaching and learning*. Portsmouth, NH: Heinemann.

Chall, J., Jacobs, V. A., & Baldwin, L. E. (1990). *The reading crisis: Why poor children fall behind.* Cambridge, MA: Harvard University Press.

Churchland, P. M. (1989). *A Neurocomputational perspective: The nature of mind and the structure of science.* Cambridge, MA: MIT Press.

Churchland, P. S. (1986). *Neurophilosophy: Toward a unified science of the mind/brain.* Cambridge, MA: MIT Press.

Churchland, P. S., & Sejnowski, T. J. (1992). *The computational brain.* Cambridge, MA: Bradford/MIT Press.

Clark, A. (1989). *Microcognition: Philosophy, cognitive science, and parallel distributed processing.* Cambridge, MA: MIT Press.

Clark, A. (1993). *Associative engines: Connectionism, concepts, and representional change.* Pittsburgh: University of Pittsburgh Press.

Cook-Gumperz, J. (Ed.). (1986). *The social construction of literacy.* Cambridge, UK: Cambridge University Press.

Darwin, C. (1859). *The origin of species by means of natural selection or the preservation of favored races in the struggle for life and the descent of man and selection in relation to sex.* New York: Modern Library

Degler, C. N. (1991). *In search of human nature: The decline and revival of Darwinism in American social thought.* Stanford, CA: Stanford University Press.

Delpit, L. D. (1988). The silenced dialogue: Power and pedagogy in educating other people's children. *Harvard Educational Review, 58,* 280-298.

Desmond, A. (1989). *The politics of evolution: Morphology, medicine, and reform in radical London.* Chicago: University of Chicago Press.

Edelsky, C. (1991). *With literacy and justice for all: Rethinking the social in language and education.* London: Falmer Press.

Fausto-Sterling, A. (1985). *Myths of gender: Biological theories about women and men.* New York: Basic Books.

Finnegan, R. (1970). *Oral literature in Africa.* Oxford, UK: Clarendon Press.

Finnegan, R. (1988). *Literacy and orality.* Oxford, UK: Basil Blackwell.

Fodor, J. A. (1975). *The language of thought.* New York: Thomas Crowell.

Fodor, J. A. (1983). *The modularity of the mind.* Cambridge, MA: Bradford/MIT Press.

Fodor, J. A., & Pylyshyn, Z. (1988). Connectionism and cognitive architecture: A critical analysis. *Cognition, 28,* 3-71.

Foucault, M. (1972). *The archaeology of knowledge* (A. M. Sheridan Smith, Trans.). New York: Harper & Row.

Foucault, M. (1973). *The birth of the clinic: An archaeology of medical perception* (A. M. Sheridan Smith, Trans.). New York: Vintage Books.

Foucault, M. (1977). *Discipline and punish: The birth of the prison* (A. M. Sheridan Smith, Trans.). New York: Pantheon.

Foucault, M. (1980). *Power/knowledge: Selected interviews and other writings 1972–1977* (C. Gordon, L. Marshall, J. Meplam, & K. Soper, Eds.) Brighton, Sussex: The Harvester Press.

Foucault, M. (1985). *The Foucault reader* (P. Rabinow, Ed.). New York: Pantheon.

Gardner, H. (1991). *The unschooled mind: How children think and how schools should teach.* New York: Basic Books.

Gee, J. P. (1991). Socio-cultural approaches to literacy (literacies). *Annual Review of Applied Linguistics, 12*, 31-48.

Gee, J. P. (1992). *The social mind: Language, ideology, and social practice.* New York: Bergin & Garvey.

Gee, J. P. (1992/1993). Literacies: Tuning in to forms of life. *Education Australia, 19/20*, 13-14.

Gee, J. P. (1996) *Social linguistics and literacies: Ideology in discourses* (2nd ed.). London, UK: Taylor and Francis

Gilbert, P. H. (1989). *Writing, schooling and deconstruction: From voice to text in the classroom.* London: Routledge.

Green, J. L. (1990). *Reading is a social process. Social context of literacy: Selected papers from the 15th Australian Reading Association Conference.* Canberra: ACT Department of Education.

Haraway, D. (1989). *Primate visions: Gender, race, and nature in the world of modern science.* New York: Routledge.

Heath, S. B. (1983). *Ways with words: Language, life, and work in communities and classrooms.* Cambridge, UK: Cambridge University Press

Hodge, R. (1990). *Literature as discourse.* Baltimore, MD: Johns Hopkins.

Hodge, R., & Kress, G. (1988). *Social semiotics.* Ithaca, NY: Cornell University Press.

Holland, D., & Quinn, N. (Eds.). (1987). *Cultural models in language and thought.* Cambridge, UK: Cambridge University Press.

Kochman, T. (Ed.). (1972). *Rappin' and stylin' out: Communication in urban black America.* Urbana: University of Illinois Press.

Kochman, T. (1981). *Black and white styles in conflict.* Chicago: University of Chicago Press.

Kosslyn, S. M., & Koenig, O. (1992). *Wet mind: The new cognitive neuroscience.* New York: The Free Press.

Knorr-Cetina, K. (1981). *The manufacture of knowledge: An essay on the constructivist and contextual nature of science.* Oxford, UK: Pergamon Press.

Knorr-Cetina, K. (1992). The couch, the cathedral, and the laboratory: On the relationship between experiment and laboratory in science. In A. Pickering (Ed.), *Science as practice and culture.* Chicago: University of Chicago Press.

Labov, W. (1972). *Language in the inner city.* Philadelphia: University of Pennsylvania Press.

Latour, B. (1987). *Science in action.* Cambridge, MA: Harvard University Press.

Latour, B., & Woolgar, S. (1979). *Laboratory life: The social construction of scientific facts.* Beverly Hills: Sage.

Laqueur, T. (1990). *Making sex: Body and gender from the Greeks to Freud.* Cambridge, MA: Harvard University Press.

Leitch, V. B. (1992). *Cultural criticism, literary theory, poststructuralism.* New York: Columbia University Press.

Lemke, J. (1989). *Talking science.* Norwood, NJ: Ablex.

Levi-Strauss, C. (1966). *The savage mind.* Chicago: University of Chicago Press.

Lorenz, E. N. (1993). *The essence of chaos.* Seattle: University of Washington Press.

Luke, A. (1988). *Literacy, textbooks and ideology: Postwar literacy instruction and the mythology of Dick and Jane.* London: Falmer Press.

Luke, A. (1993). The body literate: Discourse and inscription in early literacy training. *Linguistics and Education, 4,* 107-129.

Luke, A., & Luke, C. (1990). School knowledge as simulation: Curriculum in postmodern conditions. *Discourse, 13,* 75-91.

Luke, C. (1989). *Pedagogy, printing, and Protestantism: The discourse on childhood.* Albany: State University of New York Press.

Luke, C. (1991). On reading the child: A feminist poststructuralist perspective. *Australian Journal of Reading, 14,* 109-116.

Malcolm, N. (1989). Wittgenstein on language and rules. *Philosophy, 64,* 5-28

Martin, J. R. (1991). Critical literacy: The role of a functional model of language. *Australian Journal of Reading, 14,* 117-132.

McClelland, J., Rumelhart, D., & Hinton, G. (1986). The appeal of PDP. In D. Rumelhart, J. McClelland, and the PDP Research Group (Eds.), *Parallel distributed processing: Explorations in the microstructure of cognition* (Vol. 1). Cambridge, MA: MIT Press.

Michaels, S. (1981). "Sharing time": Children's narrative styles and differential access to literacy. *Language in Society, 10,* 423-42.

Michaels, S. (1985). Hearing the connections in children's oral and written discourse. *Journal of Education, 167,* 36-56.

Nichols, P. C. (1989). Storytelling in Carolina: Continuities and contrasts. *Anthropology and Education Quarterly, 20,* 232-245.

Perkins, D. (1992). *Smart schools: From training memories to educating minds.* New York: The Free Press.

Schiebinger, L. (1993). *Nature's body: Gender in the making of modern science.* Boston: Beacon Press.

Scollon, R., & Scollon, S. B. K. (1981). *Narrative, literacy, and face in interethnic communication*. Norwood, NJ: Ablex

Shotter, J. (1993). Conversational realities: *Constructing life through language*. London: Sage.

Smitherman, G. (1977). *Talkin and testifin: The language of black America*. Boston: Houghton Mifflin.

Stahl, S. D. (1989). *Literary folkloristics and the personal narrative*. Bloomington: Indiana University Press.

Star, S. L. (1989). *Regions of the mind: Brain research and the quest for scientific certainty*. Stanford, CA: Stanford University Press.

Sterelny, K. (1990). *The representational theory of mind: An introduction*. Oxford, UK: Basil Blackwell.

Street, B. V. (1984). *Literacy in theory and practice*. Cambridge, UK: Cambridge University Press.

Stuckey, J. E. (1991). *The violence of literacy*. Portsmouth: Boynton/Cook.

Stucky, S. (1987). *Slave culture: Nationalist theory and the foundations of Black America*. Oxford, UK: Oxford University Press.

Waldrop, M. M. (1992). *Complexity: The emerging science at the edge of order and chaos*. New York: Simon & Schuster.

Walkerdine, V. (1986). *Surveillance, subjectivity and struggle: Lessons from pedagogic and domestic practices*. Minneapolis: University of Minnesota Press.

Walkerdine, V. (1988). *Mastery of reason*. London: Routledge.

Watkins, M. (1994). *On the real side: Laughing, lying, and signifying—the underground tradition of African-American humor that transformed American culture, from slavery to Richard Pryor*. New York: Simon & Schuster.

Wittgenstein, L. (1958). *Philosophical investigations*. (G. E. M. Anscombe, Trans.). Oxford, UK: Basil Blackwell.

17
Relativism in the Politics of Discourse
Response to James Paul Gee

Mary Macken-Horarik
Sydney University

In this chapter I reflect on Gee's insights from the point of view of the classroom teacher. I shall assume my classroom population includes children like those mentioned in his chapter (Jennie and Leona) and that my tasks include assisting their control of mainstream literacy. Far more than this is necessary. Anything less would be a failure of responsibility and care for children whose parents look to the school as an agent for enabling access to the powerful discourses of the dominant culture. It is a reasonable expectation and a matter of social justice that schools and teachers play a role here. But what does this entail when it comes to school-based literacy? How do teachers establish a curriculum that is inclusive, rigorous, and critical? These are some of the problematics that confront educators as they try to imagine and practice a postprogressive pedagogy. In this response, I situate myself in relation to each point covered in Gee's chapter and then reflect on its pedagogical implications. Any more tangential issues are discussed briefly in footnotes.

IS MEANING IN THE HEAD?

Gee is anxious to overturn some of the tacit assumptions about meaning that still predominate in U.S.-style theoretical linguistics and cognitive science—for instance that meaning is a cognitive activity. His project calls for strong rhetoric and he counters traditional assumptions via a strategy of oppositional classification in which he asserts that meaning is not in the head but in social practices.[1] This is evidenced in Gee's study of children's oral narratives. For both Leona and Jennie, learning to tell stories is a social and emulative rather than an individual and originating process.

One cannot help but concur. In her story about the battle over the Transformers and Cabbage Patches, for example, 5-year-old Jennie is accessing and reproducing the meanings available within her specific sociohistorical formation. Devices like the "sympathetic fallacy" are part of the generic potential available to her and allow her to mean far beyond her private resources. Her story is much more an artifact of her experience of a particular "home-based social practice, with its ways of interacting, talking, thinking, valuing, and reading and its books and other physical props" (p. 271) than it is one of individual imagination. And, furthermore as Gee notes, Jennie will increasingly be open to attributions of intelligence and giftedness as she learns to construct narratives like this that "resonates with particular historically derived interpretive practices 'owned and operated' by certain groups" (chap. 16, p. 276).

And although we may observe that her semiotic "giftedness" comes with both positive and negative consequences for her developing meaning potential, it is the notion of the gift that is crucial here.

Pedagogical Implications: Explore the Gift

Students need informed access to textual practices (as part of the social practices they engage with in the course of their education). An enabling pedagogy will increase both their unconscious meaning potential (as

---

[1]I see no reason to exclude heads from meaning-making. If we start with a social semiotic perspective on meaning, there is no need to establish such strong boundaries between an individual's consciousness, his or her semantic potential, and the social environment in which he or she develops it. For example, operating within such a textual practice and attracting positive assessments from others as a result will definitely influence what is inside Jennie's head. She may participate "without full understanding" in social practices that naturalize gender differences of the sort legitimated in her narrative. But these differences will be internalized in the process of her formation, ensuring that Jennie comes to see a given sexual division of labor as natural and right. The meanings she gets "free" are meanings that become part of what is inside her head and that also make change so difficult. Constructing a notion of individual agency is important to the task of generic and discursive change and agency is impossible without consciousness. Jennie may want to take issue with discourses that naturalize the given order of things for women. Bringing "what is inside her head" to bear on this task will be one important part of this project—along with other textual and social actions. And learning to write about it may be an important first step in discovering that discourses are enshrined and demolished in textual practices (i.e., they can be rewritten just as they are written).

Jennie is doing when she utilizes the sympathetic fallacy in her narrative) and introduce them to a more conscious meta-discourse for reflecting on language and its sociocultural functions. This would include both a formal meta-language that is shareable, oriented to texts, and part of the specialized curriculum of the school; and it would make space for those perspectives that come from the so-called margins of the society—perspectives instantiated in texts like Leona's.

A meta-language is useful within formal education only if it is shareable. But not all of these are useful. Traditional school grammar is one such meta-language. It is oriented to written language, syntactic in focus and it has become an instrument for devaluing nonstandard dialects and meaning styles. The meta-language envisaged here is one that distinguishes but relates spoken and written language, is semantic in focus and oriented to language in use. One such is the genre-based approach to teaching literacy that draws on both systemic functional linguistics and social semiotics (e.g., Christie, 1990; Cope & Kalantzis, 1993).

Students can learn about the structuring principles of the narratives they produce and read. Within a social semiotic perspective, a text is a social construct. It has an identifiable structure that is an artifact of the occasion in which it occurs again and again. As a construct, its structure and its social function can be deconstructed. A shared meta-language is crucial to this process—especially when learners first engage in the process. Members of the particular cultures know about how narratives are built—a fact that both Jennie and Leona bear out in their own storytelling. But telling stories and reflecting consciously on their artifice are different orders of semiosis. In one primary classroom that I visited regularly in 1989, students were introduced to a Labovian approach to the fairy tales they had heard read for years at home and school. They explored the stages of the tales using functional labels like *orientation, complication, evaluation,* and *resolution.* These terms enabled them to capture the semantic contribution of each stage to the narrative as a whole. And because the meta-language was functional rather than formal, and oriented to the meanings made by the text as a whole, they could draw on it when they came to write their own tales. A shared meta-language makes it possible for students to explore textual practices and patterning, and to talk about these to one another.

Of course, classroom meta-language has its limitations. There will be forms of semiosis that it fails to recognize, and discursive effects it cannot imagine. A meta-discourse must also make space for those yet-to-be realized meanings that lie beyond the ken of life within mainstream Discourses. Students whose social location and coding orientation tend to alienate them from the process of schooling are in a much better position here. I saw the beginnings of this in the same primary school where students had been reading, deconstructing, and discussing fairy tales. During one such discussion, issues of gender and agency were raised—although not in such terms. The girls in the group simply talked about why the heroine was always beautiful and always saved by a handsome prince. They wrote their own tales after this and one student's text carries the traces of her questioning: It features an overweight princess who is agentive in her own rescue.

Stories like Leona's have a place within a meta-discursive pedagogy—not only because they are texts rich in humor and symbolic wisdom, but also because they offer an opportunity for this kind of semiotic work. A contradictory relation to hegemonic discourses can be capitalized on in the development of a working meta-discourse. It promotes a healthy capacity to sniff out the worrisome discourses inscribed in literacy practices like Jennie's and to explore the gift in less familiar ones like Leona's.

MEANING DOES NOT TRAVEL WELL: MEANING IS IN MATERIALLY SITUATED SOCIAL PRACTICES

In this section Gee argues that meanings do not "travel well" because the practices that give rise to them are not abstract systems, but networks of situated material objects and concrete actions tied to specific times and places. Using Leona's tale, Gee demonstrates that some narrative forms are not well understood or well appreciated within mainstream schooling practices. Although a "creative masterpiece," Leona transports her tale to the class sharing time with negative consequences. The meanings that have salience and value within her home community do not resonate well with the texts of "powerful mainstream institutions" like the school. And the social practices in which Leona participates are not abstract things but are "embedded in material objects (such as bodies, places, objects, institutions, and texts) and concrete actions" (pp. 278-279). Like Jennie, Leona is more than just an individual "meaner." Her subjectivity is socially and discursively constituted—a product of her membership of a particular African-American community.

There are some important issues to address here, including that of the portability of meaning.[2] But the most important issue for

---

[2]Some kinds of meanings do travel well. Written language was developed to exploit the portability of meaning. This is not to assert that meanings are fixed in text and that they communicate in exactly the same way to everyone or that the fullness of its communicative import is available to all listeners or readers. Texts are open to a variety of readings but texts that are longer than a few clauses constrain the potential readings by their own form of semiosis. Any reader who does not "split off" from a text is forced to engage with the unfolding meanings

pedagogy is how a classroom can become a site that accommodates and builds on the divergent voices and meaning styles of its members. What should schooling have to do with Leona's sharing of her story? If we accept that she should feel encouraged to tell her story at sharing time, what kind of climate is envisaged?

Pedagogical Implications: Organize for Diversity

Leona needs to belong to a classroom that will value, share, and build on her individual and community meaning styles. This requires a pedagogic openness to the sociocultural and semiotic diversity of the classroom population, a matter Gee raises in his conclusion. Given that universal schooling is mandatory, how are we going to deal with classrooms that are increasingly multicultural? Do we shut the door on the problem and argue that diversity is a matter for homes and communities to sort out and that epistemic literacy is the school's only responsibility? Or do we construct a classroom agenda that celebrates and draws on the linguistic, ethnic, and socioeconomic diversity of its students' realities?

The consequences of the latter option, if it is given proper attention, are far reaching. First, it means viewing epistemic literacy as an important extension of the functional potential of language but only one form of it. The modes of communication that are relevant to children can be incorporated in classroom interaction and study. This is a political stance because it requires an acceptance of meanings that epistemic literacy is not based on. It means making space for diversity within the classroom and this affects the curriculum, the kind of classroom interaction that takes place and the discretionary power of the students. Organizing for diversity puts orality of different kinds on the agenda—and encourages teachers to make the languages, dialects, storytelling traditions, and experiences of the children part of their classroom attention and work. It involves an inclusiveness in which student meanings—their dialects, meaning styles, and experiences—can be both the starting and endpoint of any lesson. The extra work for teachers can be daunting. They need an extensive acquaintance with the linguistic, ethnic, and socioeconomic environments of all their students.

---

of a text—to process it in terms that respond to its own developing meaning potential. And this logogenesis is not open to just any kind of semantic transformation. I have to listen carefully to Leona's text if I am to process it properly and this is even more important if I am not a member of her African-American community. The deep meanings of her narrative will be less accessible to those who are not members of her community. Nevertheless, writing them down construes her meaning potential as "shareable" because written text makes a version of her narrative accessible as written meanings. The publishing industry is based on the assumption that meanings can travel.

This realization also takes teachers beyond a simplistic "let's celebrate difference" curriculum focus. It means developing learning programs in which students investigate the contexts that give meaning to stories like Leona's; in which students investigate the functional differences between spoken and written modes of communicating; in which students analyze the role of other semiotic systems in the culture at large (media like television, radio, and video games), and in their own cultural inheritance. In short, it involves teacher and students in a systematic study of the diverse forms of meaning and their functions both in local communities and in the broader community.

Such a curriculum will go some way to addressing Gee's call for attentiveness to the "networks of situated material objects and concrete actions tied to specific times and places" that constitute the specificity of our students' social practices (chap. 16, p. 274).

KNOWING AND HEADS

In this section of his chapter, Gee develops the crux of his argument about the relation between mind, meaning, and the social. Using the example of the "Jets" and the "Sharks," he illustrates how the associationist view of cognition challenges commonplace assumptions about learning that stress "the encoding of generalizations over specifics as the basis of knowledge" (chap. 16, p. 284). The "network view" suggests that what is in our heads is not a set of mentalese sentences, but rather rich networks of associations among experiences we have had—verbal and nonverbal experiences.

And, just as I wonder whether this view suggests that generalizations emerge flexibly and unmediated from experience—in which a Jet being a regular member of the workforce and living in a gay relationship is inconceivable if I have not met one—Gee acknowledges that there is something to knowing beyond our experiences, associations and their emergent properties. This something that gives us "common experiences" and focuses us on the "relevant" features is the work accomplished by the social—the sociocultural groups and the social institutions to that we belong and that politicize and ideologize our experience.

In this move Gee integrates the connectionist and the sociocultural work of individual formation. Cognitive science really needs its sociology and it is here that he makes his strongest claims about pedagogy. What Gee wants for classrooms incorporates aspects of both progressivism and "postprogressivism": He wants a balance between immersion in "rich experience and practice" and explicit focusing on how to set up relations between your experiences and what sort of generalizations count. I do not want to take issue with his characterization of either pedagogies, except to say that the gloss he offers of both experience and explicitness begs more questions than it answers. "Experience," for example, is not well theorized within either progressivism or postprogressivism. Does it include only those things I have experienced bodily? Does it include vicarious experience and other forms of textually mediated experience? What can "immersion" mean within the constraints of the school environment? What kinds of immersions are possible and desirable? And what kinds of explicitness does he envisage? How much teacher intervention is valuable and at what stages of a learning sequence?

Some of the work going on in educational applications of systemic functional linguistics and social semiotics has attempted to deal with issues like the relationship between experience and educational intervention. Systemic functional linguistics, for example, developed in part out of the reflections of Halliday and others on systematic ties between semantics and context. Educators can draw on this model of context and text to generate learning experiences for students and also predict the semiotic demands these will make of them (e.g., see Halliday, 1978; Halliday & Hasan, 1989). A functional model of language makes it possible to imagine the kinds of semantic pressures different situations will put on students and hence to support their efforts to handle them.

Pedagogical Implications: Build a Shared Meaning Potential

Educators are paid on the assumption that they know what they are doing when they intervene in learning, and that they can justify this to others. They need a model of pedagogical practice (i.e., of interventions) that helps them to not only generate learning situations for their students, but also to reflect on how the learners handle these and the extent to which their own practices assisted them in their efforts. Only a socially sensitive contextual framework will help them predict the pedagogic significance of particular kinds of experience for students' learning.

If we consider what it is that situations have in common, we move into the area of situation types. Particular situation types become socioculturally agnate and come to be associated with general context types—which can be called macro-contexts. As children grow up within a given sociocultural formation, the range of macro-contexts they encounter increases. Formal education is one of these whether their homes are in Japan, Germany, Malaysia or Australia. And whatever their gender, class, or ethnicity, schooling is a macro-context that is inextricably linked to enculturation in specialized forms of knowledge and role relations. It is a form of educational socialization that marks certain experiences as *specialized*—whether the orientation is theoretical (as in mathematics) or practical (as in industrial arts). Explicitly focused immersions cannot avoid the challenge of specialized knowledge—along with discourse that is only metaphorically related to experience, being highly technical, abstract—frequently uncommon sense.

Different contextual readings of an experience are possible but some are more socially and pedagogically salient than others. Students who make a common sense reading of an assessment task, for example, risk penalties that most would not choose to attract if they had the opportunity to make the right (i.e., specialized) reading. The point here is that students need access not only to experience but to interpretive cues that enable them to weigh experience in productive ways. Other resistant readings of a context are possible but not always advantageous for their long-term (discursive) futures, at least for those students who want access to mainstream Discourses and that school failure closes off. An adequately powerful model of the relation between experience and social context helps teachers and their students to explore and weigh the significance of any of the experiences they share. A detailed introduction to the applications of the model here described is available elsewhere (e.g., see Hasan & Martin, 1989; Hasan & William, 1995; Macken & Rothery, 1991).

In a heterogeneous classroom, teachers must help their students to construct and act on the basis of a shared meaning potential. No members of a classroom should be in any doubt about which meanings are going to be valued and rewarded by agencies of schooling. The relevant meanings to deploy in any test situation, for example, are those of specialized knowledge domains. And in this respect, traditional pedagogy served its students more fairly than does progressivism.

Students in New South Wales, for example, face only one state examination in the 4 years of their secondary schooling—the Year 10 Reference Test. Those who take assessment tasks on their face value will often be doomed to failure. In one year, examinees were asked to do a creative writing piece, writing "in any form you please". Those who took a creative view of the task, writing an advertising text, for instance, were penalized for their failure to develop character and plot (see Rothery & Macken, 1991). A study of the corpus of texts and examinees' comments, published and distributed widely for teachers' information, revealed a hidden exam agenda that rejected some generic choices and rewarded others (like the well-formed narrative). Students who fail to recognize the requirements of assessment contexts such as this, and/or cannot produce a text of the institutionally approved type will be subject to the discretionary exclusions of mainstream discourses.

In short, students need to learn how to interpret particular tasks marking the context appropriately and complying with its generic demands. And a functionally principled model of school learning contexts enables teachers and all their students to make adequate interpretations of any task, even those that appear to encourage common sense interpretations. Of course, specialized knowledge is not socially neutral and can be construed along alternative lines, especially in those situations where such expertise affects people's lives.

A critical perspective on experience will draw on alternative meaning potentials. And there is no reason why teachers cannot be just as systematic about their interventions here as they are with specialized learning. The same contextual dimensions can inform students' work on gender and role-set bias, for example, as they analyze how narrative genres naturalize particular views of women (see Gilbert, chap. 4, this volume). A shared feminist meaning potential, for example, helps students to question the representation of femininity in fairy tales, to challenge the reading position that these texts project, and to experiment with and subvert their generic possibilities. An explicit, focused model of text and its relevant social context is a powerful means to this end.

BIRDS

In this section of his chapter, Gee exemplifies the relation between meaning and social practice by drawing an extended analogy between "birding" and other Discourses. The notion of Discourse is crucial to this relation and is far more than a language matter for Gee: it is a "material social practice with its associated people and things". He argues that the social practice that disciplines birders is far more important to their learning the activity than is the nature of their brains.

If we consider educational Discourses from this perspective, it is the social practices in which students learn rather than the contents of any forms of knowledge that must exercise their teachers' attention. But this brings us back to an earlier point. If what is inside heads is less essential than we thought, it is important to focus on what is relevant for learning in the social environment. It is here that students will need to look for guidance as they build up working cultural models on which to draw in their learning.

Pedagogical Implications: Explicit Pedagogies Encourage Learner Independence

Explicit pedagogies signpost the learning environment, assisting students to make relevant assumptions about the purposes and requirements of any classroom activity. Interpreting the signposts or cues is crucial to classroom participation. Students can learn to do anything if they understand the purpose of an activity and they are shown how. Pedagogical strategies like modeling, deconstruction, and joint construction, for example, are very helpful for learners who do not read or write texts valued in school at home (see various chapters in Cope & Kalantzis, 1993). Such strategies support students as they begin work on a new genre or in an unfamiliar context. In early days, their teacher will play a leading and guiding role in modeling the linguistic requirements of a task, for example. But they do so to encourage learners into greater semiotic independence.

In explicit pedagogies like these, students do not have to guess at what is expected. Their teachers can be up front about what they are doing and why. And this is important not least because what is up front can be argued about, challenged, and amended if necessary. An adequate model of educational macro-contexts is also important in this process. It helps teachers to reflect on the learning situations they have set up in their classrooms and on whether their own practices supported their students' learning on a day-by-day basis and over a sequence of lessons. It offers a look-forward framework for planning a unit of work and that can be construed along common sense, specialized, applied, or critical lines. And the same contextual dimensions enable them to reflect on whether their students need assistance with the generic, role, knowledge, or modal dimensions of their learning.

KNOWING IN DISCOURSES

In the final section of his chapter, Gee stresses the inherently historical and contingent nature of all Discourses and exemplifies this with an excerpt from a biologist's lecture. He goes on to consider two important developments in history that helped make the word *atrophied* a technical term in biological science: the devaluing of the feminine and the triumph of localizationist perspectives on the brain. The male finch's brain came to be seen as the norm, for example, partly as a result of these developments. Gee does not extrapolate here in any depth on the implications of this discussion for education. Nevertheless, it points ineluctably toward the need for a critical language pedagogy.

Pedagogical Implications: Pursue a Critical Orientation to Text and Context

Students need to learn to identify the relevant features of different text types they encounter but also to read the social interests and agendas behind particular generic and semantic choices made in texts. A consciousness of the historicity of meaning is only developed in students oriented to intertextuality. Genres are nascent in a culture at a given point, develop, change, and die over time. They retain traces of their historical antecedents and can be probed for these if students know how. A critical orientation to text—one that is able to deconstruct texts and the social processes they instantiate—can flourish only if students are part of classrooms that encourage this and if their own literacy formation enables this. Such a formation has its own historicity.

In fact, engagement with written language is a prerequisite for the activity that Gee proposes in his conclusion for those educators who want to "expose the limitations on meaning that all Discourses effect and open out new meanings" chap. 16, p. 296). But the linguistic price of juxtaposing texts is high. It is a strategy that presupposes an already high level of literacy on the part of student readers—an ability to process the meanings instantiated in often quite complex texts, access to a meta-language that enables them to characterize the genre of these texts, interpret its unfolding meaning potential, and name the interests and agendas of the texts' producers as well as meta-practices by which students can question, relativize, challenge, and re-construe the Discourses that such texts naturalize.

CONCLUSION

Gee is right in that prevailing views of cognition and education need to be dismantled if we are to take up a more sociocultural and critical approach to language and literacy. The foundations of "a post-progressive pedagogy" can only be built on ground that is cleared of knotty and intractable assumptions about the relation between mind, meaning, and society.

But in a project like this, teachers like me need more. We are charged with the care and education of children from diverse backgrounds—who vary widely in terms of mother tongue, ethnicity, gender, and socioeconomic circumstances. We have weathered the exigencies of tumultuous changes in the teaching profession—including wage cuts, loss of teacher inservice support, and a burgeoning responsibility for a wider and increasingly demanding set of student needs. We have experienced in one teaching lifetime the dismantling of the traditional mandatory syllabus, the ascendancy of progressivism, and new demands for a school-based curriculum that we have had to write as well as teach. And we face a diverse classroom population every day—children whose parents want us to equip them for survival in the mainstream society and to value and build on the meaning styles they learn in their home communities.

Good foundations are important but teachers need to feel that the new house is one they can live in. A useful postprogressive framework will be one that enables me to view my students' starting points and my role positively—so that I can explore with them the semiotic gifts they encounter and produce, can organize a curriculum around student diversity, can build up a meaning potential from which they can draw as they negotiate the terrain of specialized learning with all its contradictory social outcomes and, finally, so that any pedagogies I use make for greater student independence and critical discursive awareness.

REFERENCES

Cope, W., & Kalantzis M. (Eds.). (1993). *The powers of literacy: A genre approach to teaching literacy.* London: Falmer Press

Christie, F. (Ed.). (1990). *Literacy for a changing world: A fresh look at the basics.* Melbourne: Australian Council for Educational Research.

Halliday, M. A. K. (1978). *Language as a social semiotic: The social interpretation of language and meaning.* London: Edward Arnold.

Halliday, M. A. K., & Hasan, R. (1989). *Language context and text: Aspects of language in a social semiotic perspective* (2nd ed.). Oxford, UK: Oxford University Press.

Hasan, R., & Martin, J. R. (Eds.). (1989). *Language development: Learning language, learning culture: Studies for Michael Halliday.* Norwood, NJ: Ablex.

Hasan, R., & Williams, G. (Eds.). (1995). *Literacy in society.* London: Longman.

Macken, M., & Rothery, J. (1991). *A model for literacy in subject learning.* (Metropolitan East Region Disadvantaged Schools Program). Erskineville: NSW Department of Education.

Rothery, J., & Macken, M. K. (1991). *Developing critical literacy through systemic functional linguistics.* (Metropolitan East Region Disadvantaged Schools Program). Erskineville: NSW Department of Education.

18
After English: Toward a Less Critical Literacy

Ian Hunter
Griffith University

English as an Australian school subject encompasses three sorts of pedagogical activity and outcome. It teaches linguistic competences of certain kinds; it inculcates an aesthetic use of literature; and it oversees a certain affective or personal development of students. These activities can and have been organized as separate areas of the curriculum where they have been known, respectively, as rhetoric, literary criticism, and ethics. We see here that their superimposition in the English classroom is a relatively recent and contingent historical development, albeit one governed by powerful social and moral conditions.

English is thus an amalgam of different pedagogical activities held together by various unifying strategies. It is not surprising, therefore, that the discipline is periodically destabilized, as the weight of emphasis shifts between its key components and new stabilizing strategies are pursued. These shifts of emphasis are manifest in a series of debates about the nature and purpose of the subject area. We can see them in the debate over whether English should be focused in the teaching of literature or in a broader range of linguistic competences. This debate overlaps a second difference of opinion, as to whether the teaching of English should concentrate on the exploratory personal development of students or on the transmission of socially useful skills. A third debate—which may in fact be a variant of the second—concerns the issue of whether the literacy formed in the English classroom should have a critical (oppositional) or a vocational relation to the larger social and political world, with the debate illustrated across this volume.

These debates condense a mix of linguistic, ethical, pedagogic, and even political issues. Moreover, they tend to cross-cut each other, often leading to unpredicted alignments, rather than forming a single bipolar field. Nonetheless, it is the case that they are currently organized around a particular version of the literature versus language debate. On one side of this debate we find an approach to English that privileges literature, or language conceived in an aesthetic manner. This approach, which held sway over the English curriculum in Anglo-American countries during the 1970s, found its manifesto in Dixon's (1967) *Growth Through English*. Characterized by a commitment to the moral centrality of literature, a child-centered pedagogy, and by the subordination of linguistic skilling to personal inwardness, this personal growth model has recently come under increasing pressure from a more linguistically oriented approach to English.

Initially aligned with the personal growth model, this second approach has distinguished itself by submerging literature in a wider typology of language kinds and by incorporating a particular sociolinguistic model of language in its curricular frameworks and contents. Drawing on Hallidayan systemic–functional linguistics, this approach centres English in the relation between text and social context—a relation for which the idea of genre plays the key mediating role. It thus represents a shift of emphasis away from the literary and ethical components of English toward the rhetorical. Consequently, it has been criticized, from the personal growth perspective, for sacrificing personal development to disciplinary socialization and for subordinating critical to vocational literacy.

Still, despite the official antagonism, it would be premature to posit a clean break between the two models. The sociolinguistic approach maintains the commitment to a child-centered pedagogy, viewing the generic schemata as something that the student encounters and negotiates in the individual cognitive processing of experience. Moreover, despite its refurbishing of the rhetorical categories, this approach seems no more inclined than the personal growth model to divide rhetoric, literary criticism, and ethics into separate curricular areas. This is because the sociolinguistic approach continues to privilege a single category—this time "language" rather than "literature"—as a single general means of mediating "experience" and "subjectivity." Hence, literature and ethics—like everything else—are viewed as linguistically mediated phenomena, to be dealt with inside the English curriculum. The overreaching effects of this theoretical strategy are dealt with in more detail later.

In this chapter, I step back from the current debates in order to provide a brief sketch of their historical circumstances. English, I suggest, is not founded in literature or the kind of personal inwardness fostered by aesthetic cultivation. But neither is it grounded in language, or an open-ended typology of genres mediating texts and social contexts. Against these views it is argued that English emerges as a specialized pedagogical milieu. This milieu is capable (under specific technical circumstances) of forming the capacity for personal inwardness as one of its effects; but it is also capable (under similar or modified circumstances) of supporting a range of generically organized linguistic competences.

Second, in the light of this historical argument I propose a more thoroughgoing separation of rhetoric, ethics, and literature in the secondary school curriculum. Here it is argued that rhetorical, ethical, and literary capacities belong to different (although related) spheres of life and that they require different (although related) educational settings. The superimposition of these different spheres of human activity in the English classroom has arguably led to a blurring of pedagogies and purposes, as the methods and goals of one area are imposed on the others ir. pursuit of curriculum unity. Until now, this problem has been most visible in the imposition of aesthetic pedagogy in the rhetorical and ethical domains. It seems likely, however, that a similar problem will emerge if the genre-based English curriculum fails to detach rhetorical from ethical and aesthetic education.

GENEALOGY

I begin by looking at the pedagogical milieu from which English emerges. As this is something I have discussed in detail elsewhere (Hunter, 1987, 1988, 1991b) I am brief here. Consider first the following statement from the Year 12 English syllabus document published by the Senior Secondary Assessment Board of South Australia in 1985:

> Academic approaches which make unrealistic demands on students should be avoided. Detailed writing about set texts in the manner of literary examinations is much less appropriate than writing done in response to a course based on experience and analysis of books, drama, the media, and involvement in real language situations. This is not to say that some texts will not be read and discussed in detail. However, the emphasis should be on writing, and discussion which extends and explores meaning, and not on formal, evaluative responses which examine the literary structure of a work.
>
> It is suggested that teachers use the workshop approach as much as possible so that students do not have to write to a strict deadline, or to hand in uncorrected first drafts. Editing and redrafting are essential aspects of the course. (p. 9)

The acceptance of a range of genres beyond the literary suggests that here we may be dealing with a hybrid of the genre-based and personal growth approaches; but the stress on exploratory process writing indicates that the latter approach is preeminent. This statement is interesting because it shows that what distinguishes aesthetic pedagogy is not the use of literary texts per se but a particular way of deploying texts (of whatever kind) in the classroom. This is a deployment in which formal instruction concerning the text as a cultural artefact is relegated in favor of its use as a means of eliciting personal responses through the pedagogical simulation of real language situations.

Perhaps the most obvious precursor for this model of English teaching is the program outlined by Dixon (1967):

> Part of our work in written English, then, is to foster the kind of looking and the kind of talk and writing that direct observation of experience demands. We do so, not in the detached systematic way of a scientist, but by watching for, and even helping to provide moments when such experiences are of personal importance to pupils. For it is their involvement in the experience that will draw them into writing . . . Primary teachers will take pupils into the woods, encouraging them to feel and smell the bark of trees, to look at the fungi, to collect autumn leaves . . . and secondary teachers go out with cameras and sketch-pads to look at men working on bulldozers and cranes, the new concrete skyscrapers, or to stare through grated windows at children pushing prams in the alleys of black tenements. On their way and may be back in class, they talk with groups and groups talk together, sharing and probing—to see more and get it clearer—so that later they may build together, through writing, painting, photographs . . . a report of what they found. But at the same time, in the same situation and "lessons", we leave room for the symbolic representation of experience to emerge if it will. (pp. 51–52)

Here we find the same subordination of formal instruction in reading and writing in favor of the creation of specially organized learning experiences, through which children appear to discover themselves.

The idea that written texts will emerge from this process with a minimum of formal instruction has been criticized from a number of quarters. Its most convincing critics have been those who argue that the purposes and contexts governing the production of speech and writing issue in definite generic structures and formulae, which students must be explicitly taught (see Gilbert, 1991; Martin, Christie, & Rothery, 1987). Still, without disagreeing with such criticism, it would be wrong to see personal growth English as the product of 1960s libertarianism or progressivism. It has a far more interesting genealogy.

Consider in this regard the following statement on the role of drama in working-class schools; it was written in 1904 by McMillan, socialist, feminist, and advocate of aesthetic education:

Drama—Here is the great City of Refuge as well as School of almost every type of imaginative and unimaginative! And children appear to understand this far better than older people. Much of their own play is just their own way of getting a stage and being players. . .

I have seen a class of very dulled and stupefied children, who could understand only a very small range of words, begin to live at once when they were allowed to dramatise even a word! . . . A dull almost subnormal girl of eight allowed to do this became quite normal and even animated-looking within a week. (pp. 98-99)

As in its modern versions, this pedagogy is not confined to literature; visual art provides an optional equivalent device for manifesting personality in the classroom:

Art is the expression of a living force. It is true. It is an inner force that we deny to the poor. And the denial begins in the earliest years. Very soon it tells in the withering of all that, living, seeks for expression. The drawings of the slum children are saddening, not because they show a lack of hand or eye skill, but because they show us all the weakness and emptiness of the inner life, the dimness of the perception also, of which they are the shadow. (p. 57)

As in the modern personal growth classroom, the role of drama and art is to stitch the pedagogy as seamlessly as possible into the extramural life and experiences of the child. The main difference is that in 1904 the socially corrective role of personal growth pedagogy is less abashed than in subsequent versions. Nonetheless, McMillan's use of drama and art as devices for diagnosing and reshaping the deficient personality of the "stupefied" slum child is a direct anticipation of Heathcote's (1968) work with borstal boys, Holbrook's (1964) development of an English curriculum for the comprehensive secondary school and, of course, Dixon's apparently norm-free personal growth classroom. In short, there is a striking and apparently paradoxical connection between the freedom and informality of aesthetic pedagogy and its use as an instrument for the social and moral training of problem populations. (I should add, immediately, that I do not regard this connection as pedagogically or politically inappropriate in and of itself.)

One final backward step completes this brief genealogical sketch. In 1850, Stow, drawing on his pedagogical experiments with Glasgow's slum children, published these statements on the need for spaces of free play in the working-class school and on the need for a new—sympathetic and noncoercive—form of teaching:

A play-ground is in fact the principal scene of the real life of children, both in the juvenile and initiatory departments—the arena on which their true character and dispositions are exhibited; and where, free and unconstrained, they can hop and jump about, swing, or play at tig, ball, or marbles . . .

> Whilst the pupils sympathise with each other, it is important that the children sympathise with their master. For this purpose, it is necessary that he place himself on such terms with his pupils as that they can, without fear, make him their confidant, unburden their minds, and tell him any little story, or mischievous occurrence. Teachers and parents, desirous of gaining the confidence of their children, must in fact, themselves as it were, become children, by bending to, and occasionally engaging in, their plays and amusements. Without such condescension, a perfect knowledge of real character and dispositions cannot be obtained. (pp. 144, 156)

Here the reciprocities between surveillance and love, between supervision and freedom, between the disciplinary imposition of social norms and the personal discovery of them in play, are far too densely and subtly interwoven to be unthreaded by the clumsy binarisms of modern political philosophy: utility versus self-expression, social skills versus personal development, state versus community.

Notice also that (aesthetic) literature and art play no significant role in this first version of the personal growth classroom. Instead, the relations of freedom and supervision, of self-expression and noncoercive correction, are built into the architecture of the school itself, and into the carefully crafted relation between the spontaneous student and the sympathetic teacher. It is this purpose-built pedagogical milieu, which emerged in Britain and Australia in the mid-19th century, that is novel and fundamental for subsequent developments. Above all, we can see that the personal growth of the student is not the foundation of the pedagogical environment but one of its by-products, and that the use of literature to focus this pedagogy was a later and dependent development.

Where, then, did this pedagogical environment come from and under what historical circumstances did it emerge? Very briefly, studies by Laqueur (1976), Jones and Williamson (1979), and Melton (1988) leave us in little doubt that it was the product of two overlapping developments. On the one hand, this milieu emerged from the institutions of Protestant pastoral care—German Pietism and English Puritanism in particular. It was this pastoral pedagogy—still clearly visible in Stow—that provided the system for organizing conduct around individual conscientiousness; for intensifying personal inwardness; and for transforming the role of the teacher from drill master into sympathetic yet vigilant soulmate, responsible for the personal development of each and every student. It is becoming increasingly clear that the critique of rote learning first emerged not in the progressive education movement but in the practices and ethos of Protestant pastoral pedagogy. It was this pedagogy that would assume the form of child-centered educational progressivism, after it had passed through the mills of Romanticism and psychology.

On the other hand, the new pedagogy was deeply embedded in the bureaucratic systems and objectives of a series of emergent governmentalized states. Protestant pastoralism may well have provided the means of reforming conduct around the cultivation of an inner self, but only bureaucratically organized states possessed the administrative expertise, financial resources, and political will to distribute the means of inwardness to entire national populations. Needless to say, they had their own reasons for doing so. Whether they were dealing with backward rural peasantries or the chaotic populations of new industrial cities, bureaucratic states required instruments to provide their populations with the inner composure and outward skills needed for participation in rapidly modernizing economies and societies. Bureaucracies do not invent such instruments, however. The pedagogy of Protestant pastoral care was thus taken over by the emerging state school systems and bureaucratically adapted to the tasks of social discipline and modernization. (It is necessary to add, unfortunately, that this description is not intended as criticism of the development of state education systems: far from it.)

The structure and routines of personal growth pedagogy—and ultimately the modern English classroom—are direct and ineluctable products of these historical developments. In fact the child-centered classroom, overseen by a sympathetic yet vigilant teacher, was both the instrument and the effect of the marriage between pastoral pedagogy and bureaucratic social administration. It was this new pedagogical milieu— this "pastoral bureaucracy"—that satisfied the central design imperative of state schooling. In carefully and sympathetically simulating the milieus and conducts of working-class life, it allowed the "real life of the child" to be enclosed within the corrective space of the school, where new social norms could be discovered as personal conscience.

SUBJECTIVITY AND GOVERNMENT

Dixon (1991) recently attempted to protect English from such disenchanted genealogies, taking particular issue with the revisionist histories of Baldick (1983), Doyle (1989), and Eagleton (1983). Dixon attempted to rescue an earlier progressive image of the discipline from these analyses of it as an ideological cover for various kinds of social exploitation. His main criticism of such revisionist works is that in attempting to read off a history of English from its general ideological function they are too abstract, neglecting in particular the self-organizing democratic networks and groups that Dixon (1991) claimed, played the central role in the birth of English. Still, without dismissing Dixon's criticism of these other accounts, there is a clear sense in which his focus on self-organizing groups is just as far removed from the contingencies of history as is the revisionists' focus on the discipline's ideological mission.

According to Dixon (1991), the belief that English should be based in the authentic experience of literary texts—rather than in their rhetorical or philological analysis—first emerged in the context of the late 19th-century University Extension movement. This was a movement in which freelance lecturers taught short courses to self-selecting groups in provincial towns and cities. Dixon's claim is that this movement was organized outside official university channels, by self-organizing oppositional groups—women's groups, trade unions, cooperatives—driven, apparently, by a spontaneous interest in aesthetic cultivation.

Now, Dixon may well be right in suggesting that the impetus for this movement did not come from the universities. This does not mean though that it came from outside established institutions altogether—from the spontaneous enjoyment of literature apparently characteristic of women, trade unionists, elementary school teachers, and other oppositional groups. Dixon's humanism prevents him from asking how such groups acquired the capacity for advanced literacy, the interest in reading, and indeed the motivation, discipline, and organizational abilities required to run a voluntary self-improvement network.

Individuals sometimes gain such capacities through autodidactic labor, but for whole social strata to acquire them an immense work of institution building and social transformation is required. Before Dixon's apostles of culture could take up their positions in front of literate, interested, and self-disciplined lower class audiences, a few other things had to be done: A popular school system had to be built; a complex machinery of administration and inspection had to be put in place; suitable pedagogies had to be improvised; teacher-training institutions had to be established, and much more. This set of developments, which began in earnest in the 1830s, was not spun off by self-organizing oppositional groups acting out of a love of literature. It was the achievement of large-scale governmental organization and bureaucratic expertise. In this regard, the words of the emerging school system's most creative bureaucrat—spoken in 1866—turn out to be far more faithful to the historical moment than Dixon's:

> It is no small matter that the training colleges and day schools which exist have established throughout the country an idea of the organisation and form of a system of public education, which has made itself permanently a part of public opinion throughout influential classes. But the ministers of state and leaders of political opinion were in advance of the great body of the people when this system was built up. It did not spring from the people, it originated with the Government. Nor, though influential classes have accepted it, are the people yet trained to receive from the hands of the State this system, and to support it by their own voluntary contributions. (Kay-Shuttleworth, 1980, p. 85)

No doubt there will be many ready to attack Kay-Shuttleworth for his paternalism, but his remarks were in fact entirely appropriate to the historical circumstances. Before dismissing them we need to note that their target was the middle-class doctrine of *laissez-faire* which, like certain anti-statist ideologies of our time, was opposed to state schooling in the name of individual freedom. In any case, the lesson should be clear: Before "self-organizing" groups could appear, a large amount of governmental organization had to have taken place.

We should note, however, that "government" in this context is not equivalent to the notion of the state as a unified and sovereign political will. Instead, following Foucault's (1991) discussion, we use it to refer to an ensemble of political technologies—systems of economic management, public health, social welfare, education, discipline. From about the 18th-century, these technologies began to support a variety of programs aimed at knowing and managing particular governmental domains, in the name of an optimal development of the state and its population. The emergence of state schooling in England is governmental in this sense.

It is central to Foucault's discussion, however, that government does not invent the instruments through which it takes place, as pure expressions of a sovereign political will. Instead, it borrows and adapts such instruments from a variety of sources—from the economic management of estates, the military disciplining of armies, and the pastoral guidance of lay populations. In doing so, it also borrows and adapts the objectives or wills of these domains. This leads to an important insight into the emergence of popular education in states like England and Prussia. In these states, as we have already noted in the case of England, government took over and adapted the institutions of Protestant pastoral guidance, developing school systems that pursued the social training of the population through the systematic inculcation of individual conscientiousness.

We are still learning about the role of religious disciplines of inwardness and self-regulation in the development of state schooling. Laqueur's (1976) study of the 1780s Sunday school—the key precursor institution—provides an important lead. Protestantism, it will be recalled, was a "religion of the book," and moral reading—at first of the Bible but then of secular moral stories—was an important means of relating to the self and (through techniques of supervision and interrogation) of opening this relation to the pastor or the teacher. In Hunter (1988) I discussed how this use of reading as a technique of inwardness and moral supervision was adapted to the emerging state school system. At the center of an emerging literary pedagogy lay a special relation to the teacher (as a sympathetic guide and unintrusive exemplar) and to the text (as the means by which the students' personal responses were intensified and supervised).

In other words, I am suggesting that a major condition for the emergence of the literary reading as an intense personal experience—and indeed for the existence of readers with the literate and ethical abilities required to undergo this experience—was the deployment of moral reading in the emerging school system as a technique of spiritual discipline and social management. So, far from signifying an absolute or unconditional experience, beyond the reach of constraining institutions, the widespread personal reading of literature can be traced to its pedagogical transmission as a technique of individual inwardness and collective discipline. This pedagogy, with its gentle teacher and its unremitting surveillance—with its experienced text about which one is always mistaken—is the key condition of the English classroom. In speaking of English as a means of "watching for, and even helping to provide moments when such experiences are of personal importance to pupils," Dixon (1967, p. 51) provided symptomatic confirmation that personal growth English is neither more nor less than the current form of this pedagogy.

In short, English did not spring into history when the personal reading of literature at last found the right pedagogical milieu; that is, one whose democratic and communal character allowed such reading unconstrained expression. Neither did its critical moments coincide with democratic struggles or popular radicalisms. To the contrary, English started to take historical shape when a governmental pedagogy began to deploy the personal reading of literature as a disciplinary technique; and its temporality is marked by the less spectacular rhythms of bureaucratic planning and teacherly improvisation. English was not born as an institutional expression of the experience of literature; it emerged as a pedagogical institution that gave students the capacity to relate to literature as an experience. Given Dixon's own position as a teacher educator, it is hard to say what is more disturbing in his detour around the pedagogical reality of English: his failure to look squarely at its actual history; or his refusal to face up to the remorseless exercise of moral discipline involved in this (as in every) system of training.

RETHINKING THE PRESENT

What are the implications of this genealogical sketch for our understanding of the modern English classroom and the debates that surround it? In the first place, at the most general level, it should lead us to step back from the dominant political critique of state schooling. This critique depends on a series of principled oppositions between the emancipation of persons and the interests of the state, between personal development and social skilling, between critical and vocational education. As a consequence, it conceives of a progressive education in terms of a series of measures—a child-centered pedagogy, democratic control of the curriculum—aimed at freeing the complete development of the person from the heavy hand of the bureaucratic state.

But we have seen that no matter how opposed these values are at the level of principle they have long been reconciled and harmonized at the level of pedagogical regimen and social administration. The modern school emerged as a purpose-built environment in which personal inwardness was transmitted as a desirable social skill; in which personal development was tied to the state's interest in disciplining and modernizing chaotic populations; and in which the teacher supervised his or her charges with both the solicitous care of the pastor and the impersonal expertise of the bureaucrat. An oppositional critique of state schooling that relies on notions of repressed personal desires or stifled class energies is in little danger of understanding or transforming its object.

Second, we have already observed that the new pedagogical milieu was not a specialized linguistic nor, in the first instance, literary environment. Certainly, mass literacy was a prime objective but—along with numeracy, regular habits, and good grooming—this was seen as a basic civic capacity required by the citizens of a modern well-governed state. The new pedagogy was focused in the relations of self-expression and correction, inwardness and emulation that linked the student and teacher, rather than in specialized linguistic or literary training. Stow (1850) advised school builders that "the master himself is the best book" (p. 178). When literature did emerge in the progressive English classroom it was as a device for focusing these same relations. Hence, right up until Dixon, students' conversations, stories, and confessions can stand in for the literary text or literary response, playing basically the same role; while the explicit writing up of these intimate moments can be left "to emerge if it will."

This pedagogical milieu and the English classroom that in time became its specialized embodiment was, therefore, preeminently an environment of ethical formation. By *ethical* I do not mean a specific set of values or moral code. Instead, the term refers to a particular way of conducting the self; a particular means of relating to oneself and living one's life; a particular ethic or ethos. We have seen that this ethical regimen began in the Protestant mode, as a series of pedagogical settings and exercises in which events are simulated as a means of getting students to concern themselves with their own conduct; that is, as a means of transforming events into moral experiences, through which students come to adopt an introspective relation to ethical judgment.

With the increasing use of literary and artistic artifacts to achieve these ends—from the early decades of the 20th century—we begin to see the emergence of the modern English lesson. Under these circumstances, the mode of ethical self-concern becomes increasingly aesthetic, focused on the personal style—the right balance of thought and feeling—required for a truly inward and authentic response to literature. This is the point at which the ethical and aesthetic organization of the English classroom acquires a rhetorical dimension. It does so in the form of a training in kinds of writing—literary criticism, creative writing, the personal essay—that are themselves instruments for heightening, elaborating, and recording the introspective relation to ethical conduct and judgement.

The most striking feature of this rhetoric, however, is that it is neither named nor taught as a rhetoric. The generic formulae for literary appreciation, creative writing, and personal essayism must appear to emerge unforced from the same (staged) experiences through which the English classroom inculcates self-concern and the personalist ethic. The manner in which the modern English class grafts a narrow and tacit (literary) rhetorical training onto an aesthetically organized training in ethical inwardness is thus the direct outcome of its role in the state schooling of the popular classes.

Third, we can recall (although only in passing) that elsewhere there indeed existed a classroom organized around specialized linguistic education. Pre-dating the modern state's interest in mass education, the grammar schools remained separate from the new popular system throughout the 19th and into the early 20th century. The grammar schools trained a series of professional elites. They prepared middle-class and upper class boys for roles in the clergy, military, law, and bureaucracy by equipping them with the specific linguistic competences required for participation in these specialized departments of life.

Taught in an ancient foreign language, the rhetorical competences of the grammar school depended, as Ong (1971) showed, on the trained mastery of complex linguistic routines and formulae. They were thus far removed from the apparently spontaneous ethical inwardness of the popular schoolroom. If the literary exercises of the popular classroom were an ancillary means of addressing the self, then the linguistic exercises of the grammar school were a specialized instrument for addressing an audience in a civic setting. If the English lesson has been geared to the heightening of subjective states and the development of personal judgment, then the rhetorical regimen has been oriented to the perfecting of public linguistic competences associated with the legal, religious, and bureaucratic organization of social life.

The contrasts then are clear enough at one level, but it is unhelpful and misleading to carry them too far or extend them too deeply. Above all, we must resist the temptation to organize the differences between the pedagogies of English and rhetoric around the binary oppositions between personal growth and social skilling, critical, and vocational literacy. As we have seen, the cultivation of personal inwardness in the state school was itself a social skill, organized by governments as a means of preparing the popular classes for their vocation as citizens in modernizing states. The capacities for ethical inwardness and personal judgment fostered by state schooling are no more fundamental than the capacities for forensic, deliberative, or panegyric oratory trained by rhetorical schooling: they are simply different. In analyzing this difference, we must therefore resist the temptation to accord an intrinsic ethical or political privilege to the personal growth focus of modern English—as if this were inherently more democratic, critical, or human than the focus on civic participation characteristic of the rhetorical tradition.

Attempts to rescue personal growth English by attaching it to women, as untainted ethical subjects, fall prey to precisely this temptation (see e.g., Green, 1987). The notion that the emancipatory credentials of English can be rehabilitated by identifying its exploratory introspective ethic with the feminine—while simultaneously attributing the authoritative civic orientation of rhetoric to the masculine—is both historically inaccurate and politically dubious. As we have just seen, it ignores the fact that personal growth pedagogies were themselves fashioned as governmental instruments for the formation of modernized populations. At the same time, this strategy converts what is at best an historical fact concerning the social distribution of competences—that is, the alleged skewing of personalist introspective competences toward women—into a universal ethical imperative, by identifying these competences with the feminine per se. As Laurence (1991) argued, this attempt to make women go proxy for an exemplary extra-governmental subjectivity may end by locking them into a personalist conduct of life that is itself an artifact of government.

Finally, because it ascribes an essentially negative and repressive function to government, this critical strategy loses touch with political actuality and assumes the form of a morally insatiable hypercritique. When modern states developed programs for the schooling of the popular classes they borrowed a pedagogy that was dedicated not to the repression of ethical inwardness but to its intensification—not to the denial of personality but to its cultivation. This is precisely what is misunderstood in all those analyses of English—and indeed of the major literacy campaigns of the 19th and 20th centuries—that treat them as ideologies.

The mass literacy campaigns—and that special (aesthetic) form of literacy called *English*—did not consist in ideas, values, or discourses, although of course these played a part. They existed, rather, as a complex piece of social organization: an assemblage consisting of governmental programs, systems of training, ethical and aesthetic disciplines, a network of purpose-built pedagogical institutions, special pedagogies, a dedicated bureaucracy, and so on. For all its value-laden character, the machinery of literacy is not an ideology; it is a social apparatus that combines, in Foucault's (1991) words, two types of government: the political government of the population and the ethical government of the self. Above all, these forms of government do not work via some general mechanism of repression. As we have seen, the achievement of literate populations was not a work of cultural subtraction; it involved a massive labor of institution building and cultural creation. The fact that modern government works by conferring statuses and augmenting capacities makes generalized oppositional critique redundant, except for a special caste of intellectuals whose status depends on their credentials as hypercritics.

The salient political point is that personal growth pedagogy was initially targeted on the popular classes as a means of distributing basic skills of ethical self-management. We have seen that the specialized and socially powerful linguistic competences provided by rhetoric were at that time largely confined to the middle class and masculine grammar schools. It is an esoteric politics indeed that proposes to confine women to the domain of personal growth, in the name of human emancipation, and to compensate their forfeiture of powerful professional trainings by turning them into the ethical saviours of men. Moreover, it is a politics that ignores the striking increase of female participation in the legal and bureaucratic professions, the least introspective and most rhetorical of the modern professions. In short, those seeking the empowerment of subordinate social groups through the further development of personal growth pedagogies may be denying such groups access to some of the most powerful systems of training and social destinations available. We can recall that this was a political lesson not lost on Gramsci (1971), who envisaged a training in rhetoric and grammar as an important component of any future popular school system.

RHETORIC

Those advocating the establishment of a renovated rhetorical curriculum in the state school system should not be accused, therefore, of attempting to turn back the clock. Nostalgia plays no part in this program. Nor can these advocates of a genre-based language arts curriculum be tagged with the back-to-basics slogan. No one familiar with the complex compositional formulae and routines of the rhetorical genres would call them basic. In fact, what is entailed by the new program is a radical transformation of that amalgam of introspective ethics, and literary rhetoric known as English.

An examination of the senior language arts curricula being developed by the Queensland Board of Secondary School Studies indicates that significant changes have already taken place. By placing literary forms in a much wider and more diverse generic field, these curricula show the narrowness of the literary rhetoric of personal growth English. Moreover, by insisting that texts have structures appropriate to particular (often public) settings and purposes, the genre-based curriculum has begun to detach rhetorical training from the personalist ethic of the English classroom. After all, if textual structure is indeed based on definite compositional formulae, responsible for forming specific linguistic abilities, then these must be explicitly taught, rather than discovered in personal learning experiences.

Still, I think it is fair to say that this detachment of rhetoric from personalist ethics remains substantially incomplete in the genre-based program. No doubt there are a number of reasons for this, including the sheer administrative and political inertia of the personal growth classroom and the difficulty of developing alternative pedagogies. It is also possible that the new rhetoricians have taken the progressivism of modern English too much at its word, hence incorporating a personalist pedagogy in the genre-based curriculum as a standard operating procedure to the radical conscience. Nonetheless, there is a feature of the sociolinguistic model itself that tends to lock it back into the personalist ethos and render incomplete the transition to a genre-based rhetorical training. This feature is a general–theoretical model of language and a correspondingly general and abstract conception of the language user as human subject.

Broadly, the problem here is that the sociolinguistic model envisages all forms of language as the product of a single general relation between texts and social contexts. The relation forms a closed general system mediated by the concept of genre, and this leads to a radical overextension of this concept. On one side of the equation—as we can see in Christie (1987), for example—all uses of language are pictured as texts, characterized by generic patterning, discursive cohesion, and grammatical organization. This might be a theoretical exaggeration. But the real problem lies on the other side of the equation where all social contexts—that is, all human activities and departments of existence—are also given a questionable linguistic unity through their nomination as genres. (See Martin, et al., 1987, and Curriculum Services Branch, 1987).

As a result of this linguistic turn all such departments—from mass media to medical examinations, from public law to personal ethics—are theorized as discourses, accessible through language to the language user. Under these circumstances—as I have argued in detail elsewhere (Hunter, 1991a)—the language user transcends all historical conditions and practical limits and is transformed into that familiar all-purpose philosophical prop, the subject of consciousness. That this is indeed the fate of the language user is confirmed once we observe that the model has recourse to the notion of unspecified cognitive processes to explain how users negotiate between generically organized social contexts and generically patterned texts.

This has unfortunate consequences for the genre-based curriculum. In the first place, it tends to produce an open-ended proliferation of genres as, like experience, texts and contexts are held to be infinite. Second, this multiplication of genres tends to dilute the program of explicit training in the compositional formulae of a limited number of important genres. The risk here is that students will encounter and choose from a vast array of genres in an insufficiently structured experiential space. This space is of course the space of the personal growth classroom, which returns to haunt the genre-based curriculum through its too theoretical conception of language and the language user.

The contrast with the rhetorical training provided by the grammar school becomes quite marked at this point. The grammar school provided specialized training in a limited array of rhetorical genres—forensic, deliberative, argumentational, panegyric. It did so not because these were examples of language or experience but because they were the linguistic armature of the professional capacities in which the grammar school students were being trained. In lapsing back into notions of experience, negotiation, and choice the genre-based approach is in danger of forgetting that, for all their importance, purely linguistic capacities are only part of the picture. The other part is taken by range of more or less expert conducts and competences—related to various professional occupations and social destinations—that give the rhetorical genres their function and purpose.

Perhaps most importantly, rhetorical training did not trust to cognitive processes to handle the relations of composition and reception linking writer and audience or context. Ong (1971) showed us that the choice of headings or topics (*inventio*), the ordering of materials (*dispositio*), and the achievement of topical coverage and flow (*copia*), were all explicitly formed through the practical mastery of definite compositional techniques and routines. Such practices became of course the very epitome of rote learning in the context of the trained inwardness of the personal growth classroom. But we have seen that such a critique only works by disavowing the elaborate disciplinary apparatus responsible for the capacity for ethical and aesthetic introspection.

The rhetorical classroom is simply a more open acknowledgment of the fact that specialized linguistic abilities—like other human conducts and capacities—depend on the trained mastery of definite and limited cultural techniques and routines in a specific regimen or *habitus*. There is no theoretical, ethical, or political reason for the advocates of the genre-based curriculum to avoid this acknowledgment, or the more explicitly regulated teaching environment that it entails. This is a further area in which contemporary progressivism might make better use of its nodding acquaintance with Gramsci (1971), in recalling his more clear-eyed view of the role of linguistic training in the formation of human comportment and ability:

> Latin and Greek were learnt through their grammar, mechanically; but the accusation of formalism and aridity is very unjust and inappropriate. In education one is dealing with children in whom one has to inculcate certain habits of diligence, precision, poise (even physical poise), ability to concentrate on specific subjects, which cannot be acquired without the mechanical repetition of disciplined and methodical acts. Would a scholar at the age of forty be able to sit for sixteen hours on end at his work-table if he had not, as a child, compulsorily, through mechanical coercion, acquired the appropriate psycho-physical habits? (p. 37)

Needless to say, the point is not to bring back Latin and Greek. What can be taken from Gramsci's comments, rather, is a more realistic sense of the kinds of cultural technique and discipline that go into the formation and maintenance of literate conducts and capacities.

CONCLUSION: ETHICS

The preceding arguments suggest two considerations that may need to be taken into account in the program to introduce rhetorical training into state schooling. First, it may be necessary to base the writing of curricula on a less theoretical, more historical and pragmatic, understanding of genre. As long as genre is held to be a general mechanism mediating all contexts and texts there will be a tendency for the formulaic specificity of particular genres to dissolve into the general cognitive processes of an all-purpose human subject. In other words, there is a risk that the difficult pedagogical problem of how to train students in the complex compositional routines associated with specific genres will drop from sight.

Second, it will be necessary to disentangle the affective and personal development of students—that is, their ethical formation—from the emerging rhetorical curriculum. The idea that ethical formation is preeminently literary or linguistic—and hence belongs in English—is, we have seen, a residue of the aesthetically organized personal growth curriculum. Curriculum designers in this country have not yet begun to work on the problem of what a postpersonalist ethics pedagogy might look like. Before they can—that is, before the groundwork for a less introspective and personalist public ethical culture can be laid—it will be necessary to rigorously distinguish between the question of the formation of ethical conduct and the ethos of personal growth and the theory of sociolinguistics, and to provide it with its own space in the curriculum.

The concrete form of a nonintrospective civic ethics can only emerge from a painstaking process of curriculum reform, but we can already see why this process must be divorced from the critical and aesthetic ethos of English. In assuming that language and experience mediate each other in a single metropolitan space (subjectivity), the theorists of English have imagined that the discipline possesses a privileged moral insight into all the departments of ethical life—private and public, political and religious, personal and professional. The result is that the reading of literary texts is presumed to equip teachers and students of English with a general purpose moral competence, adequate to each and every sphere of existence. This aspiration to complete moral transparency wildly overreaches the real but mundane virtues of teaching children the arts of literary reading and writing. Its results, as seen in the following example from Dixon (1991), can only be described as unfortunate:

> For example, how could my own reading of the Frost poem not be lightened, in July 1990, by the winter revolutions in Europe—only to be darkened again by trigger-happy reactions to the invasion of Kuwait? It is this living context, I could say, with its deeper interests, which shapes both the reading and the dialogical evaluation—unless, of course, that is stifled and repressed in the classroom or the professor's study. (p. 197)

Why, one feels like saying, should we be interested in what John Dixon "the person" thinks about the Gulf War or the nationalist reconstitution of Eastern Europe, unless he happens to be a person trained in the histories of these regions, in international relations, or in the principles of statecraft? Moreover, what is it that makes the profession he represents presume that it possesses the range of intellectual and moral qualifications necessary to teach about such matters competently in a civic setting? It is enough to say that Dixon is not interested in wars or state reconstruction as military, political, economic or social realities. He is interested only in his own aesthetic reactions to such events. He is concerned only with the manner in which these events—once they have been tagged with the crudest of moral judgments—lighten or darken the inner state achieved through the reading of poetry.

One could comment here on a culpable degree of self-absorption. Even less fairly, one might observe how quickly the winter revolutions that served to induce Dixon's aesthetic high turned into fratricidal anarchy, and how important is the duty to acknowledge the things one can not understand. But it is the intellectual and moral grandiloquence of an entire profession and mode of intellectual conduct that we are dealing with here. At the very least Dixon's example gives us cause to question whether education in social, political and civic ethics should *de facto* be left in the hands of English teachers. There is no professional reason why English teachers should be competent in this range of ethical and political areas, any more, for example, than mathematics teachers should. We can only look forward to the day when the teaching of politics and ethics through poetry lessons will seem as odd as the teaching of history through algebra lessons.

REFERENCES

Baldick, C. (1983). *The social mission of English criticism 1848-1932*. Oxford, UK: Clarendon Press.

Christie, F. (1987). Genres as choice. In I. Reid (Ed.), *The place of genre in learning: Current debates*. Geelong, Australia: Centre for Studies in Literary Education.

Curriculum Services Branch. (1987). *How language works: The relationship between language and its social context*. Brisbane: Department of Education.

Dixon, J. (1967). *Growth through English: A report based on the Dartmouth Seminar 1966*. Oxford, UK: Oxford University Press.

Dixon, J. (1991). *A schooling in "English": Critical episodes in the struggle to shape literary and cultural studies*. Milton Keynes: Open University Press.

Doyle, B. (1989). *English and Englishness*. London: Routledge.

Eagleton, T. (1983). *Literary theory*. Oxford, UK: Blackwell.

Foucault, M. (1991). Governmentality. In G. Burchell, C. Gordon, & P. Miller (Eds.), *The Foucault effect: Essays in governmentality*. London: Harvester-Wheatsheaf.

Gilbert, P. (1991). Writing pedagogy: Personal voices, truth telling and "real" texts. In A. Luke & C. D. Baker (Eds.), *Towards a critical sociology of reading pedagogy*. Amsterdam: John Benjamin.

Gramsci, A. (1971). *Selections from the prison notebooks* (Q. Hoare & G. Nowell-Smith, Eds. and Trans.). London: Lawrence & Wishart.

Green, B. (1987). Gender, genre and writing pedagogy. In I. Reid (Ed.), *The place of genre in learning: Current debates*. Geelong, Australia: Centre for Studies in Literary Education.

Heathcote, D. (1968). *Drama in education*. Newcastle, UK: Institute of Education, University of Newcastle-Upon-Tyne.

Holbrook, D. (1964). *English for the rejected: Training literacy in the lower streams of secondary school*. Cambridge, UK: Cambridge University Press.

Hunter, I. (1987). Culture, education, English: Building "the principal scene of the real life of children." *Economy and Society, 16*, 568-88.

Hunter, I. (1988). *Culture and government: The emergence of literary education*. London: Macmillan.

Hunter, I. (1991a). From discourse to *dispositif*: Foucault and the study of literature. *Meridian, 10*, 36–53.

Hunter, I. (1991b). Learning the literature lesson: The limits of the aesthetic personality. In A. Luke & C. Baker (Eds.), *Towards a critical sociology of reading pedagogy*. Amsterdam: John Benjamin.

Jones, K. & Williamson, K. (1979). The birth of the schoolroom. *I & C, 6*, 58-110.

Kay-Shuttleworth, J. (1980). Popular education. In D. A. Reeder (Ed.), *Educating our masters*. Leicester, UK: Leicester University Press.

Laqueur, T.W. (1976). *Religion and respectability: Sunday schools and working class culture. 1780–1850*. New Haven, CT: Yale University Press.

Laurence, J. (1991). Remembering that special someone: On the question of articulating a genuine feminine presence in the classroom. *History of Education Review, 20*(2), 53-65.

Martin, J. R., Christie, F., & Rothery, J. (1987). Social processes in education: A reply to Sawyer and Watson (and others). In I. Reid (Ed.), *The place of genre in learning: Current debates*. Geelong, Australia: Centre for Studies in Literary Education.

McMillan, M. (1904). *Education through the imagination*. London: George Allen & Unwin.

Melton, J.V.H. (1988). *Absolutism and the eighteenth-century origins of compulsory schooling in Prussia and Austria*. Cambridge, UK: Cambridge University Press.

Ong, W. (1971). *Rhetoric, romance and technology*. Ithaca, NY: Cornell University Press.

Senior Secondary Assessment Board of South Australia (SSAB). (1985). *English: Year 12: Detailed syllabus statements for English*. Adelaide: Peacock Publications.

Stow, D. (1850). *The training system. The moral training school and the normal seminary*. London: Longman, Brown & Green.

19
Setting Limits to English
Response to Ian Hunter

Annette Patterson
James Cook University of North Queensland

HUNTING ENGLISH

English is a popular target of literacy theorists.[1] Taking aim from a variety of positions, contemporary theoretical critiques focus on a range of concepts: *ideology, power, democracy, subjectivity,* and *agency* but not always as targets for (inevitably unsuccessful) removal. Just as often, the intention is to bring one or other of these concepts into sharper focus through a strategic contrast with the opposition: nature, totalitarianism, organic individualism, false-consciousness. Although the positions of the various critiques appear to be different, particularly in their philosophical orientations and in their deployment of a range of methodologies and analytical techniques (structuralist, poststructuralist, humanist, linguistic, feminist) they do hold at least one set of assumptions in common: All agree that English offers the promise of an ideal unity in whatever form—personal freedom (critical or organic), full democracy; the complete subject/society—if only whatever it is that currently stands in the way of this promise could be removed.

The concept of a *block* to an ideal of completion is the trademark of the English quest: For Arnold (1964) the block is "industrialization"; for Leavis (1972) it is "our technologico-Benthamite civilisation"; for

---

[1] I make no attempt to address the issues—in this necessarily brief chapter—of the relationships between the fields of English, literature, and literacy, and the attempt to juggle them here within an uneasy alliance is by now a familiar strategy of English research.

Rosenblatt (1938) it is "behaviorism" and "logical positivism"; for Eagleton (1991) it is "ideology." In each case, the tenacious opposition between a definably hard-edged, exploitative field and the inexplicable nuances of the imaginative and creative spaces of English reappears in different guise but in the service of similar ends. Thus, critiques of English are littered with phrases suggesting the quarry is in sight: English is, or should be, about "coming to know/understand" and "seeing things as they really are" or "knowing life as it really is", and about achieving "full democracy" or "full human worth." Curiously, but perhaps not unexpectedly, these exactly worded phrases appear in the work of theorists as apparently diverse as Leavis (1972) and Dixon (1975); Richards (1973) and Rosenblatt (1938); Hirsch (1987) and Gee (1996) where they are deployed in the interests of a remarkably unified view of what English/literacy should be trying to achieve, even if the means are promoted as different.[2]

Learning theorists face similar problems when constructing accounts of literacy that oppose two types of instruction—a utilitarian or learned literacy against a freely chosen form. The following stands as a representative example only:

> Work both with teachers and pupils has convinced me that there are two models of literacy on offer in our schools: a utilitarian one aimed at giving people the ability to write little more than their name and address and to fill in forms, and a supercharged model which allows its possessors to choose and control all that they read and write. (Meek, cited in Hadley, 1992, p. 170)

It is this "supercharged model"—which Meek named *critical literacy*—that forms the centerpiece of both emancipatory liberal and emancipatory political accounts of literacy education; in the case of the latter, literacy is described in terms of an opposition between a political literacy that takes account of the ideological characteristics of its formation and transmission and a putative nonpolitical literacy that attempts to escape ideology by claiming universality or naturalness. In both cases, English is set up as a cover for the exploitation of marginalized groups or the suppression of individual creativity while simultaneously hailed as their potential saviour through its utopian ideal of a liberated society or subject/individual. Whether these ideals are to be achieved through the mechanism of a "psychosocial theory of personal development," "a social theory of language," or a "postmodern theory of the subject" it seems that theorists working from a remarkably

---

[2]See Mellor (1992) " 'Pre-theoretical' Criticism" for an extended discussion of this point.

broad range of sites share a concern to track those forces that stand between English and the true object of its desire: "the organic community/person, "cultural pluralism", "difference", "diversity", "equality".[3]

However, the work of Hunter (1988, 1993, 1994) suggests that these accounts, common in Australia, Britain, and the United States[4] are at best misguided in their subordination of literacy to an exemplary principle of personal freedom or emancipation of subjects and societies that demands a continuing opposition between such concepts as *humanity* and *bureaucracy* or *subject* and *citizen*. Hunter's argument in the last chapter—that personal development is not opposed to *government*[5] but is produced by it—undercuts the premise of these debates and positions English not as the always inadequate repository for a set of romantic (or even postmodern) ideals managed through practices of personal introspection and reflexivity, but as the name applied to a contingent set of discrete capacities whose relationship may be no more than familial—in a Wittgensteinian sense. In suggesting that the link between literature or language, and consciousness—social or personal— is not fundamental to the operation of English, Hunter opens the way for an uncoupling of "personalist pedagogies" and "English."[6] Just why English educators might want to pursue this possibility and how it might be begun are the topic of the discussion that follows.

---

[3]For a useful discussion of the ways in which feminist postmodern critiques of critical pedagogies have sought to dislodge this worrying essentialism in liberatory accounts see Luke (1992).

[4]Much of the Australian work—including my own—conducted under the auspices of critical literacy or critical pedagogies is based on appeals to a process of social change or a moral transformation of the subject and society underwritten by oppositional ideals. In Britain the work is located in neo-marxist accounts or politicized growth accounts of the London School while in the United States, as in Australia, the debate is located by a set of principles associated with resistant or critical curriculum and pedagogy.

[5]It should go without saying that the notion of *government* employed here is based on a Foucauldian understanding of the term: that is, *government* does not equal the state, rather, the term refers to any instance of disciplinary formation whether secular, religious or bureaucratic.

[6]*Personalist pedagogies* are linked to literacy debates that assume a general opposition between principles of personal/social development and government. Hunter's (1988) account of literary education shows how this arrangement effectively maintains a particular pedagogic strategy involving the techniques of personal introspection and self-problematization deployed as part of reading and writing practices.

TROUBLING CIRCULARITY

Janet Emig, chair of the U.S. National Board for Standards in English Language Arts draws attention to the confusions that arise when *personal development* and *government* are deployed as oppositional concepts within debates about English. In warning the U.S. government not to attempt interference with the work of the Board through a proposed federal panel, Emig suggested "the federal government [should instead] place its energies on ensuring that every American child come to school each day fed, clothed, housed, immunised, mentored, and in every way ready to learn in an environment free from drugs and violence" (Long, 1993, p. 6). In this recognition of the positive role of government in the formation and care of its subjects, Emig acknowledged a set of person-forming health and safety norms around which she would like the child to be arranged. Obviously, there exists another related set of person-forming learning norms around which the child is in a continuing process of arrangement: Emig, as chair of a Standards Board is involved through her capacity as a bureaucrat in the description of those norms. But in this account, the work of English learning is located outside the range of government, despite the momentous intervention that has already taken place through the establishment of the Board. In theoretically opposing public health and safety (government) and learning (personal/critical development) Emig both acknowledges and denies the conditions that make particular forms of learning possible.

If I look to political accounts to take me past expressions of a personal versus government or related opposition, I find that they are as much in evidence here as in "progressive" or "growth" English statements. Taking the form of learning but not training; facilitating but not teaching, these accounts repeat the theoretical circularity that takes hold through descriptions positioning these concepts as antipathetic. These circularities are most apparent when theorists subject what could otherwise be viewed as discretely functional strategies to the conformity of general principles; a move that results in a line of argument that does not allow for the workings of practices such as literacy, and makes it difficult to decide just how things do get done in classrooms. Thus, after asserting that the Australian government of the day desired to build a knowledge-based economy but that it did not value learning, Frow (1990) commented in terms reminiscent of Meek: "What [the government] values instead is training, which involves the application of existing knowledges. Learning, by contrast, involves the critical transformation of existing knowledges; it involves the uncertainty and doubt, and the impossibility of predictable outcomes" (p. 11).

But Frow did indicate the complexity of trying to account for literacy education in these oppositional terms when he noted in the same address: "Despite its close connection with the secondary schooling system [English] has rarely taken seriously the realities of its roles in ethical regulation and in the training of students in functional literacy . . . " (p. 8). He also suggested that schools should "start valuing the teaching of composition and writing skills" (p. 15). In accounts such as these, it proves difficult to maintain "training" and "learning" as oppositional concepts even when the implication is that training remains a necessary, if undesirably pragmatic prerequisite for learning. A common assumption is that the critical transformations attendant on learning will eventually obviate the need for training. With training out of the equation, and learning and critical transformation bracketed, it becomes difficult to imagine how students actually critically transform knowledge—unless they manage it through learning. But then, to learn they must be able to critically transform knowledge . . . ?

SOME PROBLEMS WITH DIFFERENCE AND PLURALITY

It was problems such as these that arose for a team of writers,[7] with whom I have been working developing what have been described variously as *critical curriculum materials* (Freebody, Luke, & Gilbert, 1991; A. Luke, 1991) or *poststructuralist approaches to reading* (Corcoran, 1992; Gilbert & Taylor, 1991). In working with students in classrooms, we became increasingly worried by what appeared to be an inability to explain how the reading strategies we were developing actually worked to reconstruct reading practices and "transform" readers. Working from a broad-based cultural studies approach, we assumed that an important aspect of the strategy being developed was to ensure that readers could recognize, construct, and be free to choose from a range of reading positions. We viewed these practices as radical alternatives to those traditionally offered in schools where students were encouraged to find a single reading and then learn an authoritative interpretation with little or no regard for the sociohistorical and ideological locations of texts, and readers.

The rationale for our commitment to pluralist reading positions seemed obvious. If readers were to be transformed from subjects who read "blind" to the ideological constructs of texts, to subjects who were

---

[7]This group is led by Bronwyn Mellor who also directs Chalkface Press, a Perth-based publishing company affiliated with the English and Media Centre in London, directed by Michael Simons. Both institutions publish innovative classroom materials in textual analysis with attention to the traditional concerns of critical literacy and cultural studies.

"critically aware" of their ideological positioning, then we would need to ensure they had access to a range of strategies for recognizing the ideology of texts and for constructing alternative readings. But, a concern for "difference" and "choice" was offset somewhat by the acknowledgment that we could not claim that any reading would do; we therefore had to devise ways that encouraged readers to choose wisely among the readings. This proved to be a difficult task for a group of writers committed to a pluralist position and working out of emancipatory English practices. Obviously, we could signal a preferred reading through the structure of the activities but that seemed a little directive for an approach advocating student choice. On the other hand, we could not simply provide students with the means to produce a range of readings and then leave them to choose—what if they chose an inappropriate reading, one that would disempower them in the assessment stakes? Or, worse still in its consequences for a liberatory pedagogy, what if students chose not to support say, the antiracist reading but chose instead to construct a racist reading?

Davies drew attention to this problem in relation to gender when commenting on a preschool teacher's acceptance of "aggressive superhero themes" in the play of her female students:

> From a feminist point of view, having girls take up the violent aspects of male behaviour . . . is not something that can easily be condoned. The feminist wish that girls have access to all behaviours regardless of sex clashes here with a feminist wish for a nonviolent society. (cited in Fernie, Davies, Kantor, & McMurray, 1993, p. 109)

When the ideals of pluralism run up against a different set of equity ideals there are problems and consequences for critical pedagogy. Traditionally, advocates of a pluralist position invite pedagogical attention to concepts of *difference*, assuming that if students have access to multiple subject positions then they will choose to express that difference appropriately. But, as our experiences of secondary English classrooms and Davies' observations indicate, this is not always the case.

The tendency of many critical accounts to assume that the effects of difference are positive rather than negative shaped part of the problems we faced as classroom technicians and designers of English course books. For instance, if the difference being articulated in my classroom is a version of neo-Nazism and I am a teacher committed to a pluralist position then what do I do with/about that? I cannot claim that the students do not have access to alternative readings because, as Mellor's (1992) work shows, they can demonstrate a critique of the reading positions of tolerance from within positions of intolerance, providing an unsettling reminder that this process of critique—which demonstrates access to multiple reading positions—is not always indicative of a student's attainment of critical literacy. This poses problems for a pedagogy that promotes "difference" by providing students with the means to move across multiple subject positions, a maneuver assumed to restore them to "critical consciousness."

Nevertheless, such concepts as *multiple subject positions, resistance, alternative readings*—familiar in critical literacy work and across this volume—provided the initial basis of our classroom materials. The problem was, and still is, that we appeared to be caught in similar terms to many of the accounts of English mentioned earlier. In asking students to examine the various readings made available to them by a foregrounding of ideology—and then requiring that they critically evaluate the readings and choose among them—we appeared to be doing little more than expected of a teacher well versed in the practices of critical literacy. However, what this strategy assumes is that students already have the facility to make the choice in a critical manner. But how did they acquire this expertise? An obvious answer is that they are free to choose because they have come to know the terms of that choice. But presumably they have come to know precisely because they are free to choose. That is, in order to critically evaluate the choice they must already be able to produce multiple reading positions that in turn are dependent on their being able to critically choose.

This we now consider to be a particularly unhelpful position to maintain both theoretically and practically. It is disabling on several counts. Two will suffice at this point: one is that it makes it difficult for teachers to argue for the primacy of one reading over another, and the second is that within a regime that insists on the necessity for producing multiple readings and for offering choice it becomes difficult to argue a case for the usefulness of not encouraging multiple readings on some occasions. Just as teaching multiple readings of a text advocating the dismembering of women's bodies might be dismissed in favor of teaching a specific reading of it as sexist, so might the reading of a text proposing the extermination of a particular racial group be confined to a reading of it as racist. Although censorship policy has recourse to similar arguments it seems that in English we are not able to argue explicitly for the teaching of specific readings and specific reading practices over others in either personal growth classrooms that advocate choice and response, or in classrooms committed to a critical cultural studies approach where difference is valorized.

PERSONALISM: A RICHER KIND OF HUMAN ACTIVITY?

In the English classroom where the student is the target of a positive practice for forming a self who will choose consciously among readings, the techniques for personal introspection and self-problematization that attend this production do have to be taught. But, because the emphasis here is on achieving critical consciousness—assumed to involve an inner transformation via the production of a new subjectivity—the teaching of a specific reading and how to produce that reading cannot be explicit. In a report of a 10-country study of literature education, Purves (1973, 1981) provided compelling evidence of this pedagogical ambiguity and its contradictory conjunction with definable personalist features of classroom techniques. Located within the field of statistical analysis and deploying the research strategies and vocabulary of measurement technologies, the study seems inimical to the interests and pedagogical concerns of the literature teacher. However, several points do seem pertinent to current debates. In defining the literary response patterns of students in the United States, Purves (1981) concluded that: "The moralistic interpretive pattern is the dominant pattern of American high-school students" (p. 92). Within his system for categorizing literary response the "moralistic interpretative pattern" is derived from the students' selection of a particular set of questions as being the most important questions to ask about any literary text. This set comprises the following: "Does anything in the story have a hidden meaning? Is there a lesson to be learned from the story? What does the story tell me about people or ideas in general? What emotions does the story arouse in me?" (p. 84). These data give pause for thought particularly when considered in conjunction with the teachers' rank ordering of eight possible goals of literary instruction. Teachers from both junior and senior high schools placed the following goal as the first priority: "To help the students understand themselves and the human condition" (p. 29). Twenty years after Purves' survey Luke (1991) reported a similar response by Australian teachers who, when asked to rank order "the most important goals of literacy teaching" ranked "personal expression and creativity" the "highest by a significant margin" (p. 15). Apart from providing a reminder of the crossover between literature teaching and literacy teaching, the conjunction of these events indicates the persistence of particular classroom techniques and educational ideals. It also establishes some possible parameters for describing the operation of classroom procedures relevant to particular sites.

The statistical significance of the students' selection of the "moral interpretative" set of questions in combination with the teachers' ranking of goals led Purves (1981) to draw attention to an "oddity" in his re-examination of the U.S. data: He concluded that there was "a clear indication that patterns of response are learned in secondary school" but then went on to comment: "If they are learned, they appear to have been taught, if not as a conscious part of the curriculum, at least as part of a 'hidden curriculum' " (p. 106). The ambivalence regarding the teaching of response was due to the inability of this, the most extensive study of literature education ever to be undertaken, to describe literature teaching. This difficulty resides in part in the inability of a personalist pedagogy to ascribe definable traits to specific techniques for reading— in this case, "literary response"—precisely because it is viewed as a feature of personality and therefore indefinable, and presumably unteachable. However, this ideal of response as the always incomplete reflection of the personality of the reader collides with the necessity to produce students who have the right response equipment. That is, a generally unacknowledged goal of literature teaching is to produce students who are able to respond in particular ways and whose responses are characterized by recognizable markers of "correctness," whereas at the same time this normative alignment is confronted by the necessary imprecision of the personalist origins of literary response.

It would be imprecise to attempt to account for the findings of Purves' study as prespecified generalities of the nonpolitical classroom. The questions selected by the students could just as easily be applied in politicized classrooms deploying the strategies of cultural studies approaches to text analysis, although they may be expressed in slightly different ways. In the latter case, the "emotions aroused" may take feminist or antiracist forms, the "hidden meaning" may be expressed as "the ideology of the text" and there would be less emphasis on the text as a reflection of life and more on its sociohistorical location. Although expressed in somewhat old-fashioned terminology there is ample evidence that neither the goal nor the set of questions identified by Purves' teachers and students would be out of place in many modern English classrooms.[8] Wingard (1990) provided a reminder of this when describing a pedagogical device that he instituted in his literature classes: "Basic to the response statement . . . is a heuristic that asks students the following: What was the initial effect of the text on you? How do you account for that effect, in terms of features of the text and qualities of yourself as a reader? What does your response tell you about yourself or your society?" (p. 153). There is little doubt that modern students are regularly rewarded for taking as their guide the questions and goals proposed by Purves' research team in the twilight of "old English."

At this point, it is worth reviewing a brief run of dates in order to raise some questions about two sets of related claims: one, that Dartmouth crystallized the differences between British English and North American English, and the other, that it marked a theoretical disjuncture between "old English" and "new English" in British terms,

---

[8]See Cullen (1992); Hughes (1992) for supporting data.

but that this disjuncture did not manifest itself as a significantly different form of English in the classroom on either side of the Atlantic (Allen, 1987; Harris, 1991).[9] The Dartmouth Seminar—funded by the Carnegie Corporation—occurred in 1966; the new English is assumed to have emerged around the mid-1970s; Purves' team constructed the set of instruments for data collection from 1965; the students and teachers involved in the study completed the questionnaires during 1970. Luke, Freebody, and Gilbert (1991) reported the results of their study in 1990. Hunter's genealogy, which challenges traditional historical accounts of subject English by pointing to particular pedagogical continuities, is sometimes challenged by claims to the effect that it ignores the extent of the gap between a program and its realization, or that it does not provide a recognizable account in terms of our experiences of the classroom, or that it relies on Dixon's account of Dartmouth that is specifically British.[10] But the set of questions selected by high school students across the United States as the most important questions to ask about a literary text, not only bear an uncanny resemblance to the types of questions asked within the regimes of new English, but stand as an empirical reminder of the actual techniques and strategies deployed within the apparatus of personalist pedagogies. Although Dartmouth undoubtedly marked a shift in classroom strategies—the inclusion of "relevant" texts; an emphasis on oral language; the use of group work[11]—it nevertheless kept English and its pedagogies tethered to a set of relatively unchanging formative practices.

The grandiose demeanor of English, evident in the expansive ethical claims made on its behalf, were reinforced by the Dartmouth Seminar. We do not have to look far to find many such instances of these hopes of English both in a out of the classroom and, in case there should

---

[9]Although the connections between a "Leavisite" strand of old English and a growth strand of new English seem obvious most accounts continue to theorize the continuities in terms of Dartmouth's failure to change classroom practices because of an inadequate theory of language or of the subject.

[10]These lines of critique have been drawn from audio tape recordings of discussion sessions following papers presented by Hunter at Murdoch University and The University of Western Australia (no date, but probably took place during the late 1980s). Although critiques of Hunter's work are appearing within the fields of literary criticism and cultural studies there is little evidence of critique from within English education, although Dixon's refusal to review *Culture and Government* (*Typereader* No.2 July, 1989) provides general support for my summary of concerns.

[11]A comprehensive guide to the classroom concerns and pedagogic initiatives of the new English is provided in Australia by Forrestal and Reid's Workshop Series published by Nelson between 1983 and 1986: *Room to Move* (1983); *Space to Dream* (1984); *Time to Tell* (1985); *Bridges to Build* (1986).

be any lingering doubt that Dixon's reading of world events (cited in Hunter, chap.16, this volume) is a feature of British English, one more example—this time from the other side of the Atlantic—should suffice to stress the strength and uniformity of the imperative for emancipatory transformation. In a retrospective look at a highly influential career, Rosenblatt (1990) recently commented:

> In 1938, democracy was being threatened by Fascism in Italy and totalitarian governments in Germany and Russia. This retrospect, this backward look, has not lingered on much that was dark in the intervening years. But in recent months, we have been witnessing the heartening spectacle of the liberation from within of such totalitarian states. We have seen whole peoples effect peaceful nonviolent revolutions, and we apprehensively watch their hazardous gropings toward democracy. Note that . . . their demands were first of all for freedom, for the freedoms that we enjoy. . . . Our democracy is still threatened, not by totalitarianism, but by social and economic problems that, if not solved, will prevent the education and development of a people capable of the decisions and responsibilities of a full democracy. (p. 107)

Perhaps there is a need for caution with respect to the theoretical reproductive tendencies attendant on these somewhat repetitious appeals. English teachers are faced on a daily basis with "a people" who must/should/might conceivably become "capable of the decisions and responsibilities of a full democracy." It does not seem helpful to claim that students could achieve this capability through their "transactions with literature" on the assumption that it is there that they can make the necessary transformative connections between "personal consciousness" and events, or even to claim, in more modern parlance, that fundamental links between "language and subjectivity"or "language and experience" provide the ground for the critical or linguistic transformations required for an emancipated society. It may be time for English to give up the claim for creating general, or even specific capacities subordinated to the principle of emancipation and to address, instead, the more mundane practicalities concerning the types of techniques classroom strategists need to devise if students are to acquire those capacities necessary for doing things with texts in particular departments of existence.

TRAINING READERS

If personalism is an effect of an English pedagogical milieu then does it make sense to propose that a more public engagement with various departments of existence—postpersonalism—could be an effect of a different pedagogical milieu, one in which the public, social, and civic aspects of practice are emphasized? Can critical literacy be organized around a set of explicitly acknowledged norms that do not demand the moral conversion of the subject but do require, nevertheless, an "ethical formation" tied to a specific and limited domain of practice? Keeping in mind, of course, that any proposal for change may be questioned in terms that assert the instability and contingency of the surfaces on which particular suggestions and decisions are produced it is, nevertheless, feasible within the current climate of English to suggest we lower our sights from the lofty ideals of fullness and concentrate for a time on the more pedestrian issues of how best to equip the child with a limited set of strategies and techniques for working with texts in modern social and civic settings.

Perhaps I can continue the initial set of questions as an interim means of suggesting some possible boundaries within which to work at rethinking English in postpersonalist terms. Is it possible to explicitly teach, for instance, the "feminist reading" or the "antiracist reading" as a "linguistic competence" and if so, would we want to? Perhaps we could view the production of the feminist or antiracist reading as just one technique among many—to be applied on certain occasions and under particular circumstances—in the critical repertoire of the student? What would be the advantages of this practice? It would not demand the moral transformation of the students—although it would still demand a particular type of transformation of the kind regularly demanded by education. If being able to perform the feminist or antiracist reading is considered a necessary part of the equipment required for participation in modern societies then presumably this would be just one strategy available to the student from a range of techniques for working with texts. The formation of a reader capable of deploying a specific technique effective within the apparatuses of feminism and/or antiracism does not seem such an uncritical act. Of course, within this regime, being able to perform the feminist or antiracist reading would not have to equate with being a feminist or being an antiracist (although it may do so); but then, just as equity policy in the workplace cannot legislate for employers to be fair-minded—all it can stipulate is that they be seen to act as though they are fair-minded—then English need not expect the moral conversion of its subjects, only that they be seen to be technically competent, literate deployers of the capacities for which they have been prepared.

It could be argued that real social change only comes when people are touched at the core, converted, transformed, and so on into truly feminist or truly antiracist beings. But even a passing glance at events will confirm that it is government intervention (often through legislation) that has an impressive history as an instrument for social change and the transformation of subjects within the arenas of gender and race, as well as health and the environment. Teachers are already attached to various campaigns for changing public behavior: currently in Australia these include antismoking, antilittering and sun protection campaigns. Other undertakings similarly aimed at changing values include date-rape campaigns and environmentalist campaigns, while Mabo (the Australian High Court decision on indigenous land claims) provides the opportunity for a public undertaking to change race relations. It is true that policy and legislation require support from the people to be successful but this support is not so much the result of a spontaneous insightfulness on the part of individuals or groups, or even the resistance of repressed minorities. Rather the insightfulness and resistance are an effect of a complex set of technologies—media, events, policy, education—through which the readjustment of the norms around which particular practices are organized takes place.

Literacy practitioners are continually engaged in the adjustment of pedagogic practices toward specific, although often unacknowledged, educational norms. However, even when these are acknowledged there can be unexpected or unplanned effects. Delpit (1988) drew attention to the complexities involved in juggling classroom techniques on the shifting terrain of equity education. In noting that different practices work differently for different groups of students she commented on "the negative outcry in the Black community" when "dialect readers" were introduced into the schools (p. 285). Although this move was accounted for in terms of the practices of "cultural pluralism" and "difference," Delpit reported that it was, nevertheless, greeted with hostility by the people for whom it was ostensibly designed. In a reconsideration of the "process pedagogies" within which the move to dialect readers was situated, Delpit stressed the necessity for "explicit teaching" of new information to children who have not already acquired this at home. In doing so, she noted the unfortunate tendency of many critical literacy theorists to equate this claim with "direct instruction" and "skills," a maneuver that locates what could be a positive intervention in critical literacy terms within the more conservative framework of transmission pedagogies.

In many respects, this account is promising in its refusal of a polarizing "process" versus "skills" position and in its thoughtful attention to the dilemmas of progressivism. But in keeping classroom practices anchored to an ideal of "diversity" Delpit directed her argument down a now familiar path. Although the potential of government for positive intervention on behalf of equity issues is acknowledged through Delpit's comment that she does "not believe that political change toward diversity can be effected from the bottom up" since "to encourage diversity within classrooms [does not mean that] diversity will automatically be accepted at gatekeeping points" (p. 292), it is still the case that the strategy is driven by the potential for a "true diversity" that will assist the realization of a more complete society. Rosenblatt's ideal of a "full democracy" is close to Delpit's ideal of a "truly diverse society" and although the latter account is more promising in its attention to the processes of government, both take too long a view of an English agenda that—English educators may have noted—has only piecemeal effects.

GETTING OUT OF THE LOOP

What is at stake then in turning away from accounts of English based on opposing principles of government and emancipation, and looking instead at what might be achieved within the limits of a postpersonalist pedagogy for critical literacy? Elsewhere, we have argued that the classroom is inescapably normative and that as teachers of reading and writing, we need to declare this—both to ourselves and to our students— but this need not mean that we must abandon a political project related to English education. On the contrary, Meredyth (1993) argued:

> the more prepared we are to acknowledge the historically-based argument that the classroom is a key site for the governmental adjustment of the "norms of life" the more possible it becomes to regard these pedagogic norms of life as contingent and variable. There is little reason to doubt that this would assist equity-based educational and social reforms, not least by removing some of the more curious confusions which have come to shape our educational understanding. (p. 229)

Although English continues to be conceptualized as a dialectic of ideals but not as a set of contingent, variable, and adjustable norms around which something called "English" is arranged, it remains difficult to see past "some of the more curious confusions" of both liberal and dialectical critiques. Briefly, and no doubt over simply, liberal arguments—mortgaged to concepts of "full democracy" and "complete persons"—fail to acknowledge that each achievement requires the prior completion of the other. And, although those of us working from a neo-Marxist position have traditionally looked to political accounts to advance critical debates, it seems that this position is no less beset by the "curious confusions" of liberal critiques. The suggestion that "political emancipation" will be achieved by the removal of the block of ideology or by the "play of difference" raises the question of how the misleading or marginalising effects of ideology will be shed without the prior achievement of a state of "emancipation"[12]. To stop thinking about English as the pedagogical field on which the important, enduring ideals of life are played out—but never won—could seem, for some of us, akin to giving up something fundamental to our personal and professional lives. On the other hand, it is more likely the case that to think this way is just a habit—and one that the English classroom could easily do without—but that is not to underestimate the complexity of the issues at stake here. Boomer (1988) once remarked: "teachers teach most profoundly what they are at the core" (p. 31). For many readers unfamiliar with the arguments of *Culture and Government* it may seem that "the core" is what Hunter's work has in its sights, but that is to misread the trajectory of the argument: It is the concept of "the core" and the relations between it and literary education that are under a particular kind of investigation; one that focuses on the mechanisms through which certain pedagogical techniques (self-cultivation) devolved in association with specific philosophies, concepts, ideals (Romantic aesthetics). If we are prepared to think about English as being nothing more nor less than a contingent and functional grouping of discrete practices—and to view the core as an acquired deportment—then it may be possible to think more freely and pragmatically about English as a form of moral training and its relations with the social destinations of those that it trains.

Wittgenstein (cited in Moon, 1993), in a statement which will no doubt seem offensive on a number of counts claimed: "To understand a language means to be master of a technique" (p. 86). This assertion, however, may come as a pleasant surprise for many students particularly, as Moon noted, Wittgenstein's work suggests first, that "linguistic capacities . . . are the product of local and specific trainings"; second, that "language competence is on a par with other kinds of behaviour, such as playing a piano" and third, that the "operations of language are systematised in the practices of public life relevant to a particular department of existence" (pp. 85–86). If we consider that the students who may be relieved on being appraised of the teachability of English are also quite likely to be the current targets of critical literacy angst then it may be time to set some less ambitious goals than, say, those set by teachers taking part in the studies conducted by Purves and by Luke et al., or those suggested by most current theoretical critiques. Hunter (1988, and chap. 18, this volume) argued that the origins of English are bureaucratic and pragmatic rather than ideological or voluntary and that English in its modern form inherited a particular technique for personal reading in its devolvement from pastoral care and pastoral pedagogy into popular education. If we accept this account

---

[12]See Hunter (1994) for a detailed explication of this problem within the general field of education.

and begin to treat the capacities of English—literary criticism, ethics, rhetoric—as civic capacities (rather than expressions of personal and/or social/cultural experience) then it becomes possible to think of them apart from say, the discourses of liberatory politics and subjectivity. This is not to argue that there is anything wrong with liberatory politics (far from it), but only to suggest that the requirement to discover or recover an ideal form of the society or the subject—a process that is always blocked by some force or other—would cease to be the concern of English pedagogical procedures.

If we are to avoid converting Eagleton's (1985) intransitively "sensitive subject" of literature to Mellor's (1992) "intransitively critical subject" of critical literacy then English and literacy educators could make a small beginning as "classroom strategists" by considering the possibility of constructing, within specific and limited domains of practice, a set of contingent techniques for reading and writing. These strategies and techniques would be "transformative" in that they would be linked to the formation of particular capacities—but with limited effects. Just as in any professional practice, literacy educators will continue to argue for decisions about which sets of capacities are required for participation in modern societies. To then teach these capacities—not as part of a generally transformative practice for personal or social liberation but as ways of doing things with texts relevant to particular departments of existence—will require a careful restructuring of pedagogies.

ACKNOWLEDGMENTS

I thank Ian Hunter, Bronwyn Mellor, and Denise Meredyth for their helpful comments on the first draft of this chapter.

REFERENCES

Allen, D. (1987). Dartmouth and growth through English. In V. J. Lee (Ed.), *English literature in schools*. Philadelphia: Open University Press.

Arnold, M. (1964). Selected essays. (N. Annan, Ed.). London: Oxford University Press.

Boomer, G. (1988). Struggling in English. In B. Green (Ed.), *Metaphors and meanings: Essays on English teaching by Garth Boomer*. Melbourne: Australian Association for the Teaching of English.

Corcoran, B. (1992). The making and remaking of readers and writers: A retrospect and prospect. In J. Thomson (Ed.), *Reconstructing literature teaching*. Norwood: Australian Association for the Teaching of English.

Delpit, L. (1988). The silenced dialogue: Power and pedagogy in educating other people's children. *Harvard Educational Review, 58*(3), 280-298.

Dixon, J. (1975). *Growth through English.* Oxford, UK: Oxford University Press.

Eagleton, T. (1985). The subject of literature. *The English Magazine, 15,* 4-7.

Eagleton, T. (1991, Summer). The enemy within. *NATE News,* 5-7.

Fernie, D., Davies, B., Kantor, R., & McMurray, P. (1993). Becoming a person in the preschool: Creating integrated gender, school culture, and peer culture positionings. *Qualitative Studies in Education, 6*(2), 95-110.

Forrestal, P., & Reid, J-A. (1983). *Room to move.* Melbourne: Nelson Australia.

Forrestal, P., & Reid, J-A. (1984). *Space to dream.* Melbourne: Nelson Australia.

Forrestal, P., & Reid, J-A. (1985). *Time to tell.* Melbourne: Nelson Australia.

Forrestal, P., & Reid, J-A. (1986). *Bridges to build.* Melbourne: Nelson Australia.

Freebody, P., Luke, A., & Gilbert, P. (1991). Reading positions and practices in the classroom. *Curriculum Inquiry, 21*(4), 435-457.

Frow, J. (1990). *Inaugural address: The social production of knowledge and the discipline of English.* Brisbane: Queensland University Press.

Gee, J. P. (1996). *Social linguistics and literacies: Ideology in discourses.* London: Taylor and Francis.

Gilbert, P., & Taylor, S. (1991). *Fashioning the feminine: Girls, popular culture and schooling.* Sydney, Australia: Allen & Unwin.

Hadley, E. (1992). [Review of *A schooling in English—Critical episodes in the struggle to shape literary and cultural studies* by John Dixon]. *The Use of English, 43*(2), 169-172.

Harris, J. (1991) After Dartmouth: Growth and conflict in English. *College English, 53*(6), 631-646.

Hirsch, E. D. (1987). *Cultural literacy: What every American needs to know.* Boston, MA: Houghton Mifflin.

Hunter, I. (1988). *Culture and government: The emergence of literary education.* London: Macmillan.

Hunter, I. (1993) The pastoral bureaucracy: Towards a less principled understanding of state schooling. In D. Meredyth & D. Tyler (Eds.), *Child and citizen: Genealogies of schooling and subjectivity.* Brisbane, Australia: Institute for Cultural Policy Studies, Griffith University.

Hunter, I. (1994). *Rethinking the school: Subjectivity, bureaucracy, criticism.* Sydney, Australia: Allen & Unwin.

Leavis, F. R. (1972). *Nor shall my sword: Discourses on pluralism, compassion and social hope*. London: Chatto & Windus.

Long, R. (1993, June). Emig sees proposed federal panel as intruding on standards process. *The Council Chronicle*, p. 6.

Luke, A. (1991). The political economy of reading instruction. In C. D. Baker & A. Luke (Eds.), *Towards a critical sociology of reading pedagogy*. Amsterdam/Philadelphia: John Benjamins.

Luke, A., Freebody, P., & Gilbert, P. (1991). What counts as reading in the secondary school classroom: Selective traditions of reading practices and positions. In F. Christie, B. Devlin, P. Freebody, A. Luke, J. R. Martin, T. Threadgold, & C. Walton (Eds.), *Teaching English literacy: A project of national significance on the preservice preparation of teachers for the teaching of English* (Vol. 2). Darwin: University of Northern Territory.,

Luke, C. (1992). Feminist politics in radical pedagogy. In C. Luke & J. Gore (Eds.), *Feminisms and critical pedagogies*. New York: Routledge.

Mellor, B. (1992). *English and reading practices*. Unpublished doctoral thesis, The University of Western Australia, Perth.

Meredyth, D. (1993). Marking the immeasurable: Debates on ASAT. In D. Meredyth & D. Tyler (Eds.), *Child and citizen: Genealogies of schooling and subjectivity*. Brisbane, Australia: Institute for Cultural Policy Studies, Griffith University.

Moon, B. (1994). *Reading and gender: From discourse and subject to regimes of practice*. Unpublished doctoral thesis, Curtin University of Technology, Perth.

Purves, A. C. (1973). *International studies in evaluation II: Literature education in ten countries, an empirical study*. Stockholm: Almqvist & Wiksell.

Purves, A. C. (1981). *Reading and literature: American achievement in international perspective*. Urbana, IL: National Council of Teachers of English.

Richards, I. A. (1973). *Interpretation in teaching* (2nd ed.). London: Routledge & Kegan Paul.

Rosenblatt, L. (1990). Retrospect. In E. J. Farrell & J. R. Squire (Eds.), *Transactions with literature: A fifty year perspective*. Urbana, IL: National Council of Teachers of English.

Rosenblatt, L. M. (1938). *Literature as exploration*. New York: Appleton-Century.

Wingard, J. (1990). Delivering on the promise of liberal education. In C. Morgan & E. F. Penfield (Eds.), *Conversations: Contemporary critical theory and the teaching of literature*. Urbana, IL.: National Council of Teachers of English.

20
Critical Literacies and the Teaching of English

Terry Threadgold
Monash University

A useful question from two feminists: Is it coincidence that the death of the subject is announced just as some of us are voicing our subjectivity? (Hartsock & hooks, cited in Brook, 1994, p. 276)

"Emancipatory educators," constructed around ideas of "being human," are faced with demands both to change into new-management bureaucrats and to address challenges to the political agenda which framed their/our teaching. As the "Post-Dawkins" Tertiary system makes clear an interesting disregard for the "humanities" through the allocation of funding, so theorists suggest that the explicit political agenda was anyway always contradictory to the implicit "real" function of the humanities: the reproduction of a public service. (Brook, 1994, p. 276).

People are not poor because they're illiterate; they are illiterate because they're poor. (Anderson & Irvine, 1993, p. 82).

The presence of women and girls at every level of education has crucially influenced curriculum, teaching, the organisation of schools and the value put on a whole range of educational outcomes. A beginning would be made by acknowledging this, and by acknowledging at the same time that there are serious gender implications in all forms of criticism levelled at education and in all proposals for change. (Miller, 1992, p. 26).

I have brought these quotations together to suggest some of the complexities and contradictory positions that have to be negotiated in writing today about critical literacies and the teaching of English. They also of course have to be negotiated in the "doing" of the teaching of English. I take the reference in the second quotation to the "real" function of the humanities as being the reproduction of the public service to be a reference to the recent work of Hunter (1994b) and that too is a part of the complex scenario I explore in this chapter.

Perhaps at no time in the history of literacy and popular education have more complex and heterogeneous demands been placed on English teachers, teacher educators, and teacher trainees working within the changing area of English studies. The very name Cultural Studies English (Mellor & Patterson, 1994) provides some indication of the schizophrenic nature of the exercise as it is currently formulated in the Australian (and international) contexts. Among the prominent issues are what are perceived to be a series of serious mismatches between school English and tertiary literary studies (McCormack, 1991), between school English and the curriculum documents that are supposed to specify what it is, and between school English and theoretical understandings of the economic, political, theoretical, and ethical functions and underpinnings of the discipline (or is it now an interdiscipline?; Hunter, 1988; A. Luke, 1990b; McCormack 1991; McDonald, 1991).

The factors that have brought about the changes in subject English are multiple and complex. They include the changing economic and cultural conditions that have produced new literary and critical textual theories, new vocational and technical demands from governments and in the workforce, a new focus on work as discourse (information technologies; McCormack, 1991; see also Green, chap. 13, this volume), new demographic tendencies that change the nature of secondary school populations (the dramatic increase in retention rates to Year 12) and thus require different kinds of teaching, the media and information economy that itself requires a pedagogy but also means that academic theories now circulate freely in the popular press, intruding into everyday life in new and unpredictable ways (see C. Luke, chap. 2, this volume). In ways that have barely begun to be understood, they involve the impact of theories such as feminism and poststructuralism on contemporary concepts of the self and of difference and on the feminized practice of teaching in the schools. These changes, even somewhat randomly articulated as they are here, begin at the most rudimentary levels to indicate certain obvious and emerging needs. The complex informatics and communications systems of the new social orders in which we live require a complex focus on the role of language among other meaning making processes in society, and a theoretical understanding of the politics, ideologies, and power relations involved in these processes. Perhaps more than anything else there is a glaring need for a historical sense, something we have been in danger of losing under the impact of theory (Meredyth, 1994; Steedman, 1992a). There has also to be a synchronic focus on the heterogeneity of the social groups and the different clientele that mass educational practices now need to serve. That heterogeneity is further complicated when issues of class, race, and gender are taken into account. The role of teachers in classrooms where students have no expectation of either work or further training at the end of their school days, and education must seem irrelevant or worse, and the role of teachers in trying to maintain the often tenuous relation between schooling and adult work have to be addressed. These various needs and the role of the teacher as intellectual, bureaucrat, pastoral carer, provider of basic skills or functional literacy or emancipatory educator (depending on your theoretical persuasion) often seem to sit uneasily together both in contemporary theoretical stories about teaching and in practice (Brook, 1994; Mellor & Patterson, 1994). I come back to these questions later.

In Australia at the present time, English teachers (and I continue here to refer to both secondary and tertiary teachers) are being required variously to provide training in the use of language and knowledge about language, support for all the other language-based areas of the curriculum, technical and vocational training in a range of linguistic and textual skills for use in the workforce, and a usually unacknowledged aesthetic and ethical training (Hunter, 1988) designed to produce the citizens of a democratic society. This latter training is usually exercised through the more obvious trappings of English teaching either through the teaching of literature or, more recently, through the teaching of cultural studies. It is associated with the emancipatory education and educator mentioned by Brook in the quote cited earlier, although the traditional English aesthetic auto-didact masculine version of this educator[1] has to be distinguished from the current feminist or critical theory-motivated radical pedagogy versions. This is a distinction that Hunter is not very good at making. Again I return to this later.

This catalogue of things to be taught derives from a range of often conflicting governmental, pedagogic, and economic agendas, is usually associated with a conspicuous lack of articulation with teacher-training programs (of course there are exceptions), and regularly involves a failure to provide adequate inservice training for teachers trying to deal with constantly changing demands. At tertiary level, as I suggest later, there is a different but equally problematic relation to these various agendas. The demands that affect secondary and tertiary teachers however derive from both the social and cultural changes associated with the practice of teaching English in the late 20th century and the associated theory-and government-driven and economically

---

[1]As Howard (1991, cited in Miller, 1992) pointed out, the isolated learner was more likely in the 19th century to be female.

imposed curriculum revisions and redirections. The effects of these demands are sometimes characterized as "Teaching the Postmodern" (1994) or indeed now in Australia as a condition of being "Beyond Poststructuralism" (1994). These were the titles of recent special issues of journals and again I return to them later, particularly as being beyond poststructuralism seems to be affiliated with a view of being back with the bureaucracy or back with Christian pastoral care in the way alluded to by Brook in the quote with which I began. Much of this work takes as its lead recent monographs by Hunter (1988, 1994b, see chap. 18, this volume).

Thus far I have been speaking of what is being expected of teachers. One might have expected that critical literacy or critical literacies would be something that had more to do with students or learners. But clearly what happens to teachers affects what happens to learners and has to do with various agendas that concern themselves with what should happen to learners, that is, what they should know, and why, and how they should come to know it. These things are usually formalized in curriculum documents, in national profiles or, to take one specific Australian example, *The National Framework for Adult Language, Literacy and Numeracy* (Cope et al., 1993). These documents are also written by those who are presumed to have the critical literacies that are to be imparted, through these documents, to those who are designated the teachers and learners in this scenario. The difficulties of that assumption are among the things I explore here. Suffice to say that this means that in discussing critical literacies and what they might be we cannot afford not to keep this whole complicated set of intersecting and sometimes contradictory positions in play.

It might be worth here quoting from a political document, a paper given by Rodney Cavalier to the Victorian Council of Adult Education in Melbourne in 1994. Speaking of his own role in various Federal Labor government bodies set up "to maintain a watching brief" on the progress of *Australia's Language: The Australian Language and Literacy Policy* (Dawkins, 1991; the "White Paper" referred to later) he said: "within a year of the White Paper, however, it was terribly apparent that no one anywhere was able to maintain oversight on all that was happening" (p. 1). He then spoke of the way the "new awareness of language and literacy" (p. 1) was affecting government and workplace practices even when "the adherents were quite unaware of the White Paper" (p. 1) and of the conflict between "literacy courses" and "the present obsession for credentials and certification". Addressing himself to adult literacy providers he said:

People have embarked on the courses (adult literacy courses) precisely because they contain not a smack of the schooling and measured outcomes which serve to alienate them. One wonders where the "clients" will jump if they have to choose between recognised courses provided by accredited providers and courses which they like provided by people they identify with—that is, a course content which teachers and learners agree on.

It should soon be apparent to anyone involved at the centre that the real work takes place here among your affiliates and among organizations like and unlike yours across Australia. (pp. 3-4)

And speaking of the providing of literacy generally he said:

The means of providing literacy has provided a fertile ground for division and ideological strutting. I understand factional intensity— the divisions within the literacy movement astonish even an old warrior. There is no such subject as literacy. You cannot impose a curriculum from the centre or prescribe the course contents or measured stages for satisfactory progress. Your clientele is not definable, many are not aware of their own needs. The teachers have often qualified themselves by means of their own performances. (p. 4)

I have quoted him at some length because his paper seems to epitomize the entirely problematic relationship between practices of governmental surveillance and the practices that surveillance is designed to normalize and homogenize. Literacy as a governmental technology for controlling and organizing populations, even as a technology for achieving equality, certainly as a device for avoiding wastage of talent, and all in the interests of democracy—all these things are part of the rhetoric of this paper:

John Dawkins was not inclined to overlook the potential of the nation with hundreds of thousands of persons who were unable to take their place in the mainstream of society. . . . Literacy was the perfect issue for action in the later stages of his Ministry. . . . With personal empowering, they would be able to act more sensibly as consumers—especially as consumers of information. Australian democracy was the beneficiary. (p. 2)

And yet the paper is quite clear about the voices that contest the government agendas, about the difference between the rhetoric of the centre and the places where the real work is done, and about the factional intensity in the Australian context of arguments about just what literacy, let alone critical literacy might be. The paper is also indicative of a political environment that, unlike many others in Western countries, has continued to demand that educators, administrators, and researchers address equity issues across the curriculum, and that thus allows and indeed fosters the kind of factional intensity of which it speaks. The paper is even conscious of the way theory (the White Paper) circulates in embodied, lived forms (among people who do not know the text) and in ways that are unpredictable and uncontrollable.

What it does not mention specifically is the way factional theoretical interests intersect in the making of the curriculum that teachers have to implement, a process which, in the absence of inservice courses to explain it, and in the presence of constant cultural and social change, gives rise to equally unpredictable and uncontrollable practices. Classroom practice then often produces, rather than is produced by, curriculum and critical theory. Secondary teaching practices may also motivate changes at tertiary level, in theory and practice, as the products of the secondary classroom walk into university classrooms and assert their needs and differences (see Steedman, 1992a for an account of the impact of classroom practice on the development of cultural studies in Britain).

There are particular interests in all of this for critical theory, postmodernist accounts of teaching, and feminist theory as well as for those who believe themselves to be "beyond poststructuralism" or involved in "cultural studies English." It is I think crucial to consider the gender issues (not that race and class and ethnicity are not also involved) in all that I am here exploring. The secondary and adult learning English teaching profession is a feminized profession. This is something that Cavalier also does not mention. At the tertiary level there are still more senior men than women. In fact in many English departments until very recently the dominance of male academics stood in stark contrast to the increasing numbers of gifted and successful women students. All kinds of anecdotal and research evidence suggest that women continue to provide, in both these contexts, those time-consuming aspects of pastoral care identified by Hunter (1988) as symptomatic of the profession, in many cases at some cost to their professional advancement. Women in the profession have often been responsible in this nurturing capacity for the liberalizing of pedagogy and a broadening of the curriculum (Kean, 1990; Littlewood, 1989) and have often come in for considerable criticism because of it:

> A history of the last one hundred years or so reveals a recurring pattern of utopian ambitions amongst mainly women teachers for their working-class pupils, alternating with periods like the one we are living through, when a barrage of criticism is addressed at what are seen as the soft centres of education. "Basics" and a "stiffening" of standards will be opposed to a presumed laxness. Frugality will replace prodigality. "Pleasure" becomes a word which has no place in education, and all that is "hard," "difficult," "demanding" will be set against the "informal," the "progressive" and the "popular." Above all learning for its own sake will be disparaged in the name of both vocationalism and value for money. (Miller, 1992, p. 5)

In the obviously gendered nature of these oppositional terms and agendas, it is not hard to recognize the basis for the differential funding of the humanities and the sciences (see Brook, 1994) that is characteristic of most Western countries at the present time and that makes teaching in such undervalued and feminized places an even more difficult profession.

It is interesting to compare Hunter's view of the English teacher as engaged in the ethical care and production of subjects as instrument of a governmental technology with Lovell's (1987) feminist view that as a feminized profession teachers of English have always been entrusted with the transmission, not the making of the culture and its meanings. Neither of these positions seems entirely consistent with the feminist voices in pedagogy that have always and again of late, as a paradigm case for a whole range of socially and culturally oppressed others, insisted on new places from which to speak and write, have articulated the systematic structures that have silenced and contained them as the "bearers not the makers of meanings," and have with originality and enthusiasm initiated, not followed, educational reform and change (Miller, 1992, p. 8). Given the history of the education of women and girls and the role it has played in the development of public and private forms of education here and overseas (Miller, 1992), these feminist voices have a great deal invested in insisting on their right to make meanings differently for themselves and for their students.

Part of the impetus for this work more recently has come from poststructuralist theory, from understandings of language, textuality, and semiosis, of the relations between gender and genre, of the networks that are institutions, texts, sexualities, and power, and of the possibilities of rewriting and remaking that emerge from those discoveries. Much of it, however, has come from simply being there in classrooms, needing to do the job, and, something that is often less considered and researched, wanting to do the job. Recent media attacks on theory, and indeed they have a long history ("Students Victims" 1991, Miller, 1992), generally construct the teacher, often in the form of the English department student, as being beset by a kind of theory that is not only turgid, incomprehensible, and elitist but absolutely useless in the classroom where what are demanded are absolutely foolproof practical tactics for survival and the hardness of standards. It seems that such teachers need have no politics of their own, no ideas of their own, and require a purely instrumental approach to the children that they teach. In these attacks on teachers, the fact that teachers might actually be doing the job because they are interested in the historical and theoretical issues involved in teaching, that their choice to work within an impoverished state system has to do with the fact that they believe in children's intelligence and in the possibilities of making a better world for all of us by working with that intelligence, utopian if you like, is rarely considered.

In the conclusion to her essay "Prisonhouses," Steedman (1992b) explored the location of her own experience as a primary school teacher within a history that cast her always as "that impossible figure, the watchful mother of other people's children, but never as the intellectual worker her occupation and her responsibilities inevitably made her" (Miller, 1992, p. 24):

> I don't care any more about sounding pretentious, so now I tell people who ask at parties why I did it for such a very long time, that it did seem a way of being a socialist in everyday life. I believed immensely in their intelligence, thought I could give them peace and quiet, a space of rest from the impossible lives that many of them had to lead. I read everything there was to read, later was to make myself a minor expert in children's writing. No-one cared—indeed no-one knew—what social and political theories informed my classroom practice: all I looked like was a very good teacher, doing all the things that textbooks said were right. (Steedman, 1992b, p. 60)

It is the work that goes on in the local sites of classrooms, teacher organizations, conferences, and staffrooms, but it is also the gendered nature of that work, that explains why government instrumentalities of surveillance and control can never actually contain it. What no one knows or cares about can hardly be on a governmental agenda. Perhaps governmentality would work better if it were. I say this deliberately to counter Hunter's (1994b) arguments that critical intellectuals and radical pedagogy will never achieve their goals because they do not understand that they are irrelevant to governmentality. That there are two radically different forms of ethical and personal comportment here—two radically different forms of rationality is too tidy a way of expressing it, because they are not only incompatible but actually oppositional—is clearly something with which one has to agree. Fairclough (1993) wrote powerfully of the differences and of the need for academic discourse to recognize and understand the consequences of what he called *the marketization of public discourse*, the impact of bureaucratic rationality in its discursive forms on the academy and public life in general. A. Luke (1990a); Kamler, Maclean, Reid, and Simpson (1993); and Threadgold (1993) looked at the intersections between the kind of teaching practice described by Steedman and the way the system works to discipline, control, and gender the habitus of the classroom and indeed of public and private lives.

In the face of these kinds of conflicting and competing arguments, it seems essential that we begin to understand that these oppositional rationalities are in no sense autonomous (Hunter, 1994b). Despite their mutual incommensurabilities, they constantly colonize and recolonize one another. They cannot fail to do this when they are actually lived, performed, and enacted as common sense on a daily basis by men and women, girls and boys, who constantly and regularly juggle the conflicting demands of an English curriculum that attempts to fuse the archaic and the modern, nostalgia and technology, community and entrepreneurialism, and is capable of recommending in the same breath the retention of basic skills and the ever essential Shakespeare (Miller, 1992; Sinfield, 1985). In this very complex situation it could be argued that governmentality needs to understand that its goals, indeed its technologies of control, are always part of this heteroglossia, that indeed the heteroglossia always results from deliberate or accidental attempts to subvert the system in one direction or another (Pratt, 1987; Threadgold, 1994) and that this is not something that the technologies of government have ever been able to control. This is why it will not do to argue that English teaching is about accepting that we have always been agents of the bureaucracy and therefore should now confine ourselves (Hunter, 1994a, 1994b) to the "reproduction of the public service" (Brook, 1994). That agency has always been a contested field, a field in which the opposition have always been a largely feminized profession, and where from time to time "a strange nostalgia for school-days when boys were boys and teachers were men regularly erupts" (Miller, 1992, p. 1). To suggest that a return to the rhetoric of the 19th-century grammar school as a way of increasing vocational generic competence and overcoming the narrowness of a literary education is the answer (Hunter 1994a, 1994b) is first to ignore the variety and richness of the forms of reading and writing practiced and taught in current versions of "cultural studies English" (the English syllabus in Victoria is just one Australian example) and second to participate again in that attack on theory that characterizes Hunter's recent work but has been endemic in English with respect to recent critical literacy debates.

Godzich (1994), writing in an entirely different U.S. context, discussed the way the opposition theory/literacy has come to be associated with the opposition elite/masses, so that in the rationalization of the academy that is designed to produce more marketable knowledges (cf. Fairclough, 1993), the "new vocationalism," realized in the form of new writing programs, associated with "basics" and "core" curriculum, comes to be another form of instrumentalization (Godzich, 1994, pp. 4-5). Godzich argued that this produces students with a very restricted literacy, with competence in a specific code, and the ability to write in a field, but no sense of the complexities involved in the contact between codes and languages or the unequal distribution of linguistic capital in societies. In the course of this process not only has the attack perceived to have been made by the new vocationalism against the humanistic values of English departments worked but "any pretense of addressing the needs of so-called disadvantaged school populations has quietly evaporatea" (p. 5). In all of this:

> The mapping of the distinction between the two tendencies, theory and literacy, was never made explicit as such, but it determined the mutual perceptions of both movements. Theory was a speculative, effete pursuit; literacy a crassly utilitarian one. One thing was clear: they could have nothing to do with each other, and *that*, in retrospect, *may very well have been the object of the exercise*. . . . Before universities are further "rationalised" and made into more "efficient" loci of cultural reproduction and of the production of marketable knowledge, the links between the debates on literacy and those on theory must be re-examined. (Godzich, 1994, pp. 2-3)

In his attempt to re-examine this issue, Godzich suggested that the new literacy actually participates in the realization of Hegel's conception of the historical process, a process whereby persons "ignorant of Hegel's grand design," contrive to produce a situation where:

> The final moment is marked by the advent of Absolute Knowledge, in which the intermediate figure of the state withers away to be replaced by self-regulating and autonomous institutions of knowledge that no longer need to communicate with each other, for they all partake of the spirit and do nothing more than manage its day to day investment in the world. . . . There are no longer any discoveries to be made, and neither the nature nor the direction of the historical process is worthy of speculation, for both have become manifest. (Godzich, 1994, pp. 13-14)

The Hegelian overtones in Hunter's recent work are hard to miss in this context, and they connect of course with the very modernist Weberian and Habermasian arguments about separate spheres of rationality and consensus-based communications that surface explicitly only rarely in Hunter's (1994b) work. The links between this and a "linguistics of appropriateness" are tenuous, but they are there and already have been subjected to strenuous critique (Fairclough, 1992; Pratt, 1987). They perhaps explain Hunter's predilection for Hallidayan sociolinguistics as a rediscovery of the rhetoric that was: "the traditional source of prestigious and powerful linguistic abilities in middle-class 'grammar' schools, but now surfacing in the state system in a revamped and theorised form" (Hunter, 1994a, p. 12). They may also explain his distrust of theory and humanist English teaching (which he frequently seems to conflate). Both have always been oppositional to the values implicit in that organisation of society and of bureaucratic structures, participation in which he sees as tantamount to educational success: "the occupancy of a range of civic and occupational capacities beyond the school" (Hunter, 1994a, p. 12). It is salutary here to return to the question of gender. Speaking of the continuation of the "grammar" school in the form of "private school" education, Miller (1992) said:

> Parents who pay for their sons' education may be paying for an absence of women, amongst other things. To an extent which is quite inadequately recognised, state education is provided by women; as is virtually all schooling, public or private, for young children. . . . A strange nostalgia for days when boys were boys and teachers were men regularly erupts. Fear of women's influence as teachers and of girls' academic success at school is by no means a new fear, and its contemporary manifestations are unprecedented only in so far as they are disguised by the apparent even-handedness of current educational discourse on the subject. "He and she," like so much "equal opportunities" rhetoric, can operate to deny specific and telling gender differences in teaching, curriculum, management and academic outcomes and in the debates and documents accounting for them. (p. 1)

There is clearly no direct link between the patriarchal nature of the grammar school then and now and the use of a technology of education deriving from it for an apparently "unimpassioned" (Hunter, 1994a, p. 16) intervention into the critical literacy debate, but as we research these issues we would do well to heed Miller's warnings of the ubiquitous implications of gender in our engagements and to be mindful of Godzich's story of the dangers of seeing theory and the "new writing," or in Australia the genre pedagogy, as binary and unrelated opposites. It may be crucial that the latter be theorised if it is to avoid the results Godzich reported (Threadgold, 1992). It is interesting that in his most recent writing on the subject Hunter (1994a) appears to be moving in this direction.

Certainly the situation in Australia at the present time suggests that that is largely the direction that curriculum is taking. *Teaching English Literacy* (Christie et al., 1991), commissioned by the federal government, was a typically heteroglossic document, speaking the many agendas of those who collaborated to produce it. These included critical theory and systemic-functional linguistics as well as social theory and radical pedagogy and the consequence of this has been, where it has had any influence, to keep all of those agendas in play and to rewrite in often unpredictable ways the various theories involved. For example, a critical discourse analysis that emerges from the mutual recontextualization of systemic linguistics, poststructuralist, feminist, and critical theory is not the same as genre pedagogy (see Lee, chap. 22, this volume; Lee, 1993; Poynton, 1993). This activity has not always gone on however at the level of academic theorizing about what critical literacies should look like. It has frequently been part and parcel of the actual business of making and implementing curriculum and there have been varying emphases in different states with associated differences in the provision of teacher education and inservice programs to support these initiatives. In Victoria, a secondary English curriculum motivated largely by the desire to equalize opportunities by providing critical literacy of a kind dissociated from the teaching of the literary canon—and thus inevitably informed by poststructuralist theory and the semiotics and other theoretical moves that founded cultural studies (Grossberg, Nelson, & Treichler, 1992; Steedman, 1992a)—has only very recently been overtaken by the imperative to incorporate the teaching of systemic-functional linguistics. This is an interesting case study in resistance and rewriting. I quote myself here in a recent paper where I was speaking of the explosion of interest in systemic-functional linguistics that another scholar had seen to have overtaken curriculum development in Australia:

> I was reminded of these comments (and indeed of the somewhat similar politics and dynamics of the writing of what has become known as the Christie Report in which I was also involved) when I was asked by VATE/AATE to participate last week in two full-day in-service seminars on the new Curriculum Standards Framework for the teaching of English, which is again writing systemic functional [hereafter, SF] grammar into the curriculum, the English curriculum this time. The politics was again similar—university "experts," with a somewhat ambiguous relationship to the grammatical theory being propounded, all of them known for their resistance to some aspects of the SF or genre approach, and all being co-opted to explain the new theory being imposed by curriculum writers on teachers and teaching practice in the classroom. That practice in this case is constituted through and by the VCE English curriculum which was constructed in relation to a whole set of different and in many ways contradictory theoretical positions—poststructuralism, deconstruction, feminism and so on—many of these actively inimical to the discipline of linguistics—and many of these foundational critical positions only now becoming clear to the teachers who are implementing them (with skill, resourcefulness and energy) via a curriculum (in which the theories are not overtly acknowledged) in classrooms. The situation is complicated by the tendency of certain very conservative influences, some of these with the ear of the Minister, to co-opt the linguistics in the service of a return to the teaching of "grammar" (for which read traditional grammar to which SF has always been oppositional). In this extraordinarily postmodernist context (or was it always thus) . . . the positions I discussed at the outset of this paper come back into focus. Teachers need to be doing action research in their own classrooms to establish collaboratively with other teachers what they are doing that is useful and to publish it, but they also need to do some

linguistics, some recent critical theory, some social theory—you name it—to make the ventriloquism and the heteroglossia of the situation in which they are positioned accessible, available to them. Otherwise the many uses in local sites, the local sociologies which Luke imagines will emerge and be made possible from his intervention at curriculum level, may well emerge, but may emerge in ways that have little relationship to the 'ideological' engineering, the agendas for enfranchisement and social change, which his work attempts to further. Ventriloquism, learning to mimic the discourses of the master, is, like competency scales, and as feminists and Kooris have always known, a double-edged sword, one that can colonize as well as enfranchise, and one that requires a very considerable level of critical literacy to practice (or in the case of competency scales to teach) with any degree of success. (Threadgold, 1994, p. 14)

Thus, as Cavalier recognized in his comments, the rewriting and the remaking goes on, among students (if pedagogy does not stamp it out, normalize it, refuse to hear it), among teachers who learn the theory as it circulates in books, as common sense, in the media, in university and inservice courses, and as students learn it from teachers. The system is never as monolithic or as hegemonic as certain kinds of theory would have us believe, and sexed social subjects are not the passive constructs or the reifications constructed by objectivist theory. As any parent or classroom teacher will know, all of us are perfectly capable of both critique and resistance from a very early age. de Certeau (1984/1988) reminding us of the relativity of all theories, presented the other side of Foucault's panoptic and disciplinary society, by theorizing these myriad resistances as being like the "pedestrian movements" that, untraced on any map (the system that represents the city), are the real system that makes up the city:

one can analyze the microbe-like, singular and plural practices which an urbanistic system was supposed to administer or suppress, but which have outlived its decay, one can follow the swarming activity of these procedures that, far from being eliminated by panoptic administration, have reinforced themselves in a proliferating illegitimacy, developed and insinuated themselves into the networks of surveillance, and combined in accordance with unreadable but stable tactics to the point of constituting everyday regulations and surreptitious creativities that are merely concealed by the frantic mechanisms and discourses of the observational organization. (p. 96)

My point here is that in current educational practice, theory of all, or any kind, among practitioners, is often left to circulate in this way, as social practice, like noise in the system, destabilizing it, producing unpredictable, unauthorized, and untheorized results. It is left to circulate and be taken up in ways that "no-one knows or cares about" to return to Steedman's (1992a) story. The feminized teaching profession is constructed as one that does not need theory, and perhaps even more outrageously as not having any theory. As Steedman (1992a) pointed out elsewhere cultural studies in Britain was shaped as much by teachers as by theory, informed by "their particular educational histories and their purchase on different forms of historical knowledge" (pp. 617, 619). But she pointed to the flip side of this coin, the fact that the new text-based form of knowledge was accompanied by an inadequate model of language to deal with the new textual approaches, a remarkable absence of history, and a marked tendency for governments to reorganize education in critical literacies around cheapness and practicality and accessible texts. Thus she sees the establishment of English literature as the basis for literacy education in the period 1880 to 1920, as well as Practical Criticism (The New Criticism in the United States) after 1930, and present-day cultural studies, as motivated by the need to provide education on the cheap. Teaching history or critical linguistics, or critical theory, she argued, is much more expensive. Thus, although everyone, from the policymakers to the teachers to the students in the classrooms, is immersed in theory, positioned and constructed by it, they have different, partial, competing, and more or less explicit awarenesses and understandings of that positioning. Everyone enacts theory, performs it, embodies it, debates it, contests it, as social practice, on a daily basis in the ways in which they read and write, speak and listen, see and look, behave and live. Few, however, are helped to have any explicit knowledge or understanding of what it is that they are doing:

> Practical sense, social necessity turned into nature, converted into motor schemes and body automatisms, is what causes practices, in and through what makes them obscure to the eyes of their producers, to be sensible, that is, informed by a common sense. It is because agents never know completely what they are doing that what they do has more sense than they know. (Bourdieu, 1990, p. 69)

It is my contention that it is not enough for teachers in the present situation to never know completely what they are doing, at least with respect to theory. Somehow one needs a map, something that will make the system legible, but that will do so in a way that will not cause "a way of being in the world to be forgotten" (de Certeau, 1984/1988, p. 97).

Feminist work that theorizes from a sexed and embodied position, which tries to understand how panoptic systems control what it is to "be" as woman in a patriarchal order, and that at the same time tries to capitalize on the noise in the system, the resistances that are already there, is one way of doing this. Poststructuralist and postmodernist teaching strategies that include postcolonialism and a concern with difference in all of its forms are another. One of the reasons that language about language and semiosis is so necessary is that one needs to be able to talk about theories, like other texts, to see how they are made, in whose interests, and to consider the consequences of taking them seriously.

At the end of this first section of this chapter, I suggest that a knowledge of critical theory—including structuralism, poststructuralism, deconstruction, and feminist theories but also social theory and critical discourse analysis—has to be a part of what we are calling critical literacy for teachers of English. For the learners of English, in all their variety and heterogeneity, the lived embodiment of that kind of critical practice as *habitus* ("practical sense, social necessity turned into nature" or we might say theoretical sense turned into nature) has always to be the beginnings of critical literacy. That kind of practice is never necessarily separate from critique. It is also a kind of practice that, as Steedman indicated so poignantly in the quotation presented earlier, we need to learn to understand.

That is why if teachers need to know much more about theory, theorists need to know much more about the theory that already informs teaching. Here I return to the comment made at the outset of this section that there is a serious mismatch between secondary and tertiary understandings and teaching practices where English is concerned. Action research and attempts to understand how it is that knowledges come to be embodied and lived have to be on the critical literacy agenda for all of us (Kamler et al., 1993; Lee, 1993; A. Luke, 1990a). It is also not much use knowing that our policies and political, theoretical, and personal agendas are constantly subverted if we do not make some effort to understand how and why. Of course the habitus I am talking about here is not the habitus of the panopticon—but that in itself is a somewhat paradoxical thing to assert. What is the difference between a subject disciplined in one mode rather than another, or for one reason rather than another (e.g., governmental or ethical)? What kinds of critical literacies might be involved in their production?

Here I return to an interrogation of the implications of the quotations with which I began and which this first section of this chapter now contextualizes. How does an "emancipatory educator" who sees that people are illiterate because they are poor and not poor because they are illiterate (among other things) speak when her clientele are convinced by the argument that they are poor because they are illiterate, and when theory tells her that the author is dead and that her emancipatory aims are in any case irrelevant to the role she plays as part of a government technology to reproduce the social status quo. Who is she when her role as critical intellectual is also constantly being subverted or mediated by her new role as bureaucrat in the new university or school?

THE THEORIST, THE FEMINIST, AND THE NEED FOR THEORY

It is indeed odd that just as feminist and poststructuralist/postmodernist pedagogy—for which here read one form of emancipatory pedagogy if you will—begins to have some effect, we should be told that we are wasting our time or merely replicating what English has always done (in its politically more dubious forms). That, it seems to me is what Hunter's (1994a) most recent book, *Re-Thinking the School*, is saying. This is even more relevant in this context because Hunter also took a somewhat ambiguous position among the "factional divisions" that have characterized recent literacy debates in Australia. Seeking an alternative to the aesthetic mode of literary pastoral care, an ethics of self-formation that he sees as constitutive of and complicit with the technology of governmental control of populations, he found it in what he sees as the modern descendant of the grammar school and a rhetorical pedagogy, systemic-functional linguistics (see also Hunter, chap. 18, this volume). For Hunter (1988) this discovery has the considerable implication of removing knowledge of literature from the domain of sensibility formation altogether, and reconnecting the study of English with the positive sciences of philology and rhetoric as well as reconnecting it to the needs of the workforce. He viewed literary theory as connected to the human sciences and potentially offering a way of freeing English from its "supervisory deployment," but this is only possible if theory can be disconnected from aesthetics and criticism, something which in 1988 Hunter seemed to contemplate, but which by 1994 seemed no longer to be on his agenda. Given Hunter's considerable position as a theorist and the debates that have gone on around systemic-functional pedagogy and critical literary theory in the Australian context, his work has to be central to debates about the constitution of critical literacies (see Patterson, chap. 19, this volume).

There are two things to note here. First his position seems to replicate a much earlier language–literature binarism in the history of English that seems to me to be unfortunate. Second, it is also associated with his extolling of the separation of public and private spheres in the 1994a book. Hunter described:

> Hobbes's still unsurpassed achievement . . . to have understood and faced up to what was in fact a major historical change in the political

and moral organisation of European politics. He understood that its capacity to put an end to religious civil war had allowed the state's pursuit of its own security and prosperity to float free of "higher" religious and philosophical justification. (p. 41)

This is hardly compatible with either Pateman's (1988) or Gatens' (1991) feminist reading of Hobbes's accomplishment:

> The artificial man (Leviathan, the body politic), a creation of "the word" of men united, thus renders itself free from the necessary but difficult dealings with both women and nature. This masculine image of unity and independence from women and nature has strong resonances in psychoanalytic accounts of infantile anxieties and the fantasies created to cope with them. The image of artificial man, the body politic, perfectly mirrors the infantile wish for independence from the maternal body. . . . The modern body politic has "lived off" its consumption of women's bodies. Women have serviced the internal organs and needs of this artificial body, preserving its viability, its unity and integrity, without ever being seen to do so. (Gatens, 1991, pp. 80-81)

Hunter's intervention in these debates in Australia then has to be problematic, especially when systemic-functional linguistics and genre theory were already coming under considerable attack from feminists and critical literacy theorists for upholding the status quo and ignoring the kinds of contextual, historical, and social issues being raised by critical theory (Lee, 1993; Poynton, 1993; Threadgold, 1992, 1994). Despite the apparently Marxist and left politics of the genre school, for example, they have assumed that to become part of the existing bureaucratic arrangements or disciplinary organisation of knowledges would be empowering. From this came the dubious argument that students need to know the "powerful genres" recently critiqued by A. Luke (1995a).

Hunter's (1994b) Foucauldian position equates liberal philosophy with Marxist educational sociology as sharing the same understanding of equality, based on the goal of self-reflective, self-realizing personhood. In declaring then that governmentality has nothing to do with "full personal development" (p. 101), that what matters is "self-discipline and cleanliness, literacy and godliness," and that "those who see the bureau as an alienation of human faculties have missed the point. It was a decisive augmentation of them," his arguments both complement and conflict with those of the linguists. When he asks whether "optimal social training (the ethic of the bureau)" can produce equality, his response, that equality "can be a by-product of a uniform system of ethical cultivation and social training" (p. 107) is not dissimilar to the genrist arguments, but his assertion that equality is a government objective in the interests of government and that the comprehensive school system is used to train people for the occupational hierarchy run somewhat in the face of the arguments of empowerment that are typical of genre school rhetoric.

Nevertheless his whole redefinition of equality in governmental terms as a concern to avoid "wastage," an object of concern made, produced, by technologies of government such as statistical surveys, while following his Foucauldian agenda, is much more thoughtful and thought-provoking than the genrecists somewhat (un)critical politics. For him, governmentality actually produces the (apparently Marxist) understanding that schools merely function to reproduce unequal cultural capital. It does this by providing the technologies to produce new social cartographies allowing the mapping and "problematising of unequal trajectories" (p. 111). Comparing liberal and Marxist accounts of "ability," opposing arguments that the equalization of opportunity be based on natural talent to those that say this perpetuates inequality because "natural talent" is in any case socially constructed, Hunter argued that both positions ignore the actual historical ground on which the argument is taking place. It is not he says a "moral question" but a question of statistical measurement and administrative management in the interests of government. Thus intelligence testing that demonstrated beyond a doubt that "'intelligence' is inescapably milieu-specific," indeed a name for "milieu-specific conducts and capacities" (p. 117) became, along with the statistical survey, a tool for "government to problematise its own institutions" (p. 119).

Clearly, he said, "intelligence" had then to be detached from educational and social success, and if the problem was the different milieu in which abilities were being formed then clearly government needed to intervene in the family to reconstruct it as institution. Administrative intellectuals, Hunter declared, thus proposed far more interventionist policies than their radical critics. It had become possible to "governmentalise ability" (p. 120), government could "form and distribute ability for its own ends" (p. 121), and thus "the proposal emerged to equalise the outcomes of education by reconstituting the family as an annex of the school" (p. 120).

Hunter's explorations of why this did not work, why the reconstruction of the family as habitus for scholastic ability was a failure, again denies both liberal and Marxist explanations. It was neither, he argued, that the principle of educational equality met the immovable obstacle of parents' right to bring up their children without state interference, nor was it that government sought to maintain class inequalities by allowing parents discretion and thus thwarting the egalitarian move for comprehensive schooling. It was, he said, by now predictably, a modified form of governmentality, and the only way to understand state–family relations in this context "is by situating it within the organisational contingencies of 'pastoral' government" (p. 123). In a very interesting account of the historically symbiotic and improvisational relationship of school and family, he argued that from the outset, because of the hybrid "bureaucratic-pastoral" character of the organisation of schooling, the school system could "transform the family only by embodying the latter's ideal form" (p. 125). And that form, its social and ethical organization, "imposed ethical and technical limits on what could be done with it" (p. 126). Here, I quote Hunter in full:

> Thus far we have argued—against its humanist reduction—that the so-called "social democratic" goal of educational equality was a by-product of the ethically autonomous domain of bureaucratic social governance. It is no detraction from this argument to now insist that, in the family, the educational bureau met an equally autonomous social and ethical domain. . . .
>
> The best that could be hoped for was some kind of technical and ethical trade-off between the bureau's pursuit of the interests of state schooling through the family, and the family's pursuit of its own interests through state schooling. (p. 126)
>
> The cry that we need to temper equality with diversity—which has been gaining ground since the 1970s—is very far from being what it seems. It is neither a moral balancing act between competing principles, nor a sign of the bureaucracy's tardy recognition of the principle of cultural identity and the "politics of difference." In fact it is neither more nor less than a symptom of the latest in a series of historical accommodations between state schooling and the family, reached on the basis of their hybrid, bureaucratic-pastoral, organization. (p. 127)

It is perhaps time to return to the beginning, to Hunter's (1994b) theorization of what the school system is—"simultaneously statist and personal, bureaucratic and pastoral" (p. 63). His aim in part is to demonstrate that the current mode of critiquing bureaucracy as a failed form of the "ethos of self-reflection," of morality or justice or equality conceived in those terms, is utterly misplaced. The school system, he said, is a hybrid of "'two radically autonomous 'technologies of existence'," a government apparatus that sought the social transformation of the citizenry in accordance with the objectives of the state; and a system of pastoral discipline that operated by inculcating the means of ethical self-reflection and self-cultivation. Both, however, are essentially disciplinary technologies within the school system. The pastoral intellectual brought to the school system "not the principle of self-reflection, but the disciplines responsible for forming self-reflection" (p. 90). This is why Hunter can argue that "The demand that government in general and the school system in particular obey the absolute principles of self-realising personhood thus has no place within the ethical and civic horizons of the governmental sphere" (p. 89).

Who is it then who is demanding that government be something other than its bureaucratic self, who is it who wants to insist on the importance of self-realizing personhood? It is indeed the "pastoral intelligentsia" who certainly seem to have exceeded their function if they are meant to be merely the instruments of governmentality and who are never really clearly identified in Hunter's recent writing. One hesitates to think that this may be because most of them are among his best friends, for he, like the rest of us is undoubtedly obliged to obey the demands that the modern school system makes on all who inhabit it "to act within the limits of their professional personae and to respect the fragility as well as the power of these institutional arrangements that give the system its unprincipled coherence" (p. 91). Be this as it may, there are some clues. The critical intellectual described by Weber as "oriented to the rejection of the world" (cited in Hunter, 1994b, p. 66) and emerging in the early modern period in opposition to the incommensurable sphere of radically mundane politics, the Marxist and liberal intellectuals who just keep on getting it wrong, the contemporary teacher and radical pedagogue (tertiary and secondary) informed by critical theory and unaware that the system "we have improvised is a remarkable variant of the milieu of Christian pastoral guidance" (p. 86), the "self-reflective virtuosos required by the pastoral form of modern pedagogy" who should be able to understand that their principles of self-reflection and self-determination may be valuable civic virtues but cannot possibly be the foundations for a school system—these are among some of the characters who play ephemeral roles in Hunter's story.

His agenda seems to be the total discrediting of all forms of emancipatory pedagogy. Let me quote him again:

> In the school system, therefore, we confront a machine for living whose hybrid formation means that it can neither be understood nor reformed as the expression of a coherent set of ethical or political principles. (p. 90)

> Seen in this light the demand that the whole system be made transparent to the principles of self-reflection and self-determination is not just a failure of historical understanding; it represents incompetence at the level of one's professional self-composure, and a culpable disregard for the plurality of ethical domains that compose the system. In fact, in seeking to subordinate this plurality of domains and comportments to what is in fact the status ethos of the pastoral intelligentsia, this demand is symptomatic of the latter's tendency to intellectual fundamentalism. (p. 91)

It is perhaps significant that this form of the argument comes just after Hunter explored the only actual example of teaching practice that enters the book. He wrote scathingly of an "exercise in radical pedagogy based on popular culture." The account is radically decontextualized but is used to demonstrate that the techniques of radical pedagogy and cultural studies (neither of these explored in their complexity) are the same as those of pastoral forms of pedagogy—a practice of conscience-formation involving unreserved communication between teacher and learner, mentorship, self-expression, and self-doubt.

It is a feminist reading of a teacher's reading of a popular cultural icon that provokes this response and the added accusation that those who read the teacher do not know what they are doing, do not realize that their pedagogy is "no more based on the free choices of the self-reflective subject than are the pedagogical relationships characteristic of Buddhist or Hindu 'psychagogy' " (p. 86). What they do not know, it turns out, is that they are the purveyors of a disciplinary form of surveillance of conscience which is implemented "within specially culturally elaborated environments and interpersonal relationships" (viz., the school).

What is puzzling is that Hunter should be so affronted by this discovery. It is after all what he told us the pastoral intellectual was there for. But there are more confusions than this in this account. How does it happen, one wonders, that the whole of radical pedagogy and cultural studies is reduced in the first place to "self-reflection," what amounts in Hunter's account to a pernicious form of navel-gazing. There is a curious lack of historical understanding in Hunter's conflation of literary modes of self-reflection, critical and aesthetic practices of the self, with the differently derived and theorized practices of radical pedagogy and cultural studies. There may indeed be intersections between these areas, and Hunter has been at pains to demonstrate them, but they are not reducible to the same. It seems particularly important to emphasize this when theorists like Hunter begin to contribute to a significant self-questioning among feminist scholars and teachers. Brook (1994), whom I quoted at the beginning of this chapter, is one example, but so are Mellor and Patterson (1994), who in the volume entitled "Beyond Poststructuralism" (1994) begin to demonstrate the truth of Hunter's sameness arguments almost as a self-fulfilling prophesy.

They question their own earlier position on the difference between what they call "Heritage Model" English (to appreciate literature), "Growth Model" English (to empathize with characters, learn about life), and "Cultural Studies" English. The latter they understand as operating around poststructuralist understandings of texts and readers, recognizing the possibility of different reading positions and assuming the need to make these available to students. What they come to question in this paper is actually their function as teachers, the fact that the "technology" of the classroom lesson is in each case designed to make the students think that what they have produced is their own reading when clearly the teacher and the practice of teaching have actually made it possible for/or imposed on the student the imperative to read in whatever way she finally does. If this is what the classrooms can be seen to be doing, then "theory," poststructuralist feminist theory to be specific, has just turned out to be more of the same and must acknowledge itself as having nothing to do with the development of the self, but much to do with forming and encouraging, if not insisting on, certain kinds of readings and readers. The "insisting on" I come back to, but I know no form of poststructuralist reading regime that, *if properly theorized*, would ever confuse these aims. The research that makes these women question their own directions involves looking at reading lessons across the commonly accepted "models" of English and recognizing a set of similarities in all the classrooms that they investigate. I suggest that it is Hunter's conflation of these agendas in his own theoretical work, which they are using, that projects these concerns, and their anxieties about their teaching practice, in this form, into their research. One can, I think, recognize this influence in the way they are then constrained to tell the story of the reading regimes they find in each of the classrooms:

- The imperative (laid upon readers) of "systematically misunderstanding" the text.
- The imperative (laid upon students) of "problematizing" or questioning their readings.
- The imperative (laid upon teachers) to "teach and yet not teach."
- The imperative (laid upon both teachers and students) of "freedom." (Hunter, 1994b, p. 25)

It seems to me that there are a number of possible readings of the situations that must have prompted these imperatives. I am actually forced to construct my stories from assumptions about what else the imperatives might or could mean.

Hunter himself spoke of the "rarity" or scarcity of pedagogical and administrative resources that enabled the unprincipled assemblage of bureaucracy and pastoral surveillance from which the school system was improvised and that explain the similarity of educational initiatives in Ireland in the 1830s and in Australia in the 1850s. The same arguments can be used here. If you are going to have a "reading lesson" there are only certain ways in which you can go about it, whatever your political or theoretical persuasion. You have to begin somewhere, often with a group of students who have not read the text, or who have read it hastily for the purposes of this class. Actually, what has usually failed is the imperative laid on readers to read, not the reading itself. Even if they have read there is an assumption that discussion and more detailed attention to the text and its contextualizations may produce new and different possibilities of reading. Why else would you have a reading lesson? The question of "problematizing the text" follows from this. However, I would still see big differences between the kinds of problematizing that might follow from a concern with identifying with characters or understanding plot, and problematizing that might be involved in a deconstructive classroom (Gilbert, 1989) where the concern might be about understanding the discursive make-up of the text and the ways in which it works against itself in some sense, or the kinds of things that are reported here as going on in the author's own feminist classrooms. There are certain basic contextual factors pertaining to the institutionalization of reading as a pedagogy, to the persons (teachers and learners) who participate in that pedagogy and to the conditions under which it is done that should not be forgotten in the excitement of Foucauldian argument. And if Foucault taught us anything, it was to be suspicious of totalizing categories. It is sometimes better to unsettle the familiar in the manner of Borges' *Chinese Encyclopedia* (Foucault, 1966/1973) than to categorize it too readily with nominalizations that occlude whole worlds of difference.

In a democratic classroom it is also it seems to me hard to imagine that you would not both "teach and not teach," that is, that there would not be an exchange of ideas and positions. In an actual classroom, fraught with all the difficulties of difference and likely unemployment, you might very well mostly "not teach." In a classroom informed by poststructuralist theory, however, or any understanding of critical discourse analysis or recent critical theory, including feminisms, I would have thought that "freedom" was precisely a question to be negotiated. Understanding that different reading positions are possible involves understanding more than the particular text to be read. It involves understanding how readings are constrained and produced in the complex networks of the social, cultural, and gendered realities that we live and embody. It involves understanding that the classroom is always part of those networks and that it can never be then "non-normative." Acknowledging plurality and difference is not the same thing as "claims to non-normativity" (Mellor & Patterson, 1994, p. 24). Nor is it the same thing as "freedom." Critical discourse analysis that is often part of cultural studies English would teach just how readership is constrained and produced by textuality, subjectivity, and intertextuality.

And no Foucauldian influenced cultural studies would be able to avoid being specific about the fact that the classroom is a reading regime, precisely a lesson in reading, and a lesson in reading of a very precise kind, with its own rules and practices that are specifically and generically different to those of other regimes of reading belonging to other interpretative communities and disciplines. Hence, the problem of the science text raised by Mellor and Patterson (1994) can also be addressed. One does not and never has read the same way in English and science classrooms although there are also good reasons for exploring and deconstructing that difference (Bazerman, 1988; Threadgold, 1992). The "freedom" of a poststructuralist feminist classroom is again not the same as the "freedom" of the Heritage or Personal Growth models. Words, after all, mean different things in different contexts, something that Cultural Studies English, particularly if informed by theories of language and semiosis, should be self-reflexively discussing in classrooms.

The negative terms of the Hunter critique—"readers have to be *trained or taught* to <u>doubt</u> their initial readings" (Hunter cited in Mellor & Patterson, 1994, p. 26), or "The bottom line though in all models is that the initial reading <u>fails</u> and <u>is in need of work</u>" (Mellor & Patterson 1994, p. 29; italics in original, underlining is mine), contrasts with the positive terms in their attempt to recuperate the models of reading usually critiqued by "cultural studies" as always conceiving of reading as a "struggle to see clearly" and involved with the "development of human capacities" (p. 28). It seems there is a middle ground here. And it is encapsulated in the idea I expressed: that reading lessons might be about developing understandings of the possibilities of texts and readership rather than involving students in self-doubt or in a sense of failure, or in practices that lead them to believe that only teachers know how to read and that their efforts must therefore always fall short of that goal. Indeed, as Mellor and Patterson concluded, the teacher's task is not "to reveal or allow to be produced readings that are distorted, blocked or hidden, but, instead, to alter the use of the text and teach specific ways of reading that produce particular readings" (p. 44). This has, they said, nothing to do with the "expression of inner self or critical consciousness." I would suggest that it has a great deal to do with critical literacy, one of whose aims should surely always be a focus on the contingency and relativity of concepts like *the inner self* and *consciousness*, and some understanding of the social and gendered construction of subjectivity (see Yeatman, chap. 23, this volume).

It is the confusion of these literary and critical theory aims and directions that produces the complexities of this argument and the "self-doubt," the sense that their initial reading might have "failed" and "need more work." It is the same confusion that, for teachers who have learned to live and practice these succeeding models of English without explicit theoretical teaching and training, produces the similarities in the English classrooms they have looked at. Once Mellor and Patterson sort this out they have no further problem with the concept of using texts to produce particular ways of looking and with declaring their position with respect to favored feminist readings. It is interesting, however, that they are still unclear about when to intervene in readings and when not, the matter of "insisting on" readings raised earlier. I am tempted to become even more banal at this point and to declare that "you can lead a horse to water but you can't make it drink." The reality of classrooms is that some students will hear what you are saying and some will not, some will chose to work with what you bring to them and some will not. If, as in the case cited here, a student continues to express ideas about social reality that differ from the teachers then surely the argument about "offering students different positions from which to read" has to allow her that position. Correct her writing by all means if it needs help, discuss your differences of opinion. But you cannot change the habitus by force, or the world in one lesson. The reality is that she does have a choice, and will very likely exercise it, even if the means for that choice come from another reading or living regime in another place. Again there are theories of subjectivity, habitus and embodiment that could help to deal with these questions. It seems to me that the postructuralist feminist classroom, the postmodernist classroom (Brook, 1994), the cultural studies English classroom, are all places that are not just about producing subjects who can make feminist or antiracist readings, not just about producing subjects who can critique earlier forms of reading regime, but actually about producing subjects who know the differences and the implications, the functions and consequences of doing one or many of these things, and who have a range of strategies for doing it with. This does produce subjects with choices that are additional to those with which they began that may or may not be the same thing as freedom.

What Mellor and Patterson have still not resolved at the end of the paper is whether they have taken up the position of instrumental government agent or radical feminist educator and whether there is a difference. This is made particularly problematic in the context of Hunter's (1994b) work because he argued that "equity for girls" as government policy in Australia is "another instance of the state caring for its citizens as a means of looking after itself," underutilized feminine potential being wasteful and costly to the state (p. 62).

Despite the apparent complicity in their conclusion with Hunter's (1994a) bureaucratic and instrumentalist story that declares that his ill-defined notion of the ethical role is "too big for English," I believe that they have actually taken up a position that is not the same as his. They have a very clear commitment to a form of teaching designed to change the habitus of the reading classroom, a belief that in changing the daily lived behaviors of students, the texts they read, the stories they write, the practices in and through which belief is embodied as habitus, they will change the social order and the practices that produce lived gender and racial and class inequality. This they call "constructing the reader as a social agent with particular capacities" (pp. 44-45). It may look very like Hunter's account of governmentality intervening to remake the family as environment for optimum learning, and there are similarities, but I would suggest that this particular kind of feminine and feminist pastoral care intellectual operating within the feminized profession of English becomes a very unruly element in Hunter's account of governmentality.

In fact there are no women or children at all in Hunter's stories, a remarkable fact given the feminization of the English profession and the consequent role of women educators in the reshaping and making of childhood, gendered childhood, since the beginning of the 19th century. Nor is women's experience of the state–family relationship likely to resemble Hunter's account of it. Some of the more troubling aspects of the symbiosis of state and family applauded by Hunter are suggested in the quote from Steedman that demonstrates the cost to women of being cast in the nurturing rather than the intellectual role both at home and at school. Miller (1992) wrote also of the way women's apparently "natural" maternal qualities worked both for and against them in that they were forbidden both economic independence as teachers and maternity or marriage as a result of the "arbitrary use of the marriage bar to sack teachers" (p. 11).

The incorporation of the family into the school as a government technology for the control of populations was at enormous cost to the women who represented the "family" in that context. It is also interesting to recall Miller's (1992) point that in discussions of "parents" in relation to schooling, although it is women who predominate here too in active participation in their children's schooling, gender is never articulated as an issue. What is more, this participation of women in education and in the provision of literacy has continually broken down the public and private split that Hunter (1994b) is so keen to maintain. It may also be the reason that "there are limits to the ethical and technical uses to which the family can be put" by governments, but this is something that cannot be thought in Hunter's story.

The unruly feminist intellectual then cannot coincide with Hunter's position, cannot be a feminist intellectual without having concerns about governmental rationality, or about the separation of public and private that Hunter is so pleased with. She must therefore come close to being the hard to identify problem intellectual in Hunter's (1994b) account. She is certainly someone other than Hunter's version of that intellectual. A descendant of Christian pastoral care regimes somehow does not fit with either the feminist critique of religion or of patriarchy in general. Perhaps that is why Hunter finds her so "fundamentalist" and so disrespectful of other ethical domains. Indeed there is every indication that he would find her decision to produce a social agent with the capacity to produce feminist readings of a text (Mellor & Patterson, 1994) precisely fundamentalist. He is absolutely insistent that such undertakings are to do with a morality and surveillance of consciences of a kind which are irrelevant to the "autonomous" ethical domain of governmentality where human agency is basically denied. It is the agency of the critical intellectual disturbing that system that is troubling, particularly if she is a feminist intellectual.

If there is a more accurate account of the derivation and nature of that feminist intellectual it is perhaps to be found in Yeatman's (1990) account of the femocrat or in Miller's (1992) story of the feminization of schooling. Hunter's (1994b) account of the main characters in his narrative include the impersonal official, the trained citizen, and the self-reflective moral subject. The latter is credited with regarding the former as technocrats and moral robots respectively. These characters appear to be genderless, although there are strong indications of dangerous femininity with respect to the moral subject and it is hard not to read the official as masculine, particularly in Hunter's fictional account of the bureaucracy:

> The comportment of the bureaucrat is marked precisely by the trained capacity to subordinate "personal" principles to the "ethos" of office. Let us say that it was only through the pragmatic and expert offices of the bureaucrat that education was removed from the sphere of spiritual principle and religious rivalry, to be reconstituted as a pragmatic problem of government. This is an historical lesson yet to be learned by those who today call for a more principled bureaucracy. (p. xxii)

This does not appear to refer to those contexts where the moral person has been increasingly being converted into a "new-management administrator," or many of those other contexts in which women and men teaching English increasingly work. The binary opposition he drew between intellectual and bureaucrat is hard to sustain in the present context and is made particularly problematic in the case of the femocrat (Yeatman, 1990) who must be both intellectual and manager, as indeed teachers have always needed to be, and whose position immediately problematizes the maintenance of the public/private opposition. The genderlessness of the account is also marked and participates in that same gender blindness that Yeatman (1990) commented on in relation to Marxist intellectuals:

> This indifference on the part of class analysts to the radical changes in the structural location of women extends also to an almost total neglect of the gender segmentation of the intelligentsia. . . . there has been virtually complete neglect of 'feminism' as the ideology of the feminine segment of the intelligentsia, and of its relationship to movements for revolutionary and social change. (p. 64)

Yeatman's concern is with trying to understand how, with the erosion of the old categories of public servant and academic and the emergence of a new class of technical intelligentsia the administrative state can remain democratic. Democracy is something she demonstrated to be difficult to maintain as the management culture invades all areas of activity and political control is increasingly exerted economically. The fact that the technical intelligentsia (credentialed intellectuals in the public service) lack the kind of critical literacies I talk about in this chapter is for her a real danger to democracy (Yeatman, 1990):

> Excellent technicians in the management of human and financial resources may be recruited and trained, but they are likely to be illiterate in the knowledge and skills required to comprehend and make judgements about the substantive purposes of public administration and office. Worse, they are likely to have acquired a trained diffidence to what they dismiss as "philosophical," "academic" or "abstract" questions. Needless to say this technical intelligentsia is an easy mark for credentialed salesmen of economic pseudo-science. (p. 18)

Needless to say, Yeatman's account is very different to Hunter's. It is the difference that makes me believe that we cannot think about critical literacies at all without considering this issue and the other theoretical and gendered complexities I have raised in this chapter. From what I have said thus far, however, it must be clear that I do believe that critical literacies are about social change. The problematic ways in which such change is brought about, and the need for cooperation between the various sectors of the educational community who are engaged in these activities if they are to accomplish the intentions of those working for change, are among the reasons that all of these people actually need to understand much better how the others work and why they all need to understand one another's theories.

At all levels, it is not of course only femocrats, but also male intellectuals and radical pedagogues who are engaged in these activities. It is probably true to say, however, that it is at the tertiary level that these exercises are most explicitly and self-consciously theorized. I want here to refer very briefly to the work of two male intellectuals who have become bureaucrats (interestingly Yeatman did not have a name for them— perhaps intellectocrats might do) or rather who now do both simultaneously, and as a condition of being either, at the tertiary level. Yeatman wrote of a developing "basis for integration between humanistic intellectuals and the technical intelligentsia," "which promises a much more advanced and sophisticated dialogue between technical and substantive aspects of all social activities, including those which belong to public policy and administration" (pp. 30-31). In 1992, Stephens wrote of the experience of acting as Chairperson of the New South Wales Higher School Certificate Examination Committee in 1991. A. Luke (1995b) wrote of the politics of textual subversion involved in "changing the subject of competence" in the process of collaborating with the educational bureaucracy in writing competency scales for adult education. I have written about the latter elsewhere (Threadgold, 1994) and concentrate here on Stephens' account. Both accounts demonstrate just why the bureaucracy is not autonomous and just why we all need to understand the complications of critical theory and its real effects on practice.

Like A. Luke, the intellectocrats and femocrats Stephens described as engaged in this exercise of subverting traditions in English teaching through the construction and assessment of curriculum are providing a rewritten, reframed tool to be picked up and used to change the nature of English teaching in the local sites of classroom practice. It cannot work however unless those who implement it are capable of reading its agendas, unless they share the critical literacies of its makers, whatever else of their own they may have to add to them. Reading and writing critically in these ways are not merely academic, however. They are part of a particular kind of workplace activity, in schools and universities, and they are capable of also changing the workplaces to which the students in school classrooms are headed. Once learned, they are seductive and pleasurable as well as empowering activities, something we need to be clear about as we engage in them, but something that needs also to be kept in mind in relation to the multiplicity of other than workplace uses communities find for their literacies (Hamilton, Barton, & Ivanic, 1994). Literacies for the unemployed (Davies, 1994), the discovery of language and story for aging women (Kamler, 1994), the changes wrought by literacy in ordinary women's lives (McMahon, Roach, Karach, & Van Dijk, 1994) the discovery of reading in similar contexts, adult education for all kinds of clients—these are places where the ability to read and write critically and to reconstruct or simply understand the embodied construction of the self are hardly irrelevant. They are also places where literacies still mean pleasure and are related to that sense of a "more complete" self that Hunter's (1988, 1994b) work is right to make us question, but should not make us forget (Davies, Fitzpatrick, Grenko, & Ivanic, 1994).

Critical literacies of the kind I have been exploring here then are not just elitist intellectual pastimes. The issues they try to deal with are in every classroom and in every workplace or vocational situation we are ever likely to walk into. Haraway (1991) once said:

> Cyborg imagery can suggest a way out of the maze of dualisms in which we have explained our bodies and our tools to ourselves. This is a dream not of a common language but of a powerful infidel heteroglossia. It is an imagination of a feminist speaking in tongues to strike fear into the circuits of the supersavers of the new right. It means both building and destroying machines, identities, categories and relationships, spaces and stories. Though both are bound in the spiral dance. I would rather be a cyborg than a goddess. (p. 181)

I would certainly rather be a cyborg than a bureaucrat, but because at present I have no choice but to be both, which is probably part of being a cyborg, I certainly see no reason why I should leave the bureaucracy as I found it. That is where Hunter and I have to part company and where it seems to me the future of the emancipatory feminist educator with which I began and the kinds of critical literacies I have been recommending are actually assured.

REFERENCES

Anderson, G. L., & Irvine, P. (1993). Informing critical literacy with ethnography. In C. Lankshear & P. L. McLaren (Eds.), *Critical literacy: Politics, praxis and the postmodern*. Albany: SUNY Press.

Bazerman, C. (1988). *Shaping written knowledge: The genre and activity of the experimental article in science*. Madison: The University of Wisconsin Press.

Beyond Poststructuralism. (1994). Special issue. *Interpretations, 27*(3).

Brook, B. (1994). Speculative feminist fictions: Teaching in postmodernism. *Southern Review, 27*(3), 276-284.

Bourdieu, P. (1990). *The logic of practice*. Cambridge: Polity Press.

Cavalier, R. (1994, May). *The Australian language and literacy policy—Two years on*. Address to the Victorian Council of Adult Education, Melbourne.

de Certeau, M. (1988). *The practice of everyday life*. Berkeley, Los Angeles & London: University of California Press. (Original work published 1984)

Christie, F., Devlin, B., Freebody, P., Luke, A., Martin, J. R., Threadgold, T., & Walton, C. (1991). *Teaching English literacy: A project of national significance on the preservice preparation of teachers for the teaching of English.* Darwin: University of Northern Territory.

Cope, B., Kalantzis, M., Luke, A., McCorrmack, R., Morgan, R., Sland, D., Solomon, N., & Veal, N. (1993). *National framework of adult English language, literacy and numeracy.* Canberra, Australia: Department of Employment, Education and Training.

Davies, P. (1994). Long term unemployment and literacy: A case study of the restart interview. In M. Hamilton, D. Barton, & R. Ivanic (Eds.), *Worlds of literacy.* Clevedon & Philadelphia: Multilingual Matters.

Davies, P., Fitzpatrick, S., Grenko, V., & Ivanic, R. (1994). Literacy, strength and identity. In M. Hamilton, D. Barton, & R. Ivanic (Eds.), *Worlds of literacy.* Clevedon and Philadelphia: Multilingual Matters.

Dawkins, J. S. (1991). *Australia's language: The Australian language and literacy policy.* Canberra, Australia: Department of Employment, Education and Training.

Fairclough, N. (1992). The appropriacy of "appropriateness." In N. Fairclough, (Ed.), *Critical language awareness.* London & New York: Longman.

Fairclough, N. (1993). Critical discourse analysis and the marketization of public discourse. *Discourse and Society.* 4(2), 133-168.

Foucault, M. (1973). *The order of things: An archaeology of the human sciences.* New York: Vintage Books. (original work published 1966)

Gatens, M. (1991). Corporeal representation in/and the body politic. In R. Diprose & R. Ferrell (Eds.), *Cartographies: Poststructuralism and the mapping of bodies and spaces.* Sydney, Australia: Allen & Unwin.

Gilbert, P. (1989). *Writing, schooling and deconstruction: From voice to text in the classroom.* London & New York: Routledge.

Godzich, W. (1994). *The culture of literacy.* Cambridge, MA: Harvard University Press.

Grossberg, L., Nelson, C., & Treichler, P. (Eds.). (1992). *Cultural studies.* New York & London: Routledge.

Hamilton, M., Barton, D., & Ivanic, R. (Eds.). (1994). *Worlds of literacy.* Clevedon & Philadelphia: Multilingual Matters.

Haraway, D. (1991). *A manifesto for cyborgs: Simians, cyborgs and women.* London: Free Association Books.

Hunter, I. (1988). *Culture and government: The emergence of literary education.* London: MacMillan.

Hunter, I. (1994a) Four anxieties about English. *Interpretations, 27(3),* 1–19.

Hunter, I. (1994b). *Re-thinking the school: Subjectivity, bureaucracy, criticism.* Sydney, Australia: Allen & Unwin.

Kamler, B. (1994, August). *Stories of women and ageing.* Paper presented to the Alma Unit on Women and Ageing Public Seminar, Key Centre for Women's Health, Melbourne University, Melbourne, Australia.

Kamler, B., Maclean, R., Reid J., & Simpson, A. (1993). *Shaping up nicely: The formation of schoolgirls and schoolboys in the first month of school.* A report to the Gender Equity and Curriculum Reform Project Department of Education Employment and Training Canberra: Deakin University, Geelong, Australia.

Kean, H. (1990). *Challenging the state? The socialist and feminist educational experience, the lives of suffragette teachers.* London: Pluto Press.

Lee, A. (1993). Whose geography? A feminist-poststructuralist critique of systemic "genre"-based accounts of literacy and curriculum. *Social Semiotics, 3*(1), 131-156.

Littlewood, M. (1989). The "Wise Married Women" and the teaching unions. In H. De Lyon & M. Widdowson (Eds.), *Women teachers: Issues and experiences.* Milton Keynes: Open University Press.

Lovell, T. (1987). *Consuming fiction.* London: Verso.

Luke, A. (1990a). The body literate: Discursive inscription in early literacy training. *Linguistics and Education, 4*(1), 107–129.

Luke, A. (1990b). No single method: Critical approaches to the preparation of literacy teachers. In J. Manitzky (Ed.) *Responding to literacy needs: Implications for teacher educators and training consultants.* Brisbane: Queensland Board of Teacher Registration.

Luke, A. (1995a). Genres of power? Literacy education and the production of capital. In R. Hasan & G. Williams (Eds.), *Literacy in society.* London: Longman.

Luke, A. (1995b). Getting your hands dirty: Educational politics in postmodern conditions. In P. Wexter & R. Smith (Eds.), *After poststructuralism: Education and identity.* London: Falmer Press.

McCormack, R. (1991). Framing the field: Adult literacies and the future. In F. Christie, B. Devlin, P. Freebody, A. Luke, J. R. Martin, T. Threadgold, & C. Walton (Eds.), *Teaching English literacy: A project of national significance on the preservice preparation of teachers for the teaching of English* (Vol. 2). Darwin: University of Northern Territory.

McDonald, K. (1991). Cultural innovation and economic modernisation: The context of language education today. In F. Christie, B. Devlin, P. Freebody, A. Luke, J. R. Martin, T. Threadgold, & C. Walton (eds.), *Teaching English literacy: A project of national significance on the preservice preparation of teachers for the teaching of English* (Vol. 2). Darwin: University of Northern Territory.

McMahon, M., Roach, D., Karach, A., & Van Dijk, F. (1994). Women and literacy for change. In M. Hamilton, D. Barton, & R. Ivanic (Eds.), *Worlds of literacy*. Clevedon: Multilingual Matters.

Mellor, B., & Patterson, A. (1994). The reading lesson. *Interpretations, 27*(3), 20-47.

Meredyth, D. (1994). English, civics, ethical competence. *Interpretations, 27*(3), 70-95.

Miller, J. (1992). *More has meant women: The feminisation of schooling* (The London File: Papers from the Institute of Education). London: The Tufnell Press.

Pateman, C. (1988). *The sexual contract*. Cambridge: Polity Press.

Poynton, C. (1993). Grammar, language and the social: poststructuralism and systemic functional linguistics. *Social Semiotics, 3*(1), 1-22.

Pratt, M. L. (1987). Linguistic utopias. In N. Fabb, D. Attridge, A. Durant, & C. McCabe (Eds.), *The linguistics of writing: Arguments between language and literature*. Manchester, UK: Manchester University Press.

Sinfield, A. (1985). Give an account of Shakespeare and education, showing why you think they are effective and what you have appreciated about them. Support your comments with precise references. In J. Dollimore & A. Sinfield (Eds.), *Political Shakespeare: New essays in cultural materialism*. Manchester & New York: Manchester University Press.

Steedman, C. (1992a). Culture, cultural studies and the historians. In L. Grossberg, C. Nelson, & P. Treichler (Eds.), *Cultural studies*. New York & London: Routledge.

Steedman, C. (1992b). *Prisonhouses*. London: Rivers Oram Press.

Stephens, J. (1992). The HSC Examination Committee: A view from 1991. *The Teaching of English, 2*, 22-26.

Students Victims of Education Experiment. (1991, March 23-24). *The Weekend Australian*, p. 1.

Teaching the Postmodern, (1994). Special Issue. *Southern Review, 27*(3).

Threadgold, T. (1992). Legislators and interpreters: Linguists, feminists and critical fictions. *Meridian, 11*(1), 76-91.

Threadgold, T. (1993). Feminisms, the judiciary and rape. *The Australian Feminist Law Journal, 1*, 7-2.

Threadgold, T. (1994). Linguistic utopias, political ventriloquism and ALBE. *Fine Print, 16*(4), 10-16.

Yeatman, A. (1990). *Bureaucrats, technocrats, femocrats*. Sydney, Australia: Allen & Unwin.

21

Toward a Critical Writing Pedagogy in English
Response to Terry Threadgold

Barbara Kamler
Deakin University

I begin by reflecting on the multiple layers of intertextuality that characterize this book on critical literacies. As writers located within intersecting and contradictory discourses of feminisms, critical theory, poststructuralism, postmodernism, radical pedagogy, and linguistics, we respond to the multiple texts that lie outside this text and precede it. Embodied now as chapters, we also speak to one another in and across the boundaries of this book—chapter to chapter, chapter to response, response to response. There is pleasure and tension in the exploration, a heteroglossic play of idea: Kamler reads Threadgold reading Hunter reading Halliday, reading and rewriting Patterson and Mellor's reading of Hunter.

There is also danger in bringing a range of speaking positions into play; of critique becoming its own end and irrelevant to practice. As I position myself in relation to the multi-voiced complexities that characterize Threadgold's writing, I fear speaking as the fireman in Ionesco's (1958) *The Bald Prima Donna*, who prior to departure from the stage announces to all gathered, for no ostensible reason, "THE BALD PRIMA DONNA." Although his comment provides the title of the play, it also disrupts the conversation, creating a new space that constrains and alters the possible range of texts that can be constructed thereafter.

So it is that writing a response genre is itself a problematic construction. It responds to but is different than, it is shaped by the history of the teller but is responsive to the telling of the other. As teachers, students, and/or academics, many of us have been subjected to a variety of conference response genres, the most distasteful of which might be characterized as *slash and burn* or *hit and run*. The former, favored by some of our prestigious universities, operate to show how deficient the speaker is and hence how the responder's own work is more significant, whereas the latter politely survey the speaker's main point and launch into the responder's own agenda, regardless of its relevance or connection to the text to which it is responding.

Treading a path that I hope avoids such models, I produce a written text more practice-oriented than Threadgold by locating my response in relation to my own teaching with tertiary and secondary students. In doing so, I wish to avoid constructing a dualism that sees theory and practice as binary and unrelated opposites and the feminized teaching profession as one that needs no theory. Rather, I take up Threadgold's argument that "a knowledge of critical theory—including structuralism, poststructuralism, deconstruction, and feminist theories but also social theory and critical discourse analysis—has to be part of what we are calling critical literacy for teachers of English" (chap 20, p. 367).

I explore what such a critical literacy might look like in the secondary English classroom, an important task motivated in part by Threadgold's reading of Hunter's (1994) recent intervention into the critical literacy debate, in particular "his distrust of theory," his "total discrediting of all forms of emancipatory pedagogy," his "predilection for Hallidayan sociolinguistics," and his apparent misreading of genre pedagogy.

I agree with Threadgold that "if teachers need to know much more about theory, theorists need to know much more about the theory that already informs teaching" (p. 367). I attempt in this chapter to bridge what she calls "a serious mismatch between secondary and tertiary understandings and teaching practices where English is concerned" (p. 367). To help me theorize a critical pedagogy that is accessible and possible for the English classroom, I have found it important to work in and around primary and secondary classroom sites. I report on two such teaching interactions, from my positioning as tertiary educator learning to develop a critical writing pedagogy.

My focus on writing rather than on reading is deliberate. A great deal of important work has focused on developing critical reading practices (e.g., Mellor, Patterson, & O'Neill, 1991; Morgan, 1992), including strategies of discourse critique, development of "multiple reading positions as instructional activity," and "disciplined reading against the grain of a canonical textual corpus" (Freebody, Luke, & Gilbert, 1991). By contrast, little attention has been given to developing critical writing practices. In Australia, the application of systemic functional linguistics that has come to be known as *genre pedagogy* (e.g., Martin, Christie, & Rothery, 1987) has gained currency as the dominant approach to writing that names itself *critical*. I argue here that genre pedagogy does not in itself constitute a critical literacy. The work I report on here suggests the importance of combining the systemic-analytic with feminist and poststructuralist understandings of discourse and subjectivity (Poynton, 1993) in order to develop a critical pedagogy for English that theorizes conflict, power, and difference (A. Luke, 1995).

GENRE PEDAGOGY: A CRITICAL LITERACY?

Threadgold comments that:

> Hunter's intervention in these debates in Australia then has to be problematic, especially when systemic functional linguistics and genre theory were already coming under considerable attack from feminists and critical literacy theorists for upholding the status quo and ignoring the kinds of contextual, historical and social issues being raised by critical theory. (chap. 20, p. 369)

I share Threadgold's concern with Hunter's ambiguous alignment with genre pedagogy (expressed again in chap. 18, this volume), as a solution to the problem of normativity. Genre approaches to writing have achieved a position of dominance in recent conceptions of literacy pedagogy. This dominance can be traced in the labels and assumptions of curriculum documents in a number of states, including New South Wales, Queensland, Western Australia, and the Northern Territory. The genre project's reliance on self-referencing (Lee, 1992), its absence of links with other traditions (Threadgold, 1988), and "its narrow focus on text and language to the exclusion of the institutional and disciplinary contexts within which these texts work" (Threadgold, 1994, p. 23) require critical scrutiny.

Of particular concern here to its operation as a critical literacy (Martin, 1991) is its linear conception of mastery and critique. Although social change is an explicit part of the genre project's claim to being a critical literacy, there is, as Lee (chap. 22, this volume) points out, "an explicit chronology in operation, a linear, before-and-after, means-end pedagogic logic which distinguishes the linguistic project from other 'critical' positions" (p. 420). This chronology implies that students must first learn to master genres before they can critique them; it ignores the fact highlighted by Threadgold (1993), however, that genres actually discipline and position literate subjects (A. Luke, 1992) and contribute to the making of *habitus* (Bourdieu, 1990). Once disciplined, it may be difficult or impossible for students or their teachers to see or name that which needs critiquing.

I learned about the dangers of genre pedagogy operating as a "pedagogy of deferral" (Lee, chap. 22, this volume, p. 420) when I was confronted with the following text by a third-grade writer whom I call John.

Girls into concrete

This potion will turn girls into concreate
Ingredience
1 kg of concreate
2 girls
1 eye from a bat
Method
1) tip 1 kg of concreate into tub
2) drop eye into concreate in tub
3) put girls into concreate. make sure that girls are sitting up right
Note
This potion will not work if add to much concreate

I gained access to this procedural genre through John's teacher, a student of mine enrolled in a unit I taught in 1992 on children's writing in a graduate diploma in language and literacy at Deakin University. The course materials in the unit were primarily framed within a systemic-linguistic theoretical framework and advocated a genre-based approach to teaching writing (Christie, 1989). The text in question was produced as part of an assignment that asked students to select a genre, to teach it within a curriculum context of their choosing, and to closely analyze the texts of six students, using the systemic analytic to demonstrate how these were instances of the genre taught. Based on the success with which children constructed the genre, students were asked to evaluate the success or otherwise of their lessons and make recommendations for improvement.

As requested, the teacher analyzed the linguistic features of this text to demonstrate that John had indeed created an instance of a procedural genre. I abbreviate her detailed analysis here by highlighting her summary discussion of the following characteristics of the genre:

- Transitivity processes are almost exclusively material to build the sequence of actions required to make the brew.
- Material processes are in the imperative mood (tip, drop, put) and are all in Theme position, so the action/command serves to carry the text forward to direct the reader.
- Reference is at all times generic rather than specific (referring to all girls, for example, rather than specific girls).
- A sense of sequence is made explicit by use of numbers in the method.

- The tenor is authoritative and impersonal, and the writer's identity does not intrude into the text as is common in genres of personal experience, such as Recount or Observation.

The analysis is competent in its own terms; it reproduces a number of linguistic and generic features that are characteristic of systemic analyses of text, as these are set out for teachers in a variety of genre-based materials (e.g., Christie, 1989; Christie et al., 1990; Derewianka, 1990; Disadvantaged Schools Program, 1988). What was surprising to me as her reader-assessor, however, were the absences in her discussion. Not one comment was made about the gendered meanings constructed in the text, the misogynist violence being done to girls' bodies, or the way the male writer constructs the victim as female. The imperatives certainly do build authority in the text, but they do so by directing the reader to immobilize the girl body and turn her into a stationary object. The act of making female an object is made literal in the text in the pouring of concrete, a material process, indeed, and one that presumably causes the death of the subject through this concretization. Not only did the teacher fail to see such meanings or comment on them as significant, she colluded in the construction herself by making the following suggestion at the end of her analysis:

> While I would classify text 2 as a complete instructional procedural genre, it would have been even better with a concluding step after step 3 of the method—e.g., (4) When concrete girls have set can be used as ornaments in home or garden.

Her remark demonstrates her uncritical apprenticeship to the systemic analytic and the extent to which she has been positioned by the terms of the pedagogy. In striving to make the generic structure more complete, she presents her suggestion as neutral and unproblematic. When I phoned to ask permission to use her text and raised my concerns about her silences, she suggested I was overreacting, that this kind of thing goes on all the time in primary school. Exactly the point. The construction of gender is such a dominating set of social practices in our schools that misogynist meanings are naturalized and unseen, or seen and minimized because "boys will be boys" and "after all they are only children." This ignores the fact, highlighted by Walkerdine (1981) and other theorists operating from feminist and poststructuralist positions, that boys can take the position of men through language; they can gain material power by constituting girls in text (even cementing them in) as powerless objects of sexist discourses.

My intention here is not to highlight the inadequacies of the teacher-analyst. Her response is not unique, nor is her work a poor instance of the pedagogy she was trying to implement. On the contrary, I would argue the systemic-analytic she uses is a powerful technology that prevents her from reading the gendered meanings in John's text; instead it becomes a site for the reproduction of sexist discourses. Clearly her reading of the text is dependent on the way in which she is positioned in relation to it (Kress, 1985); her positioning as docile apprentice makes it difficult for her to be critical. The practice of the instructional genre becomes difficult for her to identify because she is so firmly fixed on specifying textual characteristics and linguistic features. What is overlooked, of course, are the networks of power that are sustained and brought into existence by the text and the ways these contribute to and reproduce social injustices (Gilbert, 1993). In order to produce a more critical reading, the teacher needs access to other discourses, rather than more sophisticated understandings of the analytic templates of systemic linguistics.

In short, she cannot foreground the gendered nature of the generic conventions because the linguistic tools are not sufficient to examine the relations of power operating. Following Lee (1993), I argue that linguistics is an insufficient theoretical and methodological base from which to derive a pedagogy of writing: "What is missing is, among other things, a social theory of discourse which acknowledges simultaneously the complexity and materiality of the negotiation of power relations in social practices" (p. 132). From the perspective of genre theorists such as Wignell, Martin, and Eggins (1987) power is seen as a matter of access. It is argued that we teach the genres of power to students in order to empower them. We make explicit the linguistic and structural features of genre in order to give students conscious control over powerful forms of writing. In doing so we "directly inculcate power" (A. Luke, 1995) to those individuals who have not previously had power, and thereby achieve social change and mobility.

In the remainder of this chapter I question such assertions through my work with a Year 11 English student, in particular the simplistic notion that an individual's life can be changed by being taught to operate the genres of her culture. Furthermore, I show, following Threadgold (1993), that in developing a critical writing pedagogy "there is no Piagetian developmental chronology at work here, which says we must teach the genres 'straight' first and only then can we critique them. Teaching and critique go hand in hand . . . and detailed linguistic analysis is not actually necessary to do this effectively (Luke & Gilbert, 1991). There are other ways" (p. 10).

WORKING WITH SASHA: FAILURE AS EMBODIED SOCIAL PRACTICE

> Everyone enacts theory, performs it, embodies it, debates it, contests it, as social practice, on a daily basis in the ways in which they read and write, speak and listen, see and look, behave and live. Few however are helped to have any explicit knowledge or understanding of what it is they are doing. (Threadgold, chap, 20, p. 366)

> For the learners of English, in all their variety and heterogeneity, the lived embodiment of that kind of critical practice as habitus (practical sense, social necessity turned into nature or we might say theoretical sense turned into nature) has always to be the beginnings of critical literacy. That kind of practice is never necessarily separate from critique. (Threadgold, chap. 20, p. 367)

Sasha was a Year 11 student who attended a large metropolitan high school in Melbourne. The day I met her in February 1993, she sat at my diningroom table, body-written with the posture of failure. Shoulders forward, head inclined downward, a shifting embarrassment at direct eye contact, a smile she pulled out and put back as the moment suited, she gestured at the pile of English papers she had brought to show me. Her red-penned essays were covered with Ds and Es and a consistently negative commentary: "Expression is weak; No logical structure to the piece; No awareness of the audience shown; Not very informative; You need to enlarge upon the points introduced; You must produce more in the time allowed." She was failing English, her teacher was a bastard, he hated her she was sure. Could I help her?

I hoped I could. She was a friend's daughter and her pain and embarrassment were palpable. It is not comfortable being labeled *stupid*, believing you are and daily gaining confirmation in writing that this is the case. It was clear to me from the moment I met Sasha, however, that all the genres in the world were not going to give her power unless she could also develop an authoritative and critical position from which to speak; she needed access to other discourses that could make explicit the relations of power and how these operated to construct her failure. As I considered how I might work with her, I had to take account of the processes by which she had acquired a failing student habitus (Bourdieu, 1990), her ways of talking, acting, moving, and constructing social relations, that marked her as different, as failure.

This is not to say her writing did not need close attention. To demonstrate I present an argumentative text written by Sasha 3 weeks into her Year 11 school year. Her class had been asked to read a number of newspaper articles on David Irving and write an argument about his being denied entry to Australia. The task can be understood as a preparation for the Victorian Certificate of Education (VCE) media analysis task in Year 12, which requires English students to write an analysis of the media presentation of an issue and an argument which takes a position on the issue itself. (Sasha's texts are presented with spelling and punctuation as used by her.)

> Should historian David Irving be allowed in Australia?
>
> The historian David Irving argues that the Jewish Holocaust is exaggerated, he is not saying it didn't happen he is just saying that people have added that all the people who died in the gas chambers, where not all Jews, in fact, he states only very few of them where Jews. His statements and allergations cause some people frustration and confusion. As well, the Foreign Affairs Department has refused the right for David Irving to come into Australia. The reason given are that it may offend some people who are still mourning their losses, and also it might begin protest. The decision to refuse entery to David Irving is based on keeping the peace.
>
> A member of the Australian civil liberties union, John Bennett implies that it is wrong not to let David Irving into Australia, because Australia is a free country and feedom of speech is a right. Mr Bennett, has chaired two meetings for Mr Irving in 1986 and 1987, and say's that his lectures were well attended, and there was no protesting against his beliefs, nor was there any racial tension or provocative violence.
>
> On the other-hand Gareth Evans, the Foreign Affairs Minister disagrees with John Bennett, believing that it is an unsuitible time for Mr Irving to come, because of the elections, and also seeing that people are very moody around this time. Further-more Gareth Evans states that David Irving views are "morally repugnant" and are not based on facts, and since his last visit he has become more "offensive". The Foreign Affairs Minister believes that this will only cause problems in Australia which is not really needed, and may cause a "breach of the peace".
>
> It is intresting to note that the print-media has published articles on both sides of this question. It seems to be a matter of, freedom of speech verses potential violence unrest and breches of peace. The government of the time is obliged to protect all inhabbitants of Australia hence it's decsion to refuse entry to David Irving.

The title of this text poses a question Sasha never answers. She does not construct an argument about David Irving, but rather summarizes the ideas of a variety of male experts and puts them together paragraph by paragraph: (1) David Irving (2) John Bennett (3) Gareth Evans. Paragraph 4 highlights the media viewpoint and the issues involved with some oblique reference to her own position (*the government is obliged . . . hence its decision*). Sasha's text bears traces of the articles she has read and a few phrases she has learned are appropriate to factual genres (*it is interesting to note, on the other hand, hence*), although she does not necessarily use these appropriately. For the most part she has excluded her point of view entirely.

Her teacher's written response was brief and predictably negative. "D+ Expression—punctuation, spelling, sentence structure. What is your view?" His focus on surface features and Sasha's lack of attention to convention locate his response within a traditional skills paradigm. His only genre-specific comment, "What is your view," is misleading and could be read to mean the text will be improved with the addition of one sentence stating the writer's point of view. The teacher's failure to comment more usefully on what Sasha might actually do to construct argument lends weight to claims by genre theorists that teachers need explicit understandings of genre to more usefully guide their student's writing development.

Rather than critique the teacher, however, I would ask what other frames might he use to read Sasha's text? If we read her text from the frames offered by a genre pedagogy, we might note the absence of schematic structure signifying argument. There is no thesis, followed by a series of logically ordered arguments, concluding with a restatement of position (Derewianka, 1990). We might, therefore, set out to explicitly teach this structure to a weak student like Sasha who may have no idea there are culturally validated ways of putting forth a point of view in text. Linguistically, we might also note the absence of nominalization and a tendency for her text to present itself using the patterns of speech. As argument is central to the high school curriculum, we could help her master the conventions and linguistic patterns of the argument genre in order to achieve success.

Such a reading is useful in providing more precise ways of working than her teacher's "awkward expression" or "What is your view." It also produces, however, a naive reading with regard to issues of power and access central to Sasha's failure, and fails to acknowledge "the role of embodied subjectivity in the making of all texts" (Threadgold, 1993, p. 9). If we were to read Sasha's text from feminist and poststructural frames which theorize from a sexed and embodied position, we might ask rather, how is it possible to assert the authority required of argument when one is positioned as as inadequate failing female student?

Although Sasha was a failed writer who had no control of the recognizable patterning associated with argument, and no strategies for revising text, she was also a 16-year-old girl who felt harassed by her male teacher. She was located within a series of binary oppositions she was unaware of and had no control over: uneducated to her teacher's educated, failure to his success, female to his male, weak to his strong. Her failure to produce argument must also be understood, therefore, as a failure to believe she had an opinion worth hearing—as a problem of finding a speaking position from which she could assert any authority.

Sasha taught me a great deal about what might be involved in developing a critical writing pedagogy. Prior to working with her, my approach could be characterized as an amalgam of process, genre and critical linguistic approaches (Fairclough, 1992; Kress, 1988). I utilized explicit understandings of text structure, of the relation between text and context, and of the differences between spoken and written language, as well as process understandings of revision to teach students how to craft text and develop meaning over successive drafts. While my knowledge of genre informed the questions I asked of writers' texts, my knowledge of revision worked against formulaic notions of genre. The new challenge was to apply the feminist poststructuralist critiques of language (e.g., Davies, 1992; Haug, 1987; Lee, 1992; Walkerdine, 1990) I had been reading for some time to rewrite my teaching. Sasha provided a starting point for theorizing gender, discourse, positioning, embodiment, and critique in the teaching of writing; for opening up a more critical space that cannot be labeled either *process* or *genre* in the binary way recent debates suggest is possible (see Kamler, 1994 for an updated discussion of the old process–genre debate and the problems with advocating genre as a new and better opposition).

In the remainder of this chapter I describe two ways of working with Sasha in which "teaching and critique go hand in hand," to recall Threadgold's words. I separate these out for the purposes of discussion and thereby oversimplify the complexities. It was always the case, however, that I worked simultaneously with Sasha's inability to speak from positions of authority and her need to learn techniques for crafting an argument genre.

TEACHING CRITIQUE: POWER, POSITIONING, DISCOURSE

> When we teach writing in classrooms, or reading and writing, we are doing more than teaching language or genre, visual or verbal, explicitly linguistically or otherwise. We are engaging in sets of highly gendered and acculturated practices which involve the process of disciplining the body and mind into a predisposition of behaviour as part of a corporate body. . . . That behavior includes but is not limited to language and the learning of school genres. (Threadgold, 1994, p. 26)

> Rereading depends on being able to read all texts as makings, constructions, stories, which therefore have no epistemological authority other than as stories, and thus can be rewritten from another perspective, with a new setting, a different plot, a different hero, another ending. (Threadgold, 1993, p. 7)

Sasha needed a "map," something that would "make the system legible," that would help her read her failure differently. I saw my job in part as teaching her a meta-language that would enable her to speak about her positioning and find new positions from which to speak. The meta-language of poststructuralist theories is "explicitly not linguistic" (Threadgold, 1993, p. 7) but can make explicit

> the ways in which teachers and students are caught up in multiple discourses, positioned in multiple ways—sometimes as speaking subjects mobilising the discourses through which they have been subjected/made subject to powerful and libertory ends, at other times in ways that deprive them of choices and the possibility of acting in powerful ways. (Davies, 1994, p. 79)

I worked explicitly with Sasha to deconstruct her multiple positioning as failure, as schoolgirl, as student of a male teacher she feared. I worked to effect change in her mind and body. Regarding subjectivity as "precarious, contradictory and in process, constantly being reconstituted each time we speak or think" (Weedon, 1987, p. 33) made it possible to envisage such change and work towards it.

My own positioning in this relation is privileged. I speak as outsider to the classroom and the demands of 30 other students, working in the luxurious quiet of my diningroom to help one student critique her positioning within the classroom, school, culture. Although my aim was to help Sasha rewrite a number of bad school stories, it is important to point out that I never constructed a blame-the-teacher text. On the contrary, by using poststructuralist understandings, I attempted to shift the focus to the way individuals, including Sasha's teacher, are positioned in and through discourse. Sasha blamed her teacher, saw him as the source of her problems. I tried to give her new discourses to transform her understanding of power:

> from the dominant and monologic voice of the oppressor at the top of the hierarchy to a heteroglossia of multiple local and specific strategies and tactics, and the workings of power imposed from outside on inert minds and bodies, to stories of power internalised, lived, embodied as personal history and habitus and producing forms of embodied consciousness. (Threadgold, 1993, pp. 9-10)

I worked with Sasha in a variety of ways to help her rewrite her positioning as failed student. One of these involved the practice of rereading her teacher's essay comments as text, rather than as fact or truth; as a construct that could be analyzed and deconstructed. I provided a meta-commentary by asking questions that made explicit the positions being offered to her. So, I showed how the comments stated what she hadn't done, for example:

no logical structure to the piece
no awareness of the audience shown
not very informative

I then asked what action she was to take. How was she to improve her control of logic, audience, information? She said she didn't know. I asked if the comments told her what to do. She said no. I suggested she had been given no information to help her take action. We also examined the advice she had received, for example:

you need to enlarge upon the points introduced
you must produce more in the time allowed

I asked how she was to act on this advice. Again she said she didn't know. I attempted to locate her "I don't know" as textual practice in relation to a text that provided minimal guidance, rather than as verification of her lack of intelligence and inadequacy. I made it clear I would assist her, show her what to do, teach her strategies and structures to improve her writing.

At the same time, I provided discourses to enable her to reread her relationship with her teacher as one where she had some agency and control. We discussed her options: transferring out of the class, seeing the English coordinator, discussing her problems at parent–teacher interviews, and/or learning to cope and succeed. I pointed out this would take time, and that she would see no results for some time, given her teacher's reputation as a hard marker of even his most able students.

I also engaged in storytelling of a different kind to disrupt her elision of failure in English with failed identity. I rewrote stories with "another ending" where she succeeded, received help, and learned how to pass English. I stressed she was probably doing the best she could and if she could have done better she would have. A whole history of teacher-response texts had highlighted what she could not do and she had come to believe them. Simultaneously, I worked with her on structuring argument and power in text, on mobilizing linguistic resources she had no idea existed, some of which I detail in the next section.

A turning point occurred 3 months into working with Sasha. She arrived at my home with uncharacteristic energy and announced, "You'll be proud of me." She relayed how she received yet another D in English that afternoon, but had approached her teacher after class and said "It's no surprise to you or me that I'm failing. I don't know what to do. I need your help."

In that moment, I knew I could begin to teach Sasha to write with the authority required of argument. Her wording is significant.

Linguistically, she positions herself in relation to her teacher as less powerful, less knowledgeable, as one who requires help. He is constructed as the one with power and knowledge, the one who knows what to do. Crucially, however, she takes power by asserting her need for assistance. She thematizes (Halliday, 1985a) and makes her self, the *I*, prominent in each clause: I'm failing, *I* don't know, *I* need. No longer invisible, she speaks and is now seen both linguistically and as embodied text. She does not, for example say "You need to help me," thereby giving prominence to the *you*, her teacher, nor does she say "You never help me." She observes discourses of politeness, is not rude, and does not accuse. After 3 months of working with me, she refuses discourses that have constituted her as a powerless victim and that she has taken up as her own. Instead, she asserts her right to pass and repositions her teacher as one who can help her achieve this goal. She has, in short, begun to rewrite the story with "a new setting, a different plot."

The speaking was essential to her development as a writer and suggests the power of poststructuralist discourse to help her disrupt the usual ways of thinking about students and teachers. It was not until she could begin to speak with some authority that she could begin to construct authority in written argument. Her progress was not smooth, but from this point on she could stop blaming her teacher, stop complaining about how unfair he was, stop fantasizing about how to get out of his class and instead figure out how to survive and gain control of the genres required of her to pass VCE. The genres would not in themselves give her power, but they would help her rewrite a story of failure.

TEACHING NOMINALIZATION: WORKING WITH THE CONSTRUCTION OF POWER IN TEXT

> It seems to me that the poststructuralist feminist classroom, the postmodernist classroom, . . . the cultural studies English classroom, are all places that are not just about producing subjects who can critique earlier forms of reading regimes, but actually about producing subjects who know the differences and the implications, the functions and consequences of doing one or many of these things, and who have a range of strategies for doing it with. This does produce subjects with choices that are additional to those with which they began, which may or may not be the same thing as freedom. (Threadgold, chap. 20, p. 377)

From my perspective, the most powerful application of systemic linguistics for teaching writing is not genre pedagogy but Halliday's (1985a) work on grammatical structure, because it is not formulaic and is an analytic tool that can be used by teachers in a variety of ways (Williams, 1993). In working with Sasha, my aim was to develop explicit understandings of the textual resources available to her to assert opinion. In the following discussion I exemplify some of this work to make explicit how a linguistic meta-language might work together with a poststructuralist meta-language detailed in the previous discussion.

Sometimes I gave Sasha direct advice. Her early texts were filled with rhetorical questions that I told her to avoid. I explained that although experienced writers might use these to good effect, her questions often functioned as evasion, as a refusal by the writer to state her opinion. We also explored the power dimensions of how to assert self in text without using the first person pronoun. In doing so I was following the dictates of her teacher who discouraged the use of I.

Sasha's early attempts to include her point of view in the argument genre often involved a heavy reliance on I and sticking a final paragraph onto the end of her text. This is exemplified in the final paragraph from an essay written in March on changing the Australian flag.

> As for myself, I am apathetic to this issue. I feel that there are more important issues to consider, but if I had to decide whether or not Australia should change its flag, I would have decided that they do need a new flag.

This text provided a good opportunity to discuss the problems of stating one's opinion too honestly in a system that assesses that opinion. Sasha and I discussed relations of power between student and examiner, the kind of student subjectivity required to pass, the importance of stating opinion with conviction but not too boldly. Theme analysis was particularly helpful to show how the focus in argument needed to be on the issue, on what the writer believed, rather than the fact that the writer had a belief. I showed her the difference for example, between *I believe James is a small minded bureaucrat* where I is thematized or foregrounded and made the focus of attention, and *James is a small minded bureaucrat*, where James and an aspect of his behavior is made prominent. We discussed, however, why this construct might be too bold as assertion, especially for a VCE writer. We explored resources of modality that could help the writer qualify opinion and assert with varying degrees of probability or possibility, including conditional clauses:

> It appears that James is a small minded bureaucrat
>
> The evidence suggests that James is a small minded bureaucrat

modal verbs, such as *may* and *could*:

> James may be a small minded bureaucrat
> James could be a small minded bureaucrat

or modal adjuncts, such as *occasionally*:

> James is occasionally a small minded bureaucrat

While I sometimes worked with Sasha at the sentence level, the work was always done in the context of her texts, taking them apart, treating them like clay. The work was hard and slow, the meta-language we used was explicitly linguistic, aimed at helping her write power into her texts. Of particular use in developing her control was the work we did on nominalization (Halliday, 1985b). Nominalization is the process by which verbs in text are changed to nouns (things) and information is packed more densely into nominal group structures. Writing tends to be more nominalized than speaking, and much of the content occurs as "things" or nouns; in speaking, the tendency is for much of the content to be coded as action and occur as "process" or verbs. Sasha's writing, like that of many immature writers, was characterized by the patterns of speech and this contributed to the more casual, less forceful way of asserting. I attempted to explain this pattern as it operated in her texts and worked with her over many months to modify it.

The change that occurs as language moves from a spoken to written form, can be demonstrated by the following text (from Derewianka, 1990, pp. 65-66). This child's spoken text can be characterized as verb centered; it is divided into nine clauses because it has nine verbs (one verb per clause) and contains very simple nominal groups.

1. Um . . . ah . . . whenever people steal things . . . ah . . .
2. you go to
3. just say somebody steals something from K-Mart
4. and they find out
5. but they didn't catch you
6. and they increase all the prices
7. because if they steal something two or three hundred dollars
8. you have to pay for that
9. 'cause the prices increase

In order to convert this text into a more written form, we need to reduce the number of verbs and compress more information into fewer clauses and nominal groups, as follows:

1. Every day shops lose thousands of dollars worth of valuable items
2. This affects us all
3. because prices increase
4. and we have to pay extra

A further conversion of the same written text into one clause results in a more highly nominalized form again:

> The daily loss of thousands of dollars worth of valuable stock ultimately affects us all through an increase in prices.

I attempted to explore this principle with Sasha when helping her write an introduction to a physical education essay in May. Her first draft replicates the pattern of speech to the extent that she encodes the content in verbs (italicized), uses simple nominal groups (e.g., the sponsors, the media, the costs, the public, their personal sponsors) and no nominalizations.

> There *are* many reasons of why football *has grown* in Australia today. The sponsors which *stand* by their teams and *support* them. The media which you *would find* at every important match and the costs, of which *is* usually *covered* by either the public or their personal sponsors.

Sasha knew the paragraph did not sound right but did not know what to do to improve it. Our starting point was her ability to distinguish between verbs and nouns. Although she was very tentative in this knowledge, she could identify her use of verbs in the passage and I helped her convert some of these into a more nominalized form. We looked at each clause separately. I showed her how

> The sponsors which stand by their teams and support them

could be converted to

> the sponsorship of teams

where the action of sponsoring and supporting is assumed but not stated in the noun form *sponsorship*. I gave another example.

> The teams worked really well together

I gave her the phrase "the team's _____" and asked her to supply a noun that could mean the same as *worked well together*. She couldn't do it so I supplied *cooperation*. I showed her how the action was again implied in the noun in a more concise form, which freed her to now add another verb to the sentence and pack more information in, as in

> The team's cooperation is great

We moved back to her paragraph and worked through each clause in a similar fashion and produced four nominalizations (italics) in the following revision, reducing the number of words in her original introduction from 48 to 33, and the number of clauses from 6 to 3.

> There are many reasons why football has grown in Australia and these include the *sponsorship* of teams, the *media coverage* of important matches, the *attractive lifestyle* of football players and *high financial returns.*

Giving Sasha a simplified version of nominalization and the meta-language to talk about it helped her produce a more concise, lexically dense text. She could not have done it alone and was dependent on my intervention in her text; simply telling her about nominalization would not have helped. That is, I did not give a grammar lesson on nominalization, but rather used my understanding of nominalization to identify her problem, explain it to her and demonstrate an alternative construction. This was only one interaction; there were many others over a long period of time to establish the procedure as a tool available to her. Although both Sasha and I required explicit knowledge of language for this interaction to occur, the knowledge required was of a different kind and it was used differently.

My work with Sasha suggests the power of a linguistic meta-language for developing ways of working explicitly to improve her writing. It was equally important, however, to explore the ideological work achieved by language transformations such as nominalization, and in this regard the systemic description did not go far enough. Like the use of the passive voice, nominalization allows for the omission of the agent. The conversion of verbs into nominals has the effect of putting the action in the background and not specifying the participants. As a consequence, who is doing what to whom remains implicit. Although there may be various motivations for this, there are political and ideological reasons for hiding agency and hence causality and responsibility. These purposes as well must be made explicit to students (Fairclough, 1992) to help them develop critical literacies. In this way, grammar is used not only to gain control of genres, but to make explicit the ways in which language operates to marginalize, exclude and disempower—a central purpose of a pedagogy where "teaching and critique go hand in hand" (Threadgold, 1993, p. 10).

A HAPPY ENDING

The danger in telling any educational story lies in creating neat fictions of smooth progress without defeat. Failure is embodied, the struggle to shape what appears to be the simplest idea takes its toll on writer and teacher. The work with Sasha was demanding, the progress slow. She often retreated to a position of "couldn't be bothered" and struggled to construct new places from which to speak. This was especially difficult as she continued to receive months of negative teacher response even after her progress was evident and obvious to me.

Yet there was a happy ending, evident in the opening two paragraphs of her final argument for the year, where Sasha argues with authority about the benefits of vegetarianism.

> Vegetarianism.
>
> Vegetarianism is not only morally right but healthy and ecologically wise. Young people today are becoming more aware about the foods they eat, but importantly they need to consider the values of vegetarianism. Considering the diets, where meat is obtained, people may not realise that although it may taste good, meat is filled with excesses of fat, cholesterol and protein, whereas vegetarian foods are by far more healthy and do not require the slaughtering of animals. This way, you gain from the diet and nothing is harmed in the process.
> Taking the life of another living species so people can eat it, is not only selfish but inhumane slaughter. It would be crazy to think of killing another human-being, so you could eat them. You would probably be sent to a psychriatric jail or institution for life. But who makes it right to kill an animal and eat it, then get away with it. Try understanding how people can take a life from this beautiful, natural world, and not even feel guilty for it.

In this text, Sasha has moved a long way from tacking her opinion onto the end or avoiding taking a position altogether. Her opening statement is strongly assertive and surveys the territory she will explore; she has learned to use a variety of conjunctions to assert her reasoning (e.g., *not only . . . but, but importantly*). Although she has researched other people's ideas on vegetarian diets, she uses these as evidence for her assertions; she does not thematize the writer, as in the David Irving text, although she has yet to learn how to reference the ideas of such experts. The text is more highly nominalized (e.g., *the slaughtering of animals, inhumane slaughter*) and constructs more complex clauses in theme position (*Taking the life of another living species so people can eat it*). Of course there are still remnants of speech, particularly evident in the use of the personal pronoun you (e.g., *you gain from the diet*) and emotional ploys (*You would probably be sent to a psychiatric jail or institution for life*).

Sasha received a B from her teacher for this essay and was ecstatic at the progress she had made. I have explored in detail a number of teaching interactions with her, which were successful in producing both social and textual change. I see these as corrective to the "radically decontextualised example of teaching practice provided by Hunter" (Threadgold, chap. 20, this volume, p. 373) to dismiss the techniques of critical pedagogy. In making visible my work with Sasha, I have tried to open up questions about critical writing pedagogies that have been ignored by genre approaches to writing and discussed primarily in the context of building a critical reading pedagogy. The work here is necessarily exploratory and small scale, a first step toward changing the habitus of the writing classroom. It is my hope, however, that it gives body to many of the issues raised by Threadgold and to the "belief that in changing the daily lived behaviors of students, the texts they read, the stories they write, the practices in and through which belief is embodied as habitus, they will change the social order and the practices that produce lived gender and racial and class inequality" (p. 378).

REFERENCES

Bourdieu, P. (1990). *The logic of practice* (R. Nice, Trans.). Cambridge: Polity Press.

Christie, F. (1989). *Writing in schools: Study guide.* Geelong, Australia: Deakin University Press.

Christie, F., Gray, P., Gray, B., Macken, M., Martin, J., & Rothery, J. (1990). *Language: A resource for meaning.* Sydney, Australia: Harcourt Brace Jovanovich.

Davies, B. (1992). Women's subjectivity and feminist stories. In C. Ellis & M. Flahert (Eds.), *Research on subjectivity: Windows on lived experience* (pp. 55-76). Newbury Park, CA: Sage.

Davies, B. (1994). *Poststructuralist theory and classroom practice.* Geelong, Australia: Deakin University Press.

Derewianka, B. (1990). *Exploring how texts work.* Sydney, Australia: Primary English Teaching Association.

Disadvantaged Schools Program. (1988). *Teaching factual writing: A genre based approach.* Sydney, Australia: Metropolitan East Region.

Fairclough, N. (1992). *Discourse and social change.* Cambridge, UK: Polity Press.

Freebody, P., Luke, A., & Gilbert, P. (1991). Reading positions and practices in the classroom. *Curriculum Inquiry, 21*(4), 435-457.

Gilbert, P. (1993). *Gender stories and the language classroom*. Geelong, Australia: Deakin University Press.

Halliday, M. A. K. (1985a). *Introduction to functional grammar*. London: Edward Arnold.

Halliday, M. A. K. (1985b). *Spoken and written language*. Geelong, Australia: Deakin University Press.

Haug, F. (Ed.). (1987). *Female sexualization: A collective work of memory*. London: Verso.

Hunter, I. (1994). *Re-thinking the school: Subjectivity, bureaucracy, criticism*. Sydney, Australia: Allen & Unwin.

Ionesco, E. (1958). *The bald prima donna: A pseudo play in one act*. (D. Watson, Trans. and Adapted by). London: Samuel French.

Kamler, B. (1994). Resisting oppositions in writing pedagogy or What process-genre debate? *Idiom, 2*, 14-19.

Kress, G. (1985). *Linguistic processes in sociocultural practice*. Geelong, Australia: Deakin University Press.

Kress, G. (1988). Language as social practice. In G. Kress (Ed.), *Communication and culture: An introduction*. Kensington: NSW University Press.

Lee, A. (1992). *Gender and geography: Literacy pedagogy and curriculum politics*. Unpublished thesis, Murdoch University, Western Australia.

Lee, A. (1993). Whose geography? A feminist-poststructuralist critique of systemic "genre"-based accounts of literacy and curriculum. *Social Semiotics, 3*(1), 131-156.

Luke, A. (1992). The body literate: Discourse and inscription in early literacy training. *Linguistics and Education, 4* 107-129.

Luke, A. (1995). Genres of power? Literacy education and the production of capital. In R. Hasan & G. Williams (Eds.), *Literacy and society*. London: Longman.

Luke, A., & Gilbert, P. (1991). Reading "gender" in a teacher education program: A proposal. *English in Australia, 95*, 60-67.

Martin, J. R. (1991). Critical literacy: The role of a functional model of language. *Australian Journal of Reading, 14*(2), 117-132.

Martin, J., Christie, F., & Rothery, J. (1987). Social processes in education: A reply to Sawyer and Watson (and others). In I. Reid (Ed.), *The place of genre in learning*. Geelong, Australia: Deakin University Press,

Mellor, B., Patterson, A., & O'Neill, M. (1991). *Reading fictions*. Scarborough, WA: Chalkface Press.

Morgan, W. (1992). *A post-structuralist english classroom: The example of Ned Kelly*. Melbourne: Victorian Association for the Teaching of English.

Poynton, C. (1993). Grammar, language and the social: Poststructuralism and systemic functional linguistics. *Social Semiotics, 3*(1), 1-21.

Threadgold, T. (1988). The genre debate. *Southern Review, 21*(3), 315-330.

Threadgold, T. (1993). Performing genre: Violence, the making of protected subjects, and the discourses of critical literacy and radical pedagogy. (Plenary paper, International Domains of Literacy Conference, London Institute of Education, London University, September 1992). *Domains of Literacy, Changing English, 1*(1), 2-31.

Threadgold, T. (1994). Grammar, genre, and the ownership of literacy. *Idiom, 2,* 20-28.

Walkerdine, V. (1981). Sex, power and pedagogy. *Screen Education, 38,* 14-24.

Walkerdine, V. (1990). *Schoolgirl fictions.* London: Verso.

Weedon, C. (1987). *Feminist practice and poststructuralist theory.* Oxford, UK: Basil Blackwell.

Wignell, P., Martin, J., & Eggins, S. (1987). The discourse of geography: Ordering and explaining the experiential world. In S. Eggins, J. R. Martin, & P. Wignell (Eds.), *Working Papers in Linguistics, Writing Project Report 5.* Department of Linguistics, University of Sydney, Australia.

Williams, G. (1993). Using systemic grammar in teaching young learners: An introduction. In L. Unsworth (Ed.), *Literacy learning and teaching: Language as social practice in the primary school.* Melbourne: Macmillan.

22
Questioning the Critical:
Linguistics, Literacy and Pedagogy

Alison Lee
University of Technology Sydney

In this chapter, I consider some of the political questions and consequences of the developments in literacy pedagogy informed by systemic functional linguistics. Specifically, I examine the movement in writing pedagogy currently exerting major influence in a majority of states in Australia drawing on Halliday's (1978, 1985; Halliday & Hasan, 1985/1989) systemic linguistic theory and on subsequent linguistic theorizations of genre (e.g., Martin, 1985). At a time when literacy has achieved major government policy attention, the question of who controls the terms on which debate and scholarship about literacy are carried out is one that carries large stakes. Given the current prominence of genre pedagogies and the rhetorical claims made by genre theorists about literacy and social power, an investigation and analysis of the politics of genre-based literacy pedagogies is timely.

Although the particular site for examination of these questions is a curriculum and a classroom in a secondary school, this discussion is framed within broader questions of the projected outcomes of schooling—with the projections, that is, of different visions of the literate adult that motivate particular pedagogic interventions. Debates over literacy, curriculum, and pedagogy are, at base, struggles over the human subject. Accordingly, the particular focus of what follows is on the projected educational outcomes of a systemic linguistics-based genre pedagogy, situated within the larger debates concerning the projected outcomes of schooling. The issues are engaged in terms of their politics, in several senses. I proceed via some brief notes on the term *political* as it might apply to current debates about literacy pedagogies. Then, in the remainder of the chapter, and in the light of these notes, I consider what the possibilities and limitations of the linguistic genre pedagogic project might be, as part of an exploration of the politics of the relationship between literacy and curriculum. Specific reference is made to school geography, drawing on a larger study of the gender politics of literate practices in an Australian secondary school (Lee, 1996).

POLITICS OF LITERACY AND LITERACY PEDAGOGIES

I use the term *political* here as one that marks the constant struggle of discourses competing for hegemony in any social-institutional site. At base, to understand literacy as political is to see it as implicated in the distribution of status and resources ("capital," in Bourdieu's sense) and in the government of populations. What counts as reading, writing, and learning, and to what educational and social ends these processes are directed, are matters of fundamental contestation among scholars and theorists within the academy, in state education bodies and schools, and most recently in government policy initiatives in Britain, Australia, and elsewhere. Literacy is implicated in relations of power in manifold and complex ways. Although it is certainly not possible to sustain naive assumptions about the promise of literacy, that is, the automatic linking of literacy to social and economic development that was once promised in various policy initiatives such as those of UNESCO in the past (Levine, 1982; Street, 1984), contemporary rhetoric in policy and theory nevertheless continues to make claims about the relationship in ways that will reward continuing careful analysis. The rhetoric of the systemic linguistics-based genre movement is of particular note in this regard, as I explore in this chapter.

The macro-politics of literacy have often been broadly related in the past to the macro-political categories of Right and Left. These are most visibly realized in educational debates as polarizations between standards and equality, between traditionalism and progressivism, between applied sciences and humanities (A. Luke, 1988). In turn, these positions are related to some fundamental binaries preoccupying Western philosophy generally: speech–writing, inside–outside, private–public, individual–society, nature–culture. Of course, a representation of the history of literacy debates in terms of pure binary positions such as this is clearly a *post facto* reconstruction of what in historical actuality were much more complex and specific engagements and articulations. While in terms of current positions in Australia an analysis along the lines of a Right–Left binary is unsatisfactory, these categories nevertheless continue to exercise a particular effectivity in contemporary literacy politics.

In current debates, the relations among literacy, schooling, and social power are engaged by critical theorists in terms of their politics in several senses. The first is the issue of access to, and participation in, the discursive practices of a culture. These issues are intimately connected, on the one hand, to issues of identity and of individual social mobility and, on the other, as Foucault might have argued, to the wider social processes of citizen training and nation building. It is interesting to note that the current rhetorics of policy and government work to forge explicit connections between these twin foci of literacy training. For example, the Australian Language and Literacy Policy (titled *Australia's Language*), released in 1991, refers in its foreword to "the strategic importance of language and literacy skills to Australia's national development and to the well-being of all Australians" (Dawkins, 1991, p. iv).

A politics of access, as I argue in the next sections of this chapter, is at base a liberal politics, specifically a liberal-democratic politics of equality. Those concerned principally with questions of access to literacy argue for what Luke and Freebody (chap. 1, this volume) term *quantitative change* in educational outcomes (i.e., access to more of the more valued forms of literacy for more of a nation's population). However, there are important issues concerning the politics of access to, and participation in, official literate cultures. In particular, the interests of all individuals and those of a dominant social formation are not necessarily unproblematically congruent, as appears to be assumed in policy documents such as *Australia's Language* and the various meta-commentaries of genre linguists (e.g., Martin, Wignell, & Rothery, 1988).

Second, the politics of literacy may be enjoined in terms of the status of the meanings encoded through language and engaged in particular reading–writing practices. Those concerned with the curriculum politics of representation argue for what Luke and Freebody term *qualitative change* in educational outcomes. The currently much-used term, *critical literacy*, conceived in these terms, is concerned with social critique of the dominant forms of school knowledge and with a project of cultural rewriting (i.e., of changing the discourses and practices of dominant cultures that generate and sustain material inequality). Imperatives for such a critical literacy project have come from cultural studies, feminist, poststructuralist and postcolonial theories, and critical educational sociology. In its earlier manifestations, practices of "ideology critique" included a focus on the content of school textbooks, interrogating the naturalized narratives and explanatory frameworks of curricular texts. This work (e.g., de Castell, Luke, & Luke, 1989) draws substantially on Williams' analysis of the "selective tradition", but also on the various theorists of critical pedagogy, most notably Freire, and on American critical-sociological work such as that of Apple.

A more recent development is the use of the term *discourse critique* to characterize a range of forms of analysis of texts and readings in the name of critical literacy. These draw on various forms of linguistic analysis, including systemic linguistics, "critical linguistics" and social semiotics (e.g., Fairclough, 1989; Hodge & Kress, 1988; Kress & Hodge, 1979), as well as poststructuralist theories of discourse, most notably the work of Foucault, and various feminisms, notably in Australia, Gilbert (1993), C. Luke (chap. 2, this volume), and Mellor and Patterson (1991), and postcolonialisms (M. G. Singh, 1988; P. Singh, 1994). My own work, on which I draw in this chapter, is located broadly within a developing corpus of discourse critique from a feminist poststructuralist perspective, drawing on various linguistic-analytic technologies within this broader framework.

Within this perspective, the politics of school literacy are engaged as a complex politics of discourse and subject formation within the social project of the curriculum. Learning to read and write particular things in particular ways involves being schooled into becoming particular kinds of meaning-making subjects. This move points to a notion of a literate subject as not being merely a transparent entity, possessed of a prescribed quantity of literate competence, understood as autonomous and universalizable. Beyond this, particular kinds of literacy and pedagogies for literacy constitute the literate in particular ways; in turn, literate subjects, schooled into particular forms of literate behaviors, both serve and constitute particular sociocultural domains in their specificity. Just as different institutions are implicated in the literacy–schooling project, so the different discourses of literacy pedagogy produce and position their student-subjects in particular ways and with particular differential consequences with respect to relations of power–knowledge within a wider social formation. Within a feminist poststructuralist framework, what this means is that the politics of literacy and curriculum are crucially concerned with struggles over subjectivity, as the next sections of the chapter exemplify with respect to school geography. It is in the light of these struggles that the linguistic pedagogy for literacy will be situated and read.

LITERACY-CURRICULUM

To situate the linguistic genre movement more precisely within the contemporary theory and politics of literacy in Australia, it is now necessary to consider more generally the question of *context* and the attendant issue of the relationship between literacy and curriculum. Only in the light of this issue can the possibilities and limitations of a genre-based literacy pedagogy be assessed.

One of the important theoretical issues accompanying and informing recent moves within literacy studies and policy developments is the notion of the *context-specificity* of literate competence. There has in recent times been considerable pressure on policymakers to acknowledge what Street (1984) termed an *ideological* as opposed to a psychologically based *autonomous*, model of universalizable literacy skills. This has had a range of consequences, theoretical, sociopolitical, and pedagogical. Not the least of these has been the emphasis in the *Australia's Language* policy document and the various resulting and surrounding documents (Cope et al., 1994; Wickert, 1989) of the centrality of context in curriculum, pedagogy, and assessment for literacy.

Theoretically, the emphasis on context-specificity with respect to literate competence is connected to a notion of multiple and situated literacies. These two concepts have important consequences for a politics of literate practices. Literacy is understood both as a plural concept, involving a notion of a plural textuality, and as *transitive* in the traditional grammatical sense of the term. That is, literate practices are always directed toward the achievement of a social task; one always reads or writes something (see Luke & Freebody, chap. 12, this volume). Furthermore, that something is always situated within particular social-institutional contexts, which produce and position human subjects in particular relations of power-knowledge. Informed by theories of the discursive construction of knowledge, contemporary literacy studies thus lead logically to a necessary close linking of literacy with curriculum. That is, curricular knowledge in the classroom is constructed in and through literate practices. This is the transitivity of literacy.

In terms of the plurality and specificity of the curricular discourses of school subject-disciplines, school literacy can at the very least be construed as *subject-specific*, a term defined provisionally as "the particular literacy, or set of literacy competencies that is inextricably part of the operation of specific subject areas as contexts for learning and meaning" (Green, 1988, p. 157). The notion of subject-specificity becomes further complicated, however, with close analysis of the multiple discourses being mobilized within particular curricula (Lee, 1993, 1996). Accordingly, a refinement of this notion understands literacies as being specific to specific discourses, or discursive practices. The notion of *discourse* being used here is a poststructuralist one, emphasizing the linking of discourse with institutions and forms of government. Mobilizing different discourses in school subject curricula has differential consequences for socially differently positioned students within schools.

The notion of the discourse-specificity of literate competence raises important questions for curriculum and pedagogy. These questions are in the first instance linked historically with the concept of *language across the curriculum*, which was associated with the language and learning movements in Britain and elsewhere in the 1960s, and that reached its most explicit articulations in the Bullock Report, titled *A Language for Life* (1975) and in Marland's (1977) edited collection, *Language Across the Curriculum*. This movement, despite general in-principle agreement with the concepts of both language and literacy across the curriculum, however, has seen little actual broadly based curriculum and pedagogic development to this end (Gillham, 1986; Piper, 1988). It is possible to point to many reasons for this. One important reason, however, is that until quite recently there have been no theories of language and of discourse and discursive practices available that are sufficiently persuasive to effect required changes in structuring and resourcing the massive project of state-sponsored schooling.

In the context of these broader historical and theoretical issues, the systemic linguistics-based genre movement might legitimately lay claim to be moving toward a genuine literacy-across-the-curriculum mode of development, drawing on particular forms of grammatical and structural analysis to describe the specificities in form and function of written texts in different curricular contexts. Unlike earlier models of literacy pedagogy, genre theorists appear to be systematically engaging and theorizing the literacy–curriculum interface. On the face of it, the arguments for a linguistically informed literacy pedagogy are persuasive.

AN ACCOUNT OF THE SYSTEMIC FUNCTIONAL LINGUISTICS-BASED GENRE PEDAGOGY

Questions of genre have attained some prominence in the recent research into, and teaching of, writing in a range of different sites, including the workplace as well as the school. The linguistic genre approach to writing pedagogy in Australia differs from other work, such as the developing tradition of scholarship and debate in composition studies in North America in the 1980s. Although the North American work has grappled with many of the same issues, such as the notion of genre both as a form of social action (Miller, 1984) and as discipline-specific and political (Slevin, 1988, 1991), no substantial rapprochements have been made between it and the Australian linguistic work. Collections edited by Freedman and Medway (1995a, 1995b), which bring the various traditions into dialogue, are an important developments in this regard.

The Australian work on genre in education is singular in several respects and relies on the historical and theoretical particularity of systemic functional linguistics. This linguistics lays claim to being a social and contextual linguistic theory, where language is understood as a resource for making meaning and where genres are functional categories for the achievement of social goals. Theoretically and institutionally, the educational work based on systemic linguistic theory owes much to Halliday's long-term connection in Britain with Bernstein's work of the 1970s, that supplies what the genre movement has by way of a social theory, and it is via selective citations and partial readings of Bernstein that the genre linguists have categorized (in characteristic binary manner) major predecessors to genre pedagogy collectively and pejoratively as "progressives" (for further commentary on these classifications, see chapters by Hunter, Patterson, Gee, and Threadgold, this volume). The debates have by and large focused around the genre theorists' critique of process writing pedagogy for its lack of explicit instruction in textual production and for its pedagogic politics (e.g., Reid, 1987).

The systemic linguistic genre pedagogy developed from a corpus of texts written by primary school students that was collected in the early 1980s. It derives its major principles from a text-based linguistic analysis of this initial corpus, which produced a description and a classification of these texts into genres according to grammatical and structural regularities. The early work of Martin and Rothery (1980, 1981) documents the generation of the generic typology. Although relatively little known in international literacy studies, the early genre work nevertheless represents a significant intervention because it is one of few traditions that has developed from systematic empirical data based on what children in schools are actually writing.

One important outcome of this empirical work was the discovery of the overwhelming emphasis on narrative and recount writing in primary schools. This led to a trenchant and, I believe, apposite critique of the inadequacy of such practices to the development of the writing knowledges needed for curriculum areas other than English and for secondary and further education. The initial typology of factual genres: description, report, procedure, explanation, and exposition, as well as the recount and narrative genres—has formed the base for a subsequent development of subject-specific writing pedagogies.

In the later 1980s, the genre movement succeeded in attracting substantial funding, particularly through the New South Wales Disadvantaged Schools Program, to continue development in descriptions of, and pedagogies for, genres of school writing in specific subject areas. Related work developed descriptions of the linguistic organization of the fields of specific subject-disciplines, geography, history, science, and mathematics (notably the various papers in Eggins, Martin, & Wignell, 1987). Some publications have been developed as resource material for teachers, whereas more discursive accounts can be found in volumes such as Christie (1991) and Halliday and Martin (1993).

Broadly speaking, the "genre" approach to writing proposes a pedagogy of induction and apprenticeship using the analytic tools of systemic functional grammar and generic structuration. This position is articulated as a counterbalance to privatized notions of literacy as "personal voice," "authorship," and "self-realization," as these terms are developed in progressive pedagogies such as process writing. The espoused politics of the genre-based writing pedagogy concern teaching the "genres of power" in order to "empower" students who otherwise would not have access to these genres. Genre theorists such as Martin explicitly see power as a matter of access to the specialized registers of secret English (Martin et al., 1988), as exemplified in the following account:

> Secret English is a collection of specialised registers which have evolved to get on with different kinds of work. Though not designed to mislead and control, they are used in this way—because specialisation involves apprenticeship and the relevant apprenticeship is made selectively available to specific members of our culture. Secret English is powerful, and needs to be explicitly taught if this selectivity is to be broken down. Teaching it to empower means giving students from a range of backgrounds conscious control over its technologies. Critical literacy makes sense only in these terms. It is in bringing these discourse technologies to consciousness that linguistics has its special role to play. (p. 171)

The projected outcome of a pedagogy of apprenticeship is the notion of *mastery* of *powerful* forms of specialized language. Through mastery, it is argued, students gain power to control their world (Christie, 1987). According to this account, the genre movement argues for what Luke and Freebody (chap. 1, this volume) characterize as *quantitative* educational change, projecting, via a pedagogy of access to and mastery of secret English (i.e., through the acquisition of linguistic capital), individual social mobility. The argument is, in essence, that it is via individual social mobility that social change is achieved.

I argue generally that the linguistic work rewards engagement by critical theorists of literacy and pedagogy, in terms of the possibilities it offers for understanding the functions and effects of genres of writing and for explication of the context specificity of school-literate practices. However, I also argue that the genre pedagogic project is theoretically and politically naive. Despite the espoused Left orientation of the project, and the origins of the informing linguistic theory in a marxist position, its access politics is, as I suggested earlier, a liberal politics. Among its effects is a *de facto* endorsement of the official discourses of schooling, a reification both of curriculum and of genres of writing and the assimilation of difference into curricular discourses of the same. In the next three sections, I present a critique of this work in terms of its politics, from three different perspectives.

CURRICULUM AS A CONTESTED SITE

The linguistic work on the construction of the fields of specific school subject disciplines can be read as a direct attempt at engaging the literacy–curriculum interface. It has to be said that very little work of this kind has been carried out in the separate histories of either literacy or curriculum studies. Indeed, very little of the work in school literacy studies generally engages any specific subject-discipline other than English. In statements such as the following, in a report of an analysis of school geography textbooks, genre linguists articulate explicitly their understanding of the nexus between language and knowledge and hence between literacy and learning: "Learning the discourse of geography; learning to be a geographer entails learning the technical terms and their 'valeur' within the field" (Wignell, Martin, & Eggins, 1993, p. 165).

However, as I have argued elsewhere (Lee, 1993, 1996), there is a methodological problem with this linguistic work in school subject-disciplinary fields, as exemplified in the canonical (and much reprinted) paper from which I have just quoted. The problem stems from an inadequate theorization of curriculum and results in what I claim is a *political* problem in the second sense of the term as I outlined it earlier (i.e., in terms of the curricular politics of representation). The basic question to ask of the work is: how have the genre linguists come to identify the field of school geography in order to claim that they have found an example of it to analyze? How can the "valeur" of the technical terms within the field be established without a careful contextualization, within the field, of the texts submitted for analysis? In the larger study of gender, literacy pedagogy, and curriculum politics in school geography referred to in the introduction (Lee, 1996), I produced a detailed analysis of the contemporary politics of school geography. This analysis situates the particular texts selected for analysis by the genre linguists, producing a reading of the linguistic work as seriously skewed in terms of a geography curriculum politics of representation.

The linguistic work in Wignell, et al. (1987) is an analysis of several textbooks dealing with physical geography (i.e., the subdomains of hydrology, atmospheric studies, meteorology, climatology, geomorphology and bio-geography). However, the analysis does not claim to represent *physical* geography (let alone *school physical* geography) but geography itself. There is, in this implicit claim to representativeness, a resulting elision of difference in several senses of that word and at several levels. First, there are important disciplinary divisions between the domains of "physical" and the various "human" geographies. These are divisions concerning what geographers take to be the objects of their study, divisions that have major curriculum implications. Second, there are competing and often conflictual relations among positivist, interpretive, and critical methodologies within the discipline, rendering geography an exemplary instance of the broader technicism–humanism split in the physical and human sciences, as well as of attempts within feminist and poststructuralist work to destabilize the terms of this binary (Johnson, 1990; Rose, 1993). Within this linguistic work, and in the absence of any serious attempt at contextualization, geography is quite clearly and unproblematically represented as a natural (i.e., physical) science. This is consistent with Halliday's and Martin's more general characterizations of the subject-discipline (Halliday & Martin, 1993). A selection has been made from the discursive multiplicity that constitutes the discipline and the curriculum in the totality of its sites of practice, yet its status as selection is nowhere made clear.

That this has profound effects in terms of the history and politics of the school geography curriculum can be briefly exemplified in the following commentary by Morris (1992), a general inspector for school geography in Britain, who reflects that neo-conservative moves within the National Curriculum in that country to re-emphasize physical geography are "bizarre":

> Even to the untrained eye, the dominance of weather and landform studies is obvious. It is worth a reminder that physical geography based on these two elements is known as environmental determinism: human activity shaped by the environment. David Pepper . . . notes that this approach had its origins around the fifth century BC and reached pre-eminence in the nineteenth century. (p. 80)

School curricula can be understood in part as interested selections from available versions of disciplines, selections that are exercised in a highly political climate of competition and exchange among different participants, some located within the discipline, others within other institutions such as ministries of education and professional associations. My research into the school geography curriculum has shown how geography classrooms are sites characterized by a discursive multiplicity, including both dominant and alternative or resisting discourses about spatial relations. Student subjects are differentially located within this discursive régime in complex ways, ways that nevertheless work to reproduce relations of dominance and marginality, particularly along the lines of gender and race. The enduring dominance of physical geography within Australian school curricula is part of a discursive complex privileging technicist, masculinist, and ethnocentric modes of theorizing the spatial and writing-out more socially and culturally complex and speculative modes. For instance, through grounding geography in the physical landscape and through positing physical scientific methodologies as foundational to the discipline and curriculum, a particular curriculum logic is established. Within this logic, cultural categories are arrived at after and via physical, chemical, and biological categories, in what I call a Darwinist evolutionary curricular narrative. This has important effects in terms of constructing an imperialist and neo-colonial discursive complex about spatial relations in the curriculum. It has material and demonstrable effects in the positioning of actual students engaging the curriculum in the school classroom within asymmetrical relations of power–knowledge. In the next section, I consider some of the gender politics of this issue.

This linguistic work on geography, by implicitly elevating the analysis of physical geography textbooks to the status of representativeness of discipline and curriculum, is also implicitly participating in the process of hegemonizing and marginalizing discourses of spatial relations. If practices of induction, apprenticeship, and mastery are then mapped onto the analysis of a singular, hegemonic discourse of geography, genre pedagogy is locked into a reproductive project of discursive identity and stasis, without the possibility of meta-commentary of the status of the representations it is purveying. This would appear to efface the possibility of the genre project's effectively engaging a literacy–curriculum politics of difference.

A PEDAGOGY OF DEFERRAL: A CRITIQUE OF THE APPRENTICESHIP METAPHOR

In this section, I consider more closely some of the implications of a projected pedagogy of apprenticeship and mastery. According to Christie (1987), one of the most vocal advocates of a systemic linguistic genre pedagogy:

> An educational process in an important sense is an initiation; an initiation, that is, into the ways of working, or of behaving, or of thinking (the terms all mean similar things to me) particular to one's cultural traditions. Mastery of these ways of working, which are necessarily encoded very heavily in linguistic patternings,

represents mastery of the capacity to exercise choice: choice, that is
to say, in that one is empowered to make many kinds of meanings,
enabled to operate with confidence in one's world. And, let there be
no doubt about this, without capacity to exercise choice in this sense,
one cannot change one's world. Learning the genres of one's culture
is both part of entering into it with understanding, and part of
developing the necessary ability to change it. (p. 30)

The notion of "change" is explicitly a part of the genre linguists'
project of critical literacy. However, there is some slippage in what it is
that can/should be changed. According to Christie's account, an
individual's own life can be changed by means of the confidence
acquired in the ability to operate the discourses and genres of the
culture. Furthermore, the genres can also be changed in this process.
Indeed, "the culture" itself can be changed by means of an individual's
operation on it. It is not clear what the relationships among these forms
of change are. What is clear, and what is of most importance for this
discussion, is that no change can occur without mastery. Thus, there is
an explicit chronology in operation, a linear, before-and-after,
means–end pedagogic logic that distinguishes the linguistic project from
other critical positions: "Once the genres are understood explicitly,
students can use them to serve their own ends and . . . they can also
change the genres in the pursuit of other goals" (Christie & Rothery,
1989, p. 10).

In this sense, genre pedagogy might best be termed a pedagogy
of deferral, where a project of critique or of rewriting of the genres and
discourses of dominant knowledges can only be envisaged and
countenanced after mastery.

Apart from the issue of chronology, the notion of *choice* invoked
by Christie is problematic here. Within systemic functional linguistic
theory, the term *choice* is generally used, following Saussure, to indicate
linguistic selections from paradigmatic sets of linguistic categories. What
seems to be suggested here, however, is something of a different order.
The notions of *choice* and *use* in these two passages appear to refer to
larger scale choices of discursive self-positioning with respect to the
world. Upon attaining mastery, students can choose, in stable, self-
present consciousness, to pursue their own ends. The unified subject of
humanism can readily be read from these accounts (cf. Threadgold,
1993). Yet it is difficult to imagine this kind of freely choosing subject
being produced out of a pedagogy of induction and mastery. If, in the
case of the successful outcome of a pedagogy of mastery, a student
subject is "properly" constructed as the "good subject" of a discourse, in
what sense might that subject be envisaged moving outside that framing
to take up another position within an alternative, resisting or competing
discourse? In other words, how can a student's "own ends" be

conceived outside the obedient and docile subject position, required for and achieved through apprenticeship? At the very least, this issue requires careful and sustained inquiry.

Notions of desire and of subjective investments in particular positionings within discursive practices problematize the notion of mastery more generally, within the complex politics of identity and of difference. In effect, only a certain proportion of students will, in any local site, envisage taking up a position of mastery. A generation of feminist scholarship in education, as well as research on and by minority and "disadvantaged" groups, demonstrates powerfully that this is not a simple matter of access or of degrees of teacher efficiency. On the contrary, for many students, it is often difficult to see the point of participating in, and constructing themselves as subjects of particular dominant forms of knowledge and of textual practice. Indeed, many may well see a point in not doing so. For many, it may simply be too stressful, in terms of the work involved in accommodating subject positions that are in considerable conflict with other significantly internalized notions of self and of group membership (Green & Lee, 1995; Lee & Green, 1990). Lewis and Simon (1986) articulated the gender politics of this point well with respect to particular forms of academic exchange in their paper titled *A Discourse Not Intended for Her*, while the following brief account of a case study in school geography in South Australia demonstrates the material effects of the politics of discourse and subject production in curricular practice.

GIRLS AND SENIOR GEOGRAPHY: A SOUTH AUSTRALIAN CASE STUDY

In 1991 it became clear to researchers within the Senior Secondary Assessment Board of South Australia that some major gender issues had emerged from analysis of assessment data in geography. Here, I focus on just two of these, of particular concern for a discussion of the complex politics of the literacy–curriculum interface: (a) the gendering of student choice within the geography curriculum, and (b) the gender specificity of outcomes within the written examination.

In South Australia, geography, together with other academic subjects, is structured, taught, and assessed in two different ways at senior secondary level. Publicly Examined System (PES) geography is the higher status tertiary entrance qualification, whereas School Assessed System (SAS) geography is a lower status certification: Only one of the three South Australian universities counts it in aggregate scores for purposes of tertiary entrance. The main "core topic" of PES geography is physical geography; additionally, teachers have some flexibility to turn a "physical" focus to the other "core topic," economic geography. For example, a common approach to economic geography is the analysis of statistics of the urban–rural split in resource production and distribution. This approach is commonly explained in terms of a "lack of time" to introduce more complex analyses such as those afforded by a study of the political economy of geography. SAS geography, on the other hand, is strongly oriented to human and social geographies, has an explicitly speculative, sociopolitical orientation and is assessed internally on a continuous basis.

Although the overall numbers of girls in senior geography is consistently lower than that of boys, there has been, over a number of years, a slight majority of girls enrolled in SAS geography. Importantly, interviews with girls gave a strong indication that girls chose to enroll in SAS geography even when they were aware of the status differential. The reasons they consistently gave were those of "personal" interest in the curriculum content and orientation.[1] In terms of assessment outcomes, girls typically performed significantly better than boys in SAS geography, whereas the reverse was the case in PES geography (Whitehouse, 1992).

In 1991, some startling examination results in PES geography prompted the initiation of the research project carried out by Whitehouse for the Senior Secondary Assessment Board of South Australia. An unusually high number of girls had not passed the examination. Analysis was undertaken that suggested that the questions were gendered in significant ways, including the use of illustrative examples. Part of this analysis is produced in the draft report (Whitehouse, 1992). The PES examination paper is divided into two parts. The first, worth 60%, consists of short-answer questions involving interpretation of data and mapping. The second, worth 40%, consists of two essays. Girls have traditionally performed badly on the first section and well on the second (essay writing) section of the paper, whereas the reverse is the case for boys (Whitehouse, 1992). Drawing on a range of theorists, the draft report states:

> Girls are far more likely to see ambiguity, which leads them to see no right answer or to think of several possible responses. The general process of abstracting and focusing down on a right answer reflects a more 'male' style of thinking. Boys as a group find it easier to judge a problem in isolation and consider the context of an activity to be idiosyncratic. (Whitehouse, 1992, p. 37)

---

[1]These interviews are part of an incomplete investigation carried out by researchers within the Senior Secondary Assessment Board of South Australia. As the decision has been made not to publish this work, no details are available. My comments draw on a draft-in-process, sighted in 1992.

As a result, girls were considered by examiners to write with "less precision" than boys. Male teachers typically privileged the computational aspects of the subject in PES geography and, while acknowledging that girls often write well, claimed that that was not what was valued in geographical training. It was not uncommon, in the experience of Senior Secondary Assessment Board geography curriculum specialists, for male geography teachers to claim to be "illiterate" and to lay claim instead to skills in practical and analytical aspects of the subject discipline. Interviews with girls indicated a strong preference for more socially complex topics and a dislike of mapping, computational and short-answer questions. A common comment by girls with respect to the first section of the examination paper was that they "did not have enough space" to answer the questions to the depth that they understood the question to be demanding.

The most likely outcome in the South Australian case was predicted by the researchers to be, in the short term at least, that more classroom time in PES geography would be spent during the year on preparing students better for answering the short-answer section of the examination paper. This was predicted to have the result of further marginalizing girls' interests and strengths in essay writing and more considered exploration of geographical social issues, and subjecting them further to what can clearly be characterized as a masculinist-technicist regime within the subject discipline. Together with the deprivileging of human geographies in their relegation to the lower status SAS subject, this additional devaluing of the more socially complex aspects of the publicly examined curriculum appeared to be seriously working against girls' interests, as these were articulated through such means as subject choice and preferred modes of textual practice.

The gender political implications of this study for a projected pedagogy of induction, apprenticeship and "mastery" should be clear. Only by seeing the field of the curriculum as a representational given, and student participation in that field as a matter purely of access, can apprenticeship metaphors be sustained in any straightforward way. The problem is that such metaphors locate literacy pedagogy outside the politics of curriculum. This is a problem because, as I have briefly demonstrated, there is never a single identity to be attributed to a subject-disciplinary area. It is also important to note that the means by which access to and successful participation in a curriculum are achieved cannot be reduced to questions of literacy, defined in relatively conventional ways in terms of competence in the production of written texts. In PES geography, mapping and statistics were more highly valued than more discursive textual productions. A very particular kind of student subject is projected through this curriculum, one that appears to sit easily with the predispositions and investments of a particular kind of masculine subjectivity. For girls, on the other hand, the importance of social complexity in the curriculum means a clear orientation to and investment in discursive and textual complexity. There is a great deal to consider here concerning the feminization of textuality more generally (Lee & Green, 1990; White, 1986). By ignoring the politics of representation in curricular content, language, and textual practice, what happens is that another form of inequitable selection is being exercised, one that is merely different in kind from that being opposed by advocates of access.

GRAMMAR AND THE POLITICS OF RIGHT AND LEFT IN LITERACY PEDAGOGY

Although it is important to avoid a too easy reduction of the complex politics of literacy and curriculum to agendas of the macro-political Right and Left, there are several contemporary instances in which such an analysis has a particular salience and effectivity. In the current climate of the rapidly increasing incorporation of literacy into various macro-political agendas of economic restructuring and reform, what will reward close scrutiny is the redrawing of the lines of debate around questions of political difference and the rapprochements being effected between unlikely allies. In this section, I consider some of the political consequences attendant on the forging of such rapprochements and alliances, in terms of their unforeseen effects in the workings of policy and government and the press. In particular, I am concerned to track the progress of the genre movement in the contemporary macro-political arena.

So what are Right politics of literacy? Australia has its own inflections of two major Right agendas within the international politics of literacy: that of "cultural literacy" (after Hirsch, 1987), most notably in the position articulated by Leonie Kramer, chancellor and former professor of English of the University of Sydney, and that of the ubiquitous "back-to-basics" movement. This movement has, in such places as the daily press, consistently denounced falling standards of literacy and called for the teaching of reading and writing through a return to formal grammar and spelling. The most common back-to-basic positions are articulated in opposition to various progressivist pedagogies such as the whole language movement and process writing. What is of particular interest here is the potential congruence of the agendas of the genre linguists and the back-to-basics lobbyists (see Threadgold, chap. 20, this volume)—allies in their opposition to "progressivism."

This congruence was foreshadowed in 1987, the occasion of the first extended dialogue between genre and what was then being oppositionally enjoined by the various parties as process, the pedagogy par excellence of progressivism. At that time, Green (1987) sounded the following note of caution: "[genre] has the ability to tap into both popular and bureaucratic sensibility, having 'Right' on its side for one thing in its concern and calls for greater rigour and structure in literacy education" (p. 85).

The notions of *rigour* and *structure* do not, of course, automatically translate into cruder notions of back-to-basics. Linguistic conceptions of genre and the analysis of the structures and functions of genres of school writing are potentially a useful focus for a socially critical literacy project. However, both "bureaucratic" and "popular" sensibilities, as these are articulated in newspapers and policy documents, are over–determined in their institutional commitments to closure in the service of, respectively, the pragmatics of government and of a good story.

The rapprochement between Right agendas and the espoused Left orientation of genre is in part strategic and in part implicit and possibly unintended. It is worth considering briefly one articulation of the Right opposition to progressivism, in order to give some substance to the pedagogical-political issues. In the following excerpt, the U.S. commentator, Simon, invokes, with considerable offensiveness, "the four great body blows to traditional literacy standards":

> (1) the student rebellion of 1968, which, in essence, meant that students themselves became the arbiters of what subjects were to be taught, and grammar by jingo (or Ringo), was not one of them; (2) the notion that in a democratic society language must accommodate itself to the whims, idiosyncrasies, dialects and sheer ignorance of underprivileged minorities, especially if these happen to be black, Hispanic and, later on, female or homosexual; (3) the introduction by more and more incompetent English teachers, products of the new system (see items 1 and 2 above) of even fancier techniques of *not* teaching English, . . . and (4) television. (Simon, 1980, p. xiv cited in Faigley, 1992, p. 64)

With the possible exception of television (currently enjoying something of a lull in literacy crisis discourses), the other three "body blows"—the lack of grammar, the valorization of nonstandard forms and discourses, and incompetent and/or noninterventionist teaching— are salient features of both Right-oriented back-to-basics and cultural literacy advocates and also the genre position—although with espousedly different pedagogical-political agendas at stake. I should add that nowhere in any of the literature produced by genre linguists or their followers is there evidence of the attachment to bigotry characteristic of much Right rhetoric.

It is worth briefly considering the success of the linguistic genre movement in the light of these issues. In accordance with the Australian Labor government's growing focus on literacy, linked to the larger agenda of rationalizing and articulating education and training on a national basis, there were in the early 1990s rapid changes in curriculum and syllabuses for literacy development in schools. An examination of these developments readily shows a growing influence of systemic functional linguistics-based literacy pedagogies. Furthermore, these developments occurred separately in four of the six Australian states, with very particular inflections as a result of local politics and institutional histories. That is, the highly centralized control of knowledge production and curriculum development that characterized the systemic work in education in the 1980s in Sydney gave way to a dispersal into state systems in a manner characteristic of Australian cultural politics more generally. Through these developments, it is very clear that the best intentions of academic linguists, either as researchers or as pedagogues for literacy, were not able to control the outcomes of bureaucratic and cultural-political processes.

There are two related consequences of this situation with respect to the genre project, both revolving round the concept of *grammar*, perhaps the transcendental signifier of the moral panic around literacy. The first of these is the appropriation and transformation, in recent policy developments and syllabus documents in several states of Australia, of the initial linguistic/pedagogic meta-language that has been developed by the Sydney-based genre linguists to articulate their position. To take just one of several recent examples, in the Western Australian *First Steps* project (a primary school writing syllabus), the structuring and description of the textual forms and functions of written genres has been partly adapted from the elaborate work developed through the New South Wales Disadvantaged Schools Program, which is theoretically informed by linguistic theories of genre. In fact, *First Steps* resembles, in many ways, the Disadvantaged Schools Program genre project without the functional grammar. In its place is a short handbook of a traditional-descriptive formal grammar, a familiar enough looking document used traditionally in prescriptive ways to correct students' errors and non-standard forms in language and writing.

This is not to say that *First Steps* is not a potentially useful development in writing pedagogies for Western Australian schools. However, what is of concern is the question of what a syllabus projecting a writing pedagogy based on genre will be like in practice, without the possibilities for analysis offered by a functional grammar. Systemic functional grammar allows a systematic analysis of ways in which representations, relations among writers and readers and textual forms themselves are constructed; these are the theoretical building blocks of the systemic linguistic theory and practice of genre. Although I argue here and elsewhere that much of the genre work has been far too uncritically oriented to discursive reproduction, this has by no means been a necessary outcome of the linguistic theory informing the textual analyses. Indeed, as I indicated at the beginning of this chapter, systemic linguistic analytics has much to offer for a project of discourse critique. Without the possibilities offered by the analytic technologies of systemic functional grammar, however, as in the case of *First Steps*, it is difficult to see how teachers and their students can be in any position other than that of reproduction, reification, and rigidity in the teaching and learning of writing.

It is worth pointing out briefly here that these processes might have been predicted by the very complexity and unwieldiness of the conceptual and techno-analytical apparatus of systemic-functional linguistics itself. It is a pertinent criticism of systemics as a text-analytic technology, that its complexity and redundancy militates against its political effectiveness in very pragmatic ways (Poynton, 1993). It takes a great deal of time and effort to gain even a modicum of control yet teachers would often appear to have little choice but apprenticeship to (read: dependence on) linguistically credentialed masters in front of whom, so long as only linguistic knowledge is the knowledge that really counts about literacy, a teacher will not and cannot ever be "one who authoritatively knows."

The second consequence, related to the first, is that the notion of grammar signifies so powerfully in Right discourses about literacy that in press and other populist accounts, the genre movement became rhetorically incorporated in the service of a neo-conservative move against various forms of libertarian, critical or transformative pedagogies. In the first half of the 1990s there was some evidence that the term *grammar* was indeed being construed by press and politicians in ways that connected it back to back-to-basics agendas, where the significant differences between functional and formal grammars was elided in the process of what A. Luke (1988) termed the *ritual symmetrization* of swings between polarized binary opposite positions. For example, in a lengthy article in the national press, outlining the new New South Wales *K-6 English Syllabus*, headed "Grammar Comes Back into Fashion," the journalist, Carolyn Jones (1993), began as follows:

> In a move that has been hailed as a back-to-basics approach to the teaching and learning of English, NSW students are about to get their first taste of what educationists are hoping will mark a sea change for school literacy education.

> From next year, teachers will begin phasing in a new English syllabus which will require them to rely more on conventional language teaching methods to introduce children to grammatical theory and concepts. By 1996, the new syllabus, which stipulates the teaching of grammar, spelling, reading and writing, will be compulsory in all NSW primary schools. (p. 8)

Not until later in the article is it made clear that teaching functional grammar is different from "the traditional, Latinate style of teaching" grammatical theory that focuses on individual, decontextualized sentences. Grammar, it seems, signifies powerfully as Grammar, invoking a ritualized discourse of standards and basics in a return to convention—here the proper and the real, against which progressivist concepts such as whole language and process are marked as temporary deviations.

The current extension of the space within which literacy concerns are being articulated, however, calls for a careful re-examination of notions of the real. In the next section, I conclude with a consideration of the political implications of an expanded field of operation for this particular reading of literacy.

CONCLUSION: THE BROADER CONTEXT

This chapter has, in considering some questions of the contemporary politics of literacy in Australia, been concerned with articulating what is at stake from a number of different, and commonly separate, perspectives. In particular, in drawing attention to the context-specificity of literate practices and the notion of multiple and contested literacies, what becomes clear is the necessary articulation of literacy studies with curriculum studies, whatever the site of literacy instruction under review. The chapter considers two major ways in which the relations among literacy, education, and social power are engaged by critical theorists in terms of their politics. The first is the question of access to and participation in the formal discursive practices of a culture; the second concerns the politics of representation. By demonstrating that literacy pedagogy cannot sensibly be studied outside the politics of curriculum, I argue the need for a more complex engagement with the politics of literacy and curriculum across a broad front.

This is particularly the case as the rate of change in education continues to increase. What is at issue more broadly is that educational debates are, at base, struggles over the human subject. Which projection of the outcomes of schooling and training—which vision of the literate adult—is to be incorporated into government policy and practice, given the moves to place literacy in centre stage in the educational and economic restructuring and reform processes currently being undertaken? What are the consequences and effects of such projections within contemporary social movements and policy developments? In the 1990s, demands for literate competence are being acknowledged and addressed in increasingly broad and diverse contexts: in technical, further and higher education, in vocational training, in workplaces, labor market programs, in Aboriginal and rural communities and in adult basic education—in addition to the more traditional site for literacy instruction, the school. Given changing conditions of employment and indeed unemployment, school education can no longer be effectively marked off from what might collectively be termed *not-school*.

In the light of these developments, it has been one of the tasks of this chapter to articulate a degree of concern about the potential for conflation of old agendas concerning "functional" literacy and "back to basics" with new agendas such as competency-based standards for education and training in conjunction with new analytic technologies such as systemic-functional grammar and genre analysis. For bureaucratically motivated imperatives for closure in the form of implementation of policy developments, any technology and associated pedagogy that appears to be structured and systematic looks immediately attractive, particularly when appearing to offer a return to former "standards" of "traditional" literacy pedagogies with a renewed emphasis on grammar. In particular, linguistic notions of genre, with clear-cut technical descriptors according to grammatical and structural features as well as to function, appear to map readily onto a competency agenda. I have argued that the systemic linguistics-based genre pedagogy, with all its potential usefulness in providing a tool-kit of appropriate linguistic technologies for understanding the construction of texts, suffers problems of political naiveté, connected with its theoretical and institutional insularity (Lee, 1996). In much of the work, the promise of illumination with respect to matters of text construction is countered by a lack of a sufficiently complex understanding of context, of issues of discursive and institutional practice, and of the politics of identity and of difference.

In particular, genre pedagogy raises problems because of a lack of rigorous theorization of subject production. Implied in the various meta-commentaries concerning access, apprenticeship, and mastery is the idealized abstraction of the subject/agent of liberal democracy. In contrast, contemporary poststructuralist, feminist and postcolonial theories argue for the theoretical and political necessity of diversity and differentiation. There is an urgent need, in the contemporary politics of literacy and curriculum, to confront liberal-democratic notions of equality with rigorous questions of difference. There may be a productive role for a social linguistics to play in such a project.

REFERENCES

Bullock, A. (1975). *A language for life*. London: Department of Education and Science.

de Castell, S., Luke, A., & Luke, C. (Eds.). (1989). *Language, authority and criticism: Readings on the school textbook*. London: Falmer Press.

Christie, F. (1987). Genres as choice. In I. Reid (Ed.), *The place of genre in learning: Current debates* (pp. 22-31). Geelong, Australia: Deakin University Press.

Christie, F. (Ed.). (1991). *Literacy for a changing world*. Melbourne, Australia: ACER.

Christie, F., & Rothery, J. (1989). Genres and writing: A response to Michael Rosen. *English in Australia, 90*(3), 75-85.

Cope, B., Kalantzis, M., Luke, A., McCormack, R., Morgan, B., Slade, D., Solomon, N., & Veal, N. (1994). *Communication, collaboration and culture: A national framework of adult English language, literacy and numeracy competence.* Canberra, Australia: Department of Employment, Education and Training.

Dawkins, J. (1991). Australia's language: *The Australian language and literacy policy*. Canberra: Australian Government Publishing Service.

Eggins, S., Martin, J. R. & Wignell, P. (Eds.). (1987). *Working papers in linguistics: Writing report 5.* Sydney, Australia: Linguistics Department, University of Sydney.

Faigley, L. (1992). *Fragments of rationality: Postmodernity and the subject of composition.* Pittsburgh & London: University of Pittsburgh Press.

Fairclough, N. (1989). *Language and power*. London: Longman.

Freedman, A., & Medway, P. (Eds.). (1995a). *Genre and the new rhetoric.* London: Falmer Press.

Freedman, A., & Medway, P. (Eds.). (1995b). *Learning and teaching genre.* Portsmouth, NH: Heineman.

Gilbert, P. (1993). *Gender stories and the writing classroom.* Geelong, Australia: Deakin University Press.

Gillham, B. (Ed.). (1986). *The language of school subjects.* London: United Kingdom Reading Association & Heinemann Educational Books.

Green, B. (1987). Gender, genre and writing pedagogy. In I. Reid (Ed.), *The place of genre in learning: Current debates* (pp. 83-90). Geelong, Australia: Deakin University Press.

Green, B. (1988). Subject-specific literacy and school learning: A focus on writing. *Australian Journal of Education, 32*(2), 156-179.

Green, B., & Lee, A. (1995). Writing geography: Literacy, identity and schooling. In A. Freedman & P. Medway (Eds.), *Learning and teaching genre* (pp. 207-224). Portsmouth, NH: Heinemann.

Halliday, M. A. K. (1978). *Language as a social semiotic.* London: Edward Arnold.

Halliday M. A. K. (1985). *An introduction to functional grammar.* London: Edward Arnold.

Halliday M. A. K., & Hasan, R. (1989). *Language, context and text: Aspects of language in a social-semiotic perspective.* Oxford, UK: Oxford University Press. (original work published 1985)

Halliday, M. A. K., & Martin, J. R. (1993). *Writing science*. London: Falmer Press.

Hirsch, E. D. (1987). *Cultural literacy: What every American needs to know.* Boston: Houghton Mifflin.

Hodge, B., & Kress, G. (1988). *Social semiotics*. Cambridge, MA: Polity Press.

Johnson, L. (1990). New courses for a gendered geography: Teaching feminist geography at the University of Waikato. *Australian Geographical Studies, 28*(1), 16-28.

Jones, C. (1993, November 27-28). Grammar comes back into fashion. *The Weekend Australian*, p. 8.

Kress, G., & Hodge, B. (1979). *Language as ideology*. London: Routledge & Kegan Paul.

Lee, A. (1993) Whose geography? A feminist-poststructuralist critique of systemic "genre"-based accounts of literacy and curriculum. *Social Semiotics, 3*(1), 131-156.

Lee, A. (1996). *Gender, literacy, curriculum: Rewriting school geography*. London: Taylor & Francis.

Lee, A., & Green, B. (1990). Staging the differences: On school literacy and the socially critical curriculum. In R. Giblett & J. O'Carroll (Eds.), *Discipline-dialogue-difference*. Perth, Australia: 4-D Duration.

Levine, K. (1982). Functional literacy: Fond illusions and false economies. *Harvard Educational Review, 52*(3), 249-266.

Lewis, M., & Simon, R. (1986). A discourse not intended for her: Learning and teaching within patriarchy. *Harvard Educational Review, 56*(4), 457-472.

Luke, A. (1988). *Literacy, textbooks and ideology*. Lewes, Sussex: Falmer Press.

Marland, M. (Ed.). (1977). *Language across the curriculum*. London: Heinemann.

Martin, J. R. (1985). *Factual writing: Exploring and challenging social reality*. Geelong, Australia: Deakin University Press.

Martin, J. R., & Rothery, J. (1980). *Writing project report number 1*. Sydney, Australia: Department of Linguistics, University of Sydney.

Martin, J. R., & Rothery, J. (1981). *Writing project report number 2*. Sydney, Australia: Department of Linguistics, University of Sydney.

Martin, J. R., Wignell, P., Eggins, S., & Rothery, J. (1988). Secret English: Discourse technology in a junior secondary school. In L. Gerot, J. Oldenburg & T. van Leeuwen (Eds.), *Language and socialisation: Home and school* (pp. 143-173). Sydney, Australia: Macquarie University.

Mellor, B., & Patterson, A. (1991). Reading character: Reading gender. *English in Australia, 95*, 4-23.

Miller, C. R. (1984). Genre as social action. *Quarterly Journal of Speech, 70*, 157-178.

Morris, J. (1992). "Back to the future": The impact of political ideology on the design and implementation of geography in the National Curriculum. *The Curriculum Journal, 3*(1), 75-85.

New South Wales Board of Studies (1994). *K-6 English Syllabus.*

Piper, D. (1988). Perspectives on language in content area teacher education. *English Quarterly, 21*(3), 174-182.

Poynton, C. (1993). Grammar, language and the social: Poststructuralism and systemic-functional linguistics. *Social Semiotics, 3*(1), 1-22.

Reid, I. (Ed.). (1987). *The place of genre in learning: Current debates.* Geelong, Australia: Deakin University Press.

Rose, G. (1993). *Feminism and geography: The limits of geographical knowledge.* Cambridge, UK: Polity Press.

Singh, M. (1988). Becoming socially critical: Literacy, knowledge and counter-construction. *Australian Journal of Reading, 11*(3), 155-164.

Singh, P. (1994). Generating literacies of difference from the "Belly of the Beast." *Australian Journal of Language and Literacy, 17*(2), 92-100.

Slevin, J. F. (1988). Genre theory, academic discourse and writing within disciplines. In L. Z. Smith (Ed.), *Audits of meaning: A festschrift in honour of Ann E Berthoff.* Portsmouth, NH.: Boynton/Cook.

Slevin, J. F. (1991). Depoliticising and politicising composition studies. In R. Bullock & J. Trimbur (Eds.), *Politics of writing instruction: Postsecondary.* Porthmouth, NH: Boynton/Cook.

Street, B. (1984). *Literacy in theory and practice.* Cambridge, UK: Cambridge University Press.

Threadgold, T. (1993). Performing genre: Violence, the making of protected subjects and the discourses of critical literacy and radical pedagogy. Plenary paper delivered at the International Domains of Literacy Conference, University of London Institute of Education, September 1992. *Domains of Literacy, Changing English, 1*(1), 2-31.

Western Australian Ministry of Education. (1992). *First steps.* Melbourne, Australia: Longmans.

White, J. (1986). The writing on the wall: Beginning or end of a girl's career? *Women's Studies International Forum, 9*(5), 561-574.

Whitehouse, H. (1992). *Girls and the year 12 geography examinations: A research project.* Adelaide: Senior Secondary Assessment Board of South Australia.

Wickert, R. (1989). *No single measure: A survey of Australian adult literacy.* Sydney, Australia: Institute of Technical and Adult Teacher Education.

Wignell, P., Martin, J. R., & Eggins, S. (1993). The discourse of Geography: Ordering and explaining the experiential world. In M. A. K. Halliday & J. R. Martin (Eds.), *Writing science: Literacy and discursive power.* London: Falmer Press.

Anna Yeatman
Macquarie University

Lee's intervention in current literacy, curriculum, and pedagogy debates is of a recognizable kind to me even though I am not a linguist and do not understand the "fine print" of her argument in relation to genre analysis and its wider intellectual context: systemic functional grammar. Lee argues that genre analysis has been relatively easily "co-opted" by conservative approaches to curriculum, specifically those that are emphasizing the acquisition by Australian school students of the basic competencies required for maintaining Australian national society's place within an advanced postindustrial capitalist order. Conservative in this context does not signify only or primarily the cultural conservatism and "back-to-basics" classicism advocated by some prominent educators. More significantly, in the light of dominant policy agendas, it signifies the combined technicist-economistic agendas of a competency approach to education and training.

Both the social relational and the representational features of the dominant competency discourse work to depoliticize its agendas. The social relational features are both centralized and bureaucratic— centralized because they operate in terms of corporatist modes of political decision making, and bureaucratic because they presuppose bureaucracy as the most appropriate mode of policy delivery (for discussion of a post bureaucratic paradigm, see Barzelay, 1992). The representational features of the dominant competency discourse work to technicize all aspects of competency, its acquisition and its assessment. Competency is made to appear as though its knowledge, skill, and outcome components are all objectively based and assessable. In both social relational and representational terms, the dominant competency discourse works to effect the closure rather than the opening of contestation and dialogue as to what competency is to mean and how it is to be institutionalized.

The genre movement, Lee argues, "fits" this dominant policy approach because it tends to read literacies in terms of their functional contexts. Although the virtue of this approach is its insistence on literacy in context, when context is read in a functionalist manner, the inevitable result is a technicist conception of literacy in adaptive relationship to the dominant discourse of the context concerned. In the case of schooling, a functional context is equated with what is taken to be the given subject matter of a particular disciplinary area, geography in the instance discussed.

Here we need to follow Lee more closely, and to use another of her publications (Lee, 1993). Lee argued that genre analysis conforms to the dominant positivistic understanding of the relationship between intellectual disciplines and their delivery as school subjects. The dominant understanding is that the university is the institutional site responsible for the intellectual advancement as well as custody of the discipline. When this understanding operates, universities have to be permitted the intellectual freedom required to expand the frontiers of knowledge of the particular discipline concerned. If the university represents the advanced level of disciplinary knowledge, the school as an institutional site of knowledge is associated with the elementary forms of transmission of this knowledge. These are conducted in terms of a passive and deferential relationship to what is presupposed as the site of advanced disciplinary knowledge, the university. Hence, schools operate in terms of pedagogies, universities in terms of *disciplines.*

When schooling is understood in this way it follows that a particular pedagogy is committed to normalizing the intellectual discipline concerned. Any project of normalization inevitably works to privilege those aspects of disciplinary knowledge that appear to invite consensus rather than contestation. These aspects, equally inevitably, are those that appear to be objectively based, that is conducted in terms of the canons and procedures of normal, positivistic science. Lee (1993) cited Gilbert's (1984) study of school textbooks in England:

> In particular, the treatment of an important issue was often seen as an opportunity to focus on a technical skill with the loss of the real significance of the problem, an example being when a topic "Contrasts in living standards" became a study of the problems of deriving indices to measure standards of living. At other times, hypothetical models seemed to become ends in themselves rather than partial aids to understanding. The impression resulted largely from the common practice of presenting and explaining the model first, rather than focusing on the problem which the model attempted to solve. (p. 149)

Thus, the normalizing effect of school pedagogy works to homogenize a discipline, and to marginalize those areas of it that being overtly politicized are necessarily committed to the interpretive and dialogical art of understanding (see Gadamer, 1977). These effects are not simply intradiscipline specific. The same logic works to hierarchize school subjects in such a way that the positivistic disciplines such as the sciences and mathematics appear to instantiate normal knowledge in a way that the discursive disciplines of history, english and social studies do not.

Lee makes the point that the normalizing effect of school pedagogy is deeply implicated in the hierarchical constitution of the human subject. Dominant ethnic group and middle-class males are positioned as subjects whose privilege is conferred to the extent that they learn to operate comfortably within "normal" knowledge while simultaneously disdaining and marginalizing the discursive disciplines. Females and nondominant ethnic group males, in different ways, are positioned as subjects who are more likely to find their subjectivity confirmed by the discursive disciplines than to achieve the transcendental knower status presupposed by normal positivistic models of knowledge.

We have come to know these vicious circles well. The strength of Lee's contribution is to insist on a close examination of how they work. In so doing, she opens the way for interventions that can disrupt this vicious circle, and by so doing, open up space for different kinds of knowledge-power practices with different kinds of subject effect.

As we have seen, Lee's primary intervention is to repoliticize the terrain by bringing out the depoliticizing closure effect of approaches to literacy that, however technically sophisticated, treat it as a technical-functional matter. If literacy is to be seen in context, then this context has to be the complex and contested domain of its disciplinary-pedagogic fields of practice. A condition for this is sustained critique of the discipline–pedagogy binary itself. The hierarchical relationship between university and school that is inscribed in this binary can be challenged only if is understood that schools are sites of the production of disciplinary knowledge, and universities sites of pedagogy. This allows for a reciprocal, reflective, and critical relationship between disciplinary and pedagogical features of knowledge in ways that ensure that neither is accorded the status of "truth." A reminder is due at this point that inverting the usual binary merely reconfirms the hierarchy of disciplinary knowledge (science, theory) in relation to pedagogy (practice).

This repoliticizing gesture is the deeply familiar one of all those who have positioned themselves as belonging to that aspect of the legacy of the enlightenment that Foucault (1984) and Arendt (1982) called *critique*. For Arendt, the features of critique are made to reside in a publicly accountable and thus dialogical mode of critical thinking, which after Kant, she called *selbstdenken*:

> To think, according to Kant's understanding of enlightenment, means Selbstdenken, to think for oneself, "which is the maxim of a never passive reason. . . . To be given to such passivity is called prejudice," and enlightenment is, first of all, liberation from prejudice. (p. 42)

Critical thinking cannot claim the authority of truth; all it can offer is reflectively oriented "opinion." The value of this opinion is arbitrated or judged by the common sense of the intersubjective community or jurisdiction within which it is oriented. The quality of judgment is relational, depending as much on the imaginative leadership and intellectual quality of the opinion proffered as on the degree of critically reflective reception it gets. The vitality of this dialectic is dependent on what Arendt (1982) called "the factor of publicity" (p. 41), namely the opening up of a "public space" for critique. For Arendt, opening up a public space (Melucci's, 1988) can occur only if the normative principle of what she called after Kant, *publicness*, is satisfied. Kant (cited Arendt, 1982) formulated a transcendental principle of publicness in the following way:

> All actions related to the right of other men [sic] are unjust if their maxim is not consistent with publicity . . . [for a] maxim which I cannot divulge publicly without defeating my own purpose must be kept secret if it is to succeed; and, if I cannot publicly avow it without inevitably exciting general opposition to my project, the . . . opposition which can be foreseen a priori is due only to the injustice with which the maxim threatens everyone. (p. 48)

Thus, political action is that which can satisfy, at least by the nature of its commitment to certain principles of accountability, this criterion of publicness.

Incidentally, *public*, as used here, does not denote a domain or space that is already given as public, and thereby set off from space that is already given as private. Any relational domain or setting can be politicized in Arendt's sense, and thus opened up as a public space in Melucci's sense. For Melucci, public spaces are ephemeral, historically contingent, and plural. They open up under historically specific conditions of critique, and they close down, when critique for some reason subsides. It follows that kitchen tables can become public spaces, and classrooms can become private spaces. That is, no social space is already constituted as public or private. Social spaces become public or private, depending on what is happening to politicize or depoliticize them.

Foucault's (1984) conception of critique also works with Kant's legacy, taking over the Kantian question and refusing to allow Kant's own Critiques to be regarded as doctrine or canonical tradition:

> We are not talking about a gesture of rejection. We have to move beyond the outside-inside alternative: we have to be at the frontiers . . . if the Kantian question was that of knowing what limits knowledge has to renounce transgressing, it seems to me that the critical question today has to be turned back into a positive one: in what is given to us as universal, necessary, obligatory, what place is occupied by whatever is singular, contingent, and the product of arbitrary constraints? (p. 45)

The positive feature of this critique resides in its enabling us to practically test the limits of our present situation: "this critique will be genealogical in the sense that it will not deduce from the form of what we are what it is impossible for us to do and to know: but it will separate out, from the contingency that has made us what we are, the possibility of no longer being, doing, or thinking what we are, do, or think" (Foucault, 1984, p. 46).

For Foucault, critique withdraws the authority of dogma from truth. It deontologizes truth, as it were, and relocates truth within the historically contingent domain of discourse. This deontologizing function of critique also frees the subject for what Arendt regarded action, namely the principle of beginning. For Foucault, as for Arendt, the principle of beginning is always in relation to a context of what is, and what might be, "between past and future," as Arendt put it in the title of a book of her essays. Foucault (1984), referring to the work on the limits of our "present-ness" that critique enables, called it "a patient labor giving form to our impatience for liberty". This work is informed by the contingency and historical specificity of its context. It is not part of any accumulative work on behalf of a teleological principle of progress. Both Arendt (1982) and Foucault rejected the historicist doctrine of progress, and see it as antipathetic to what they respectively called *action* and *liberty*. The doctrine of progress belongs to the depoliticized domain of metaphysics, not to the repoliticizing gesture of critique. Critique "is not seeking to make possible a metaphysics that has finally become a science; it is seeking to give new impetus, as far and wide as possible, to the undefined work of freedom" (Foucault, 1984, p. 46).

What is the status of this repoliticizing gesture of critique? This is an important question to ask for a number of reasons, not least of which is the proposition that we cannot know what politics is unless we know what it is not. To know what politics is not, is to accept that there must inevitably be a depoliticizing gesture—a gesture in which we all, equally inevitably, participate. Let me explain.

In setting out the nature of Lee's intervention, I reiterated her representation of the "genre movement's" contribution to official literacy discourse as "conservative." However, I carefully indicated that "conservative" here does not signify classicist, "high-culture" conservatism. The signification is instead the conservative effect of closure that follows on technicist and functionalist logics. I suggested *normalizing* as a more apt term for this effect of closure.

Toward the end of her discussion, Lee invokes, against the neo-conservative thrust of the genre movement, what she calls "libertarian, critical, or transformative pedagogies." We can wonder whether this bracketing together in the same phrase of "critical," "transformative," and "pedagogy" is a little too hasty, threatening to operate more as incantation than as critique. I would have liked Lee to engage more closely with the issue of how critique and pedagogy may be reconciled. Given the longstanding tradition of progressivist moralizing in radical education movements, a moralizing that depends on ontologizing moves no different in character from those made by a conservative progressivism, this is no simple issue. In particular, nothing guarantees the critical nature of an intervention just because its agent is committed to "libertarian, critical, or transformative pedagogies."

When Lee's work is read by those who are committed to the binary of disciplinary knowledge and pedagogy, they will not understand what it means to attempt to bring pedagogy and critique together within the one discursive practice. These critics will be working to reinstate a rationalist metaphysics, where the doctrine of progress works to offer a guarantee that "critique" somehow naturally resides within the working out of the laws of reason. In short, theirs is the defense of pedagogy *qua* transmission of scientific knowledge.

When this defense is operating, critique in the politicizing sense of Foucault's and Arendt's use of this term is forced to dwell in the margins, and to disrupt from time to time the regular workings of scientific pedagogical discourse. Those who occupy the marginalized subject positions of critique are forced to play out a "soft," overtly political game vis-à-vis those who are positioned as participant in the "real" business of disciplinary knowledge: politically neutral, scientific inquiry. The binary of critique and pedagogy is confirmed as it is reproduced, not least by those who understand their positioning as self-evidently *political*.

Although this is a game many of us know too well, it is not the only game in town. Those of us who are committed to critique are also positioned as proactive and creative contributors to a politics of curriculum. An extraordinary number of us who profess commitment to critique are able to shape curriculum in the sense of individual units of study, and many of us have influence over variously extended contexts of individual units of curriculum.

This being the case, it is important to ask the question whether pedagogy and critique can come together to permit disciplinary knowledges to be transmitted, but transmitted in ways which are accountable to critique. This is not a simple question because it is inevitable that all transmission of knowledge work in ways that "forgets" (see Spivak, 1974) the perspectivalist, historically contingent, and arbitrary features of knowledge. It forgets that question of critique that Foucault named: "in what is given to us as universal, necessary, obligatory, what place is occupied by whatever is singular, contingent, and the product of arbitrary constraints?" Thus, each of us transmits a particular version of a disciplinary knowledge, but when we do this we inevitably tend to ontologise the categories that organize this knowledge, and to normalize this version. This is not simply because we are better at critiquing the views of others than holding our own up to critique. Rather, in order to act at all in the transmission of disciplinary knowledge we must work to normalize, and in this sense depoliticize, those aspects of the discipline we regard as most central, as least negotiable—the bottom line, as it were.

It matters, accordingly, how this bottom line operates. Is ours a metaphysical or postmetaphysical understanding of the discipline at hand? By which I mean: Do we make a positivistic acceptance of the ontological categories by which we allow the discipline (or, subdiscipline) to be defined, or do we enter into what Riley (1988) called an attitude of deconstructive irony in respect of these categories? Riley had in mind the category "women" as the necessary organizing ("ontological") category of all and any feminisms. She argued that we do not have to ontologically install this category, to invest it with a metaphysics. On the contrary: Having accepted the category as the necessary presupposition of women's studies, we can work to deconstruct this category by showing how all the ways in which it homogenises women in binary relationship to the homogeneous category, men, do not work, and are contested. With regard to my own, current discipline of institutional operation—Sociology—the same work can be done with respect to its presuppositional category: the social. As it can be done and is being done (see Best, 1995; Longhurst, 1994) with the presuppositional category of Geography: space or the spatial.

These postmetaphysical ways of operating the metaphysics of the disciplines mean, among other things, that we are prepared to operate with a plurality and discontinuity of traditions as making up the discipline. That we can invest the presuppositional category itself with a discontinuous and contested set of histories.

A postmetaphysical relationship to disciplinary metaphysics is, then, a necessary condition of reconciling (if that is the word) pedagogy and critique. There can be no programmatic orientation for bringing together pedagogy and critique without running the risk of subjecting critique to pedagogy. We can work to understand what critique seems to mean and to involve but its work is open-ended. Its achievements, in responding to a "present-ness" that has already become past, follow on behind and threaten to corral what Foucault called "the undefined work of freedom."

REFERENCES

Arendt, H. (1982). *Lectures on Kant's political philosophy* (R. Beiner, Ed.). Chicago: University of Chicago.

Barzelay, M. (1992). *Breaking through bureaucracy: A new vision for managing in government*. Berkeley & Los Angeles: University of California Press

Best, S. (1995). Sexualizing space. In E. Grosz & E. Probyn (Eds.), *Sexual bodies: The strange carnalities of feminism*. New York & London: Routledge

Foucault, M. (1984). What is enlightenment? In P. Rabinow (Ed.), *The Foucault reader*. London: Penguin.

Gadamer, H. (1977). *Philosophical hermeneutics* (D. Linge, Trans. & Ed.). Berkeley & Los Angeles: University of California Press.

Gilbert, R. (1984). *The impotent image: Reflections of ideology in the secondary school curriculum*. Lewes, UK: Falmer Press.

Lee, A. (1993). Whose geography? A feminist poststructuralist critique of systemic "genre"-based accounts of literacy and curriculum. *Social Semiotics, 3*(1), 131-157.

Longhurst, R. (1994). The geography closest in—the body . . . The politics of pregnability. *Australian Geographical Studies, 32*(2), 214-223.

Melucci, A. (1988). Social movements and the democratization of everyday life. In J. Keane (Ed.), *Civil society and the state*. London: Verso

Riley, D. (1988). *Am I that name? Feminism and the category of "women" in history*. London: Macmillan.

Spivak, G. (1974). Translator's preface. In Jacques Derrida, *Of gramatology*. Baltimore & London: Johns Hopkins Press.

Author Index

Subject Index

CPSIA information can be obtained at www.ICGtesting.com
264097BV00007B/3/A

9 781572 731035